THE AIR WAR AT SEA IN THE SECOND WORLD WAR

THE AIR WAR AT SEA IN THE SECOND WORLD WAR

MARTIN W. BOWMAN

Pen & Sword
AVIATION

First published in Great Britain in 2023 by
PEN AND SWORD AVIATION
An imprint of
Pen & Sword Books Limited
Yorkshire – Philadelphia

Copyright © Martin W. Bowman, 2023

ISBN 978 1 52674 635 1

The right of Martin W. Bowman to be identified as Author of this work has been asserted by him in accordance with the Copyright, Designs and Patents Act 1988.

A CIP catalogue record for this book is available from the British Library.

All rights reserved. No part of this book may be reproduced or transmitted in any form or by any means, electronic or mechanical including photocopying, recording or by any information storage and retrieval system, without permission from the Publisher in writing.

Typeset in Ehrhardt 11/14.5 by
SJmagic DESIGN SERVICES, India.
Printed and bound in the UK by CPI Group (UK) Ltd.

Pen & Sword Books Limited incorporates the imprints of Atlas, Archaeology, Aviation, Discovery, Family History, Fiction, History, Maritime, Military, Military Classics, Politics, Select, Transport, True Crime, Air World, Frontline Publishing, Leo Cooper, Remember When, Seaforth Publishing, The Praetorian Press, Wharncliffe Local History, Wharncliffe Transport, Wharncliffe True Crime and White Owl.

For a complete list of Pen & Sword titles please contact
PEN & SWORD BOOKS LIMITED
George House, Units 12 & 13, Beevor Street, Off Pontefract Road,
Barnsley, South Yorkshire, S71 1HN, England
E-mail: enquiries@pen-and-sword.co.uk
Website: www.pen-and-sword.co.uk

Or
PEN AND SWORD BOOKS
1950 Lawrence Rd, Havertown, PA 19083, USA
E-mail: Uspen-and-sword@casematepublishers.com
Website: www.penandswordbooks.com

Contents

Chapter 1	Thank God for The Navy! (April 1940)	1
Chapter 2	Biplanes Against Battleships – Operation 'Judgement' (11–12 November 1940)	36
Chapter 3	Operation 'Excess' (January 1941)	57
Chapter 4	Hunting the *Bismarck* (May 1941)	72
Chapter 5	Unternehmen 'Donnerkeil-Zerberus' (February 1942)	94
Chapter 6	Sink The *Tirpitz*! (9 March 1942 – 29 August 1944)	116
Chapter 7	Hunting the Hunters	145
Chapter 8	Pearl Harbor and the US Pacific Fleet	163
Chapter 9	Attack On Davao (19 December 1941)	180
Chapter 10	Battle of the Coral Sea (4–8 May 1942)	189
Chapter 11	The Battle of Midway (4–7 June 1942)	205
Chapter 12	The Battle for the Solomons (August–November 1942)	223
Chapter 13	The Battle of the Philippine Sea (June 19–20, 1944)	234
Chapter 14	The British Pacific Fleet	244
Chapter 15	Towards the Final Downfall	256
Index		273

Chapter 1

Thank God for The Navy!

On Sunday, September 3rd, 1939, a few hours after the Pedantic but Right Hon. Neville Chamberlain announced over the wireless that German aggression had compelled Great Britain to go to war the torpedoing without warning of the passenger liner Athenia *indicated that the German submarine campaign would be just as ruthless as in the First World War. The first blow struck by Germany was a danger signal to Great Britain.*

However, much Hitler was bemused by the opinion that the British Empire was crumbling, he was not so self-hypnotized by wishful thinking as to cease to take precautions in case the imponderable English failed to behave as he hoped. He gave instructions to the German Naval Command that the U-boats were to take up their war stations in the North Sea and the Atlantic where they could hit instantly at British shipping if the British Premier, whom he had deceived and betrayed, had the temerity to accept the German challenge. 'It is evil things we shall be fighting against, brute force, bad faith, injustice, oppression, persecution – and against them I am certain that the right will prevail,' said Mr. Chamberlain over the wireless on that sunny Sunday morning.

In the early days of June 1940 when Great Britain, owing to the breakthrough of the German armoured divisions across the Meuse and the capitulation of Belgium, was forced to abandon the entire equipment of the British Expeditionary Force in order to save the lives and liberties of that superb army of men by performing the miracle of Dunkirk, Britain and the British Empire were in jeopardy. The British army after a retreat which out-rivalled that of Mons escaped destruction only because at that

THE AIR WAR AT SEA IN THE SECOND WORLD WAR

vital moment the seas abated into a flat calm and all the seafaring experience of a seafaring people crystallised into a stupendous effort which welded the Royal Navy and all the big and little ships afloat in home waters into a fleet of deliverance. Britain had an army without arms, but she had still the finest navy the world has known.

David Masters

When the German invasion of Norway commenced on 9 April 1940, the only carrier in Home Waters was *Furious*, re-fitting in the Clyde. She cut short her re-fit and embarked her two Swordfish Squadrons, 816 and 818, with a total of 18 aircraft and sailed on the 10th to join the Home Fleet sailing off Norway. But so little time was available that she left behind her Skua squadron, with the result that the Fleet and the first contingent of the Allied Army ashore were without fighter cover for the first fortnight of the campaign. *Ark Royal* was training aircrew off Gibraltar at this time, but 16 Skuas of her 800 and 803 Squadrons, left behind at Hatston in the Orkneys to supplement the local defences undertook a dive-bombing strike on the light cruiser *Königsberg* in Bergen Fjord at 0720 on 10 April during Unternehmen (Operation) 'Weserübung', the German invasion of Norway. Operating at maximum range, 29-year-old Lieutenant Commander William Paulet Lucy commanding 803 Squadron, leading with nine aircraft and Captain Richard T. Partridge RM of 800 Squadron with seven Skuas took the defences by surprise, half of the dive bombers completing their dives before the German crew realized they were under attack. *Königsberg* was hit by at least five 100 lb bombs, which caused serious damage to the ship. One penetrated her thin deck armour, went through the ship and exploded in the water, causing significant structural damage. Another hit destroyed the auxiliary boiler room. Two more bombs exploded in the water next to the ship; the concussion from the blasts tore large holes in the hull. She took on a heavy list almost immediately and the captain ordered the crew to abandon the ship. It took slightly less than three hours from the start of the attack for the ship to completely capsize and sink. Only one Skua was lost. The raid was remarkable in that it was the first to result in the destruction of a major enemy surface vessel by aircraft alone. These two mostly Skua squadrons suffered heavy losses during an attempt to dive bomb the *Scharnhorst* at Trondheim on 13 June 1940. Of 15 aircraft on the raid, 800 Squadron lost four Skuas out

THANK GOD FOR THE NAVY!

of six, with Captain Partridge taken prisoner, while 803 Squadron lost four Skuas from nine.[1]

In Britain Sunderland crews were tasked to monitor German naval activity off Norway and reconnoitre the coast to obtain intelligence for possible future operations. On 30 January 1940 a Sunderland of 228 Squadron had laid claim to the first U-boat kill for Coastal Command when Flight Lieutenant Edward John Brooks attacked *U-55* in the North Sea after the enemy submarine had been depth-charged to the surface by the sloop HMS *Fowey*. The destroyer HMS *Whitshed* and the French destroyer *Valmy* escorting a convoy arrived on the scene. As the warships opened fire the U-boat crew scuttled their boat and were all rescued except the commander, 31-year-old Kapitänleutnant Werner Heidel. By 1 April 204 Squadron were at Sullom Voe, 201 Squadron at Pembroke Dock and 10 Squadron RAAF at Mount Batten.

On 4 April a reconnaissance flight over the Elbe estuary discovered German naval vessels and 60 merchant ships in the Schillig Roads moving northward in formations of five ships. The naval vessels were attacked by six Blenheims without visible result. A patrol sent to the same place on the next day had to be recalled on account of weather; but its leader got through and flying just below clouds, which were down to 200 ft, found the Roads almost empty. On Saturday, 6 April a photographic reconnaissance showed that several units of the German Fleet, including the 26,000-ton battle cruisers *Scharnhorst* and the *Gneisenau* were in the harbours of North-Western Germany. On 8 April at 2 o'clock in the afternoon, a Sunderland of 204 Squadron flown by Squadron Leader Ernest Leslie 'Johnny' Hyde, who was on a reconnaissance of the Trondheim Fjord, was attacked by two enemy aircraft and damaged before the Sunderland was able to escape. Hyde crawled into the wings and stopped up holes in the fuel tanks, thus enabling the aircraft to make it back to base.[2]

At 1400 hours another Sunderland flying boat sighted a battleship of the *Scharnhorst* class accompanied by two cruisers of the *Leipzig* class and two

---

1. William Lucy DSO had been lost on 14 May when his aircraft blew up while attacking a He 111 off Skånland near Tranoy. His Swordfish was one of two shot down.
2. Wing Commander 'Johnny' Hyde DFC was killed flying a Beaufighter over Norway on 29 April 1942 when he was attacked by German aircraft. Hyde and his co-pilot were alive following the crash but were later reported dead.

destroyers. They were 130 miles from the Alsboen Light off the West coast of Norway. The ships saw the Sunderland almost at the same moment and opened anti-aircraft fire which was both heavy and accurate. The Sunderland was hit almost at once; two of its tanks were holed and the hull gradually filled with petrol. When it landed at its base it had lost 300 gallons. That same day German destroyers had been seen at various times in the neighbourhood of the Horns Reef, steaming on a Northerly course. The German attack on Norway had begun.

Although it was not until 9 April that German ships of war were seen in Norwegian harbours, they had sailed on the 7th. Bomber crews were brought to a state of readiness when it was realised that German ships sighted heading for Norway and Denmark the day before were part of an invasion force. During the afternoon 12 Blenheims in two formations of six saw an enemy cruiser and four destroyers at sea. They followed them and four minutes later caught sight of most of the German Fleet, which was then 76 miles NNW of the Horn's Reef. The Blenheims wheeled into the sun and attacked either the *Scharnhorst* or the *Gneisenau*. The leader sent out a message giving the position and course of the German Fleet. This information never got through and only became known some hours later when the aircraft returned. 'The German Fleet was a very grand sight,' said the leader of the Blenheims. 'When they shot at me it was like lightning flashing in daylight all about me.'

Detachments of Wellingtons that had been sent to Lossiemouth and Kinloss in Scotland sought in vain to find the German ships that same afternoon when they were thwarted by bad visibility. Two Wellingtons were shot down with no survivors by Bf 110s and three other Wellingtons were damaged. Another force that was detailed for the same task the next day was weather-bound.

In the small hours of 9 April, the Germans crossed the Danish frontier and simultaneously German troops landed at Narvik, Trondheim, Bergen and Stavanger. That afternoon 12 Wellingtons and 12 Hampdens went out to attack the enemy naval forces now in Bergen. Twelve aircraft were recalled and two of the remaining dozen dropped 30 armour-piercing 500lb bombs from between 4,000 and 6,000 ft at dusk. The Wellingtons were met by heavy fire, but thought that they had scored one direct hit on the cruiser's stern.

Aircraft of Coastal Command were very busy reconnoitring the new area of battle. Before midday a London flying boat had reported the presence of a German cruiser of the *Köln* class in Bergen. This intelligence was

THANK GOD FOR THE NAVY!

confirmed later by a Blenheim and a Wellington. A Sunderland flown by Flight Lieutenant Edward John Brooks having detached to 18 Group in the Shetlands flew an afternoon reconnaissance to Trondheim Fjord. Brooks made use of a cloud cover approach from the north, inland and made the reconnaissance whilst flying in a westerly direction. Landfall at Vikten Island was made at 1600 and the flying-boat proceeded inland above broken cloud at 7-9,000 ft. Through cloud gaps vessels were seen at anchor in harbour, identified as a heavy class cruiser, two destroyers and three large MVs. To the northeast of the harbour was lying the *Nürnburg* and in a fjord North of the town, one destroyer. Engines were de-synchronized and the aircraft constantly retired into cloud. Considerable icing was experienced and heavy snow storms were encountered. Brooks set course due West at 1750 and landed at the Shetlands at 1955.

On the morning of 11 April *Furious* mounted what was to be the first co-ordinated torpedo strike in the history of naval warfare when 16 Swordfish set out to attack the heavy cruiser, the *Admiral Hipper* in Trondheim harbour. But unbeknown to *Furious*, the *Hipper* and one of its destroyers had already left Trondheim and there were only three enemy destroyers remaining. At first light, Lieutenant Commander Henry Gardiner leading 816 Squadron and Lieutenant Commander J. E. Fenton leading 818 Squadron took off to carry out their attack. The strike was not a success, principally because of lack of knowledge of the area and most of the torpedoes grounded in shallow water.

The Commanding Officer of *Furious*, Captain Thomas Hope Troubridge, wrote: 'It is difficult to speak without emotion of the pluck and endurance of the young officers and men, some of them Midshipmen, who flew their aircraft to such good effect... All were firing their first shots in action, whether torpedo, bomb or machine gun; many made their first night landing on 11 April, and, undeterred by the loss of several of their shipmates, their honour and courage remained throughout as dazzling as the snow-covered mountain over which they so triumphantly flew.'

Next day *Furious* flew off Swordfish of 818 Squadron at 1615 hours to attack enemy ships at Narvik. Disappointed with the failure of the torpedo attacks the previous day, bombs were carried instead. The weather was terrible, with sleet and snowstorms in winds of 30-40 knots; visibility was at times less than a quarter of a mile and the average cloud ceiling of 1,000 ft was frequently down to around 200 ft but the crews found and attacked five German destroyers with 250 lb and 20 lb bombs, claiming hits on two of them. They also reported six merchant ships and logged the positions of sunken ships, mines and shore batteries. Six Swordfish were damaged and two that were hit by flak ditched in the sea although the crews were rescued by the cruiser *Penelope* and the destroyer *Punjabi*. At 1705 hours 816 Squadron was launched to make another attempt, but the weather this time was even worse and the Squadron was forced to turn back by heavy weather. While landing back on, Lieutenant Marcus David Donati went over the side as *Furious* pitched heavily. He survived in the sea for 45 minutes in sea temperatures of 28F until picked up by *Hero*.[3]

The Swordfish would subsequently take part in both Battles of Narvik and were very active in the strike and reconnaissance roles, providing the only air support for the Allied Expeditionary Force ashore.

It was on 12 April that the largest bombing operation of the war so far was mounted when 83 Wellingtons, Hampdens and Blenheims swept a wide area in search of some of the main units of the German Fleet including the *Scharnhorst*, the *Gneisenau* and a cruiser of the *Nürnberg* class discovered heading south across the entrance to the Skagerrak. There was fog and the ships were not seen, but two warships in Kristiansand South were bombed. A swarm of Bf 109s and 110s pursued the attackers 200 miles out to sea and in a running fight shot down six Hampdens and three Wellingtons. Another dozen Wellingtons which attacked the *Köln* and the *Königsberg* in Bergen harbour, fared little better. None of their bombs did any lasting damage. This was the last major daylight raid for the Hampdens and Wellingtons. German radio admitted the loss of five Bf 109s.

One of the pilots, quiet and unassuming Squadron Leader Duncan Charles Frederick Good, was born in Adelaide in South Australia in 1916 and commissioned in the RAF in 1937. His survival from the trip on 12 April savours of the miraculous. Five Hampdens on 50 Squadron and seven more on 44 Squadron crossed the North Sea at around 300 ft due to low cloud but the formation entered clearer weather a few miles from the Norwegian Coast almost exactly on target at Lister Fjord. However, as cloud was considered too low for safe bombing by the formation leader, the formation turned south and followed the coastline making for Kristiansand harbour. Climbing to

---

3. Donati died on 17 January 1941 aged 25, on SS *Almeda Star*, enroute to HMS *Goshawk* in Trinidad.

THANK GOD FOR THE NAVY!

8,000 ft two cruisers and other shipping were spotted at anchor. Approaching in line astern from inland the formation attacked the two cruisers in four sections. 50 Squadron made up No. 3 and No. 4 Sections, while 44 Squadron made up No.1 and No.2 Sections. All aircraft were loaded with four 500 lb General Purpose bombs internally. It is believed that all 12 aircraft dropped their bombs but no hits were reported. Fire from an anti-aircraft ship was reported as 'intense'. Two aircraft of No. 4 Section were reported as being seen going down into the sea in flames as the Hampdens attacked in flights of four. One of these crews was never found and are all commemorated at Runnymede. The other crashed near Mandal killing the observer. The pilot, Flying Officer Mathew Wilson Donaldson and two crew survived and were taken prisoner.

The Hampdens closed their ranks and the leader dived to sea level at full speed for the escape with the formation following. Nine Bf 109Es of II./JG 77 continued to attack until the bombers were 60 miles out at sea and a third Hampden was seen to crash in flames. None of the crew was ever found. One enemy pilot made a bad mistake by flying right over the top of the aircraft piloted by Squadron Leader Good, presenting a nice blue belly as a perfect target for Sergeant Walter George Smith and Corporal Wallace who promptly shot it down, amid much jubilation.[4] Two further aircraft, which were thought to be two 44 Squadron machines were reported to have been shot-down.

All but two Hampdens received damage of varying degrees. The combat lasted for 25 minutes after which the formation of seven remaining aircraft set course for Scotland. Of these, only six made it back. One aircraft force-landed at Acklington while another, escorted by Squadron Leader Good ditched into the sea 120 miles east of Newcastle having run out of fuel at around 1420 hours. Looking down on the North Sea, Good saw three of the crew launch their yellow dinghy. He circled round while his navigator marked the exact position so that help could be sent to pick them up. However, a search found no trace of the dinghy or its occupants.

When Squadron Leader Good landed, his aircraft was very much shot about. But the unbelievable thing was that the petrol tank had been pierced and the petrol had caught fire. The tank itself was all blistered and there was

---

4. Two enemy aircraft were claimed shot down and a third 'damaged'. German radio admitted the loss of five fighters this day.

an area of the wing 5 ft long by 4 ft wide all burned. Somehow, in some way the blazing petrol was put out. How it happened nobody knows. It was the only known instance of a petrol tank catching fire and going out again. Everyone was amazed. It was one of those things which the experts considered to be impossible. That day it was surely a miracle which saved Squadron Leader Good and his crew.

Meanwhile, a Wellington put at the service of Coastal by Bomber Command was flown from Northern Scotland over a thousand miles of sea to the north of Norway for a daylight reconnaissance of Narvik which lies 30 miles up the fjord near the entrance to Rombaks Fjord.

On 13 April a major naval action was fought in what became known as the Second Battle of Narvik. During early morning *Warspite* passed through the entrance of Ofot Fjord, screened by nine destroyers. There was a strong German naval force of destroyers in the area. *Furious* flew off an anti-submarine patrol ahead of the British ships and dispatched a strike force of ten Swordfish for a possible synchronised attack. In spite of the bad weather prevailing the strike force arrived at its predetermined time and dive-bombed from 2,000 ft through a partial clearance in the clouds. Thirty-five 250 lb and 70 20 lb bombs were dropped but no hits were made and two Swordfish were lost due to enemy action. Three enemy destroyers were observed moving along under a smoke screen. Moving up, the British ships overwhelmed the *Giese* and *Roeder* at Narvik, setting them on fire. The British destroyers then raced on, with the Swordfish overhead reporting the enemy positions. At 1500 hours the *Eskimo* engaged two enemy destroyers only to lose her bow to a torpedo, but by then *Forrester* and *Hero* had opened fire and a German destroyer ran aground, to be finished off by gunfire and by bombs from the Swordfish. *Warspite* was engaging the enemy at distance, but smoke from her exploding shells combined with low clouds, sleet or snow and the steepness of the cliffs on either side of the narrow fjord, made flying and observation very hazardous. Four more German destroyers were located and attacked with torpedoes fired from four British destroyers. However, two of the enemy destroyers had been scuttled and a third was sinking while another was sent to the bottom by a torpedo.

A Swordfish floatplane piloted by Petty Officer Frederick Charles Rice with Lieutenant Commander W. L. M. 'Bruno' Brown as observer and Leading Airman Maurice G. Pacey as Telegrapher-Air Gunner (TAG) was launched by catapult off the *Warspite* to search for German destroyers which

THANK GOD FOR THE NAVY!

had landed troops on the Norwegian coast and act as a spotter for the ships guns as well as other ships. The son of a tailor, Rice, known as 'Ben', was born at Ipswich on 17 March 1916 and educated briefly at Colchester Technical College before becoming an apprentice at Redwing Aircraft. After the firm went broke, he joined HMS *Ganges* as a boy seaman in 1932. He served on the lower deck for two years in the cruiser *York* on the American and West Indies station and then off Spain during the civil war. When the Fleet Air Arm began to expand rapidly, the Admiralty decided to train ratings as pilots and Leading Seaman Rice volunteered to join the first course in May 1938. In February 1939 Rice became the first rating pilot to land on an aircraft carrier. On his second attempt to do it, on the same day, his tailhook broke and the aircraft bolted over the side of *Courageous*; but he managed to land safely on his third attempt, using only brakes. Rice was selected to fly floatplanes and practised landing by night in the flat water of the slick created by a ship turning a circle. Once he cut across the bows of the destroyer *Eskimo* which was forced to go astern: the captain was doubly indignant when he learned that the pilot was not even an officer!

Flying up Ofot Fjord, Rice soon spotted an enemy destroyer, which was lying in ambush and destroyed it by gunfire. Turning in low cloud, between the steep sides of Herjangs Fjord, Rice next saw a U-boat on which he dived to make a copybook attack with two 50 lb armour piercing bombs, despite heavy enemy cannon fire. The bombs struck at the base of the boat's conning tower, sinking it immediately. Rice remained airborne to direct *Warspite*'s fire as she sank six large destroyers and then dived again to help sink a seventh. His rudder was damaged, and after struggling to keep airborne for several hours, he found one of his Swordfish's floats had been riddled with bullets on landing on the water. Although it started to sink, he managed to taxi it to *Warspite* where the Swordfish was hauled onboard. They had reported enemy positions for four hours, permitting the RN destroyers to calculate fall of shot and torpedo tracks. This action led to the destruction of seven enemy destroyers. Rice and his crew also sank the *U-64* at anchor in Herjangs Fjord north of Narvik. This was the first U-boat to be destroyed by the FAA during World War II. The Commander-in-Chief wrote: 'Rarely has a ship-borne aircraft been used to such good purpose.' Rice was awarded the DSM, his observer, the DSC and Pacey was Mentioned in Dispatches.

On 15 April a Sunderland flown by Wing Commander Gilbert Nicholetts, commanding 228 Squadron took the Chief of the British Expeditionary

THE AIR WAR AT SEA IN THE SECOND WORLD WAR

Force in Norway, General Carton de Wiart VC, the one-eyed and one-armed soldier who suffered from the same disabilities as Nelson and possessed similar dauntless courage, to a rendezvous with a Tribal-class destroyer in Namsos Fjord. The Sunderland landed in the fjord at 1645 - just in time to see the destroyer under attack from four Ju 88s and two He 111s, a number of which then machine-gunned the flying boat. Second Lieutenant Elliott was wounded and one enemy aircraft dropped a long stick of bombs ahead of the manoeuvring Sunderland but the pilots managed to evade this attack with no significant damage being caused.

Since the German occupation of Norway, aerodromes at Kristiansand, Oslo and Trondheim had been attacked twice, nine and five times respectively up to the middle of June. In the opening month of the campaign Fornebu was attacked whenever possible. At the end of April, it was bombed four times in four days. In all, Stavanger was bombed 16 times by aircraft of Bomber Command between 11 and 24 April besides being repeatedly attacked by aircraft of Coastal Command and by the Fleet Air Arm. Operations against ports in Germany were also flown by Bomber Command aircraft. On the night of 20/21 April 23 Hampdens laid mines in the Elbe estuary and some of them patrolled seaplane bases at Borkum and Sylt. Thirty-six Whitleys were detailed to bomb various airfields and shipping and 22 bombed targets including airfields at Stavanger and Kristiansand and at Aalborg in Denmark. Shipping was not located and all the aircraft dispatched returned safely. At dawn on the 17th Stavanger aerodrome was shelled by HMS *Suffolk*; a Hudson spotted for her and had to fight a Ju 88 over the target. Later in the day 12 Blenheims flew in two formations at different heights to Stavanger airfield and that night 20 Wellingtons and Whitleys were sent to bomb Stavanger, Trondheim (Vaernes) and Oslo airfields. One Wellington was lost. Thirty-three Hampdens meanwhile, laid mines off north-west Denmark and all returned safely.

Airfields in Norway were attacked on four nights running, 21/22 April to 25/26 April and minelaying was carried out on two of these nights by Hampdens. On 31 days/nights from 9 April to 9/10 May 1940 Bomber Command flew a total of 93 night and day sorties, from which 36 aircraft (3.9 per cent) were lost. Night-time minelaying or 'Gardening' operations as they were code-named proved highly effective, experiencing a low casualty rate of less than 1.9 per aircraft sortie despite many of these being flown by the twin-engine and poorly armed Handley Page Hampden. The cramped

THANK GOD FOR THE NAVY!

accommodation of the three-man crew led to fatigue on long flights and it carried no power-operated gun turrets, earning it the unwelcome nickname 'The Flying Suitcase'. Just how dangerous these flights were was brought home on the night of Saturday, 4 May when five Hampdens on 50 Squadron operating from their forward base at Kinloss were detailed to mine the 'Onion' area in the waters of Bonne Fiord in Norway.

At Kinloss Squadron Leader Good sat on one of the bomb trolleys by his Hampden waiting while the ground staff completed their preparations for the night's operations. It was just after 1900 hours. The sky was red and the Squadron Leader felt decidedly uneasy. He had been briefed to mine the port of Oslo and it was a long sea crossing from Scotland to Norway and back again.

The crew got aboard, Sergeant Smith the rear gunner sitting in the 'tin' with an angle of fire below the tail to deal with attackers who came up from below, Corporal Wallace, the wireless operator sitting in the turret above him with an angle of fire over the tail to cope with attacks from above, while Pilot Officer Walter George Gardiner - 'nothing could shake Gardiner,' Good once remarked - was the second pilot, navigator and bomb-aimer seated in the front cockpit.

Taking off about 2000 hours the pilot set course for Norway to help to make Oslo as dangerous as possible for the German supply ships using the port. Throughout the long journey across the North Sea, he remained uneasy, looking round for fighters all the time. It was as though he had a foreboding.

About 2330 the Norwegian coast came into sight. Good was by no means sure of his position after the long crossing. Flying at 8,000 ft, he saw above him a layer of stratocumulus clouds at 10,000 or 12,000 ft; below him the mountains of Norway were covered with snow. Changing course, he flew inland across Norway in search of his target. The crew of the bomber were quite undisturbed. No searchlights sought them, not a gun fired at them. Squadron Leader Good scanned the land below him all the time to try to pick up Oslo Fjord. The navigator in the front cockpit was bent on the same task.

'Finally, about 50 miles away, I saw a whole packet of searchlights and flak go up and decided that was the place, so I went across to have a look,' Good said afterwards. The Hampden was then about 20 miles away. Maintaining the same course, he started to lose height until he was down to 2,000 ft. The tongue of land running up to Oslo and dividing the fiord into two was plainly visible. Good decided to use that tongue of land to mask his approach to the port, dart from its cover at top speed, deposit his mine and do a steep turn away to head for home.

With the plan firmly fixed in his mind, he took the Hampden down until it was just below the level of the spit of land. Everything remained quiet, and the pilot was convinced that the enemy had no idea of his approach or that the port was likely to be attacked. Boosting the speed, the pilot flew out from the cover of the point into the open fjord with bomb doors open. As he did so a searchlight from the opposite cliff caught the pilot and navigator and nearly blinded them. At once the defences came into action. 'The ack-ack was the heaviest I've ever seen. You would not think an aircraft could fly through it without being cut to pieces. There were a lot of light guns as well as machine-guns firing tracer,' Gardiner stated after his return.

Good saw streams of pink shells like fireworks spraying out from the opposite sides of the fjord ahead. He observed the two streams of fire crossing each other in the centre and, knowing that no aircraft could possibly run that gauntlet of fire, decided on the instant to drop down almost to water level in order to run in underneath the fiery arch of shells and tracer.

The Germans were firing directly across at each other and somebody must have suffered badly that night.

Moving the stick forward Good dived under the barrage of fire. The masts of ships rushed past just above the level of his wing tips. Ahead was the spot where he was to lay his mine. Just as he was about to shout to Gardiner to drop it, there was a crash like the breaking of windows, an enormous flash of light which blinded him so that he could not see what he was doing, and an acrid, sulphurous, burning smell.

He knew he had been hit. The aircraft started to run away from him. Yet even at that moment the task he had come so far to perform overshadowed everything else. 'Let it go – I'm hit!' he shouted to advise Gardiner to deposit the mine and tell him that he was wounded. 'I'm hit! I'm hit!' he repeated. But no one could hear him. The intercom was severed by the explosion.

The Hampden ran on past the island where the mine was to be dropped and did a steep turn. The senses of the pilot were so clouded that he could never afterwards recall anything that happened from just after he was hit until he came out of the turn. He must have been flying the aircraft subconsciously according to the plan so firmly fixed in his mind. Coming out of the turn, he

THANK GOD FOR THE NAVY!

sought to climb, but when he tried to pull the stick back, he discovered that his arms were powerless. Wounds in the left wrist and right elbow rendered both arms useless. The Hampden's nose dropped and pointed straight toward the sea. Unable to use his arms to pull back the stick, in that desperate emergency he thought of the trimming wheel at the right-hand side of his seat. The trimming wheel is a device which acts upon the tail plane in order to take the physical strain off the pilot. Directly he has found the correct amount of control required to hold the aircraft on her course at the desired height, by turning the trimming wheels he could hold the rudder and tail planes in position without having to endure the strain all the time on his arms and legs.

Unable to use his arms, which hung down helplessly, Good managed to hook one of his fingers in the trimming wheel and, by swaying his body, gradually moved it round and gained a little height. A gigantic effort was required to do this, but he managed it. Then he started to kick on the rudder, thinking that the noise made by the escape of the compressed air would attract the attention of other members of the crew. All this time the searchlights were flashing and the guns were doing their best to blow the Hampden out of the sky. He looked at the altimeter and saw that they were climbing. He knew something was wrong with his face. Dimly he saw the blood dripping out of his cuffs.

Although so sorely wounded, he still remained conscious. It must have been through sheer will-power that he clung to his senses. He kicked again on the rudder, but the crew merely thought that he was taking the usual evasive action.

Less than a minute earlier as the Hampden made its run up under the cover of the spit of land, Gardiner saw the ships slipping by. They were moored close inshore parallel with the cliffs, no doubt to protect them from air attack. How he regretted that they had no bombs with which to attack them, for there was no one on board and the ships were quite undefended. Dazzled by the searchlight as they ran out into the open fjord, amazed by the heaviness of the gunfire which greeted them, he waited patiently for the island to turn up where he had to drop his mine. 'I think it was a Bofors gun which hit us,' he stated later. 'It was the last shell of a burst of five - they fire in clips of about five. I could see them - bang! bang! bang! - and the last got us. They must have had our range nicely. I thought it had hit the outer fuselage and did not worry very much.'

THE AIR WAR AT SEA IN THE SECOND WORLD WAR

The Hampden ran on its course as he expected. Although he received no order, he automatically dropped the mine on the right spot and reported that it was away. Then the bomber banked in a right-hand turn and began to sway and dive. Gardiner remained there quite cool, thinking the captain was just doing his best to dodge the shells. Not until the wing nearly hit the mast of a ship, did he suddenly wonder if all was well. Quickly he switched on the light in his cockpit to have a look round. To his surprise there was a pool of blood in the tunnel under the pilot's seat and he saw the blood steadily dripping down. Instantly he realized that the pilot was wounded. He realized also that he would have to pilot the Hampden back to its base. He had already worked out the two courses to take them back to Britain. Knowing these would be essential to him, he rapidly noted them on a piece of paper - it shows how cool he was, how calmly his brain was working - and then he crawled through the tunnel and stood up behind the pilot.

A glance revealed the serious face wounds of his captain and then his eye caught sight of the altimeter. Swiftly he thrust his arm past the wounded pilot, caught hold of the stick and pulled it back. The aircraft was so low that he anticipated hitting the edge of the cliff at any moment. As soon as he pulled the stick back, the bomber started to climb, but not until he had taken the aircraft to a safe height and knew it was no longer in danger of hitting anything, could he attend to the pilot. With difficulty he unbuckled the captain's parachute harness; then he undid the straps which held him in his seat, after which he was able to pull down the back of the seat - for with the pilot strapped into his seat and his feet in the pedals, the back cannot be let down.

Wriggling over the wounded man, the navigator grabbed the stick to take the Hampden to a higher level. Eventually he attracted the attention of Corporal Wallace, the wireless operator, who had no idea that anything was wrong. He heard the bang, as did Sergeant Smith, the rear gunner who was also a trained navigator, but they were so busy firing at the searchlights and guns on the ground that they paid little attention to it.

In the pilot's cockpit blood was everywhere. 'Pull him out from under me,' Gardiner said. With considerable difficulty Wallace succeeded in drawing the wounded man backwards until his head lay on the padded top of the main spar, on which the back of the pilot's seat rests when it is pulled down. After further efforts, he manipulated him so that the back of the pilot's seat could be raised again.

THANK GOD FOR THE NAVY!

The remarkable thing is that Squadron Leader Good had made his crew practise this exact manoeuvre in case something like this ever came to pass, in which event they would know exactly what to do. It almost looks as though he had a sense of prevision.

Somehow Wallace and Smith managed between them to lower Good down the well leading to the front cockpit. The wounded man was bleeding very badly from one arm and it was obvious that unless this was stopped quickly, his chances would be small. Obtaining the bandages and dressings from the first-aid kit, Smith improvised a tourniquet with a small bottle and succeeded in checking the loss of blood. Then he gave him an injection of morphine in the calf of the leg, and covered him up with fur coats to make him as comfortable as possible.

The extraordinary thing was that in spite of the morphine and the loss of blood, the wounded man did not lose consciousness. He was very weak, and in a sorry condition. He had a hole in his cheek, his tongue itself was torn, and part of his nose was nearly off; he swallowed a tooth or two that was knocked out and a lot of blood, yet he still knew what was going on.

Meanwhile Gardiner had taken the bomber up to 8,000 ft to fly across the country to Stavanger. Asking the wireless operator to see if the tanks were holed, he was thankful to learn that they were intact. Wallace did his best to repair the intercommunication system, but could only succeed in passing messages through to the pilot. Smith, who remained in the front cockpit to check the navigation, could not speak to the pilot, so he had to pass slips of paper up to him from the tunnel under the seat.

Leaving Stavanger behind, the bomber sped homeward across the North Sea. The wounded man lay with his back against the bulkhead listening to the hum of the engines. A sudden flapping disturbed him.

'It's all right,' shouted the pilot down to him. 'We're on our way home.'

And they were. Advising the base that they were returning with a casualty on board, the wireless operator got a fix by which they checked their course, and they duly touched down and taxied right up to the tarmac where an ambulance was waiting to take Squadron Leader Good to hospital. Before he knew what was happening, they were cutting off his Royal Australian Air Force uniform, which was something he prized beyond anything.

No words could express his gratitude to the surgeons whose skill left him almost unscarred. In ten days, he was out of hospital. That is how he and Pilot Officer Gardiner came to receive the DFC. It was an amazing adventure

THE AIR WAR AT SEA IN THE SECOND WORLD WAR

which shows how skill and courage and fortitude can save an aircraft from disaster when all seems lost.[5]

* * *

After the bulk of the Home Fleet had returned to Scapa Flow on 15 April *Furious* remained behind to support the land forces. She departed the Narvik area escorted by three destroyers, to refuel at Tromsø. Her Swordfish were constantly airborne, attacking targets ashore and afloat in the Narvik area, bombing destroyers and jetties and carrying out anti-submarine and photographic reconnaissance patrols. En route to Tromsø, nine of her Swordfish attacked Junkers Ju 52 transports that had landed on frozen Lake Hartvikvatnet approximately ten miles northeast of Narvik. Two of the Ju 52s were destroyed and several others damaged. Flying was extremely hazardous because of enemy fighters, steep mountains, no proper maps and abysmal weather, usually with prolonged snow or sleet squalls and fog. Aircrews frequently returned frozen through, but still had to land on to a pitching and slush-covered flight deck in winds up to 50 knots. *Furious* reached the port on 16 April with only 27 per cent of her fuel remaining and remained there until 18 April when she headed south to scout the Narvik area. She was attacked en route by a single Heinkel He 111 of II./KG 26 wing from very high altitude. Two large bombs narrowly missed the ship, the closest only eleven yards off the port side aft. The shock shook her propeller shafts out of alignment and jarred the port inner high-pressure turbine so she was limited to 20 knots (23 mph). *Furious* remained off the coast of Norway despite the damage and attempted to fly off aircraft on 22 April, despite severe weather, to discourage German aircraft from delivering supplies to the German forces in Narvik. One aircraft was shot down by the Germans and the others returned reporting heavy snowstorms between the ship and Narvik. The weather worsened the next day and

---

5. Adapted from *The Copper Dingo* by David Masters. Squadron Leader Good was killed on 28/29 April 1941 during a 'Gardening' trip off La Rochelle. The last major operation on targets in Norway by RAF Bomber Command was on the night of 9/10 May when 23 out of 31 Hampdens dispatched laid mines off Kiel, Lübeck, Warnemünde and in the Elbe. In June and July Whitleys, Hampdens and Wellingtons of Bomber Command continued to raid German ports and sow mines in enemy waters.

THANK GOD FOR THE NAVY!

Captain Troubridge decided to head to the military base at Harstad on the island of Hinnøya to check the damage from the near miss. It proved worse than anticipated and *Furious* was ordered to return to Scapa Flow. Only six of the nine remaining Swordfish were serviceable, but during the 14 days of operation in Norway her Swordfish had flown 23,870 miles, fired 18 torpedoes, dropped 409 bombs and taken 295 photographs; seventeen Swordfish had been damaged by enemy action, nine being lost in the process with 12 casualties, three of them fatal.[6] On 24 April *Ark Royal* and *Glorious* arrived from the Mediterranean and the following day *Furious* left Norwegian waters for Great Britain.

Ark Royal and *Glorious* were recalled from the Mediterranean and dispatched on 23 April to relieve *Furious* on station and to give support off Namsos and Åandalsnes. *Glorious* was built as a light battle cruiser in 1916 and served with valour during World War I. It was even present when the German High Seas Fleet surrendered in 1918. The ship was decommissioned after the end of the war, but was rebuilt as an aircraft carrier in the late 1920s. *Ark Royal* and *Glorious* arrived on 24 April. *Ark*'s aircraft complement was 810 and 820 Squadrons with 12 Swordfish each, 800 Squadron with 12 Skuas and 801 Squadron with six Skuas and six Blackburn Rocs embarked. Derived from the Skua and developed in parallel, the Roc had its armament in a turret. It came to be viewed as inferior to existing aircraft such as the Skua and the type had only brief front-line service.

On 11 May *Glorious* embarked 823 Squadron with 12 Swordfish, 802 Squadron with 12 Sea Gladiators, 803 Squadron with six Skuas and 804 Squadron with six Sea Gladiators which had been used in defence of the naval base at Scapa Flow. They were to provide air cover for 18 brand new Gladiator IIs of 263 Squadron RAF that had been based at Filton which were also embarked on *Glorious* and were destined for Lake Lesjaskogsvatnet in Oppland, 40 miles from Åandalsnes in central southern Norway. Eighteen Hurricanes of 46 Squadron destined for the airfield at Bardufoss were also embarked. This squadron's CO was Squadron Leader Kenneth Brian Boyd 'Bing' Cross. Born on 4 October 1911 at Portsmouth, where his father was a surveyor and estate agent, young 'Bing' was educated at Kingswood School, Bath until his father fell on hard times and he had to leave at 16 to work at a local garage for ten shillings (50p) a week. His squadron had prepared to

---

6. *Swordfish At War* by W. A. Harrison (Ian Allan Ltd, 1987).

go to France but had been suddenly issued with Arctic clothing and sent to Scotland with orders to embark on *Glorious*. During the next two days their Hurricanes were hoisted aboard the carrier. The ground crews and advance party embarked in the troop carrier *Batory* in Glasgow on 13 May and on the following day *Glorious* sailed again. The Swordfish were to carry out daily strike and support sorties while the equally obsolescent Gladiator biplane fighters had been selected because they could operate from small landing grounds nearer to the Army's positions, at that time in the Namsos area and ease the load on the Fleet Air Arm but they lasted for less than 48 hours, by which time they were all out of action.

So desperate was the British need for landing grounds that the squadron of Gladiators strove to function from the frozen lake of Lake Lesjaskogsvatnet, a long, narrow lake, about eight miles by a half mile, bounded by woods and high and desolate mountains skirting the southern shore. In all that area there was not a flat space of ground. The servicing flight arrived there in two parties on 23 and 24 April, having experienced great difficulty in sorting their stores (which were neither listed nor labelled) and getting the essential items sent forward by the only two lorries which could still be found in Åandalsnes. Among the advance party sent to prepare a runway was the famous racing motorist Whitney Straight, who was naturalized some years before the war and had been flying in a RAF fighter squadron since the outbreak of war. His efforts in preparing the lake and his courage during the ensuing attacks earned him the award of the Military Cross.

A runway measuring about 800 by 75 yards had been prepared with local labour, which had also swept the snow from a track between the main road and the lake edge. Unfortunately, only one inadequate route had been swept from the edge to the runway; this was half a mile long and a foot deep in snow and the stores had to be conveyed over it on three horse-drawn sledges, intermittently available. The village of Lesjaskog was two miles away, so that even the provision of forage for the horses involved difficulties.

However, by 1700 hours on 24 April, the servicing flight had laid out fuel and ammunition along the runway in small dumps and collected every possible tin, jug, or other container for refuelling. It had at once been perceived that the essential work of refuelling and starting machines would be difficult: only two refuelling troughs had been despatched, and the starter trolley could not be used as the batteries were uncharged and no acid had been sent with them. Moreover, the ground staff included only one trained

THANK GOD FOR THE NAVY!

armourer to maintain 72 Browning guns for the squadron. Two guns from a naval battery of Oerlikons, which was landed at the same time as the RAF stores, had also arrived for anti-aircraft defence and a platoon of Marines to guard the petrol supply.

In a blinding snowstorm, 18 Gladiators took off from the deck of the *Glorious* with four maps among 18 pilots, none of whom had been in action previously, 180 miles from shore, in a snowstorm. Escorted by two Skuas of the Fleet Air Arm, they descended on the lake at 1800 without serious mishap, although the heaped-up snow at either side of the runway had melted during the day so that its ice surface was half covered by trickling water. Meanwhile, the Germans had flown high above the lake and reconnoitred it. The Gladiators were immediately refuelled and one section placed at instant readiness. Their arrival was soon discovered by the Luftwaffe, who sent over two aircraft disguised by Norwegian markings, which were promptly intercepted and driven away by the Gladiators.

At three o'clock on the morning of the 25th the pilots and few available staff fought to get the first Gladiators in the air, a task which the intense cold made practically impossible. The bitter cold of the night froze the engines of the Gladiators. It was two hours after first light before the first aircraft could take off. Although two more were brought in to service later it was not enough to protect the airfield, much less provide air support to British troops as intended. A series of German bombing raids during the day destroyed or seriously damaged 13 of the Gladiators. By 26 April the squadron, now positioned at Setermoen, was down to five serviceable Gladiators and then finally, only one remained airworthy. Nothing remained but to withdraw the pilots in a cargo vessel and they reached Scapa Flow safely on 1 May. Their Norwegian sojourn had lasted exactly ten days. The re-equipped squadron would return to the far north of Norway on 21 May, flying from Bardufoss airfield.

Ark Royal meanwhile, withdrew on 28 April to replenish and by this stage the Skuas and Gladiators from the carriers had accounted for nearly 40 enemy aircraft, destroyed and damaged, for the loss of one Skua in combat. On 13 April the Royal Navy had entered the fjord and sank seven German destroyers but by 14 April the Luftwaffe was in occupation of all the aerodromes in Norway and Denmark. *Ark Royal* returned on 4 May and stayed until 24 May, by which time *Glorious* had ferried out more Gladiators and the 18 Hurricanes of 46 Squadron to be based at Bardufoss. HMS *Furious* carrying 263 Squadron and its Gloster Gladiators also set course for Norway to reinforce the already faltering Norwegian campaign. On the 21st, the carriers entered their fly-off position outside Lofoten. *Furious* then flew off her Gladiators, which landed at Bardufoss. Conditions on the ground were very basic with poor runways and primitive servicing and repair facilities. The airstrip at Skånland near Narvik proved boggy however and was not able to take the Hurricanes, so 46 Squadron returned in *Glorious*.

The carriers withdrew from Norway and *Glorious* arrived at Scapa Flow on the 23rd, refuelled on the 24th and sailed again the same afternoon. On the 26th, the landing strip at Skånland was finally reported ready. Despite doubts that a Hurricane could take off from a carrier flight deck in a flat calm, they all took to the air for the 40-mile flight without difficulty, thanks to the efforts of the ship's engineers, who managed to get the *Glorious* up to a speed of 30 knots. But the surface at Skånland was still too soft. 'Bing' Cross damaged his propeller in landing and another Hurricane was flung on its back. Cross declared the strip unfit. He instructed Flight Lieutenant 'Jamie' Jameson, who was already airborne, to lead the rest of the squadron 50 miles north-east to Bardufoss. Patrick Geraint Jameson, born at Wellington, New Zealand in 1912, had become an assistant clerk after leaving school and had learned to fly privately at Rongotai in 1933. In January 1936 he travelled to England on the SS *Aorangi* at his own expense, joining the RAF on a short service commission. After training he was posted to 46 Squadron in January 1937, becoming a flight commander in March 1939. He had flown daily from the *Glorious* to patrol over Narvik since the battle began, destroying two Dornier Do 26 four-motor flying boats and a Ju 88.[7]

Patrols were maintained over the land and naval forces at Narvik without respite, some of the pilots going without sleep for more than 48 hours. The Gladiator squadron from *Glorious* also used Bardufoss, working with astonishing persistence and heroism at Narvik in defence of British troops

---

7. For his services in Norway Jameson was awarded the DFC in July 1940. His citation read: 'This officer led his flight with determination over completely strange country during operations in the Narvik area. He discovered and set on fire, two four-engine enemy flying boats which were concealed against the almost vertical side of Rombaksfjord, in a position most difficult to attack. No trace of them was found during a reconnaissance shortly afterwards. The following morning, he destroyed a Junkers 88 over Ofotfjord...'

THANK GOD FOR THE NAVY!

against the German bombers. The Fleet Air Arm could work from closer at hand, but its aircraft were not suitable for army co-operation.

After quick repairs, which included the removal of several rows of turbine blades, *Furious* returned to Norway on 18 May carrying the Gladiators of a reformed 263 Squadron. These were flown off on 21 April once their base at Bardufoss was ready. One Gladiator and the guiding Swordfish crashed en route, killing all crewmen. The ship returned to Scapa Flow once all the Gladiators had been flown off, carrying only six Sea Gladiators of 804 Squadron and nine Swordfish of 816 Squadron for self-protection while ferrying 263 Squadron. *Glorious* followed a few days later with some Hurricanes. Narvik was at last taken on 28 May. But it was too little, too late though the defenders fought gallantly to the last. From 29 May to 1 June the RAF was busy, but mainly with single enemy aircraft. Then, throughout 2 June, wave after wave of a dozen enemy bombers or dive bombers, escorted by Me 110s, sought to destroy Allied shipping and the military base at Harstad; but the Gladiators and Hurricanes so harassed every attempt that the German crews either jettisoned their bombs or aimed them wide. By the end of the day the two squadrons had flown 75 sorties, fought 24 engagements and claimed at least nine enemy aircraft, all for no loss to themselves. Many of the actions took place in full view of the troops; and General Claude Auchinleck was moved to send a handsome message of thanks. Unfortunately, the general situation had become untenable, while in the west, the German Blitzkrieg in the Low Countries was threatening to overrun British forces and her Allies and that evening the Norwegians were informed of the British intention to withdraw.

Ark Royal and *Glorious* arrived off the Norwegian coast to begin Operation 'Alphabet'. Royal Air Force patrols were to be flown over the vital areas until evacuation was virtually complete. The movement presented a most tempting series of targets, for many of the troops had to be picked up by the local fleet of fishing boats called 'puffers' which stank of fish and were ferried from ship to shore to land at the small port of Liland, thence to be transferred to liners standing off the coast. But a kindly cloak of mist and low cloud concealed the vessels for many hours and until the last day the enemy's effort in the air was very small. Such as it was, it was well contained by the RAF and by the aircraft from *Glorious* and the *Ark Royal*.[8] The outcome for the Allies can

---

8. *Royal Air Force 1939-45, Vol.1 The Fight at Odds* by Denis Richards (HMSO, 1953).

perhaps be summed up in the words of the historian of the Irish Guards: '...hopes and plans ended in failure and depression. The campaign was a tragedy, made more grievous by the endurance of the few troops who did the fighting with inadequate material. From the beginning of May a sense of ineluctable fate hung over Norway.'

On 7 June 263 Squadron flew its ten surviving Gladiators on to the *Glorious*. The Squadron had flown 249 sorties and claimed 26 enemy aircraft destroyed. For the Hurricanes at Bardufoss though, it appeared that the fate of their Hurricanes was sealed. Cross was told that after his last sortie had been flown, he could burn his aircraft to prevent them falling into enemy hands, or he could fly them further north to Lakselv where there was a possibly that they could be loaded aboard a Norwegian tramp steamer. Cross looked for another way out. He found it when he heard that the *Glorious* which had carried his squadron to Norway was still deployed not far from the Norwegian coast. He immediately asked Group Captain M. Moore, commander of the RAF Component of the North Western Expeditionary Force, for permission to fly his Hurricanes on to *Glorious* so that both pilots and aircraft could be saved to fight again. 'I hoped you'd say that,' Moore replied when asked, 'but I didn't want to suggest it because the Fleet Air Arm has already decided that such a feat is impossible!' A Hawker Hurricane had never before landed on an aircraft carrier and was not fitted with an arrester hook.

Cross found time to fly out to *Glorious* in a Walrus, where he and Captain Guy D'Oyly-Hughes, a former submariner who had been executive officer of *Courageous* for ten months, made detailed plans for the deck landing. The *Glorious* was in company with the *Ark Royal* and it was arranged that, if the *Glorious*'s deck should prove too short, the Hurricanes would come down on *Ark Royal* which had a slightly longer deck. The drawback to the *Ark Royal* was that her lifts could not accommodate the Hurricanes which would have to have their wings sawn off before the deck could be cleared for the next aircraft to land. The *Glorious* was the better choice.

By early morning on 7 June plans were complete and the evacuation was timed for that day. The ground parties embarked on HMS *Vindictive* and SS *Monarch of Bermuda* and they would reach England safely. The battle against the Germans, meanwhile, continued. At 3 am 'Bing' Cross and another Hurricane pilot spotted in the Arctic daylight four Heinkel 111K bombers beginning a shallow dive attack on their airfield. Cross damaged one himself,

THANK GOD FOR THE NAVY!

then the port tank on his Hurricane was blown to pieces and a bullet hit the side of the windscreen; but it missed Cross's head because he had failed to put on his harness and was crouched forward over the control column. He managed to glide back from a height of 4,000 ft to the airfield with a shattered windscreen and a punctured oil tank.

For one hour during the morning 'Jamie' Jameson carried out special flying tests in his Hurricane, the tailplane having been loaded with a 14 lb sandbag in the hope that it would keep the tail down during violent braking to shorten the landing run on the carrier. At 1800 hours that evening, 'Jamie' Jameson led his flight of three Hurricanes towards the *Glorious*. None had ever in their flying careers landed on a carrier. If they failed, as naval experts had predicted they would, they would plunge into the icy waters off the coast of Norway or crash into the stern of the carrier.

High, grey cloud covered the sky and a good strong wind was blowing as Jameson began his approach. A little below and a few hundred yards ahead of his Hurricane he could see the *Glorious*, churning her way through heavy seas in a valiant attempt to give him as much wind over the deck as possible for the landing. They were led out by a Swordfish aircraft of the Fleet Air Arm. The deck loomed large to meet Jameson as he came in on a steep approach. 'Watch out for the down-draught,' the Navy pilots had said, 'it'll suck you into the stern before you know where you are.' If he kept his approach steep, Jameson knew that he should escape the worst of the turbulence. The boiling waters in the wake of the great ship flashed under his wing and he concentrated every nerve on keeping his aircraft steady. The stern now rushed up to meet him and a gentle surge of power from the engine foiled the down-draught which snatched at his aircraft. He was now over the deck. The down-draught had been overcome, but one question remained to be answered - without an arrester hook, could his aircraft stop before it reached the end of the deck, which must have seemed all too short to the pilot in his fast-moving aircraft? Jameson was confident, however. With the sandbag attached he knew that he could brake violently, if necessary, without tipping the aircraft on to its nose. But violent braking was unnecessary. The experts were proved wrong as the Hurricane rolled to a halt with a third of the flying deck still in front of it. Jameson had landed successfully. Within a few minutes two other Hurricanes piloted by 21-year-old Flying Officer Herbert H. Knight and 23-year-old Sergeant Bernard L. Taylor had made landings equally successfully.

THE AIR WAR AT SEA IN THE SECOND WORLD WAR

It had been arranged that Jameson should signal back the results as soon as he had landed, but the Navy were keeping strict radio silence and so Cross remained ignorant of the success of the landings until sometime later. Because Bardufoss was so far north it was still daylight when, at midnight a lone Swordfish landed on the airfield. The pilot jumped down and handed a message to Cross. Then, for the first time he knew of Jameson's success. Three-quarters of an hour after midnight Cross and the six other chosen pilots flew their Hurricanes behind the Swordfish out to *Glorious*. It was not an easy flight. The biplane plodded along at a steady 90 mph and to fly at this speed the Hurricanes had to put their props into fine pitch and keep 20° of flap down. The pilots sent up a cheer when at last the flashing beacon of the carrier was seen. A Marine who was on the carrier has left this description of the next few minutes: 'The *Glorious* began to get up tremendous speed into wind to help the "Hurri" boxes land. Round they'd come at about 200 ft so we could see they were OK and then they'd circuit again and line up for the landing, coming in with a mighty gust and lather of spray. One by one the pilots dragged themselves out and vaulted down to the deck for the official de-briefing.'

The vicious down-draught trapped two pilots, but still they managed to make the deck. The only damage caused to any of the ten aircraft which landed was to two tail wheels which were broken. The operation had been entirely successful. Cross and his men went to bed in the early hours of 8 June after nearly 24 hours of continuous action, satisfied that they had saved their aircraft. Perhaps the most delighted men on the *Glorious* that night however, were the Fleet Air Arm pilots. 'Now we shall be getting Hurricanes,' they said. The Fleet Air Arm did get the Hurricane before the war was over.[9]

On the afternoon of 8 June the *Glorious* was steaming at 28 knots, proceeding independently of the main convoy with only two destroyers, *Acasta* and *Ardent*, as escort, when, about 180 miles west-northwest of the Lofoten Islands at about 1546, in a choppy sea, with light wind, good visibility and no cloud, the funnel smoke from *Glorious* and her escort was sighted by the *Scharnhorst* and *Gneisenau* patrolling undetected between Jan Mayen Island and the Norwegian coast on the way through the Norwegian Sea. *Glorious* apparently did not have a lookout posted; nor did not have an aircraft on patrol, which would have given her all round visibility of

---

9. *Deck Landing - by Hurricane! RAF Flying Review*, October 1956

THANK GOD FOR THE NAVY!

approximately 40 miles and did not have any of her aircraft on deck ready for immediate launch. In the memorable words of the German lookout who sighted the British carrier: 'I had never seen an aircraft carrier before this moment - then we sank her!'

The German battle-cruisers were not spotted until shortly after 1600 and *Ardent* was dispatched to investigate. *Glorious* did not alter course or increase speed. *Glorious* sent out her first radio signal at 1615, fired up the boilers, which had been shut down and slowly increased to full speed in an attempt to run to the south-east. Five Swordfish were ordered to the flight deck but Action Stations was not ordered until 1620. Unfortunately, the Swordfish were loaded with anti-submarine bombs, with a view to taking off at a moment's notice to attack any submarines that were sighted and time was necessary to unload the bombs and reload with torpedoes which would have made an effective attack on the cruisers possible. No combat air patrol was being flown, no aircraft were ready on the deck for quick take off and there was no lookout in the crow's nest on *Glorious*. She was easy prey for the powerful enemy ships.

The German battle-cruisers opened fire at 1630 hours at long range, firing a ranging salvo, which missed. Two minutes' later *Scharnhorst* then switched her fire to *Glorious*. *Scharnhorst* scored her first hit six minutes later on her third salvo, fired at an approximate range of 26,450 yards, possibly the longest gunfire hit on any enemy warship ever achieved, when one 11.1 inch hit the forward flight deck and burst in the upper hangar, starting a large fire which set the stowed Hurricanes alight. This hit also destroyed two Swordfish which had been brought up on deck after Action Stations to be prepared for flight by armourers frantically changing the bomb racks for torpedo racks. The hole in the flight deck also prevented any other aircraft from taking off. Splinters penetrated a boiler casing and caused a temporary drop in steam pressure. Fire-fighting and damage control countermeasures included turning on the hangar sprays and lowering the fire curtain, to contain the initial fire raging in the upper hangar forward.

'Bing' Cross had turned in at 1630 after a warming mug of cocoa. He was awakened by the sounding of action stations. He reached the flight deck as a shell tore a hole only 15 ft away and more landed around him as he made for the quarterdeck at the stern of the carrier. The hangars caught fire. 'Bad luck your Hurricanes got it with the first salvo,' shouted a passing Fleet Air Arm pilot over the din of the continuing crashes and explosions. Then the public address system packed up and the word to abandon ship was passed from man to man.

Able Seaman 'Ron' Doyle was at his Action Station in the 'B' Transmitting Station (TS) which was directly alongside the 'B' Gun Director Tower, which was about half a dozen steps down from the flight deck (approximately 100 ft above the waterline).

'Making my way to the TS I had to pass the tower, but before entering the TS I spent about 30 seconds or so talking to the Director Layer and what he then made of the enemy sighting, which was on our starboard quarter. As I looked in the direction to which the Director was trained, I could just catch sight of two masts and the upperworks of what I could only guess were very large ships, especially when the Layer was looking in the direction in which the crew of the tower were directing their telescopes. It was then that I could pick out two masts and the superstructure of at least two large ships. He also told me that the range was estimated at 18 miles.

'When the German heavy ships were sighted no aircraft were on patrol, on deck alert or even ranged on the flight deck. The ship was at the fourth degree of readiness (cruising stations) with air crew at ten minutes alert. There was no radar fitted and no lookout closed up in the crow's nest, despite perfect visibility.

'While I was still chatting to the men in the tower, I distinctly saw the flash of the (enemy) guns opening fire – within a matter of seconds I was through the armoured door and into the TS. We realised we were in real trouble and unable to do anything to help.'

Scharnhorst opened fire on *Ardent* at 1627 at a range about 16,000 yards, causing the destroyer to withdraw, firing torpedoes and making a smoke screen. *Ardent* scored one hit with her 4.7-inch guns on *Scharnhorst* but was hit several times by the German ships' secondary armament and sank at 1728. While this tragedy was happening, *Acasta* steamed at speed to lay a smoke screen round the *Glorious* to hide her from the enemy cruisers and obscure their target. Even as the smoke screen was being laid, orders were given on the *Glorious* to take up stations and prepare to abandon ship. The aircraft carrier was still moving at full speed. The laying of the smoke screen brought a lull in the firing and the captain, no doubt thinking there might still be a chance of escaping, ordered the men back to action stations. At 1658 a second shell hit the homing beacon above the bridge of the *Glorious* and killed or wounded the captain and most of the personnel stationed there. The smokescreen became effective enough to

THANK GOD FOR THE NAVY!

impair the visibility until 1720 when *Scharnhorst* hit the centre engine room on *Glorious* and this caused her to lose speed and commence a slow circle to port. The carrier also developed a list to starboard. The German ships closed to within 16,000 yards and continued to fire at her until about 1740.

Acasta broke through her own smoke and fired two volleys of torpedoes at *Scharnhorst*. One of these hit the battleship at 1734 abreast her rear turret and badly damaged her. *Acasta* also managed one hit from her 4.7-inch guns on *Scharnhorst*, but was riddled by German gunfire and sank at 1808. Without hesitation, the commander of the destroyer sacrificed his ship in his attempt to save the *Glorious*.

Estimates were that about 900 men abandoned *Glorious*. Leaving the ship was carried out almost routinely, the men calm and collected, without panic. Those who could lashed themselves to the overloaded, open Carley floats, replacing men who died from wounds or exposure in the icy water. The secrecy involved in the evacuation from Norway included keeping Coastal Command uninformed, so that no additional RAF reconnaissance patrols had been flown, which might have detected the German units at sea and assisted in finding the survivors. The German ships did not pick up any survivors and withdrew from the area. A rating on *Scharnhorst* recalled that: 'Our flags flew at half-mast and the whole bridge stood to attention because of the courage of the English sailors.'

'The thing which struck me most was the way the ordinary seamen carried out orders – absolutely no sign of panic or anything,' a survivor remarked. 'Then the salvoes of six-inch and eight-inch shells started again, hitting all the time. They shattered the bridge, wrecked the forward part of the ship, started up fires everywhere. The German cruisers had the *Glorious* at their mercy and it was impossible for her to escape.

'Once more orders were given to prepare to abandon ship. This time she was burning so fiercely that those on board knew she could not last. Without the slightest fuss and without waste of time they began to prepare to save themselves.

'Carley floats and rafts and planks were got up on the quarter-deck and thrown over to support survivors until they were picked up. The only boat that got away was a little dinghy which was pushed over the stern from the quarter-deck. Men quickly jumped over and clambered into it.'

'I know that when I was finally helped onto the raft after clinging on to the raft lashings', recalled Able Seaman 'Ron' Doyle, 'one of the men I took to be a senior rating took count at that moment and made it 47. Quite a large number had already succumbed to the bitter cold, thereby creating room for us latecomers.'

Among those who succumbed was the 263 Squadron CO, Squadron Leader John W. Donaldson along with nine other pilots, including Flying Officer Herman Francis Grant Ede DFC, the first Bermudian to die in the war, and eight of the ten Hurricane pilots on 46 Squadron.[10]

When the *Glorious* began sinking 'Jamie' Jameson remembered that his life-jacket was in his cabin down below along with his log book, which contained the notes of all his flying operations and flying times. A pilot's log book is his most precious possession, as it is to the captain of a ship. At that moment of jeopardy, he was apparently determined to save his log book, if he lost everything else.

He was seen to go down to his cabin, while 'Bing' Cross and two other members of his squadron were on the quarter-deck. Moving rapidly, he attempted to reach his cabin, only to find that he was shut off from it by a water-tight door. Running up to the quarter-deck again, he found that his companions had all disappeared over the side.

He took off his flying boots and was just about to jump over when he saw a raft, which was being towed by the *Glorious*, strike a rating who was swimming in the water, a terrific blow on the head and lay open his brow. He moved along to avoid a similar danger and then jumped over. For a quarter of a mile, he swam to a Carley float on which he saw his Commanding Officer. 'Hello, sir, can I come on your raft?' asked the New Zealand pilot.

There was still one destroyer floating and they were not worrying at all. They thought they would be picked up either by the destroyer or the Germans. A couple of ratings soon reached down and helped him on the raft.

By that time there were about 27 on it. But there were no oars. A rating pointed to one floating about ten yards away and the young New Zealand pilot was seen to dive in and recover it. That oar helped quite a lot, for they were able later to rig it with a sail made out of a pull-over and a shirt. Then the man who was injured by the raft swam along hanging to a plank. He must have been as tough as nails, for it was a great feat of his to get to the Carley float.

---

10. 802 Squadron lost 16 ground crew MIA; 823 Squadron, 12 ground crew MIA and 825 Squadron, one MIA.

THANK GOD FOR THE NAVY!

Many men were floating in their life-jackets; many were hanging to planks of wood; the sea was dotted with them. The German cruisers came to within a mile and a half of them, still firing at the remaining destroyer which fired back as hard as it could. It continued firing right up to the time it sank. The men on the float saw it disappear; they were watching it very intently, hoping when the Germans went that it would pick them up.

So the second destroyer went down with colours flying, firing to the end. The Royal Navy on that black day lived up to its finest traditions.

By now the *Glorious* was stopped. She was absolutely obscured by smoke. From the Carley float they could see no portion of the ship at all, only those great clouds of smoke on the surface of the sea, so they did not actually see her sink. Amid that shroud of smoke from her burning debris, she vanished beneath the waters, unseen by any human eye.

In those northern latitudes it was light all night. The Carley float was crowded and the waves continually washed right over the men. So cold was the sea that within four hours men started to die from exposure. The strongest among them did what they could to help and comfort the others. They held the heads of the dying men out of the water and when they died the bodies were committed to the sea. Some of the survivors had on so few clothes that it was necessary to remove some of the clothes from the dead to clothe the living in order to keep the spark of life in their frozen bodies.

When the men first got on the Carley float some of them started to sing cheery and popular songs. As the hours went by, they sang a hymn or two. Then as the cold gripped them, they fell into silence. They were drenched to the skin and lacked water and food. By next morning ten men were left on the float, among them three members of the RAF; Jameson, his Commanding Officer and an aircraftsman. Eighteen succumbed during that first night. On another float which provided about 60 men with a refuge directly the *Glorious* went down, only five men came through that terrible ordeal. One or two officers of the Fleet Air Arm who flew the Swordfish on the *Glorious* were also among the 36 men who were picked up, while five more men were saved and imprisoned by the enemy.

In the afternoon of the next day, it became calm and one survivor remarked that it would have been quite pleasant if they had possessed something to eat and drink and a few more clothes. One man went to sleep and fell overboard, but they were too weak to pull him back. Two others died from exposure. They spoke very little and there were no complaints at all. They just endured and hoped. On the second day 'Bing' Cross made a suggestion which did much to aid their ultimate survival. 'If we cut the bottom out of the float and put it across the top, we may be able to get a little sleep,' he said. Without delay they set about this task and they found that it was a big improvement. It not only enabled them to snatch a little sleep, but to a certain extent it kept their legs out of the water. That day there was talk of reaching the Shetlands, although the officers knew it was impossible, for they were at least 600 miles away and drifting in the wrong direction. But it was something to talk about and it gave the others something to think about. 'Do you think we'll make the Shetlands tonight?' a rating asked.

'Not tonight, but we'll probably make them tomorrow,' was the encouraging reply. Several times the same question evoked the same answer. It gave hope and helped the weakening men to endure a little longer.

'One of the things which got us down was the fact that we saw a British cruiser squadron of three or four ships searching for us. They put up an aircraft and we saw it taking off and landing, but it did not come in our direction,' one of the survivors stated. 'We saw several of our own aircraft as well as those of the enemy, but they never spotted us.' Who can plumb their agony of mind as they saw those searching ships turn and vanish from sight?

'The rating with the injured head clung grimly to life. He grew weaker under the exposure, but he was still alive next day, although he began to wander in his mind. No one could help him. Some were weaker than others, but all were suffering from the exposure and strain. Then a corporal of marines dropped asleep, lost his balance and fell over into the sea. Weak as they were, they managed to grab him before he floated away and after a big struggle dragged him out of the sea to safety. A couple of hours afterwards one of the ratings sighted a trawler. 'There's a ship!' he said.

'We'd been seeing ships before,' said one of the survivors. 'We looked round and saw the ship about two miles away. It was coming towards us. We could see the masts in line. When it got to within one mile of us it turned off – it was an awful moment – but the trawler [the Norwegian tramp steamer the *Borgund* on passage to the Faeroe Islands, arrived late on 10 June] only stopped to pick up people off another Carley float and then it came on towards us. By this time one of the officers was waving his yellow Mae West and we all shouted as much as we could.'

Able Seaman 'Ron' Doyle: 'Our raft, when found by the trawler at approximately 0230 (from the Norwegian sailor's watch) with just seven of

THANK GOD FOR THE NAVY!

the original 47 – and I believe they reckoned we were more dead than alive. I was one that had to be lifted out of the raft by the wonderful Norwegian sailors, who also acted as our nursemaids.'

The *Borgund* soon came alongside the second Carley float and one of the Norwegians got down the ladder on to the float and made a loop of rope in which he hoisted the worst cases up on board. Those who were not so weak were helped up the ladder. Of the 27 men who originally scrambled on this float, only nine remained alive.

'No one could have been kinder to us than those Norwegians', wrote one survivor. 'Their kindness was beyond praise! They gave up their bunks for the worst cases – there were 36 survivors in all. They gave us cigarettes, shared out their only half bottle of whisky among us and made tea and coffee for us. Then they pointed out the best and warmest places in which to sleep, while they slept on deck or anywhere else they could find.'

After picking up the survivors of the *Glorious*, the fishermen set their course for the Faeroes, while the cook in the galley made some Scotch broth for them which was the finest food they had ever tasted in their lives. It was rather sad that the injured seaman who had clung so desperately to life should die after being taken on board.

The trawler was not equipped with wireless, so her skipper could not inform the British authorities that he had picked up the survivors of the *Glorious*, thus for nearly a week it was feared that there were no survivors at all. So the trawler plugged along in fairly heavy seas at about eight knots, while the Norwegian fishermen lavished all the care and attention in their power upon the men they had rescued, nursing them and feeding them and making them as comfortable as they could in the circumstances.

All on board had a bad moment when they heard the sound of an aeroplane. Presently a Heinkel 115 appeared and circled low over them. But it dropped no bombs and they breathed freely again as it turned away. Five hours later they saw it returning and this time they felt sure that it had come to bomb them. But again, it merely circled over them and flew away, much to their relief.

After a rough passage lasting three days, the *Borgund* arrived at Tórshavn in the Faeroe Islands, where British army officers met the 37 survivors of whom two died. *Svalbard II*, also making for the Faeroes, picked up five survivors but was sighted by a German aircraft and forced to return to Norway, where the four still alive became prisoners of war for the next five years. It is also believed that one more survivor from *Glorious* was rescued by a German seaplane. Of 1,474 men on board the three RN ships, only 45 survived.[11] Jameson and Squadron Leader Cross were two of only three officers and 41 other ranks rescued out of the three ships' companies. They were taken to the Faroes where they returned to the UK on the destroyer *Veteran*. Suffering from considerable pain in their feet, Cross and Jameson were landed at Rosyth a week later and sent for treatment.

Jameson spent six weeks at the Gleneagles Hotel, which had been turned into a military hospital, followed by six weeks sick leave, some of which he spent with relatives in Ireland. He was awarded the DFC and on 17 September 1940 he was given command of 266 Squadron at Wittering.

Able Seaman 'Ron' Doyle concludes: 'Chatting amongst ourselves (that is, the 30 plus survivors) for the ten months we were in the Aberdeen hospital was very enlightening. None of what was said went further than our ward, after the dire warnings we had been given. The only other person that survived who was in any position to know how things really were was Lieutenant Commander Hill who gave the order 'Prepare to abandon Ship'. He would have known the actual state the ship was in. (Incidentally, he was the officer who gave me the order to 'Abandon Ship').[12]

---

11. Two survivors from the *Acasta* were rescued by a German seaplane and taken to Norway.
12. The Admiralty Board of Enquiry was held within days of the 34 available survivors returning to Britain, its findings then sealed until 2041. The Board of Inquiry determined that not all the boilers were connected and that ready use shells at the guns were only for AA attack. Controversy began almost immediately, with questions first being asked in Parliament on 31 July 1940 culminating in a debate on 7 November. Why was *Glorious* returning home independently of the main convoy? Why was she so badly prepared? In 1946 a brief official account described a ship 'travelling independently due to shortage of fuel on a normally safe route that had simply run out of luck and been caught in the wrong place at the wrong time'. Winston Churchill was the first to contradict this, writing in his account of the war that the fuel explanation was 'not convincing. The *Glorious* presumably had enough fuel to steam at the speed of the convoy.' The fact remains that had *Glorious* remained under the protection of other warships, she would have been steaming at convoy speed, which would have consumed less fuel.

THANK GOD FOR THE NAVY!

British and French troops had to withdraw at Åandalsnes and Namsos and Narvik was besieged and finally captured on 8 June. On 10 June, two days after the evacuation of Narvik a Blenheim, one of three on reconnaissance over Trondheim Fjord, sighted the *Scharnhorst* and two cruisers, one of which they thought might not be a cruiser but a pocket-battleship of the *Deutschland* class. The warships were back from their successful encounter with the *Glorious* two days before. It was decided to assault them where they lay at anchor near a supply ship and 12 Hudsons carried out a pattern bombing attack from 15,000 ft. They dropped 36 250 lb armour-piercing bombs, losing one of their number to anti-aircraft fire and another to an enemy fighter. The *Scharnhorst* was probably missed, but both the cruisers and the supply ship received direct hits. This was on 11 June.

On the night of 13/14 June *Ark Royal*, escorted by the *Nelson* .and other units of the Home Fleet, arrived at a position 170 miles off Trondheim. At midnight 15 Skuas took off for the attack. Long-range Coastal Command Blenheims provided fighter cover over the objective, while Beauforts of the same Command created a diversion by attacking the nearby aerodrome at Vaernes in order to prevent, if they could, German fighters from taking off to engage the Skuas. At that time of the year and in that latitude, daylight is perpetual. It was not possible, therefore, to effect surprise. The enemy were prepared and waiting. The Skuas pressed their attack with the greatest determination. Eight of them - more than half - were shot down, but two hits were scored on the *Scharnhorst*.

Two days later a reconnaissance showed that she was still at Trondheim. On the 16th and 17th June two attempts by Coastal Command were made to attack her, but clouds, lower than the hill-tops, obscured the harbour. It was not until 21 June that the *Scharnhorst* was again sighted. This time she was at sea - eight miles west of the Utyoer lighthouse - steaming south at 25 knots, with an escort of destroyers. Flight Lieutenant Phillips on 204 Squadron piloting a Sunderland took off from Sullom Voe at 1237 initially escorted by three Blenheims from Sumburgh. A Do 18 flying boat was sighted and was attacked by the Blenheims to no effect; a gunner was killed in a Blenheim and all three returned to base, abandoning the Sunderland. While circling to await the Blenheims, five Fairey Swordfish were sighted by the Sunderland. Continuing alone, Phillips altered course and at 1435 sighted an unidentified submarine, submerging fast.

THE AIR WAR AT SEA IN THE SECOND WORLD WAR

At 1445 the Sunderland sighted the *Scharnhorst* accompanied by seven destroyers and their position was reported to base. The flying boat was at once attacked by heavy fire which endured for an hour. During this time its crew watched a torpedo attack on the battle cruiser by the five naval Swordfish which began at 1510. One of the Swordfish was seen to crash into the sea. At 1610 the Sunderland was being shadowed by a He 60, which dropped a bomb falling about 50 yards away. Between 1520 and 1620 Phillips was under heavy and continuous AA fire. At 1625 first three and then one more Me 109 appeared and carried out attacks on both quarters. The Sunderland captain was the same officer who had piloted the Sunderland which had fought six Ju 88s when protecting a convoy on 3 April. The combat with the Me 109s lasted about half an hour. All the Messerschmitts were hit and at 1640 one of these was shot down into the sea in flames. Meanwhile, in the Sunderland, the rear turret had been put out of action very early in the engagement and tanks were punctured. Phillips broke off the engagement and made off for its base shortly before the arrival soon after 1430 of nine Coastal Command Beauforts from a squadron which had been grounded because of trouble with their engines. On hearing that the *Scharnhorst* was at sea every pilot volunteered to take up his aircraft. They were allowed to make the attack.

When they saw these Beauforts, it is probable that the Germans thought that, like the Swordfish, they were carrying torpedoes and that another torpedo attack was imminent. The destroyer escort was seen to deploy so as to intercept, if they could, the torpedoes launched against the capital ship. The Beauforts, however, were loaded with armour-piercing bombs and, flying in a crescent formation, made a dive-bombing attack. At least three bombs hit the *Scharnhorst*, one on its stern, another nearly amidships and the third forward on the port side. The Beauforts were forthwith attacked by 45 to 50 Bf 109s. Three Beauforts were shot down; the rest got back to their base. There were no cases of engine failure. Hudsons, one of which was lost, renewed the attack, but encountered fierce opposition from an enemy now fully ready to meet them, for the warships were by then only 25 miles from Stavanger. In this action five aircraft were lost altogether, but the *Scharnhorst* had received sufficient damage to cause her to retire to a floating dock at Kiel. She remained out of action for the rest of the year and did not put to sea again until early in 1941.

THANK GOD FOR THE NAVY!

The last Fleet Air Arm action of 1940 around Norway was during September and October when *Furious* flew off Swordfish of 816 and 825 Squadrons to attack Tromsø and Trondheim, the former being the first large-scale night torpedo attack carried out by the Fleet Air Arm. Almost one month later Swordfish crews would etch their name in history in another battleground, at Taranto in the Mediterranean.

Chapter 2

Biplanes Against Battleships – Operation 'Judgement', 11 November 1940

*My Stringbag flies over the ocean,
My Stringbag flies over the sea.
If it weren't for King George's Swordfish,
Where the hell would the Royal Navy be?*

Nobody ever called the Fairy torpedo bomber by its designation (TSR 2). Even 'Swordfish' was rarely used. Instead, a nickname made in jest by someone commenting on its ability to carry a highly respectable range of weapons had stuck - permanently: *No housewife on a shopping spree could have crammed more into her string bag.* The Swordfish first flew in 1934 and was obsolete even when it joined the Fleet Air Arm in July 1936 but it was immensely flexible, durable and reliable, which enabled it to make an important contribution to the allied victory at sea. Its radial engine and ungainly array of struts, wires and fabric-covered tubing was anything but aerodynamic. (The wire and steel-tube frame had been stressed to permit use as a dive bomber to meet a Greek Air Force requirement before it lost interest). Supposedly, the 'Stringbag' could attain 138 mph, preferably with a following wind (however, encumbered with a torpedo and long-range fuel tanks, 'Stringbags' reportedly struggled to register just 93 knots (107 mph). Officially the aircraft had a service ceiling of 10,890 ft and a range of 1,028 miles carrying a single 18-inch, 1,550 lb Mk.XII torpedo or a 1,500 lb load of depth charges, mines or bombs. For self-defence, it was armed with a .303 Vickers machine gun above its engine and another .303 Vickers machine gun operated by the rear

BIPLANES AGAINST BATTLESHIPS

gunner. The two- or three-man crews - a pilot, a navigator-observer and a radioman-rear gunner - flew in an open cockpit exposed to the elements and enemy action. Enemy fire often passed through while the biplane wings made the Swordfish extremely manoeuvrable.

Even before the war, Captain Arthur Lumley St. George Lyster (later Vice Admiral, Sir Arthur Lyster KCB CVO CBE DSO) of the Fleet Air Arm had been studying the possibility of an air attack on the Royal Italian Navy, or Regia Marina (RMI) at anchor in Taranto Harbour. Born in Warwickshire on 27 April 1888, after leaving Berkhamstead School in 1902, Lyster joined HMS *Britannia* to train for a naval career. He was to see active service in the First World War, his ship fighting at Gallipoli in 1915. Lyster began his association with the Fleet Air Arm in December 1937 when he was given command of the aircraft carrier HMS *Glorious*, then attached to the Mediterranean fleet. This was not his first experience of naval aviation however. As a Lieutenant Commander during World War I, Lyster had been seconded to the Italian Fleet, where along with Wing Commander Arthur Longmore, he established the 'English Camp' at Taranto flying seaplanes, for which the Italians awarded him the Order of the Crown of Italy. Lyster's knowledge of the naval base and its surrounding geography would prove vital as the strategic situation with Italy deteriorated and Europe headed for war. In 1938 in response to the German invasion of Czechoslovakia, Lyster was tasked by Admiral Sir Dudley Pound to review the plans that had been drawn up three years previously to attack the Italian fleet at Taranto, which is located in southern Italy facing the Ionian Sea. Lyster oversaw the preparations and training of the two Swordfish squadrons embarked in *Glorious* to successfully conduct night time flying operations and torpedo attacks on static targets close to shore. After several months of practice, using the Grand Harbour in Malta for his exercises, Lyster came to the conclusion that with the right preparations, an attack on Taranto was possible.

Lyster left *Glorious* in June 1939 on promotion to Rear Admiral in charge of Scapa Flow and from there he played a strategic role in the Royal Navy's Norwegian campaign, during which he was Mentioned in Dispatches. When Italy declared war on 10 June 1940, the Royal Navy was operating only a reduced squadron of cruisers and the old carrier HMS *Eagle* in the Mediterranean. The Royal Navy now had to run convoys from Gibraltar to Malta and again from Malta to Alexandria, which meant running a gauntlet including airbases in Sardinia and Sicily, the narrow waters around Pantelleria and more airbases on the south of the Italian peninsulas well as along the north coast of Africa. Taranto Harbour lies in the Gulf of Taranto 320 miles from Malta. The inner harbour (Mar Piccolo) was completely landlocked except for a narrow channel, which would admit ships only of cruiser size or smaller. It contained extensive dock facilities and its small size made surface ships within it virtually safe from attack with torpedoes. The larger outer harbour (Mar Grande), which opened to the west and where capital ships were obliged to moor, was protected from surface attack by long breakwaters. Taranto was conveniently close to the Malta-to-Suez run and easily guarded by land-based aircraft but the Regia Marina strategy being a 'fleet in being', there was never any intention for the battleship fleet to engage with the Royal Navy. The Italians however, were running their own heavily protected convoys - inevitably crossing the path of the British in the waters between Italy and Libya. The first clash came on 9 July. HMS *Warspite* hit the battleship *Giulio Cesare* with a 15-inch shell at extreme range during the Battle of Calabria. HMS *Eagle* - operating just 18 Swordfish and three Sea Gladiators - launched several torpedo attacks against Italy's capital ships, but none struck home. Italy retaliated by dropping more than 400 bombs on the British fleet.

On 22 August the new armoured fleet carrier HMS *Illustrious*, just four months old and the first aircraft carrier in the world to be fitted with radar before completion, headed down the river Clyde and set course for Gibraltar. On 30 August she joined 'Force F', along with *Valiant* and the old cruisers *Calcutta* and *Coventry*. They would sortie with Force 'H' - the carrier *Ark Royal*, the battle-cruiser *Renown*, the cruiser *Sheffield* and 12 destroyers - along with a convoy of three merchant ships to Malta. As *Illustrious* slipped past the Pantelleria narrows and cruised by Malta on 2 September she would deliver six Swordfish and a large stock of spare parts to the FAA unit based there.

Lyster meanwhile had returned to the Mediterranean in August, as Flag Officer Aircraft Carriers flying his flag in HMS *Illustrious*. His immediate task under direction from Commander-in-Chief, Mediterranean Fleet, Vice Admiral Sir Andrew Browne 'ABC' Cunningham, was to bring the Taranto strike plans to full readiness and work up the air groups in both *Illustrious* and *Eagle* to undertake the mission, part of which was to help reinforce

BIPLANES AGAINST BATTLESHIPS

British maritime supremacy and to deter Italian interference in the Western Mediterranean and North Africa. Lyster's plan called for a moonlit attack against Taranto Harbour, with a force of 30 Swordfish in two waves. Each wave would have six aircraft armed with torpedoes to attack the battleships, five with bombs to dive-bomb the cruisers and the destroyers and one armed with a combination of bombs and magnesium parachute flares for ships and installations in the inner basin as a diversion.

The decision limiting the number of Swordfish carrying torpedoes had resulted from a mistaken belief that balloons and net obstructions would restrict suitable dropping places in the harbour. Originally, 90 balloons, tethered by steel cables, had been deployed across the harbour in three rows, but a lack of hydrogen and strong winds on 6 November had blown away 60 balloons and reduced the number to 27 by the night of the attack. An aircraft from the *Illustrious* operating from Malta then picked up full details of the enemy's dispositions, together with photographs showing the anti-torpedo nets and barrage balloons and four battleships - *Cavour*, *Littorio*, *Duilio* and *Vittorio Veneto* and the heavy cruiser *Gorizia* were singled out for torpedo attacks. *Cavour* was targeted by three Swordfish; *Littorio* by five aircraft; *Duilio* by one; *Vittorio Veneto* by only two and the *Gorizia* by one. *Giulio Cesare* and *Andrea Doria* were not targeted either by bombs or torpedoes.[13]

The 18-inch torpedoes were set to run at 27 knots at a pre-set depth of 33 ft. (Taranto's battleship harbour had an average depth of 49 ft.) This was calculated to enable the torpedoes to pass under anti-torpedo netting while still allowing the secret Duplex magnetic/contact warheads to detonate on contact or explode under a warship by 'sensing' its magnetic presence while passing beneath. The warheads were extremely sensitive to rough seas and

---

13. An attack on the harbour facilities at Taranto by RAF Wellingtons, with their heavy bomb loads, would have allowed the FAA, with its torpedo-armed Swordfish, to concentrate a maximum effort against the battleships. Arming six more Swordfish with torpedoes would have allowed all the battleships to be targeted with multiple attacks [which] would very likely have proven devastating. Two days later, on 13 November, ten Wellington bombers from Malta attacked the port facilities at Taranto. *The Attack at Taranto* by Lieutenant Colonel Angelo N. Caravagio, Canadian Forces. (US Naval War College Digital Commons, 2006).

there was also concern that the torpedoes would bottom out in the harbour after being dropped.

The torpedo attack was to be made from the west and toward the rising moon. The date for the attack was therefore dependent on the phase of the moon and time of moonrise. Based on the time and distance factors required to achieve surprise – getting the carriers to the launch point under the cover of darkness, launching and recovering aircraft in darkness and then exiting the area – the planners determined that the complete naval task force consisting of *Illustrious*, 2 heavy cruisers, 2 light cruisers and 4 destroyers, could not be north of a line from Malta to Kithera before dark. The run north had to be made before moonrise and the aircraft launched by 2100 hours. A further restriction involved the speed and endurance restrictions of the aircraft; their return trip could be no greater than 400 miles. The launch point for the attack was established as 40 miles from Kabbo Point, just west of the Greek island of Cephalonia, about 170 miles southeast of Taranto. *Illustrious* also had Fairey Fulmar fighters of 806 Naval Air Squadron aboard to provide air cover for the task force, with radar and fighter control systems.

Taranto was defended by 101 anti-aircraft guns and 193 machine guns and the loss rate for the bombers was expected to be fifty per cent. A repeat of the operation was planned to take place the following night with a single strike force of 15 Swordfish comprising six torpedo aircraft, seven dive-bombers and two flare droppers.

Operation 'Judgement' the initial plan, was originally set for Trafalgar Day (21 October) with 36 Swordfish from *Illustrious* and *Eagle*. But the strike had to be delayed until November after a fire broke out in the 60-gallon auxiliary fuel tank of one of the Swordfish in the hangar aboard *Illustrious*. The tanks were fitted in the observer's position on torpedo bombers to extend the operating range of the aircraft enough to reach Taranto; the observer taking the air gunner's position. 'One's back and head rested on it (the fuel tank)' wrote A. W. F. 'Alfie' Sutton, the observer on Lieutenant Michael Alexander 'Tiffy' Torrens-Spence's Swordfish, and it was the explosion of one of these that had set off the hangar fire three weeks earlier. 'The tank was hardly a morale-booster to have with you when going in to face intensive anti-aircraft fire.'[14]

---

14. A.W.F. Sutton, *'The Attack'*, in *Air Pictorial*, October 1967.

BIPLANES AGAINST BATTLESHIPS

The fire spread and destroyed two Swordfish. And then *Eagle* became unavailable after she had suffered damage to her aviation fuel system from recurrent near misses.[15] Five of *Eagle's* Swordfish were transferred to *Illustrious* to strengthen the available force, planned to consist of 21 aircraft, to be flown off in two ranges, at hourly intervals.[16] All this activity did not go unnoticed below decks. Air Mechanic Rayburn for one was not alone in thinking that something was 'on'. 'We were soon busy getting as many aircraft as possible serviceable. All the ammunition was brought up from the magazine, plus torpedoes and bombs and extra planes were on board. It was pretty crowded. We worked 18-20 hours a day to get it all ready.'

The attack was rescheduled for 30 October, but again it had to be delayed, since on that night the moon would not provide the required illumination. Any night from 11 – 19 November would offer suitable moonlit conditions. The Royal Navy's experience of aviation doctrine during the 1930s, largely aboard *Glorious*, had ruled out the idea of dawn and dusk torpedo attacks because enemy ships would be silhouetted against the sunrise or sunset while the attacking aircraft would be lost against the gloom of the dark sky. But, at least in the Mediterranean, the sun would rise and set very quickly. Timing the attack therefore needed to be impractically precise and so the RN began practising night carrier-launched air attacks; the only nation so to do. Cunningham devised a cunning deception, which also served to further Britain's growing needs in the Eastern Mediterranean. Two carriers, five battleships, nine cruisers, 27 destroyers and eleven merchantmen would put to sea at the same time. These were divided into five task forces and three convoys – each with different objectives and destinations.[17]

---

15. '…the weight of the attack could have been significantly increased by a second carrier. Admiral Lyster deeply regretted the unavoidable absence of *Eagle*. "Her fine squadrons," he wrote in a private letter, "would have increased the weight of the attack considerably, and I believe would have made it devastating." In fact, Cunningham could have replaced *Eagle* with *Ark Royal*.' (*The Attack at Taranto* by Lieutenant Colonel Angelo N. Caravagio).
16. *Illustrious* also had Fairey Fulmar fighters of 806 Naval Air Squadron aboard to provide air cover for the task force, with radar and fighter control systems.
17. Force 'A': *Illustrious, Warspite, Malaya, Valiant, Ramillies, York, Gloucester* and *Nubian, Mohawk, Jervis, Janus, Juno, Hyperion, Hasty, Hero, Hereward, Havock, Ilex, Decoy and Defender*. This force was to cover convoy MW3 to Malta,

THE AIR WAR AT SEA IN THE SECOND WORLD WAR

For several days before the attack Martin Marylands of 431 General Reconnaissance Flight on Malta maintained watch over the Italian naval base and its approaches. The Short Sunderland flying boats of 228 Squadron based in Malta were too slow and flew too low to survive flying over such a heavily protected shore facility, but in September three Marylands had arrived. These were capable of 278mph with a ceiling greater than 28,000 ft which put them out of reach of any fighter the Italians then possessed. On 10 November, in appalling weather, Pilot Officer Adrian Warburton flying a Maryland from Malta made two low-level photographic reconnaissance sweeps over Taranto, noting the names of five battleships, 14 cruisers and 27 destroyers along with their precise locations. Born in Middlesbrough on 10 March 1918, the son of a WWI submarine captain, 'Warby' was christened on board a submarine in Grand Harbour, Valletta. Warburton made his passes at about 50 ft, so low that the Italians were unable to train their ack-ack guns on him. He returned to Malta with a ship's radio aerial dangling from the Maryland's tail wheel and after 20 minutes' running combat with a Cr.42. The latest air reconnaissance photos, which reached Cunningham and Lyster by air on the afternoon of 11 November, showed that five of the six Italian battleships then in commission were berthed in the harbour.[18] The RAF kept Taranto under nearly continuous observation until 2330 hours on 11 November. Warburton circled the harbour several times and when the cameras failed, he flew so low that his observer was able to read off the names of the battleships as they passed over the fleet. There was a sixth battleship entering. 'All the pheasants had gone home to roost', wrote Cunningham with satisfaction. The 'pheasants' moored in the harbour were the brand new *Littorio* and *Vio Veneto* and four older battleships, *Giulio Cesare, Duillio, Andrea Doria* and *Cavour* that had been modernized in the 1930s.

The *Illustrious* had left Alexandria with 24 Swordfish, but three had experienced engine trouble and dropped into the sea. The problem was traced to bad fuel from one of the tanks on board the carrier, so only 21 were available for the attack. Sub Lieutenant John W. 'Tweeny' Neale, the observer

---

rendezvous with 'Force F' and then detach *Illustrious, York, Berwick, Glasgow, Gloucester* and *Hasty, Havock, Hyperion* and *Ilex* as 'Force X' for the Taranto raid.

18. Photographs taken on 11 November revealed that six Italian battleships and three cruisers, together with some destroyers, were moored on the shoreward side of Taranto's outer harbour, with two more cruisers, 21 destroyers, 16 submarines, nine tankers, and many more, smaller craft, in the inner harbour.

who was crewed with Sub Lieutenant Philip Donald Julian Sparke DSC and would fly in the first wave, wrote: 'Our morale was very high and we had a wonderful briefing about Taranto. I reckon I knew more about the harbour at that time than the harbourmaster himself.' By the time the first flight left *Illustrious*, all of the observers would know the exact positions of the six battleships in the outer harbour and the latest arrangements of the balloon barrage and net defences.

Lieutenant Commander John William 'Daddy' Hale the 819 Squadron Commander felt extra anxious because of the contaminated petrol in *Illustrious*. 'Three aircraft had been lost because of this during the previous two days and on the morning of 11 November the carburettors on all the aircraft were stripped down and cleaned and then refilled with petrol. The feeling was that someone else might go into the sea from the same cause. Apart from this, I felt much calmer than at other times when we had taken off for a night raid. I suppose this was because we all realised the terrific magnitude of the occasion and this dwarfed the feeling of what might happen to me.'

At 2035 on the 11th, from a point 170 miles from Taranto, the first wave of 12 Swordfish led by Lieutenant Commander Kenneth 'Hooch' Williamson commanding 815 Squadron with his observer Lieutenant Norman John 'Blood' Scarlet-Streatfield, lifted off the flight deck of the *Illustrious* in radio silence and without navigation lights to avoid detection. The first wave, consisting of six Swordfish armed with 18-inch torpedoes, two carrying 16 parachute flares and four 250 lb bombs, and four Swordfish with six 250lb bombs, was split into two sections when three of the bombers and one torpedo bomber strayed from the main force while flying through thin clouds. Captain 'Ollie' Patch DSO of the Royal Marines, flying one of the four Swordfish carrying six 250 lb bombs (one of which had a Royal Marine boot strapped to it), was one of the senior men. His observer, Lieutenant D. Goodwin, was even older. The torpedo carrying aircraft carried an extra fuel tank in the second seat immediately behind the pilot and the bombers carried one suspended below the fuselage. All the Swordfish carried a second officer, an observer/navigator.

It was the first duty of the flare aircraft to lay the flares in a line along the eastern shore of the harbour so as to show up in silhouette the Italian battleships for the torpedo-carrying aircraft coming in from the west. The bomb carriers were to find targets of opportunity ashore or afloat as a diversion for the torpedo aircraft. British planners were worried that searchlights aimed at low angles might dazzle the pilots of the torpedo-armed aircraft so it was decided that a distraction was needed to keep the searchlights directed upward. Originally, this distraction was to have been provided by Wellington bombers from Malta that were to attack the dockyard and ships in Mar Piccolo between 0830 and 0915.

The main group approached the harbour at Mar Grande at 2258. Sixteen flares were dropped east of the harbour, then the flare dropper and another aircraft made a dive-bombing attack to set fire to oil tanks. The next three aircraft, led by Lieutenant Commander 'Hooch' Williamson, attacked over San Pietro Island. As soon as Williamson was abreast of the southern tip of the entrance to the outer harbour, he would detach two flare droppers who were to fly behind the Italian battleships, drop their flares and light up the battleships. At the same time the sub-flight which carried bombs only were to go full speed – about 100 knots for the inner harbour. This was in the hope of making the enemy think that the main attack was being made on the cruisers and destroyers which were anchored there. This attack was to be under way before the torpedo aircraft went in at low level. Then torpedo aircraft were to delay slightly and then make a double attack, half from the southern tip of the outer harbour and the other half from the northern tip. In this way the battleships were to be attacked from both sides at once.

'The theory was', wrote 'Hooch' Williamson 'that the bombers would create such a diversion that the torpedo-carrying aircraft would be able to sneak in, deliver their attack and get away unobserved. 819 Squadron was to repeat this surprise half an hour later. When I propounded this theory to my squadron, I am afraid that they greeted it with a considerable amount of ribald merriment.'[19]

On the way up to their height the first wave passed through a thin layer of cloud at about 4,000 ft and the four bomber Swordfish became detached. They proceeded independently to Taranto arriving there shortly before the main body. One Swordfish, piloted by Flight Lieutenant H. A. L. Swayne RN, with Sub Lieutenant John Buscall RNVR as observer, finding themselves alone, sped ahead, fearful that they had dropped behind. Swayne's engine triggered Italian diaphone sound detectors and anti-aircraft gunners opened

---

19. Quoted in *Swordfish At War* by W. Harrison (Ian Allan Ltd 1987).

fire. The skies lit up and the rest of the formation, only minutes behind, clearly saw their approach path.

'As we approached the southern tip of the half-moon', continues 'Hooch' Williamson, 'the two flare droppers were detached and the two torpedo-aircraft on the port side of the leading sub-flight fell back astern of the leader. These three torpedo-aircraft then turned in and headed for the southern portion of the battle fleet. A few moments later the other torpedo-carrying sub-flight, led by Lieutenant Neil M. Kemp, turned to the east and approached the enemy ships along the northern tip of the half-moon - all according to plan. We had to fly low for about 3½ miles through the barrage and there was something morbidly attractive about those bullets. They appeared to approach very slowly until they were just short of the aircraft, then they suddenly accelerated and whistled past, if you were lucky, at whatever speed bullets do whistle past. This is all very exciting and not unduly alarming, as all pilots as a race have an extraordinary and totally unjustifiable belief in their own personal immortality. The observer however doesn't share this sublime faith and for him it must be rather like being a passenger in a car without any brakes, which is careering down a steep hill with a learner driver at the wheel. Worse, all the observer could do was to crouch at the bottom of a totally un-armoured open cockpit with a still partially filled long-range petrol tank, shaped like an inverted 'U', immediately over his head.

'All the torpedo aircraft reached the battle fleet and all, skimming over the water, dropped their torpedoes from heights varying between 30 and 15 ft above the surface. Just about then the short-range anti-aircraft fire was intense and as every bullet has to come to rest sooner or later, I've often wondered how many finished up in the town and dockyard. In the meantime, the bombers and flare droppers were bombing ships in the inner harbour, the three cruisers to seaward of the battleships, a seaplane base and some oil storage tanks.

'I doubt if any of the aircraft were under fire for more than five or six minutes, yet in that short space of time half the Italian battle fleet had been put out of action.'

'Daddy' Hale particularly remembered the great cloud of flak that went up to greet Williamson when the second wave was still about 70 miles away and Lieutenant G. A. Carline, his observer, said 'There's Taranto'. 'This flak never stopped from then until we arrived about an hour later and I thought at the time the Italians must be very worried and frightened. There were no searchlights, which surprised me because they would have blinded us. Apart from some fires ashore, there was nothing to indicate what damage had been done.'[20]

About 20 seconds after Williamson had dropped his torpedo at the *Conti de Cavour* that blasted a 27 ft hole in her side below her waterline he ran into 'a lot' of flak from the destroyer *Fulmine* which opened up from about 1,000 yards and his Swordfish crashed in the harbour, although his observer was not entirely convinced that they had been shot down at all. 'We [might have] put a wing-tip in the water whilst turning in the middle of the harbour in order to make our getaway. I couldn't tell. I just fell out of the back into the sea. We were only about 20 feet up. It wasn't very far to drop. I never tied myself in on those occasions. Then old Williamson came up a bit later on and we hung about by the aircraft which still had its tail sticking out of the water. Wops ashore were shooting at it. The water was boiling so I swam off to a floating dock and climbed on board that. We didn't know we'd done any good with our torpedoes. Thought we might have, because they all looked a bit long in the face.

Williamson eventually surfaced and swam to a floating dock, hotly pursued by armour-piercing and incendiary bullets. 'I climbed on to the dock and was immediately set upon by about six Italians and I feel I enjoy the doubtful distinction of being the first British naval officer to be captured by enemy dockyard workers. My observer and I became prisoners of war after that, first with the Italians and later in Germany.'

Of six torpedoes dropped, two scored hits - the *Conti de Cavour* sinking in shallow water - one near miss damaged the *Littorio* and the *Caio Duilio* too was damaged. Sub Lieutenants P. D. Sparke DSC and 'Tweeny' Neale had run to within half a mile of the *Cavour*, dropped their torpedo and spun round for the return. Neale remembered timing the torpedo's run with his stopwatch. 'The little explosion I saw after 110 seconds was most disappointing and it was not until afterwards, we realised that the new magnetic pistol on the warhead was set to run too deeply to show much result. Sparke and I were

---

20. The Italian defences fired 1,430 12.5 cm rounds, 313 10.7 cm and 6,854 8.8 cm from the heavy guns. The 20 mm cannons fired 2,635 shells and 40 mm 931. And that was the shore batteries alone. The number of shells fired by the warships is not recorded.

the first ones back to the ship and I can remember great surprise when all the aircraft but one, were eventually flying round and landing back on. I thought that we would have been the only ones to come away from that lot alive. Also, I can remember feeling thankful to the Italians for leaving the light on in the lighthouse, Santa Maria di Leucia on the heel of Italy. It helped my navigation considerably on the way home.'

The bombers had less success, destroying a seaplane hangar and starting a fire at an oil-tank farm but failing in attacks on ships. Several bombs hit cruisers or destroyers but despite being fused nose and tail, few of the 42 bombs dropped appear to have detonated. The most successful bombing run was by Sub Lieutenant William. C. Sarra in the first wave on the seaplane hangars and slipway. All six bombs fell on their target, igniting large fires and demolishing the hangars. Two aircraft were destroyed.

'Ollie' Patch and Goodwin, his observer would be the last aircraft from the first strike to land. Patch had kicked his Swordfish bomber into a dive, released his bombs and was forced to dodge behind a hill and weave close among the rooftops of Taranto itself to evade an intense barrage of following gunfire.

The first wave was followed by a second wave of nine led by 'Daddy' Hale about 90 minutes later. Five Swordfish were carrying a torpedo and four more carried 16 parachute flares and four 250 lb bombs while one 'Stringbag' carried six 250 lb bombs. These aircraft began taking off at 2128. Eight were airborne by 2134. However, as Lieutenant Edward W. Clifford and his observer Lieutenant G. R. Going in Swordfish eight began to move forward for a take-off run the ninth and final aircraft, piloted by Lieutenant William Douglas Morford with his observer, Sub Lieutenant R. A. F. Green, had its chocks prematurely removed and began to roll forward and its wings tangled with those of Clifford's Swordfish, causing the latter to be struck below. Morford's auxiliary fuel tank located between the wheels of the aircraft detached from the aircraft and the engine cut. Morford only managed to get it re-started after a drop of 1,000 ft and returned with his six 250 lb bombs intact. Fired on by nervous gunners on board the *Illustrious* and *Berwick*, he flew around the carrier at a safe distance for 15 minutes before the correct identification lights were shown and he was cleared to land.

Clifford pleaded with mechanics to patch up the fabric covering its wing and fuselage which had been torn and it returned to deck in just 25 minutes. With the encouragement of US Navy Lieutenant Commander

THE AIR WAR AT SEA IN THE SECOND WORLD WAR

John N. Opie III, who had just three days training for his new role of naval observer, on board, Clifford argued with the commander (flying) that he should be allowed to take off late and join the attack. Opie had come aboard the *Illustrious* on 22 August, when she departed Britain bound for Alexandria. During the intervening months he had sailed on board a number of Royal Navy ships on combat operations. He was in the heavy cruiser HMS *Kent* when she was torpedoed and he would spend time on board the battleship *Warspite*, destroyer *Jervis* and light cruiser *Sydney*. Opie's plea for Clifford to be allowed to take off was approved and he took off at 2158.

Thus, eight Swordfish made up the second wave. The five torpedo-carriers crossed north of Capte Rondinella, avoiding the guns of San Pietro Island, swooping in over the merchant ship anchorage and drawing a heavy barrage of light flak.

The second wave had arrived over Taranto around midnight, dodging the steel cables of barrage balloons and coming under fire from over 800 anti-aircraft guns. 'Alfie' Sutton and his pilot 'Tiffy' Torrens-Spence sighted the Santa Maria di Leucia lighthouse on the way in to the Gulf, fixed his Swordfish on it and then held off to the west. 'But', 'Alfie' wrote,[21] 'we were detected – the enemy had very good sound detectors – and anti-aircraft guns hopefully opened fire as we passed along 15 miles offshore. When we were about 60 miles off Taranto we saw the place – a great greenish-coloured cone of anti-aircraft fire, for the Italians were still keeping things going after the first attack had retired. We made to the northwest of the town, crossing the coast at around 9,000 ft and then crossed and re-crossed the coastline to put off the anti-aircraft guns which had started to get uncomfortably accurate as we approached the harbour. The noise of the breaking waves on the beach tends to confuse the sound locators if you do that.

'The flare droppers had been detached as we crossed the coast and 'Daddy' Hale now ordered their release, with him starting his dive as they did so. At this moment the dive bombers should have run in to bomb the cruisers in the inner harbour to attract their fire, but we did not have enough aircraft in the ship to provide bombers for the second wave so there was nothing to draw the Italians' fire from us. As we went down, they put up an intense box barrage for us to fly through. The rest of the sub-flight of three followed him down and then over we went and down in that screaming torpedo dive.'

---

21. Quoted in *Swordfish At War* by W. Harrison (Ian Allan Ltd 1987).

BIPLANES AGAINST BATTLESHIPS

Of the four remaining Swordfish that carried torpedoes, Hale and Carline and Lieutenant S. C. Lea with his observer Sub Lieutenant P. D. Jones aimed their torpedoes at *Littorio*, one of which hit. Lieutenants Gerald W. Bayley and his observer Henry J. Slaughter appeared to branch off to attack *Andrea Doria* or *Vittorio Veneto*, despite having been hit twice by anti-aircraft fire, but their torpedo missed. Sutton and Torrens-Spence saw Bayley and Slaughter get hit by anti-aircraft fire from the *Gorizia*, the only aircraft lost from the second wave. There was an orange flash of flame and their Swordfish spun away out of control before exploding and crashing into the harbour between the *Goriza* and the destroyer *Gioberti*. It is thought they may have tried to drop their torpedo on *Goriza* as one was found floating nearby – its warhead crushed from impact. Both men were killed. Only the body of Bayley was recovered. Bombs hitting ships again failed to explode and further bombing of the oil-tank farm did little damage. Lea and Jones hit the *Caio Duilio* alongside the 'B' turret on the starboard side with their torpedo which they dropped from just 600 yards. It blew a large hole in her hull and flooded both of her forward magazines before they safely made their escape, weaving past the heavy cruisers *Fiume* and *Zara*.

The final aircraft to arrive on the scene 15 minutes behind the others made an unsuccessful dive-bombing attack on one of the Italian cruisers despite heavy anti-aircraft fire, then safely returned to *Illustrious*, landing at 0239. Lieutenant John W. G. Wellham with his observer Lieutenant Patrick Noel 'Pat' Humphreys dived into what appeared to be a 'hole' in the anti-aircraft fire and then suddenly struck a drifting barrage balloon cut loose during the battle. The son of a retired petty officer, Wellham was born on the Isle of Bute on 2 January 1919. After his mother died in childbirth when he was six, he was brought up by his grandmother. His ambition to fly was ignited by reading Captain W. E. Johns' *Biggles* novels and was fanned when he won, in a spot dancing competition, a flight in a Fox Moth. He joined the RAF at seventeen. After a near-fatal crash in a Hawker Hind in 1937, he was visited by a premonition that he would not die flying; he also conceived the notion that he was under the personal protection of a spirit called 'Joey'.

Tumbling towards Taranto city John Wellham managed to regain control and he spotted the *Vittorio Veneto* looming to his right. The battleship had also spotted the Swordfish. The Italian flagship opened up with everything she had as Wellham was pulled into a 180-degree turn with one wing dragging in the water. The torpedo was dropped and Wellham carried out a sharply

THE AIR WAR AT SEA IN THE SECOND WORLD WAR

climbing turn to starboard. The torpedo missed but it might have continued on to hit *Cavour*. The Swordfish was then hit by an exploding shell in the lower port wing, breaking wooden ribs and tearing a hole in the fabric. 'Pat' Humphreys bellowed at Wellham through their Gosport tube: 'That was a bit exciting. I think that you've bent the plane somewhat. Do you think she'll get us home?'

'It wasn't my fault,' Wellham replied indignantly. 'It was those bloody Eyeties!'

Wellham flew 150 miles back to *Illustrious* without difficulty. But, as he throttled back to landing speed, his Swordfish became uncontrollable, flopping through the air and threatening to stall until he cut the engine early to thump on to the deck. As the Swordfish was taken down into the hangar, Wellham heard a sailor say, 'Fuck mate, look at that!' Looking over the aircraft's side, he saw that the port aileron rods were broken into two jagged pieces and, through the broken fabric, he noted several bent wing ribs.[22]

'Daddy' Hale and 'Tiffy' Torrens-Spence aimed at the *Littorio*. Because of his 'innate nervousness', Torrens-Spence always forced himself to press home his attacks to a suicidal degree[23] and this attack would be no exception. Hale's torpedo hit the battleship's starboard bow but the second was later found stuck in the mud. Torrens-Spence had spotted his target at a less than perfect 45° angle amid heavy defensive fire, as 'Alfie' Sutton recalled: 'All the close-range weapons had opened fire. We could see multiple batteries by the entrance to the inner harbour pouring stuff out – right next to our dropping position. We pulled out a bit to starboard; tracer and incendiaries and a horrible thing we called 'flaming onions' came streaming up at us. We came down a bit short, found ourselves down over the cruisers and pulled out – with that terrific jolt in the stomach as you pull out of a full torpedo dive – over the masts of the cruisers and down to our dropping height on the other side. The cruisers saw us and opened fire. We could see the tracers streaming along past us, seeming to float along. We found we had been in too close to one of the old *Cavour* battleships to attack her but now we were motoring in over the water towards one of their fine new *Littorio's*. She saw us and opened fire – the flash of her close-range weapons stabbed at us as, first

---

22. Lieutenant Commander John Walter George Wellham MiD died on 9 May 2006 aged 87. He was the last surviving pilot of the raid on Taranto.
23. Quoted in *War in a Stringbag* by Charles Lamb.

one and then another opened up along her entire length. We were coming in on her beam and were at the centre of an incredible crossfire from the cruisers, battleships and shore batteries. No worries about clear range or gun zones for the Italians, they just fired everything they had, except the 15-inch ones. I could see the shots from the battleships bursting among the cruisers and merchant ships and the place stank of cordite and incendiaries with smoke everywhere. Torrens-Spence fired the torpedo - it did not come off - the magnetic release had failed!

'He finally managed to release at 700 yards, by which time that *Littorio* battleship just about extended over the whole horizon and we seemed to be looking down the muzzles of the close-range guns. A steep turn to starboard, straighten out and then "smack", we had hit the water, we're down, but we weren't; we hit with wheels only and "Tiffy" Torrens-Spence pulled away through the balloon barrage flying between the floats and eventually out of that cauldron of fire. Suddenly everything was quiet. No one was firing at us. Relaxing, we set course for the gap between the forts out of the moon path and got away really low down - so low we did not see two defence ships in the harbour entrance. We sailed up over their masts as they opened up with just about every gun they had - to no avail, we were clear and on our way home.'

By the time the last aircraft had completed the attack, the first Swordfish had reached *Illustrious*; it was 0120. The carrier recovered the first-wave aircraft by 0155. The only landing incident of the night, after intense combat, six-and-a-half hours flying and a night deck landing, involved Lieutenant Neil Kemp. After catching the arrester wire his Swordfish was released to join the forward deck park. He opened the throttle a little too far - and crashed into the back of the aircraft before him.

The second wave began landing at around 0200. Edward Clifford was the last to land, touching down at 0250. His observer, Lieutenant Going said: 'It was the biggest firework display we had ever seen and we were awestruck by it.' Italian defences fired 13,489 shells from the land batteries, while several thousand were fired from the ships. The anti-aircraft barrage was formidable, having 101 guns and 193 machine guns. There were also 87 balloons, but strong winds caused the loss of 60 of them. The Italian fleet had 22 searchlights (the ships had two searchlights each) but Captain Denis William Boyd DSC, a veteran of Jutland, commanding *Illustrious*, stated in his after-action report, 'It is notable that the enemy did not use the searchlights at all during either of the attacks.'

THE AIR WAR AT SEA IN THE SECOND WORLD WAR

Diving into Mar Piccolo just as his 16 parachute flares began to stutter out, Clifford spotted the darkened cluster of heavy cruisers by the glow of the burning seaplane base. Dropping from 2,500 ft to 500 ft he released his four 250 lb semi-armour piercing bombs. The destroyer *Passagno* and the cruiser *Trento* were hit, but the bombs failed to detonate though *Trento* was left with a large hole in her main deck with torn bulkheads and ventilation trunking. (It transpired later that despite being fused nose and tail, few of the 42 bombs dropped at Taranto appear to have detonated). Italian records show that the destroyer *Libeccio* was hit by an unexploded bomb dropped by Lieutenant J. Murray and Sub Lieutenant S. Paine. Her bow structure was fractured and needed structural reinforcement.[24]

'It was wonderful to hear next day that three battleships had been hit and a few cruisers,' recalled 'Daddy' Hale. 'I think the reason for the success was the great experience of all the aircrews. We were all peacetime trained and came from four squadrons undiluted even after a year of war and I believe that all the pilots had at least 800 hours flying experience.'

Air Mechanic Rayburn was among those that had waited anxiously. 'Then after a couple of hours came the first roar of a Pegasus engine, then another. Finally, all had returned but two, one of these being Lieutenant Commander Williamson. We were elated when RAF reconnaissance showed one battleship sunk, two more heavily damaged and other damage. This was what we had joined for, but later there would be a price to be paid.'

On the morning of the 12th one of the precious Marylands again ran the gauntlet of flak and fighters at Taranto and the crew brought back proof, in the form of photographs, that three of Italy's six battleships would not be troubling the Royal Navy for some time to come. The *Littorio,* which was hit by two live torpedoes on the first strike, was badly damaged on the second wave strike. The third hit had struck low on the starboard side further forward than the first torpedo. It blew open a hole 40 ft by 30 ft under 'A' turret, at the bottom edge of its bulge and it caused heavy flooding. The torpedo that failed to explode after it was dropped by 'Tiffy' Torrens-Spence was later found

---

24. Clifford was killed in action on 10 January 1941 when *Illustrious* came under sustained air attack by newly arrived Stuka dive bombers (see next chapter). Going had to have a leg amputated. Lieutenant W. D. Morford, who had been involved in the on-deck collision with Clifford's Swordfish, was so badly burned that he required plastic surgery.

in the mud. There was a dent in *Littorio*'s starboard stern quarter above it. Defusing this torpedo delayed salvage operations for a month and it was not until 11 December that she began her journey to dry dock.

The battleships that could still steam - *Vittorio Veneto* and *Giulio Cesare*, which had escaped damage and *Andrea Doria* having survived the attack, departed Taranto with cruisers in escort for Naples to avoid being caught by a second attack by the Royal Navy. Sceptical about the reported success, senior British officers debriefing the pilots had begun to plan a repeat attack for the next night. One pilot drily remarked, 'They only asked the Light Brigade to do it once!' As the day wore on, however, bad weather moved in and Cunningham decided against a second attack and the task force turned away for Alexandria. Late that day, radio messages were received that confirmed the damage: three of the Italian navy's six battleships were severely damaged, out of action for at least several months. *Littorio* had considerable flooding caused by three torpedo hits and she was saved only by running her aground. Even so, in the morning, the ship's bows were totally submerged. Casualties were 32 crewmen killed and many wounded. Although actual damage to the ship's structures was relatively limited, the machinery was intact but she would not be repaired until the end of the following March.

One aircraft, despite having been hit twice by anti-aircraft fire, aimed a torpedo at *Vittorio Veneto* but the torpedo missed. The *Caio Duilio* and the *Conte Di Cavour* were both beached. The battleship *Duilio* was hit by a torpedo that blew a large hole in her hull, flooding both of her forward magazines. Repairs to *Duilio* would take seven months. The *Conte Di Cavour* had a 39 ft × 26 ft hole in the hull, and permission to ground her was withheld until it was too late, so her keel touched the bottom at a deeper depth than intended. Twenty-seven of the ship's crew were killed and over 100 more wounded. Only her superstructure and main armament remained above water. Her main guns and large chunks of her armour had to be removed to lighten the ship and she was not re-floated until July. She was partially repaired and towed to Trieste for further repairs and upgrades, but still undergoing repairs when Italy surrendered. Two cruisers were heavily damaged and the seaplane base and oil depot badly damaged.

The *Illustrious* and her escorts re-joined the rest of the fleet, all ships arriving at Alexandria on 14 November. Admiral Andrew Cunningham was triumphal, announcing, 'The zeal and enthusiasm with which these deliberate and accurate attacks were carried out in comparatively slow aircraft in the face of intense fire cannot sufficiently be praised. It was a great day for the Fleet Air Arm and showed what they could do when they had their chance. Taranto and the night of 11/12 November 1940 should be remembered for ever as having shown once and for all that in the Fleet Air Arm the Navy has its most devastating weapon. In a total flying time of six and a half hours - carrier to carrier - 20 aircraft had inflicted more damage upon the Italian fleet than was inflicted upon the German High Seas Fleet in the daylight action at the Battle of Jutland.'

Count Ciano, Mussolini's son-in-law announced that it was 'A black day. The British, without warning, have attacked the Italian fleet at anchor in Taranto and have sunk the dreadnought *Cavour* and seriously damaged the battleships *Littorio* and *Duilio*. These ships will remain out of the fight for many months. I thought I would find 'Il Duce' downhearted. Instead, he took the blow quite well and does not, at the moment, seem to have fully realized its gravity.' The Regia Aeronautica Italiana had promised no Royal Naval ship would ever be able to approach within 180 miles without being sighted. *Illustrious* had launched her Swordfish 170 miles from Taranto.

In London on 13 November Winston Churchill declared enthusiastically to the House of Commons, 'The result affects decisively the balance of naval power in the Mediterranean and also carries with it reactions upon the naval situation in every quarter of the globe. I feel sure the House will regard these results as highly satisfactory and as reflecting the greatest credit upon Admiral Cunningham and above all on our pilots of the Fleet Air Arm.'[25]

The German naval command intimated that Britain would now have complete freedom to reinforce their positions in the Mediterranean and Middle East, transfer ships to the Atlantic and mount offensive operations that would place the Italian land operations in Egypt in jeopardy. The balance of power had swung to the British Mediterranean Fleet which now enjoyed more operational freedom: when previously forced to operate as one unit

---

25. The miserly scale of awards to air and ground crew left a lasting sense of resentment however. Six months' later Williamson and 'Daddy' Hale each received the DSO (many felt that they deserved the Victoria Cross) and 16 DSCs and 20 Mentions in Dispatches were awarded. By then one-third of those taking part were dead.

to match Italian capital ships, they could now split into two battlegroups; each built around one aircraft carrier and two battleships. But the Taranto attack had very little effect in disrupting Axis convoys to Africa, Italian shipping to Libya actually increasing during October 1940 - January 1941. British naval authorities had in fact 'failed to deliver the true knockout blow that would have changed the context within which the rest of the war in the Mediterranean was fought.'

The attack on Taranto was avenged a year later by the Italian navy in its raid on Alexandria, when the Mediterranean fleet of the Royal Navy was attacked using midget submarines, severely damaging HMS *Queen Elizabeth* and HMS *Valiant*.

Lieutenant Commander John Opie meanwhile sent back numerous reports to the Office of Naval Intelligence (ONI), reporting on his own observations and also forwarding almost any Royal Navy document he could get his hands on. On 14 November, he quickly made his way to the American Legation in Cairo and wrote a four-page report on the Taranto attack. He had obtained a copy of the report by the commanding officer of the *Illustrious* and added his own observations to 'supplement the enclosed report'. In America, as in Britain the Taranto attack was front-page news. The *New York Times* ran a six-column headline on page one. The *Washington Post* gave the story similar space and *Time* magazine published three pages of coverage. On 22 November Chief of Naval Operations Admiral Harold R. Stark wrote to his commander in Hawaii, Admiral James O. Richardson, mentioning the Taranto attack and asking him about installing torpedo netting to protect the ships anchored at Pearl Harbor but nothing was done. In the days and months that followed the American officers serving as neutral observers with the Royal Navy were obtaining and forwarding the facts about these successes to the US Navy in the States but the American admirals nor anyone else ever made a Taranto-Pearl Harbor connection.

The battleships' HMS *Ramillies* and HMS *Malaya* were now no longer needed in the Mediterranean and could be transferred to equally vital duties in the Atlantic, where the Kriegsmarine was beginning to recover from its losses at Narvik. But the reduction in the Regia Marina Italiana battle fleet from six to two battleships was only temporary and the Royal Navy would fail to capitalize on the operational-level opportunities resulting from the success of the attack at Taranto. Advantage would finally be ended with the arrival of Fliegerkorps X from Norway in January 1941. Admiral Lyster deeply regretted the unavoidable absence of *Eagle*. 'Her fine squadrons,' he wrote in a private letter, 'would have increased the weight of the attack considerably and I believe would have made it devastating.'[26]

The lessons of the Battle of Taranto were not lost on those who observed the effects of the operation however. While in Italy from 18 May to 8 June 1941, the naval members of a Japanese delegation, headed by Rear Admiral Koki Abe, the Japanese Assistant Naval Attaché in Berlin spent many days in Rome talking with Supermarina officers, then travelled to Taranto to see the fleet. They inspected *Littorio* which had just completed its repairs and interviewed many eyewitnesses to the Taranto attack. The Italians wanted to learn about carrier operations because Benito Mussolini had recently approved the conversion of two liners to aircraft carriers. The Japanese wanted to know about the operation of the Italian navy, providing a list of 83 topics for discussion. The Commander-in-Chief of the Imperial Japanese Navy, Admiral Isoroku Yamamoto ordered reports on the attack from his attaché in Berlin and tactical air chief Minoru Genda in London. Lieutenant Commander Naito was quickly sent from Berlin to Italy with orders to report what he could find about the British attack plan. This was submitted direct to Yamamoto. Upon Naito's return to Japan, he provided a personal briefing on what he had found to Commander Fuchida – the pilot who would lead the attack on Pearl Harbor on 7 December 1941. The Japanese Assistant Naval Attaché's findings then fed into the planning process for the massive surprise air raid against the US Navy at Pearl Harbor.

---

26. Cunningham could have replaced *Eagle* with *Ark Royal*, which had been undergoing a refit for most of October and had returned to Force 'H' on 6 November.

Chapter 3

Operation 'Excess' (January 1941)

Of all my memories of this gallant island of ours, the strongest and the one that stands out indelibly in my mind and has left the deepest and longest impression are those fearful days in 1941 with the German air assault on the aircraft carrier HMS Illustrious.

Lino Bugeja, referring to bombing attacks on his homeland, the island of Malta.

Two months after the attack on the Italian fleet at Taranto and seven months after Italy had entered the war, Valletta at Christmas was full of shoppers. Warships of the Royal Navy were back in Grand Harbour and there was a general feeling of euphoria. Air attacks on Malta had eased somewhat. The nightmare was over, or so the Maltese thought. There were even strong rumours that the war was over or would soon be. As a result, people who used to live in the vicinity of the dockyard in the majestic port and who had left the area in the early days of the war felt it was safe enough to return to their homes. Many did, with fateful consequences. In early January 1941 the word quickly spread throughout the dockyard that while escorting a convoy to Malta, a big aircraft carrier had been savagely attacked at sea by enemy aircraft and had suffered severe damage and loss of life. The aircraft carrier was hit six times while escorting the convoy in the Sicily channel and was hit a seventh time in another attack as it approached Malta.

Two further carrier operations had been carried out before the end of 1940. In December Swordfish from *Illustrious* attacked airfields in the Aegean and the Dodecanese while *Eagle* struck at Tripoli harbour. On the night of 16th/17th December, eleven Swordfish bombed Rhodes and the island of Stampalia but with little effect. Four days later six Swordfish from *Illustrious* attacked two convoys near the Kerkennah Islands bound for Cyrenaica with vital military stores and sank two large Italian merchant ships. On the morning of 22 December, 13 Swordfish attacked Tripoli harbour, starting fires and hitting warehouses multiple times. The *Illustrious* arrived back at Alexandria two days later.

In addition to the attacks on the harbours, the Swordfish squadrons from both carriers were employed in the night interdiction and support roles in the Western Desert, tasks in which other Fleet Air Arm units specialised in later months. Meanwhile Hitler had become increasingly dissatisfied with the setbacks experienced by the Italians in Cyrenaica and with the direction of the war taken by his ally. At sea also *Illustrious* and *Eagle* were threatening to cut off the Italian armies in Africa from metropolitan Italy. Advance elements of the Afrika Korps arrived in Tripolitania before the end of 1940 and with them came the first units of the Luftwaffe, including, from Norway to Sicily, Fliegerkorps X, equipped with 500 Ju 87 Stuka and Junkers 88 aircraft, which had just finished intensive training in the anti-shipping role, with particular emphasis on the tactics for dealing with carriers.

On Tuesday, 7 January 1941, ('Force A'[27]) was operating in support in the Eastern Basin and covering the passage from Alexandria to Malta of a convoy as part of Operation 'Excess'. Concerned about the Luftwaffe, Captain Denis William Boyd and Admiral Lumley Lyster, aboard *Illustrious* as Fleet Air Arm commander, had repeatedly advised Admiral Sir Andrew Browne Cunningham it would be better if *Illustrious* kept its distance from the convoy while still providing air cover. Senior Observer Lieutenant Desmond Vincent-Jones, the temporary squadron leader of 805 Squadron, agreed. He recalled: 'We in *Illustrious* felt it would have been tactically more sound if the carrier had been detached to act independently and at speed 20 to 30 miles to the southward of the main fleet, thus keeping us further from the air threat in Sicily. The fighter CAP (Combat Air Patrol) could be maintained over the fleet from a range of 20 miles with little greater difficulty than if the carrier was in company.' But Admiral Cunningham wanted the carrier stationed between the two battleships *Warspite* and *Valiant* as a morale boost. He knew the Luftwaffe had moved onto Sicily,

---

27. 'Force A' comprised *Warspite* and *Valiant* and the destroyers *Nubian*, *Mohawk*, *Dainty*, *Gallant*, *Greyhound*, *Griffin*, *Jervis* and *Illustrious* to sail from Alexandria, covering convoys MC 4, MW 5 and ME 6 east of the Skerki Banks.

OPERATION 'EXCESS' (JANUARY 1941)

but Air Chief Marshal Tedder had assured him that RAF fighters could easily handle the Stukas. 'Our fighter pilots weep for joy when they see them,' the Air Chief Marshal had said confidently. While it was true that a Spitfire could easily outclass a Stuka, a Fulmar was an entirely different matter.

Illustrious was carrying a squadron of 12 Fulmars (806 Squadron), along with a detachment of three Fulmars of 805 Squadron. This was regarded as the standard fighter complement for the fleet carriers. There also were 20 Swordfish (in 815 and 819 Squadrons). 'There was never anything wrong with the eight-gun Fulmar', wrote Terence Horsley.[28] 'It was a fine aeroplane, manoeuvrable, with a good take-off, moderate climb and plenty of endurance. It satisfied the demands for a navigator's seat and several wireless sets considered essential for Fleet work. It merely lacked the fighter's first essential quality - speed. Unless the pilot's first burst made a kill, he rarely got a second chance.' On 7 January, when a reconnaissance bomber was sighted shortly after 0800, a section of Fulmars, which had been kept ready on deck for just such an eventuality, failed to intercept.

Ratings like Sydney Millen on *Illustrious* felt confident however. Seeing the escorts including *Warspite* practising an air defensive exercise on Thursday, 9 January he felt 'to all our eyes nothing could penetrate that barrage. How wrong could we be?'

From first light on the morning of 10 January the action started. Swordfish from the *Illustrious* attacked an Italian convoy off the Italian island of Pantelleria without significant effect. For many aboard *Illustrious*, like Air Mechanic Rayburn, it was to be a baptism of fire. 'As always, we had read orders of the day. There was a message from the C in C commenting that units of the German air force had been sent to airfields in Sicily and we might expect rather more activity than hitherto. When we arrived off Pantelleria things started to hot up and the ship's Tannoy system kept us informed of events as they unfolded. The cruiser *Bonaventure* engaged enemy units to the westward.[29] The destroyer *Gallant* struck a mine and

---

28. *Find, Fix and Strike* (Eyre and Spottiswoode, 1945).
29. When the Italian submarine *Settimo* and two Italian torpedo boats *Circe* and *Vega* attempted to attack, the *Vega* was sunk by *Bonaventure* and *Hereward*.

her bows were blown off.[30] I remember standing in the well deck, a grey sea surging past. There seemed to be an eerie still air over the ship. I have often thought about that since ... Fear? Premonition? I know I had a very strange feeling.'

Sydney Millen on duty in the after end of the hangar remembered that towards noon, 'action stations' was sounded 'and from then on all hell broke loose'.

'Suddenly the fleet came under heavy air attack mainly directed at *Illustrious* by squadrons of Stuka dive bombers' recalled Air Mechanic Rayburn. 'All the guns of the fleet opened fire. The tannoy told us that large numbers of aircraft were in the air over Sicily. The ship was all closed up at action stations and then all the ships guns opened up. The steel box of the hangar was like a huge sound box. My action station, as with all maintenance crews, was in the hanger with the aircraft, which by the way were all heavily armed and loaded with torpedoes ready for an attack on the Italian Fleet. *Illustrious* was armed with 16 4.5 dual purpose guns and eight six-barrelled 2 lb quick-firing AA weapons. The ship kept jumping and shaking. Several large bombs hit the ship aft and the after hanger was on fire. The noise was indescribable. In my baptism of fire, all that sticks in my mind are impressions.'

At 1220 hours two Savoia-Marchetti SM.79 torpedo bombers were detected on radar six miles from the fleet. It had been no accident. Their orders were to draw off the Fulmars on Combat Air Patrol (CAP) patrol as a prelude to the main attack on the Fleet. They approached from below the radar horizon and raced low through the fleet towards the starboard side of the carrier, met only by light anti-aircraft fire and then dropped their torpedoes 2,500 yards distant from *Illustrious*, which took urgent evasive action by swinging to port. Both torpedoes passed astern and went on to narrowly miss *Valiant*. The attack had achieved its aim however. Five Fulmars dived from

---

30. The mine had detonated her forward magazine, killing 65 and injuring 15 more of her crew. Her sister *Griffin* rescued most of the survivors and the destroyer HMS *Mohawk* towed her stern-first to Malta where she was beached in Grand Harbour at dawn on the 11th and never repaired. As *Mohawk* and the 'Force B' cruisers steamed from Malta to re-join 'Force A', they were surprised by 12 Stuka dive bombers of II/St.G.2 attacking out of the sun at 1520. *Gloucester* was hit by a bomb which failed to explode and *Southampton* was hit by two bombs, which killed 80 men and started fires, requiring the ship to be scuttled 210 miles east of Malta.

OPERATION 'EXCESS' (JANUARY 1941)

14,000 ft onto the low-level bombers and three of these chased and then engaged the SM.79s as they fled the fleet, the CAP fighters expending all their ammunition in the effort and claiming one shot down. One Fulmar was damaged and forced to return to their carrier, while the other two exhausted their ammunition and fuel during the combat and landed at Hal Far airfield on Malta. The remaining pair engaged two torpedo-carrying SM.79s, damaging one badly enough that it crashed upon landing. They were low on ammunition and out of position, as they chased the Italian aircraft over 50 miles from *Illustrious*.

When *Illustrious* had detected a second - much larger - raid at 1225, the Fighter Direction Officer knew the fleet was in trouble. The four Fulmars on air patrol were out of position and low on ammunition. The enemy formation was only 28 miles away, to the north. The fleet itself was about 85 miles west of Malta. *Illustrious* recalled the four Fulmars as soon as the raid was detected. The FDO also ordered them to climb. But the fighters had a long way to fly and a lot of height to regain.

Four Fulmars and three Swordfish were already in position on *Illustrious'* deck for a scheduled 1235 take-off for an air patrol just as 18 He 111s of II/KG 26 and 43 Stukas of I. Gruppe/Sturzkampfgeschwader and II. Gruppe escorted by ten Bf 110s of ZG 26 came into sight at 12,000 ft to begin the second attack of the day. Oberstleutnant Karl Christ, Kommodore of the Stukagruppen ordered that '*Illustrious* mussen sinken! ('The *Illustrious* has got to be sunk!') No other warship had ever been delivered such a blow, but the Stuka crews were confident that four direct bomb hits would destroy the armoured carrier and to make certain, the crews had practised their dive-bombing techniques over an outline of the carrier's shape marked by buoys in the sea not far from their new base.

The attack was carefully planned. Ten of the Stukas went after the battleships as a diversion to split the anti-aircraft fire while a group of Stukas forming into three clover-leaf formations headed towards *Illustrious*. It was difficult to count the numbers exactly but the first formation consisted of 15 and the second of 20 to 30 aircraft. Their actions demonstrated the value of experience, planning and training. They flew in a very loose and flexible formation, constantly changing their height, speed and position to evade anti-aircraft fire. Some of the Stukas began their dives ranging from 65 to 80° and checked at 6,000 to 8,000 ft before going into the aiming dive. Bomb release varied from about 1,500 ft in the first wave to 800 ft in later ones.

THE AIR WAR AT SEA IN THE SECOND WORLD WAR

Others delayed their bomb release until they pulled out lower than the height of *Illustrious*' funnel. Most continued to dive after releasing their bombs and flattened out low over the water having crossed the flight deck. At least one Stuka machine gunned the *Illustrious*.

A crewman of one of the Swordfish ranged on deck recalled: 'Suddenly there was a loud explosion on my right-hand side and I felt the whole plane shake as a shock wave buffeted me too - the twin 4.5inch gun turret a few feet away had opened fire, its barrels pointing vertically over the flight deck, and following their line, I looked up to see a mass of aircraft coming in fast immediately over the fleet, and they were not ours. We were frantically waved off and up the deck, even though the ship was still swinging rapidly to starboard to turn into the light breeze. By now all our 4.5-inch guns and pom-poms were blazing away straight above my head. We rumbled off as the enemy, gracefully it seemed, wheeled over in succession and dived straight down, almost as if they wanted to look down the funnel. As we passed the island the first bomb exploded at the after end of the flight deck where we had been parked seconds before. The sea around *Illustrious* was boiling with falling shrapnel and I saw that another direct hit had been scored, this time plumb in the middle of the flight deck.'

By 1237, the last aircraft left the deck even as the first bombs fell. One of these was piloted by Sub Lieutenant Alfred 'Jackie' Sewell, who together with Lieutenant Robert S. Henley in another Fulmar shot down a SM.79 earlier that morning. During this combat Sewell's Fulmar was slightly damaged from return fire but he managed to depart for *Illustrious* and landed successfully. He changed aircraft and was in the air when *Illustrious* was damaged by a Stuka. Leading Aircraftman Denis Tribe, his observer, recalled: 'We were at readiness on the flight deck and took off before *Illustrious* was to wind. Before we were at 2,000 ft the first bomb from a Ju 87 hit the ship. It went into the open lift well and exploded in the hangar - it was really horrific to watch as you realised how many would be blown to bits - also a very close escape. As we climbed to attack the Stukas were diving to bomb. When we reached height, the air seemed full of aircraft. From the rear seat I saw one go down and another was damaged. It wasn't long before we were out of ammunition and landed at Hal Far.' (Some of the Fulmar pilots, which despite having no ammunition, made dummy attack runs in an effort to disrupt the enemy's aim and successfully forced two Stukas to jettison their bombs early.)

OPERATION 'EXCESS' (JANUARY 1941)

The first of five bombs (550 or 1,100 lb) that hit the *Illustrious* had penetrated the deck armour just forward of the un-armoured aft lift and had detonated 10 ft above the hangar deck in the lift well, causing many casualties among aircraft maintenance personnel and starting a severe fire which destroyed nine Swordfish and five Fulmars, ruptured the rear fire sprinkler system, bent the forward 300-ton lift like a hoop and shredded the fire curtains into lethal splinters. It also blew a hole in the hangar deck, destroying a Fulmar which had been hauled out of line after its engine had failed to start and damaging areas three decks below. The boilers were still untouched but the stokers were working in temperatures of 130°F. A shell splinter had jammed the sprinkler system full on which was flooding the ship and for a time could not be shut down because the fires were out of control.

Sydney Millen in the after end of the hangar recalled: 'There was a terrific explosion for'ard and what I am sure was the forward lift was struck. Luckily, despite the debris etc I was unhurt and left the hangar. After that the ship shuddered many times as she was hit and like many of my comrades I helped in the rescue of the many injured. One of the after-gun turrets suffered a near direct hit and the carnage was awful. After a period owing to damage to our steering gear we were just going in circles, quite a target for the aircraft attacking, our escort had I presume decided to keep a fair distance as they were not conspicuous by their presence.'

Air Mechanic Rayburn had been standing more or less in the centre of the hanger. 'A chap came down from the flight deck; his rubber suit was full of holes with blood leaking from all of them. I helped carry him down to the casualty station in the washroom flats. The surgeons were busy. Blood washed from side to side with the sway of the ship. I returned to my action station in the hangar. The ship continued to rock and sway. I looked up with fear and apprehension. Then there was an almighty flash as a 1,000 lb bomb pierced the 4-inch armoured deck and exploded. I was only aware of a great wind and bits of aircraft, debris, all blowing out to the forward lift shaft of 300 tons, which was also blown out. There were dead and wounded all around. My overalls were blown off and I had small wounds to the back of my head and shoulder. I was probably 10-15 ft away from the bomb when it exploded. Luck I survived? I prefer the thought of someone looking out for me.

'The hangar by then was burning all over. The ship's commander came and said, "Come on lads close the armoured doors." The overhead sprays then flooded the hanger. The ship started to sink by the stern and everyone had to blow up lifebelts. Then came a spot of humour in all that chaos. Poor old Corporal Gater came through a side door white as a sheet saying 'I wish I hadn't bloody joined.'

Another bomb which passed through the forward-most port 'pom-pom' mount closest to the island failed to detonate, although it did start a fire. One bomb penetrated the outer edge of the forward port flight deck and detonated about 10 ft above the water, riddling the adjacent hull structure with holes which caused flooding in some compartments and starting a fire. The multiple hits at the aft end of the carrier knocked out her steering gear. Two near misses caused minor damage and flooding.

The main assault had lasted just seven minutes.

At 1320 another attack by 13 Ju 87s hit the carrier once more in the aft lift well, which again knocked out her steering and reduced her speed to 15 knots (17 mph). This attack was intercepted by six Fulmars which had rearmed and refuelled ashore after they had dropped their bombs, but only two of the Stukas were damaged before the Fulmars ran out of ammunition. *Illustrious* now had to be steered only by using her engines and her three screws as the rudder had been smashed but steerage was regained by 1303 through use of auxiliary steam mechanisms. She was attacked again between 1600 and 1700 in a second dive-bombing attack by about 30 Stukas in which another hit was believed to have been made on *Illustrious*. *Valiant* had one killed and three wounded from near misses.

During this attack Fulmars from *Illustrious* which had refuelled at Malta, claimed six or seven Stukas shot down or damaged with the fleet's anti-aircraft fire claiming three others. Germans records however, show the loss of just three Stukas, with another forced to make an emergency landing. One Fulmar and one Swordfish were shot down; their crews being saved and two enemy aircraft were shot down by gunfire. Eleven Swordfish and five Fulmars stowed in the hangar were destroyed by fire. One additional Swordfish, piloted by Lieutenant Charles Lamb, was attempting to land when the bombs began to strike and was forced to ditch when it ran out of fuel; the crew was rescued by the destroyer *Juno*.

Illustrious' radar had been put out of operation by the bomb hits but the second wave was detected by *Valiant* and the escort and fighters warned. Captain Boyd's report says the raid by seven Italian high-altitude SM.79 bombers began at 1329. The bomber formation at 14,000 ft was engaged before bombs could be released accurately. Splashes were observed scattered

OPERATION 'EXCESS' (JANUARY 1941)

around the fleet. But as *Illustrious* manoeuvred to evade the bombs her steam steering gear failed. The carrier was again out of control, steaming slowly in circles to port.

'The battering carried on for six to seven hours', recalled Air Mechanic Rayburn. 'There were many wounded piled up. The aft surgeon's station had been destroyed and the forward station was unable to cope quickly with so many casualties.'

Captain Boyd later concluded: 'This attack came at a bad moment for the fighters. Those in the air had already been engaged in two combats and were low down, and with little ammunition remaining. Relief fighters were ready on deck, but as the whole fleet had to be turned by signal from the Commander-in-Chief before they could be flown off, valuable minutes were wasted. In any case the Fulmar has not sufficient climbing speed to ensure being able to counter this type of attack, particularly if a heavy attack is launched shortly after a minor or diversionary attack.'

Four Fulmars struggling to get airborne at only 1,200 ft per minute against mass formations of Ju 87s in coordinated dives was asking too much of its pilots.

Illustrious listed toward Malta 75 miles away for the next nine hours, still afire, its burned and wounded men trapped and screaming below decks. Fires raged around the forward magazines but Captain Boyd made a daring decision: he would not flood the magazines. This enabled the ship to continue defending itself. He would later write: 'The guns crews (with about 60 per cent of the armament) beat off the subsequent attacks.' Her engines still intact, at a steady 17 knots, *Illustrious* limped towards Malta.

While still 45 miles from Valletta several more enemy strikes were hastily organised to apply the coup de grace but *Illustrious* now could receive intermittent air cover from Malta where three of her Fulmars were now operating from Hal Far with nine Hurricanes and *Valiant* and *Warspite* were still in company along with the destroyers *Hasty* and *Jaguar*. Late that afternoon, at 1604, another strike was reported on radar by *Valiant*. About 15 Italian Stukas from 237a Squadriglia with an escort of about five Italian single-seat fighters, and three Ju 88s of LGI attacked. *Illustrious* was unable to take effective evasive manoeuvres because of her damage and her fires were still burning out of control. The first wave of six Ju 87s attacked from astern shortly after coming into view at 1609. A second wave of three Stukas dived on the starboard side a minute later. A near-miss abreast the conning-tower funnel shook the *Illustrious* violently. Another burst just off the quarterdeck, killing and wounding those assembled there to tend the injured. Fortunately, the attack was nowhere near as well executed as the first and the enemy planes were chased off by Malta's Hurricanes and *Illustrious*' forward 4.5in mounts and four remaining pom-pom mounts despite being hampered by thick haze and smoke from the hangar fire. Only two bombs fell near the carrier.

At 1710 a fifth attack was made on the carrier, *Valiant*'s radar having detected enemy aircraft at 52 miles at 1656. Seventeen enemy aircraft came into view and then proceeded to circle the fleet to make an approach from up-sun and astern. The combined high-level and dive-bombing attacks appear mainly to have been directed at the battleships. None came close. After refuelling and rearming at Malta, several of *Illustrous*' Fulmars arrived a little too late and a long stern chase developed. Lieutenant Vincent-Jones described the scene: 'We soon sighted *Illustrious* on her way towards the Grand Harbour with smoke pouring out of her but still making a good 20 knots. She had parted company with the rest of the fleet. We were not in time to intercept before the attack developed but we caught up with the enemy on their way back to Sicily…'

Illustrious had to nose her own way through the swept channel leading to the entrance at Grand Harbour as the requested tugs were nowhere to be seen. Only two anti-submarine patrol vessels came out to assist. But the Axis air attacks were not over. An hour after sunset as *Illustrious* limped within five miles of the entrance to Valletta harbour, yet another attack developed. Malta radioed an urgent air-raid warning. Two aircraft were at first heard and then briefly sighted off the starboard bow at 1922. The 4.5 inch and pom-poms fired a blind barrage as a deterrent and the enemy aircraft withdrew. *Hasty* reported a sonar contact at 1930, depth-charges were fired but no torpedo tracks were seen. Finally, at 2104, just after nightfall, *Illustrious* was towed into the breakwater by tug boats, its hotspots glowing orange in the dark. 'The ship was quiet at last', wrote Air Mechanic Rayburn. Sydney Millen remembered 'crowds of people, cheering us in, I often wondered if they would have been so enthusiastic if they had realised that this day would have been the start of the terrible ordeal which they would have to suffer in the coming months.' The first dive-bombing raids by the Luftwaffe in January were so brutal and devastating that they reduced the inner harbour area, particularly Senglea and Vittoriosa, to a vast heap of ruins.

OPERATION 'EXCESS' (JANUARY 1941)

'The next morning', wrote Air Mechanic Rayburn, 'we cleared lower deck and a roll call was taken. An announcement on the Tannoy ordered in case of further attacks on the ship, all hands other than gun crews etc. should go over the side and into the big caves in the hillside. No sooner said when over the enemy came again, so over the side we went!'

Later, after leaving Malta for Alexandria on 10 March, Captain Dennis William Boyd[31] (known in the family as 'D. W.'), wrote a letter[32] to his brother 'E. B.' (Edgar Boyd): 'Your very kind letter of 16th January has just arrived. I knew how you would feel it and longed to be able to assure you that all the team you knew were still alive. I not only could not but dared not say anything until we left Malta and got to Alex as our expectation of life was not very high. But, as you know, we all survived and live to fight again.

'How the buzz about Bill started I have no idea as he was full of life more than anyone! My chief sorrows were Lieutenant [Peter M.] Gregory whom you may remember was very sweet to Elizabeth. He was hit on the spine by a bomb splinter and fell down saying, 'I think something has hit me.' He then turned very grey and asked for morphine knowing he was dying. Keevil gave him a shot and then he had to be moved as a fierce fire was raging under the quarter deck where he was lying. A marine picked him up and his back was heard to break. He was, I think, already dead.

'Luddington, ex-England and Navy rugger and our Master at Arms, was blown to bits in the hanger where a bomb exploded. He was a golden man.[33]

'Clifford, a Lieutenant and pilot who had done very well at Taranto, was wounded in the first attack and then devoted himself to the other wounded. After the third attack he was never seen again. Either he was blown overboard

---

31. Who had been promoted to rear admiral on 18 February and relieved Lyster as Rear Admiral Aircraft Carriers. He transferred his flag to *Formidable* when she arrived at Alexandria on 10 March.
32. This letter was discovered in 2000 by some friends of Andrew Wilson who decided that the 'raw and powerful document' deserved to be seen more widely as 'a vivid memorial of what these men went through'. It is available on the 'World War II Today' website.
33. Bill Luddington had won 13 caps for England at rugby in 1923-26 while playing for Devonport Services and the RN. His father, Private Thomas Levi Luddington of the Army Hospital Corps was at Rorkes Drift in 1879. He died in 1934.

or he disintegrated. He was a pattern of gallantry and gentility and one of the best three-quarters we have had for a long time.

'Our young marine [Lieutenant Anthony G.E.] Manisty... was killed by a bomb which did not wound him but just blasted him. The other officer casualties you would not know unless you remember Mr. Anstis our gunner. He was blown to bits by a bomb which hit the pompom just in front of the bridge. He and all the crew were in an awful mess but were clearly killed instantly. I ordered them to be thrown overboard as they were dreadful sights. Arms, legs, heads and trunks going over the side were awful to see but were better there than lying about the deck where they chilled the stomachs of others.

'Analysing one's feelings afterwards I felt no sorrow at the time as my feelings were that the dead had perhaps the easiest job. Nor was I afraid, it was all so terrific and one's responsibility so great that I had no uncomfortable feelings other than intense sorrow for the ship as I never expected her to be of any use again. I was on the wing bridge watching the bombs come down and I saw both lifts fly into the air like leaves. An amazing sight.

'Fear came later when I realised, we must have more attacks before reaching Malta. I then felt utterly sick for a while and trembled from head to foot. I went down to my sea cabin, took a good hold of myself, offered up a prayer that I'd do my stuff and then went back and was waggling the engines to steer her for the next 8 hours and through 2 more attacks without any particular feeling other than an unsatisfied desire for food. From breakfast until 10 pm, when we secured, I only had cocoa and a biscuit which Lloyd the Padre brought me.

'Our real strain came with the repeat attacks at Malta. On one occasion I was ashore not 20 yards from a cave shelter and the ship was 100 yards away. On the warning I walked to the gangway saying to myself after all there is nothing I can do and when I got to the gangway I stopped, feeling utterly cowardly and bloody nearly ran for the shelter. However, I climbed slowly and reluctantly up the gangway and then felt alright. The others were the same, I think. I allowed no one on board (there were wonderful shelters) except the gun crews and supply parties. Some of them failed to turn up and we manned the guns with four commandos, six Lieutenant Commanders, two Paymasters Seamen and Westmacott, four petty officers and six first class able seamen.

'"Rosey" Barker and I went to the air defence position on the top bridge where we directed the guns on to the targets until the attack developed and

OPERATION 'EXCESS' (JANUARY 1941)

then we just watched. However, if you have seen Bill, you will have heard as stirring a yarn as ever was spun. I sent Bill home because we did learn a lot and I wanted the powers that be to know what we learnt. To say I was indifferent to the fact that Bella had had a baby would be a ruddy lie, but Bill must never know that I thought of that first! He was splendid and deserved a little thought of that kind.

'I think my worst job was to see people suffering from strain. It was horrible and some got it badly. Tamplin the Chief, a fat cheerful self-indulgent bachelor went ashore and just couldn't come back so I sent him to hospital. Duckworth, who was badly blasted, cried at the least excuse and yet stuck at it and was always there though I think useless. Men I thought tough were no good at all, in fact the only really good ones were the team and a few sailors and engineers of the quiet nice type. Martin ... was the senior engineer and was the supreme man of the whole show. His guts and skill were quite remarkable and he was quite delighted when owing to the chief cracking he was left with the whole responsibility.

'The senior gunner went to the hospital to see the wounded and collapsed staying there! Others in varying degrees were looking like death but they stuck it well. I think I saved them all from going really potty by abandoning ship for three days after the Sunday attacks. It was a ghastly thing to do but I had to do it and as usual got away with it as during those three days we were not attacked. Had I not done so half of us would have been loonies and in any case, we would not have saved the ship. On the Thursday they all came back gladly and were able to produce the goods for an awful passage to Alex. I have often had to bear responsibility but never anything to equal this. To them the three days were a rest, to us they were just hell but I knew it was right...'

As soon as *Illustrious* reached Grand Harbour and berthed at Parlatorio Wharf in French Creek beneath Corradino Heights for emergency repairs, the dead were transferred to a minesweeper and the great majority of the casualties were rushed to Bighi Naval Hospital by boats and ambulances and to Mtarfa. Dockyard workers rushed aboard, bringing with them breathing and fire-fighting equipment to tackle the blaze still burning in the aft of the hangar. They only managed to put out the fires at 3am the following morning. Massey Anderson, a Reuters correspondent aboard the *Illustrious*, cabled his newsroom: 'The HMS *Illustrious*, battle scarred but triumphant, made port today after fighting off waves of German dive-bombers for seven hours in the Straits of Sicily. Goering's Luftwaffe had swooped out of the sky in this first

Mediterranean action and had given her one of the severest poundings ever delivered from the air against a single ship.'

On Sunday, 126 bodies and assorted body parts were sewn up in canvas bags and then taken out again and buried at sea in the deepest water around the island, between Dingli Cliffs and the tiny island of Filfla. The funeral service was a hurried affair and not enough weight was put in the bags. Many remained afloat, so the minesweeper circled them at speed to sink them with its wake. Some resurfaced, only to wash up days later, a grim tide against Malta's limestone cliffs.

At 1355 on Thursday, 16 January radar on Malta picked up a large contact – the largest so far in the war. While under repair *Illustrious* was bombed in two separate attacks by 17 Ju 88s and then 44 Stukas, which were escorted by ten Macchi C.202s, ten CR.42s and 20 Bf 110s. The RAF managed to send up four Hurricanes, three Fulmars and two Gladiators. The pilots were instructed to stay out of the harbour area and pick off stragglers. The pilots of 806 Squadron claimed to have shot down two Ju 88s and possibly damaged another pair. Despite the RAF pilots being told not to enter the harbour area a Fulmar chased a Stuka right through the barrage. After the Ju 87 released its bombs, it swept off down the harbour so low to the water that the pilot had to climb to get over the 15 ft breakwater. The Fulmar pilot eventually shot it down and when he returned to Hal Far, he remarked 'Don't think much of Malta's bloody barrage.' His aircraft however was so badly damaged that it had to be written off. One of three Fulmars that intercepted an Axis air raid on the Maltese airfields was shot down with no survivors. A 500 kg bomb penetrated *Illustrious*' flight deck aft of the rear lift and detonated in the captain's day cabin; several other bombs nearly hit the ship but only caused minor damage but a bomb exploded in *Essex*'s engine room killing 15 men and wounding 23 more. She was loaded with 4,000 tons of torpedoes and ammunition. Bombs exploding in Grand Harbour killed numerous fish that were collected after the raid and eaten.

There was another heavy air raid on 17 January and the next day *Illustrious* was attacked again. Only one Fulmar was serviceable on 19 January, when *Illustrious* was attacked several times and it was shot down. *Illustrious* was not struck unduly during these attacks (one bomb that hit the quarterdeck caused little damage) but several near-misses resulted in shock waves and dislodged enough hull plating to cause an immediate 5° list and crack the cast-iron foundations of her port turbine and damaging other machinery.

OPERATION 'EXCESS' (JANUARY 1941)

It was only her armoured deck that had saved *Illustrious* from complete destruction during the series of raids. No other carrier taking anything like this level of punishment would have survived, but she would be out of operation for several months. With repair stages still slung over its sides *Illustrious* departed Malta under cover of darkness on 23 January for Alexandria, escorted by four destroyers. Her Fulmars remained for the defence of the island.

After reaching Alexandria on 25 January *Illustrious* was able to complete additional repairs but as the Portsmouth naval yards in Britain were too exposed, she sailed for America via Durban in South Africa (where her underwater damage was assessed in the dry dock) to undergo restoration of full combat effectiveness, finally reaching the Norfolk Navy Yard in Virginia on 12 May. *Illustrious* put to sea again in November, Radio Berlin claiming that the British carrier was at the bottom of French Creek. Despite colliding with *Formidable* in a moderate storm on the night of 15/16 December, neither ship was seriously damaged and *Illustrious* arrived back in Britain on 21 December for permanent repairs at Cammell Laird's shipyard in Birkenhead. On 19 March *Illustrious* had her work-up cut short to enable her to prepare to join the Eastern Fleet in the Indian Ocean.

Chapter 4

Hunting the *Bismarck*

For the next 30 hours the Bismarck *sailed at full speed towards the French coast, without the Royal Navy being aware of her position or intentions; but at 1030 hours on Monday morning the* Bismarck *sighted a British flying-boat in a cloudless patch of sky and opened fire. The flying-boat vanished into cloud cover, but the* Bismarck *– which might have escaped recognition because of her second funnel and knowledge of British recognition signals – had given away her identity by shooting at the aircraft.*

It was now obvious that the enemy would bring attack-planes against the Bismarck, *and these planes could only come from the* Ark Royal, *which was stationed at Gibraltar. The day passed in anxious calculation of* Ark Royal's *probable position – and then at last the air-raid warning came at 2045 hours. The* Ark Royal's *planes made two strikes with their torpedoes, diving down on us from all angles out of low cloud. One torpedo which hit amidships caused no damage, but the second affected the rudders disastrously, jamming the port-side rudder at a 15-degree angle. Immediately, the* Bismarck *became no longer manoeuvrable.*

The torpedo-hit on the rudder shook the ship so badly that even in my zone of action in the turbine-room the deck-plates were thrown into the air, and the hull vibrated violently. Shortly after the blow, water flooded through the port-side gangways into the turbine-room, and clouds of gas and smoke filled the room until the forced ventilation cleared it.

The stern compartments of the ship were now flooding, but the men who had been stationed there could still be saved, and soon the carpenters and repair-crew came through, making their way aft. But the ship pitched so violently in the strong sea swell that it was impossible to keep a foothold in the turbulent water surging through the companion-way.

All possibilities were now being considered to restore the ship's manoeuvrability - even if only temporarily. The Commander, Kapitän zur See Lindemann, considered reports from Chief Engineer Lehmann, who was in continual contact with the repair and rescue teams. There was much gesticulation, and at one point the Chief Engineer stepped out of the circle, walked away, turned about, and made a sign of complete refusal. What this was about I am not certain, but eventually it was found possible to connect the hand rudder. But the old rudder would not budge, and to attempt to cut it away with underwater saws was quite impossible because of the heavy swell. A proposal to force the rudder out from below with the help of explosives was rejected, because of the proximity to the propellers. Thus, all experiments with the auxiliary rudder were given up as completely hopeless, with the old one immovable.

Despite all attempts to steer with the propellers, the ship could no longer be kept on a south-easterly course; it was therefore necessary to turn head-on to the sea - towards the north-west - at a slow speed, and into the face of the enemy.

One cannot help wondering whether everything humanly possible was really done in order to try and save the Bismarck on this critical night. The ship had gone to sea well-constructed and it is possible that the damaged rudder might have been blown out of the stern of the ship without damage to the propellers. But this risk was not attempted - nor was there any attempt to improvise a sea-anchor to stabilise the course. With three propellers capable of driving Bismarck at 28 knots, it is difficult to accept that there was no alternative but to head straight for the enemy at a slow speed.

The Last Hours of the Bismarck by Kapitänleutnant Gerhard Junack, commanding the Centre Turbine Room (Section VIII) on board *Bismarck*. The *Ark Royal*'s planes were Fairey Swordfish biplanes, which were built as 3-seat, open cockpit torpedo-bombers. A flying anachronism when it entered service in 1934 and already obsolescent at the outbreak of the Second World War, when embarked on five aircraft-carriers, the

THE AIR WAR AT SEA IN THE SECOND WORLD WAR

'Stringbag' as it was affectionately nicknamed, would become legendary in the Second World War for decisive torpedo attacks on enemy shipping in the Atlantic and the Mediterranean.

On Sunday, 18 May 1941 Schlachtschiff *Bismarck*, the largest warship ever built in Germany and pride of the Kriegsmarine, together with the heavy cruiser *Prinz Eugen* sailed from Gdynia for Unternehmen Rheinübung ('Exercise Rhine'), Grand Admiral Erich Raeder's attempt to concentrate a German naval force against the Allied Atlantic convoys. On board the *Bismarck*, her skipper, Kapitän zur See Ernst Lindemann, in consultation with the Flottenchef (fleet chief) Admiral Günther Lütjens, elected to take *Bismarck* and the accompanying *Prinz Eugen* into the shipping lanes by way of the Denmark Strait between Greenland and Iceland. *Bismarck* was laid down on 1 July 1936 at the Blohm & Voss Yards, in Hamburg. She was launched on 14 February 1939 in the presence of Adolf Hitler and a large concourse of High German Naval, Army and Air Force officers and leading personalities of the Reich. When Frau von Loewenfeld, grand-daughter of the 'Iron Chancellor' broke a bottle of German sparkling wine on the bows of the ship, *Bismarck* did not move and there was an anxious pause for three or four minutes before the ship slowly slid away from the launching platform. It was a current joke in Hamburg at the time that Field-Marshal Goering was forced to push her before she could move. *Prinz Eugen* had been completed during 1940, but had experienced some difficulties with her turbines. She was named after the French-born Prince Eugéne, brother-in-arms of the great Duke of Marlborough.

Fast-forward to Spring 1941. On 18 May the *Bismarck* and *Prinz Eugen* sailed after dark from Gdynia and the Baltic was cleared of merchant shipping for their passage. They were well up the Skagerrak at dawn on the 20th. At 2000 hours, Admiral Sir John Tovey the C-in-C, Home Fleet, flying his flag in the battleship *King George V*, learned that the *Bismarck* and *Prinz Eugen* had been sighted and he ordered the recently commissioned aircraft carrier HMS *Victorious* to put to sea from Scapa Flow in the Orkneys. Sailing at dusk in thick weather the enemy warships reached Korsfjorden near Bergen in Norway at 0900 hours on 21 May. That morning an extensive photo reconnaissance of the Norwegian coast by RAF aircraft reported seeing two warships. The subsequent photographs confirmed that they were the *Bismarck* and *Prinz Eugen*.

HUNTING THE *BISMARCK*

At 0052 hours on Thursday, 22 May the battle cruiser *Hood* and *Prince of Wales*, escorted by six destroyers hauled anchor and departed Scapa Flow. Final confirmation that *Bismarck* and the *Prinz Eugen* had already sailed, came late on the 22nd, as the result of a difficult and hazardous reconnaissance sortie in foul weather by a Fleet Air Arm Maryland target-towing aircraft of 771 Squadron from RNAS Hatson in the Orkneys with a volunteer crew. Lieutenant Noel Ernest Goddard, the Senior Pilot of 771 NAS, volunteered to captain the sortie, with Commander Geoffrey Alexander Rotherham, the Air Station's XO, an extremely experienced observer; Leading Airman John Walker Armstrong as TAG-WO (Telegraphist/Wireless operator: TAGs on Swordfish aircraft had to be able to work the Morse hand-key operated wireless and the Vickers 0.303 machine gun) and Leading Airman J. D. Milne as TAG-AG (Telegraphist/Air Gunner). Attempting to radio their discovery back to Coastal Command, they received no reply. Rotherham decided to alert the Air Station directly with their Towed Target frequency and also fly directly to Sumburgh, Hatston's forward airfield, where the Albacores were ready to intercept. Acting on this message, the Home Fleet and *Victorious* sailed from Scapa with Tovey aboard at 2245 hours. At noon on Friday, 23 May *Bismarck* and *Prinz Eugen* entered the Denmark Strait. Instead of the fog that had been forecast, there was patchy mist with large clear areas. British minefields off the north-west coast of Iceland forced the two German warships well out into the middle of the Strait, where the weather was unusually clear.

Accompanied by *Victorious*, the battleships' *Hood* and *Prince of Wales* raced at top speed with their accompanying destroyers to prevent the *Bismarck* from breaking out into the Atlantic to attack convoys. Until a few hours before the sailing, *Victorious* had been laden with 48 crated RAF Hurricanes and was under orders to accompany a troop convoy for delivery to Egypt and so only had space for nine Swordfish of 825 Squadron and six Fulmars of 800Z Flight. The Fulmars were intended only for the defence of the ship during the Mediterranean operation. Neither 825 Squadron nor 800Z Flight was up to full strength nor trained in the art of attacking large warships at sea, 825 having had little chance for recent torpedo strike practice or training. The Albacores of 828 Squadron that were based in the Orkneys at the time, were fully worked-up in the strike role, but they came under the operational control of the local AOC Coastal Command and he would not release the squadron in time for embarkation.

THE AIR WAR AT SEA IN THE SECOND WORLD WAR

At 1922 hours on 23 May, at a range of 7 miles, *Bismarck* and *Prinz Eugen* were sighted by the cruiser HMS *Suffolk* who pinpointed the position of the German ships to *Hood* and *Prince of Wales*. *Norfolk*, which picked up the report of the sighting closed to make contact. One hour later Norfolk too sighted the two enemy warships at a range of 6 miles. *Bismarck* fired a few salvos at the *Norfolk*, which all missed and the *Norfolk* turned away. She used her Walrus for shadowing for almost 48 hours, until the enemy was lost again.

On Saturday, 24 May, *Hood* encountered *Bismarck* and *Prinz Eugen* between Greenland and Iceland at a range of seventeen miles. A Special Correspondent with the Royal Navy who watched the unfolding 'battle of the giants' wrote: 'It did not get dark at any time that night. Until two or three o'clock it was nearly as light as day. Then for the next few hours a leaden greyness settled down and it was like a dull winter's afternoon in Britain. Blinding snowstorms lashed the black sea and at times visibility fell to a few yards. It was expected to make contact with the *Bismarck* at about 2 am, but at the last moment she altered course. For four more hours *Hood*, for 20 years the world's biggest warship, and *Prince of Wales* continued on a course roughly parallel to the enemy.

'Most of this time a thick curtain of snow enveloped the scene. Then, as if nature was taking a hand, this curtain suddenly lifted. There was the sea, like black treacle, and there, in the sombre murky light of dawn, appeared two black specks on the horizon - *Bismarck* and her accompanying cruiser. For some minutes our ships sped on towards the Germans to shorten the range. They, too, turned in towards their pursuers. The world's biggest warships were thundering towards one another at a combined speed of probably over 60 mph. Their specks grew rapidly into recognisable shapes, with masts, bridges, funnels - and the guns. The tension of waiting for the battle to begin became acute.

'"Open fire" was ordered by signal. Almost simultaneously with the order orange-gold flame belched with a roar from the *Hood*'s great forward guns. Within three seconds puffs of black smoke shot out from the *Bismarck*. She had also opened up. The *Prince of Wales*'s guns then began firing. Dense clouds of yellow cordite smoke enveloped her bridge momentarily blotting out the view. To the left the *Hood*, two or three hundred yards away, was still surging forward on a parallel course. Fountains of water shot up in her wake - the first about 100 yards astern, the second, 50. The *Hood* thundered on. The shell or shells appeared to fall just ahead of one of her after-15-inch gun turrets and a large fire broke out with thick black smoke. The *Hood* continued to fire and to race forward. [*Hood*, according to *Bismarck* prisoners, fired first, the salvo being over. A second salvo fell short, but the third hit and three shells in all struck *Bismarck*.] What happened next was a strangling, sickening sight. There was a terrific explosion [a 15-inch shell from *Bismarck* had penetrated the ship's armour belt and exploded in an after magazine] and the whole of the vast ship was enveloped in a flash of flame and smoke which rose high into the air in the shape of a giant mushroom. Sections of funnels, masts, and other parts hurtled hundreds of feet into the sky, some of them landing back on the ship, most falling in the sea and quickly disappearing.

'The end of the *Hood* was an almost unbelievable nightmare. Standing on the bridge of one of HM ships, I saw *Hood* go down only two or 300 yards away with her guns still firing. *Hood*'s bows tilted vertically into the air and three or four minutes after she was hit all that remained apart from bits of wreckage was a flicker of flame and smoke on the water's surface. A destroyer was diverted to rescue work and managed to pick up three of the ship's company – two seamen and a midshipman [1,415 officers and ratings died]. In a few minutes all that remained was a patch of smoke on the water and some small pieces of wreckage. All this time *Prince of Wales* had continued pouring shells at the *Bismarck*. More than once spurts of water showed she was straddled. Again, the *Bismarck*'s shells crashed near the *Prince of Wales*, which was hit by a 15-inch shell soon after *Hood* sank but no serious damage had been done. The *Prince of Wales* never lost her fighting efficiency and her speed was not impaired.' [*Prince of Wales* was in fact badly damaged before she threw up a smoke screen and retired from what became known as the Battle of the Denmark Strait.]

'After the sinking of *Hood* and the withdrawal of *Prince of Wales*, the atmosphere aboard the *Bismarck* was jubilant', wrote Kapitänleutnant Gerhard Junack a 31-year-old Berliner and commandant of the Centre Turbine Room. 'The successful defence against the aircraft from the *Victorious* and the shaking-off of the shadowing cruisers, further increased this feeling. Admiral Lütjens, however, felt that this exaggerated air of victory should be moderated and as it was his birthday that Sunday [the 25th of May], he addressed the crew shortly before midday. In precise military language he thanked the crew for their good wishes and then proceeded to speak his mind. He praised the crew's magnificent discipline and fulfilment of duty which had already accomplished so much, but said the worst still stood before them – for the whole of the British fleet had now been commanded to sink the killer of the *Hood*. Now it was 'win or die' - but before the *Bismarck* went down, she would meet and send many of the enemy before her.

'The Admiral wished with these words to rid the crew of their over-exuberance and bring them into a more realistic frame of mind; but in fact, he overdid it, and there was a feeling of depression among the crew which spread through all ranks from the highest to the lowest. The deeper they looked into the reality of their situation, the deeper became the general distress of the officers, the older ones speaking openly in the company of their younger comrades, saying that they no longer believed in a 'way out'. Junior officers appeared in life-jackets when going to their duty stations, despite the fact that to wear them with normal uniform was forbidden. The crew began to brood and neglect their duties.'[34]

Any elation on board the German ships was tempered by the knowledge that the entire Home Fleet was now pursuing them. Lindemann favoured following up the *Prince of Wales* in the hope of sinking her but was overruled by Lütjens. 'Then the *Bismarck* turned away, but only to be pursued all that day and night and next day at high speed. Twice during the night *Prince of Wales* pumped out salvoes. Attacks were also made then and later by torpedo bombers from the aircraft carriers *Victorious* and the *Ark Royal*. Altogether these attacks were delivered intermittently for three days and four nights.'

Instead of returning to Norway through the Denmark Strait, Lütjens had decided to make a run for the French port of Sainte Nazaire where the damage sustained during the engagement with the *Hood* - including some ruptured fuel tanks - could be repaired and it would also be easier to return to the Atlantic battleground from France than from Norway. During the afternoon of 24 May, Admiral Tovey detached *Victorious*, with the second cruiser squadron, to a position about 100 miles from the *Bismarck* with the intention of attempting to slow the enemy down with a torpedo attack by Swordfish aircraft.

Finally, at 2210 hours on Saturday, 24 May, all nine Swordfish of 825 Squadron set off, organized in three sub-flights led by 33-year-old Lieutenant Commander Eugene Kingsmill Esmonde, to attack *Bismarck*, which had parted company with *Prinz Eugen*. Esmonde was born on 1st March 1909 in Thurgoland, Yorkshire, near Barnsley. His parents were from Ireland

---

34. Ibid.

and he returned to his family's ancestral home of the Esmonde baronets in Drominagh, North Tipperary as a boy. He was educated in London and then in County Kildare, Ireland before being commissioned into the Royal Air Force on 28 December 1928. He became a flying instructor in 1932 and then left the Service in 1934, when he joined both the RAF Volunteer Reserve and Imperial Airways, where he trained as a flying boat pilot and carried the first surcharged airmail to Australia. In January 1939 he received a letter from the Admiralty offering him a commission in the newly formed Royal Naval Air Branch. He asked to be released from the Reserve and reported to RNAS Lee-on-Solent for refresher training and was appointed to 754 Naval Air Squadron (NAS). He had been a survivor from the first Royal Navy ship sunk in the Second World War, the carrier HMS *Courageous*, which was lost on 17 September 1939. In May 1940 he took command of 825 NAS on board HMS *Furious*. Esmonde led attacks on Trondheim and Tromsø, before receiving orders to embark on board HMS *Victorious*. She was destined for the Mediterranean but, following the sinking of the battleship HMS *Hood*, was diverted to help the search for the German battleship *Bismarck*.

At 2300 three Fulmars of 800Z Flight followed the Swordfish formation with orders to observe the attack and then maintain contact at all costs so that, if necessary, another strike could be flown off the next day at dawn. The faster Fulmars soon overtook the lumbering Swordfish and the combined force continued towards *Bismarck* at 85 knots.

The weather was showery with fresh winds and squalls but visibility remained good. At 2327 hours ASV a contact 16 miles ahead of the formation was established and *Bismarck* was sighted briefly through a gap in the clouds only to be lost again seconds later. Descending below the clouds with his squadron, Esmonde located the cruisers still shadowing and HMS *Norfolk* directed the aircraft towards their target, now 14 miles ahead on the starboard bow.

At 2350 hours a further ASV contact was made and Esmonde again led his squadron below the cloud cover to begin his attack but the contact proved to be the United States Coast Guard cutter *Modoc*. *Bismarck*, now only six miles to the south, spotted the Swordfish formation and on the stroke of midnight her flak guns opened up with a 'very vigorous and accurate' barrage of heavy and light AA, which hit Esmonde's aircraft on the starboard lower aileron as he closed to within four miles of the battleship. Undaunted, he abandoned his original intention to attack from starboard, deciding to drop there and then, whilst he was still in a good position on the target's port

THE AIR WAR AT SEA IN THE SECOND WORLD WAR

beam and *Bismarck* was ideally silhouetted against the rays of the setting sun. Esmonde and 27-year-old Sub Lieutenant John Chute Thompson attacked *Bismarck*'s port bow and released their 18-inch MK XII torpedo from 100 ft. Lieutenant Neal Gordon MacLean, the third member of the flight, became separated during the descent through the clouds and attacked the port side too. *Bismarck* managed to dodge all three torpedoes and though one Swordfish lost contact in the dense cloud covering the area, the remaining aircraft determinedly pressed home their attacks.

Next, approaching from starboard were the three Swordfish of the second sub-flight led by 5F skippered by Lieutenant Philip David 'Percy' Gick, senior pilot of 825 Squadron, with Sub-Lieutenant Valentine Kay Norfolk as his observer and Petty Officer Leslie Daniel Sayer, a qualified Telegrapher-Air Gunner instructor manning the Vickers machine gun. Leslie and his brother Victor were brought up in Bures, Suffolk where they were fostered as Barnardo's boys after the death of their mother. Leslie attended the Watts Naval School, Norfolk from the ages of 9 to 16 years before joining the Royal Navy as a boy seaman at HMS *Ganges* at Shotley in 1931.

'If anyone was going to score a hit, it would surely be "Percy" Gick the No. 1 Torpedo Attack Instructor in the Fleet Air Arm', Les Sayer later recalled. 'The *Bismarck* started throwing everything at us, but we got away with it because the German rangefinders were not calibrated for enemy aircraft approach speeds below 100 knots. We were also flying so low that the German guns could not achieve the necessary depression. At first, I thought our torpedo had got hung up, but as if in answer, back came this Dartmouth voice: "I am not lined up properly. I am going in again." We therefore wheeled away to a distance of about fifteen miles. The Germans must have thought that the attack was over and that all the Swordfish had departed. Taking up position just below the *Bismarck*'s port bow they did not see us; they did not know we were there. So, we dropped our "fish" from about 500 yards and at a height of 20 feet.'

Percy Gick was able to score a hit on the armoured belt amidships of the *Bismarck*. Oberbootsmann Kurt Kirchberg who was standing on the starboard side was thrown by the blast and killed, thus becoming the first casualty aboard. Six other men were injured. The torpedo had inflicted damage and caused an oil leak and a subsequent slick, which reconnaissance aircraft and ships could sight and follow. Les Sayer saw what he thought was a hit because 'there was a huge spurt of water coming from the hull of the *Bismarck*', and he thought to himself, 'that's us and that's our hit.'

HUNTING THE *BISMARCK*

'We turned away and by the time the gun crews had woken up we were twenty miles away' says Sayer. 'They then opened-up with their 15-inch main armament. They did not hit us, but we could not avoid the massive waterspouts thrown up by the shell splashes and when we hit one of them all the fabric at the bottom of the aircraft was torn away. We had a very cold trip back! As we approached *Victorious*, she had put on her searchlight and amazingly we all got back on board - three of the pilots had never carried out a deck landing at night before. We were probably the least prepared torpedo squadron to do the job required of us, but our No. 1 aircraft did hit the *Bismarck* amidships.

'It was getting on for 2am before we returned to *Victorious* in a squall which reduced visibility to zero. Miraculously not one of the Swordfish was shot down or even badly-damaged. Given that the attack had taken place at night, at extreme range and in appalling weather and sea conditions, it was remarkable that any torpedoes had hit at all. Although the attack did not cause any direct damage, the explosion caused by Percy Gick's hit, together with the violent zigzagging evasive action taken by the ship to avoid the torpedoes, ripped apart the repairs made in the ship's oil tanks earlier in the day, crucially slowing her down and delaying her escape towards safety.'[35]

Lieutenant William Francis Cuthbert Garthwaite RNVR with his observer, Sub Lieutenant William Anthony Gillingham RNVR and Leading Airman Henry Thomas Albert Wheeler settled on the starboard bow of the *Bismarck* and Sub Lieutenant Patrick Bernard Jackson dropped onto her starboard quarter. But once more *Bismarck* avoided the torpedoes. The two remaining Swordfish in the third sub-flight meanwhile, appeared on the *Bismarck*'s port quarter and were greeted with heavy AA fire. 24-year-old Lieutenant Henry Charles Michell Pollard and Sub Lieutenant Robert Graham Lawson[36] released their torpedoes but they too missed their target.

---

35. Percy Gick, who received the DSC for his part in the action, would serve in eight aircraft carriers and retire as a rear admiral with the DSC and bar and twice mentioned in dispatches. Les Sayer was awarded the Distinguished Service Medal for his actions on 24 May. After the war he flew as navigator for British European Airways and in 1947 became the first chairman of the Telegraphist Air Gunner's Association, being appointed MBE for his services.
36. With Lawson was his observer, Sub Lieutenant Frank Leonard Robinson RNVR and Leading Airman Iowerth Llewelyn Owen (TAG).

THE AIR WAR AT SEA IN THE SECOND WORLD WAR

A German account of the attack, summarized from an eyewitness report, stated: 'They came in flying low over the water, launched their torpedoes and zoomed away. Flak was pouring from every gun barrel but did not seem to hit them. The first torpedo passed 150 yards in front of the *Bismarck*'s bow. The second did the same and the third. Helmsman Hansen was operating the press buttons of the steering gear as, time and time again, the *Bismarck* manoeuvred out of danger. She evaded a fifth and then a sixth, when yet another torpedo darted straight towards the ship. A few seconds later a tremendous shudder ran through the hull and a towering column of water rose at *Bismarck*'s starboard side, amidships. The nickel-chrome-steel armour plate of her ship's side survived the attack ...'

As the Swordfish departed, Petty Officer Stanley Edgar Parker, Esmonde's TAG, signalled: 'Have attacked with torpedoes. Only one observed.' As the Swordfish formation turned away each TAG sighted his Vickers machine gun and raked the *Bismarck*'s gun positions and superstructure with 0.303 rounds at almost point-blank range. Later, one of the air gunners jokingly said that: 'It didn't sink the *Bismarck*, but it certainly kept their heads down and, in any case, it relieved our feelings.'

Just after midnight the single hit was confirmed by one of the Fulmars, which reported a 'great, black column of dense smoke rising from the starboard side' and also that 'the battleship's speed was reduced'.

At 0100 hours *Victorious* launched two more Fulmars to relieve those on duty and continue shadowing *Bismarck* until dawn. But in the terrible conditions prevailing the pair soon became separated and neither was able to locate the *Bismarck*. Both crews eventually had to ditch and one was never seen again. The other crew was miraculously saved after floating in the sea for 36 hours. The Home Fleet meanwhile, searched to the northwest of the last known position of the *Bismarck* while Force 'H' was hurriedly moved into the Atlantic to cover a troop convoy to the south-east of the Home Fleet but contact with *Bismarck* was lost in bad weather about three hours after the torpedo attack and would not be regained for 30 hours.

Throughout the night of 24/25 May *Bismarck* was fired at by destroyers. Two Swordfish aircraft were lost during the air searches on 25th and 26 May. At 1810 hours in good visibility, three Swordfish from *Victorious* were flown off to search an arc between west and north-east to a depth of 100 miles but the weather had worsened and nothing was seen. *Norfolk* and *Suffolk* too drew a complete blank. Two Swordfish managed to make it back to the *Victorious*. The third, crewed by Sub Lieutenant Patrick Bernard Jackson, Acting Sub Lieutenant David Anthony Berrill and Leading Airman F. G. Sparkes were fortunate to come down alongside a lifeboat floating on the sea and after boarding it they discovered to their joy that it was fully stocked with water and provisions! For eight days they bobbed about on the sea until, on 3 June, the Icelandic steamer *Lagufoss* sighted the boat 50 nautical miles off Cape Farewell and all three crew were picked up unharmed! Lieutenant Brian Donald Campbell and Sub Lieutenant Matthew Gordon Goodger were never seen again. Lieutenant Francis Charles Furlong and Sub Lieutenant John Edward Melville Hoare RNVR were more fortunate. After bobbing in the stormy North Atlantic in their small raft for 36 hours, they were ultimately rescued by the SS *Beaverhill*. Less fortunate were the two Fulmars of 800Z. Operating at night, in horrific weather, without radar, they soon found themselves separated; neither was able to locate their target. Lost at sea, with little hope of survival short of a miracle, both aircraft eventually were forced to settle into the Atlantic. One of the crews was rescued by a passing merchant ship. The search for the *Bismarck* on the 26th by three Swordfish resulted in the loss of Lieutenant Henry Charles Michell Pollard, his observer, Sub-Lieutenant David Musk Beattie RNVR and Leading Aircraftsman Percy William Clitheroe DSM (TAG). Their bodies were never found.

Aircraft of Coastal Command too were involved in the search that followed for the German battle group. Weather conditions were in the enemy's favour with high winds and extensive cloud cover. Three Catalinas of 210 Squadron took off from Oban at 1345 hours on 25 May with orders to provide a search pattern to cover any possible return to Norway by the *Bismarck* but the ship was not sighted. On 26 May however, *Bismarck* was finally spotted by 'Z-Zebra', a patrolling Catalina aircraft of 209 Squadron, RAF Coastal Command based at Loch Erne in Northern Ireland and piloted by Pilot Officer Dennis Alfred Briggs. The United States, still neutral at this time, had attached seventeen airmen to the RAF, partly to assist with the familiarisation with the new PBY-5 Consolidated Catalina flying boats and Ensign Leonard B. 'Tuck' Smith was officially a 'co-pilot and special observer' on 'Z-Zebra'. The navigator was 19-year-old Gaynor Williams, the lone Canadian aboard the aircraft. Normally for reconnaissance missions, the flying boats' anti-submarine loads of four depth charges were removed. But time was of the essence. The depth charges stayed on.

THE AIR WAR AT SEA IN THE SECOND WORLD WAR

The weather was foul, with a ceiling as low as 100 ft when, at 0325, Smith and Briggs' Catalina lifted off the waters of Loch Erne and, along with the rest of the squadron's Catalinas, headed west in search of the *Bismarck*. The long range of the Catalina meant that they were way out in the Atlantic at 1010 when 'Tuck' Smith glimpsed what was first believed to be the *Bismarck* through the clouds, much further south (690 miles from Brest) than had been expected and under full steam for Brest on the Brittany coast. When the Catalina emerged from cloud at a height of 2,000 ft, it was engaged by accurate aircraft fire from a large capital ship which was unmistakeably the *Bismarck*. Wireless operator Alan Martin transmitted the signal indicating the discovery immediately, as the crew fully expected to be shot out of the sky at any moment. 'Tuck' Smith had at once taken control from 'George' and started a slow climbing turn to starboard for a closer look, keeping the battleship sited to port. 'My plan', he recalled, 'was to take cover in the clouds, get close to the ship as possible; making definite recognition and then shadow the ship from best point of vantage. Upon reaching 2,000 ft [at 1036 hours] we broke out of a cloud formation and were met by a terrific anti-aircraft barrage from our starboard quarter. I immediately jettisoned the depth charges and started violent evasive action which consisted of full speed, climbing and "S" turns.'

Dennis Briggs went aft again to send the contact report. 'When making an 'S' turn I could see the ship was the *Bismarck*, which had made a 90° starboard turn from its original course, as evidenced from the wake made by his manoeuvering and was firing broadsides at us. The anti-aircraft fire lasted until we were out of range and into the clouds. It was very intense and were it not for evasive action we would have been shot down. The barrage was so close that it shook the aircraft considerably (one man was knocked from his bunk) and the noise of the burst could be heard above the propeller and engine noise. Numerous bursts were observed at close quarters and small fragments of shrapnel could be heard hitting the plane. The fitter came forward to our compartment saying we were full of holes.

'As soon as we were well clear of *Bismarck* we investigated the damage, which consisted of a hole in after port hull (about two inches in diameter) and one in bottom hull directly below instrument panel (about one inch in diameter). No other damage was visible at the time. I made short flight test (several turns, checked engines, etc) and finding everything satisfactory returned to area to resume shadow of *Bismarck*.'

HUNTING THE *BISMARCK*

The *Bismarck* was by now running short of fuel following hits by two 15-inch shells from *Prince of Wales* which had damaged some of her tanks, flooded the ship forward and reduced her speed and the Admiralty anticipated her next move: a run for Brest. Therefore, when the *Bismarck* had been sighted and her position reported by the Catalina, a search pattern had been made by Swordfish from HMS *Ark Royal*, which was en route to the scene with Force 'H' from Gibraltar. Together with the cruiser *Sheffield*, *Ark Royal* and her five squadrons of aircraft (807 with 12 Fulmars, 808 with another dozen Fulmars and 810 with 12 Swordfish and 818 and 820 Squadrons each with 9 Swordfish) was moved north to cover such an escape. Vice-Admiral Sir James Fownes Somerville KCB DSO had detached *Sheffield* to make contact with and shadow the *Bismarck* and *Ark Royal* was ordered to steer for a position 50 miles distant, from which an air torpedo attack could be made with Swordfish. The *Ark Royal* reached her position at about 1430 hours and with her torpedo bombers ranged on deck was ready to launch from 1500 hours with a wave off from the green flag of Commander H. A. Traill up on the bridge. But the weather worsened very quickly. The flight deck was rising and falling as much as 56 ft with the rough sea raging, and he then had to find the way in the prevailing bad visibility. Fortunately, the leading aircraft's radar quickly located a ship 20 miles from the last known position of the *Bismarck* (it had only been 45 minutes since the Catalina had regained contact during the forenoon) and the Swordfish took over the shadowing until the first of 14 Swordfish from all three squadrons formed up.

The striking aircrew were not briefed as to *Sheffield*'s new disposition however, and all the torpedo-carrying Swordfish, led by Lieutenant Commander James Andrew Stewart-Moore, knowing that only *Bismarck* herself was in the target area, commenced the attack. There was some excuse for the aircrew in that low cloud and poor visibility prevented identification after a radar approach. Fortunately, *Sheffield*'s captain, Charles A. A. Larcom, who stood shaken on the bridge of his fast-manoeuvring cruiser, ordered that none of his guns were to fire on the formation and neither they or the *Sheffield* was hit. Two of the torpedoes launched had exploded prematurely on hitting the sea. Three others exploded in the *Sheffield*'s wake and the remainder were avoided thanks to Larcom, who had ordered 'full speed ahead.' Admiral Somerville, no less disturbed, indulged in a tirade of four-letter expletives which would have shocked the ears of the roughest stoker. As the strike force returned to the *Ark* one of the aircraft sent a signal to the *Sheffield*: 'Sorry for the kippers!'

THE AIR WAR AT SEA IN THE SECOND WORLD WAR

Landing conditions had worsened and the Deck Control Officer on *Ark Royal* had to attach a rope to his waist before he could stand back to the wind, holding up the 'bats'. Three Swordfish crashed on the flight deck as they landed on, the stern rising and falling 50 ft and smashing their undercarriages. The wreckage had to be cleared away before the others could be safely landed. Fortunately, there were no crew casualties and by 1720 all the returning Swordfish crews were safely back on board. The Swordfish were speedily refuelled and re-armed and pilots re-briefed, this time being ordered to make contact before the attack with *Sheffield*, which would then direct them on to the target.

At 1910 hours 'Tim' Coode, the Striking Force Leader, opened up the throttle of his Swordfish and sped off. The carrier deck was being deluged by heavy squalls of rain driven by a north-westerly gale and the deck was still pitching badly but the 15 pilots that formed into two squadrons of three sub-flights each chose their moment to take off as the bows rose and all took off safely. Circling over HMS *Renown*, Tovey's flagship, Coode was gratified by all the elements of his fragile task force. Picking up a course to HMS *Sheffield*, his second rendezvous point, he waved the formation on.

Sheffield was sighted and home on to the ship was made by wireless until contact was lost but then re-established and the Swordfish were directed by visual signal from 12 miles distant on to the *Bismarck*, which was by now blanketed by thick cloud down to about 700 ft which split the formation into two. The coordinated attack that had been briefed was changed to individual attacks by sub-flights and thirteen torpedoes were directed at the *Bismarck* under intense gunfire. In spite of the lack of recent torpedo attack training 825 Squadron did extremely well to obtain one hit on the *Bismarck*'s armoured belt, while a second torpedo struck the starboard quarter of the battleship, damaging propellers and jamming her rudders. Another pilot achieved a probable hit and one other torpedo hit the warship amidships on the port side but did no damage. Two of the shadowing aircraft, observing the attack, saw the enemy ship turn two complete circles and drop her speed to little more than 8 knots. Her steering gear had been destroyed and *Bismarck* was reduced to steaming an unpredictable track.

Sunset, which in the northern latitude was not until after midnight, was at 0052 hours and the returning strike force was forced to make their return to *Victorious* in darkness. The homing beacon aboard the carrier was unserviceable but Captain Bovell decided to risk the danger from enemy submarines and shone his 20-inch signal projector lights vertically upwards onto the clouds to guide the aircraft in until Rear-Admiral Sir Alban Thomas Buckley Curteis KCB CVO DSO ordered him to turn them off. Bovell did as ordered but he could not resist using his brightest 20-inch signal projector to do so! Even so, all nine Swordfish found the *Victorious* at 0155 hours and between 0200 and 0230 hours each of the aircraft landed on the flight deck, which was rising and falling 30 ft in the swell. After one Swordfish had landed a huge wave swept over it, filling the cockpits with seawater. The pilot later remarked that 'It was alright; the bottom of the fuselage had been shot away by the *Bismarck*'s gunfire, so it soon drained.'

Lieutenant David Frederick Godfrey-Faussett DSC, piloting Swordfish 2B of 810 Squadron, with Petty Officer Vivian Read Graham, born in Gateshead, Durham on 20 August 1909, as his TAG and Sub-Lieutenant L. A. Royall as observer, was one of those assigned to the second wave of the attack. Graham later reported: 'Attacked from the starboard beam with two aircraft under intense and accurate anti-aircraft fire. Long range anti-aircraft fire on approach and on return. Aircraft 2A and 2B attacked together coming out of the cloud one mile away. First engaged by close range (red tracer). Fire was also opened with heavier stuff evidently time fused. Some of this went into the sea and some burst beyond and above. Aircraft was hit in tail plane and port lower main plane. The heavy fire continued with accuracy up to four miles and appeared to be predicted all the time as bursts followed the aircraft, going off just above ...'

At 0306 hours, just after the last Swordfish had landed, the two shadowing cruisers, HMS *Norfolk* and HMS *Suffolk* lost contact with *Bismarck*.

It was debatable whether further air operations could proceed in the steadily worsening weather but a second attack would have to be made, whatever the cost and it came at 1850 hours on Tuesday, 27 May when 15 Swordfish from 810, 818 and 820 Squadrons led by Lieutenant Commander Trevenen Penrose 'Tim' Coode, was launched. The battle had begun at 0847 that same morning, when Rodney opened fire on *Bismarck* from a distance of about 12 miles. The *Bismarck* answered with her forward turrets and scored some hits, but it was a hopeless situation. Forty-five minutes after the shooting began, all four of *Bismarck*'s 15-inch batteries were out of action, allowing the Royal Navy to move in even closer. For 74 minutes they pounded *Bismarck* with their big guns (which it is estimated was hit by more than 500 shells of 13.3 cm or larger). By 2125 the attack was over.

THE AIR WAR AT SEA IN THE SECOND WORLD WAR

The weather was still horrendous when at 2300 hours the last of the Swordfish was aboard *Ark Royal*. The carrier reported A/A fire to have been 'heavy and accurate and was experienced even when the aircraft were in cloud at a height of 3,000 ft but no aircraft was lost and only one pilot and one air gunner were wounded.' Five of the attacking aircraft had been hit by the AA fire. Swanton managed to get back and land on in one piece, but on closer inspection his Swordfish was found to be damaged beyond repair and it was jettisoned. Three others crashed on landing, but miraculously no one was hurt. Only six of the Swordfish remained serviceable and, expecting the possibility that another attack would be necessary, they were re-armed and ranged for yet another strike.

It had first been reported that the 13 aircraft that got their torpedoes away had scored no hits and the chance of success had gone – Coode reported immediately after the attack that he did not think the *Bismarck* had suffered any significant damage – but even as the last of the aircrew headed for the ready room for debriefing, the damage was confirmed by a signal from the shadowing Swordfish that at 2130 *Bismarck* had made two circles at slow speed and was staggering off to the north-north west. *Bismarck* headed for Brest at high speed.

It was thought at first that one hit and possibly two had been obtained on *Bismarck*. In reality at least two and possibly three hits were made. One torpedo (probably fired by 21-year-old Sub Lieutenant John William Charlton Moffat RNVR) had struck amidships on its port side resulting in slow flooding, and the second in the steering area.

'Jock' Moffat was born in the village of Swinton in the Scottish Borders. When he was a child, his parents moved to Earlston where his father opened the first garage. Mr. Moffat had served in the Royal Navy during the First World War, joining in 1914 to qualify as an aeronautical engineer for the Royal Naval Air Service.

'When Churchill gave the order to sink the *Bismarck*, we knew we just had to stop her trail of devastation at all costs. We dived through the murk, into a lethal storm of shells and bullets. *Bismarck*'s guns erupted and in the hail of hot bullets and tracer, I couldn't see any of the other Swordfish, I thought the closer we were to the water the better chance we had of surviving so we flew in bouncing off the tops of the waves – and it worked. The great thing about the Swordfish was that the bullets just went straight through. After all, it was only made of canvas. It was like David and Goliath.'

HUNTING THE *BISMARCK*

One torpedo hit on the *Bismarck*'s starboard quarter and possibly a third on the port quarter. Moffat's observer was Sub-Lieutenant John. D. 'Dusty' Miller, and Leading Aircraftman Albert J. Hayman, was the telegraphist/air gunner. The torpedo which struck the stern on the port side, according to prisoners, exploded without doing damage but that on the starboard quarter wrecked the steering gear jamming the rudders at an angle variously estimated at between 10° and 15° and damaging the propellers, causing *Bismarck* to turn slowly in circles to starboard. This hit was stated by one prisoner to have been outside an unarmoured trimming compartment, below the steering motor compartment on the starboard side and resulted in this section being flooded to the main deck. Although her main armament remained intact, Bismarck was reduced to steaming an unpredictable track.

'During the night,' wrote Kapitänleutnant Gerhard Junack, 'the British destroyers appeared once more, coming in close to deliver their torpedoes again and again, but the *Bismarck*'s gunnery was so effective that none of them was able to score a hit. But around 0845 hours [on the 27th] a strongly united attack opened and the last fight of the *Bismarck* began. Two minutes later, *Bismarck* replied, and her third volley straddled the *Rodney*, but this accuracy could not be maintained: because of the continual battle against the sea, and attack now from three sides, the *Bismarck*'s fire was soon to deteriorate. Shortly after the battle commenced a shell hit the combat mast, and the fire-control post in the fore-mast broke away. At 0902 hours both forward heavy-gun turrets were put out of action. A further hit wrecked the forward control-post, the rear control-post was wrecked soon after – and that was the end of the fighting instruments. For a time, the rear turrets fired singly, but by about 1000 hours all the guns of the *Bismarck* were silent.

'Shortly after the beginning of the battle I realised, from my station in the middle of the turbine room, that water was pouring down through the ventilation shafts; obviously the enemy's shells were landing very close to the ship and flooding the decks with water. Perhaps it was lucky that we below could not differentiate between the enemy's hits and our own firing; but after a time, the ventilator emitted a reddish-yellow smoke and I stopped to put on my gas-mask. Obviously, a serious fire was raging somewhere.

'Gradually the noise of combat became more irregular until it sank, to become nothing more than a series of sporadic crashes; even the control bells from the bridge stopped ringing. All three turbine-rooms were filled with smoke from the boiler-room; fortunately, no shells had yet come through the plating protecting the engine-room or the electric generators (though the electric plant on the port side had been hit on the Saturday morning by a shell from the *Prince of Wales*).

'Somewhere about 1015 hours, I received an order over the telephone from the Chief Engineer, Korvettenkapitän Walter Lehmann: "Prepare the ship for sinking."' That was the last order Junack received on the *Bismarck*. 'Soon after that, all transmission of orders collapsed', he wrote.

'As it became quieter up above, I sent my best petty officer to the engine-room to ask for further instructions, but the man apparently perished on his way, for he never returned. I felt compelled therefore to get an answer myself. One last look round to check that all the bulkheads were unfastened and then I sent the crew to the centre deck, giving my chief turbine-engineer orders to connect the explosive charges. Eventually I left with the turbines still moving slowly in compliance with the Engineer's orders.

'The lower decks were brilliantly lit; a peaceful mood prevailed, such as that on a Sunday afternoon in port – the silence broken only by the explosion of our own demolition charges below. I myself saw the result of the battle on the battery-deck. There was no electric light, only the red glow from numerous fires; smoke fumes billowed everywhere; crushed doors and hatches littered the decks and men were running here and there, apparently aimlessly: it seemed highly unlikely that one would survive.

'Astern, I came across a large and seemingly purposeless crowd who obviously had no instructions or any idea what to do. I worked my way through them and signalled for order and quiet; it then appeared that the metal hatch leading to the upper decks was jammed half-open, with men in their gasmasks and inflated life-jackets squeezing through slowly and with great difficulty. After I had thrown away all the unnecessary combat equipment and deflated the life-jackets, the men got through far more quickly.

'Cadet officers and more than 100 petty officers and men were collecting between the rear turrets, but amidships there was a smoke-screen which prevented us from seeing what was happening forward; only the combat mast stood out from the dense black smoke. The flag was still waving from the rear mast, and the barrels of the rear turrets stood out starkly against the sky; one barrel had been split by a tremendous explosion. Only occasionally did I see dead or wounded comrades.

'Meanwhile the ship sank deeper, and we knew that it would eventually capsize. As senior officer I told the men to make the last preparations and

HMS *Ark Royal* in 1939 with Swordfish of 820 Naval Air Squadron overhead. The 'Ark' was torpedoed on 13 November 1941 by U-81 and sank the following day after all but one of the 1,488 crew members had evacuated the carrier while under tow to Gibraltar when the order 'abandon ship' was declared again when the vessel began listing before capsizing and then sank.

Above Left: New Zealand-born Flight Lieutenant Patrick Geraint 'Jamie' Jameson who flew Hurricanes in the ill-fated Norwegian campaign in May-June 1940.

Above right: Squadron Leader Kenneth Brian Boyd 'Bing' Cross, Hurricane pilot and OC, 46 Squadron during the ill-fated Norwegian campaign in May-June 1940.

Above: HMS *Glorious*, which was sunk in Norwegian waters on 8 June 1940.

Left: Squadron Leader Duncan Charles Frederick Good RAAF on 50 Squadron who was KIA at sea 28 April 1941, age 24.

Sunderland L5798 of 204 Squadron at Bathhurst, Gambia at Gibraltar following an engine service.

T785 FAA Squadron Swordfish Mk.Is on a training flight from NAS Crail.

Above: Five eight-gun Fairey Fulmars of 806 Squadron and a Swordfish ranged on HMS *Illustrious* in November 1940. Note the two Sea Gladiators of 813 Fighter Flight aft of the island that were transferred from *Eagle* for Taranto. While it was true that a Spitfire could easily outclass a Stuka, usually a Fulmar was an entirely different matter.

Left: HMS *Illustrious* landing Swordfish in June 1940. (FAA Museum)

Above left: Taranto Mar Grande outer harbour taken by a 431 Flight RAF Maryland flying from Luqa just before the attack on the night of 11/12 November 1940.

Above right: Sub Lieutenant Alfred 'Jackie' Sewell, a Fulmar pilot on HMS Illustrious in the Mediterranean during 1940-41 usually flying with Leading Aircraftman Denis J. Tribe as his observer.

Arming a Swordfish with a 18-inch torpedo.

The *Bismarck* from the *Prinz Eugen*.

Swordfish landing on.

AH545 WQ-Z, the PBY-5 Catalina flying boat piloted by Ensign Leonard B. 'Tuck' Smith USN and Pilot Officer Dennis Briggs on 209 Squadron (seen here landing on Loch Erne) which spotted the *Bismarck* on 20 May 1941 and ultimately led to the successful pursuit of the German battleship by the Royal Navy which resulted on 27 May 1941 in her being scuttled following incapacitating battle damage.

Martin Maryland Mk.I photo-recce aircraft of 771 Squadron FAA from RNAS Hatston.

Fairey Swordfish in a dive.

Awards ceremony for the officers and ratings of 825 Squadron FAA who were decorated for the part they played in the sinking of the *Bismarck*; left to right: Lieutenant Philip David 'Percy' Gick (DSC); Lieutenant Commander Eugene Kingsmill Esmonde, (DSO); Sub Lieutenant Valentine Kay Norfolk (DSC); Petty Officer Airman Leslie D. Sayer (DSM); Petty Officer Ambrose Laurence 'Ginger' Johnson, (Esmond's TAG) (DSM) who attacked the *Bismarck*. Esmonde was awarded a posthumous Victoria Cross for his heroic sacrifice during the Channel Dash operation of 12 February 1942.

Unternehmen "Zerberus", German heavy ships steaming up the English Channel, en route from Brest to Wilhelmshaven, 12 February 1942. Photographed from the heavy cruiser *Prinz Eugen*, the *Gneisenau* is next ahead, with *Scharnhorst* visible in the distance.

Tirpitz in Kafjord-Altafjord photographed surrounded by torpedo nets by a Mosquito on 12 July 1944.

Left: New Zealander, Lieutenant Commander Archibald 'Arch' Richardson RNZVR, a 27-year-old Hellcat pilot in 1840 Squadron in *Indefatigable* who was awarded a posthumous MiD for exceptional bravery and determination in the attack on the *Tirpitz* on 24 August 1944.

Below: Corsair damaged by flak makes a safe landing escaping only with a bent propeller on *formidable* during raids on the *Tirpitz* in Alten Fjord.

Corsairs and Fairey Barracuda torpedo bombers ranged on the flight deck of HMS *Formidable* off Norway in July 1944.

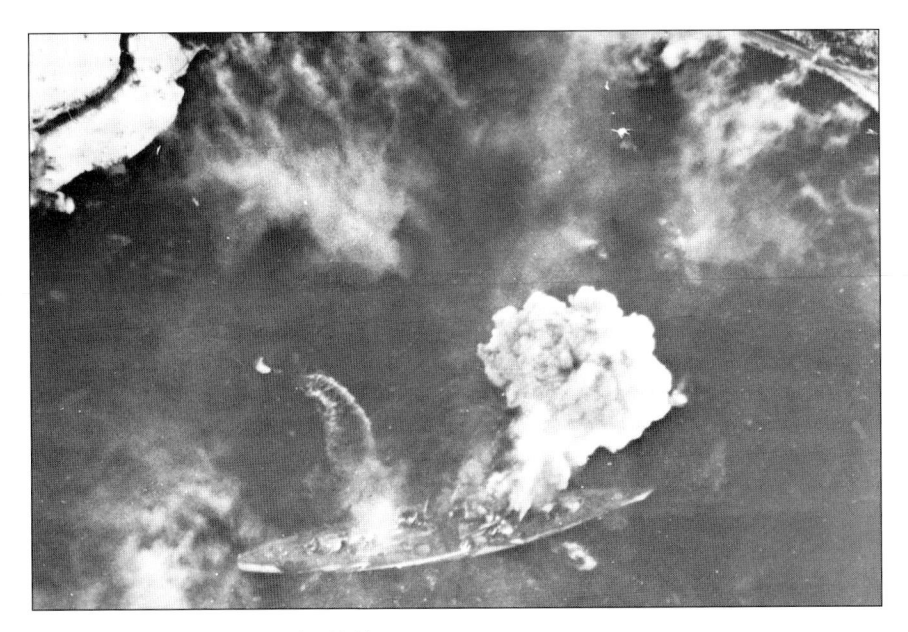

FAA attack on the *Tirpitz* in 1944.

Above: Hawker Sea Hurricane Mk I 'catafighter' aboard a Catapult Armed Merchantman (CAM).

Left: Australian Flight Lieutenant Harold Graham Pockley DFC*, the skipper of a Sunderland flying-boat of 10 Squadron RAAF. Returning to Australia in 1942 Pockley was reported MIA flying a Liberator on 25 March 1945 after failing to return from a successful operation to insert personnel and supplies into the jungles of Sarawak.

SBD-3 Radioman 1st Class William Cicero Miller of VMF-211.

VF-6 CO (*Enterprise*), Lieutenant Commander Clarence Wade McClusky.

Above: B5n2 Kate Akagi.

Left: Lieutenant Clarence Earle Dickinson, Executive Officer of VS-6 on the *Enterprise*.

Right: Lieutenant Commander Eugene E. Lindsey, Commanding VT-6 (TBDs) on the Enterprise.

Below: A6M2 Zero on the carrier *Akagi* on 7 December 1941 during the Pearl Harbor attack.

Ensign (later Captain) James G. Daniels of Fighting Squadron 6 (VF-6) who was one of the Grumman F4F Wildcat pilots on Combat Air Patrol during the attack on Pearl Harbor.

Pearl Harbor on 7 December 1941 (l-r) USS *West Virginia* (sunk), USS *Tennessee* (damaged) and the USS *Arizona* (sunk).

then gave a few simple orders – stay together in the water, keep calm, don't give up hope, and be careful when interrogated by the enemy. After a triple Sieg heil! I ordered 'abandon ship'.

'Hardly were we free of the ship when it keeled over to port, rolling the deck-rail under and bringing the bilge-keel out of the water. A pause – then the *Bismarck* turned keel-up, and we could see that its hull had not been damaged by torpedoes. Then, slowly, the bows rose in the air, and, stern first, *Bismarck* slid down to the bottom.

'While still on deck, we had seen an English cruiser coming towards us. She was the *Dorsetshire*, and she approached the wreckage and stopped to pick us up. Some 85 of the 400 who were in the water were saved – but then a look-out reported a U-boat periscope, and the *Dorsetshire* left at full speed, leaving our comrades in the water. Unfortunately for us the look-out had been wrong, for there were no U-boats in the area. Later, HMS *Maori* saved another 25 men. A U-boat saved another three ten hours later and a German weather ship picked up two more crew-members 40 hours later.'[37]

Prisoners stated that Kapitänleutnant Gerhard Junack, when in the water, shouted to all those near him to 'keep their mouths shut' should they be picked up. Another officer, who was without a life-belt, was seen by prisoners to shoot himself in the chest.

Admiral Karl Dönitz, commander of the German U-boat fleet, ordered all submarines in the vicinity to render what aid they could, even if it just meant recovering the *Bismarck*'s war diary before she went to the bottom. Kapitänleutnant Herbert Wohlfarth, commander of *U-556*, rushed to the scene even though all his torpedoes had been expended during the boat's month-long patrol. It was a frustrated Wohlfarth then who watched helplessly as the *Ark Royal*, accompanied by the *Renown*, passed directly before his periscope.

---

37. *The Last Hours of the Bismarck*, an article by Kapitänleutnant (Ing.) Gerhard Junack originally published in Purnell's *History of the Second World War*, Vol.2, No. 5, 1967. From 1947 to 1956 he was chief engineer for a steel construction firm in Hamburg. Gerhard Junack resumed his naval career in 1956, serving with the rank of Fregattenkapitän at Kiel, in the sphere of damage control. Promoted to Kapitän zur See in 1962, he served at Wilhelmshaven as Chief-of-Staff (Logistics), retiring from the navy in January 1966. He died in 1977.

THE AIR WAR AT SEA IN THE SECOND WORLD WAR

A third strike of Swordfish witnessed the final battle and were obliged to jettison their torpedoes unused before returning to *Ark Royal*. Captain T. Shaw wrote: 'The CO of 818 led 12 of us to torpedo the *Bismarck* but when we arrived it was not allowed because of the proximity of HM ships. The squadron passed half a mile astern of *Bismarck* at 1,000 ft and as we watched she rolled over and sank. When we got back to *Ark Royal* the flight deck was moving through 65 ft but we had only one undercarriage collapse - and that was because he had not jettisoned his torpedo. Shortly after that a Junkers 88 joined the circuit, but eventually he gave up, jettisoned his bombs and flew away.'

The coup de grace was given by a torpedo from the cruiser *Dorsetshire*; just 24 hours after firm contact had been regained, by the Swordfish. It remains unclear to this day whether *Bismarck* sank as the result of British gunfire or was scuttled by her crew.

Admiral Sir John Tovey said: 'The *Bismarck* had put up a most gallant fight against impossible odds, worthy of the old days of the Imperial German Navy, and she went down with her colours still flying.'

That same week a visit was arranged to South Kirkby Colliery in Yorkshire by the Air Ministry after the receipt of a telegram of congratulation on behalf of the colliery company and their employees. At an unusual pit-head meeting, 1,500 miners were treated to a visit by the captain of the Catalina who had located the *Bismarck* in the Atlantic.

The local newspaper reported that: 'Black faced miners who had just come out of the pit and others about to start work gave a great welcome to the airman. He told them that the aircraft started its search early on Monday. Three quarters of an hour later, in the mist they saw a dull black shape ahead which looked like the *Bismarck*. 'We were not quite sure so we climbed up to about 1,500 ft into a cloud. The cloud was not continuous and we came out right on top of the darned thing and it was a bit hot for us for a time. They let up with all the guns they had, knocked a few holes in us and blew us around a bit. I handed a message to the wireless operator giving her position and it was transmitted immediately.

'I was lucky to come across the enemy but I reckon I have an easier job than you. This war depends on your work. The more coal you get out, the more aircraft we can produce.'

On 1 June *Prinz Eugen*, which had been detached with engine-room defects and her captain having refused to carry out independent commerce raiding as ordered by Lütjens, reached Brest safely. Aware that she was

HUNTING THE *BISMARCK*

at large, the carriers *Victorious* and *Ark Royal* searched for her and the attendant supply ships. *Eagle*, recently transferred from the Mediterranean Fleet and *Nelson* covered the area to the west of the Cape Verde Islands and the carrier aircraft had some degree of success in their searches. On 4 June *Victorious*' Swordfish sighted and stopped the supply ship *Gonzenheim*, awaiting *Bismarck* 200 miles north of the Azores. *Gonzenheim* escaped owing to her superior speed, but was later stopped by *Renown*, who sent a boarding party on board, but the crew had already taken steps to scuttle their ship. The ship was eventually sunk by two torpedoes and gunfire from *Neptune*. Before surface forces could reach the position however the German ship was scuttled. On 6 June *Eagle*'s aircraft found and sank by bombing the U-boat supply ship *Elbe*, following this up with the detection and surrender of the tanker *Lothringen* on 15 June 1941.

As soon as it became certain that *Prinz Eugen* had reached Brest, *Victorious* and *Ark Royal* were returned to their normal duties, the two ships joining for a ferry operation in early June, 47 Hurricanes being flown off to Malta on the 10th.

In England, Kapitänleutnant Gerhard Junack began five years in PoW camps first in England and later in Canada. He was one of the lucky ones on the crew of the *Bismarck*. Out of a total of between 2,300 and 2,400 officers and men believed to have been on board the battleship when sunk, only 110, including four officers, survived.

Chapter 5

Unternehmen 'Donnerkeil-Zerberus' February 1942

The Swordfish flew right into the German air umbrella, which was on the look-out for some such British force and almost immediately things began to happen. In a moment the air was filled with criss-crossing lines of tracer... The 'Stringbags', truly living up to their name, for that first swarming attack had punished them badly, flew straight on through the flak screen and across the billowing cloud of oily murk towards the Scharnhorst *and* Gneisenau *gleaming dully. The destroyers and other escort vessels began pumping up flak in a more closely woven curtain. Esmonde went through it and the other two machines in his flight, torn and battered, were still close behind him, the warheads of their torpedoes pointing threateningly at the enemy. The warships put up their own barrage and the fire from the escorts redoubled as the German gunners sweated to keep the guns firing. Esmonde was holding course for the others, who were following. He kept going, though he knew that at any moment his aircraft would be shot to pieces above the waves. The inevitable happened.*

The Stringbags' Greatest Flight **by
Leonard Reginald Gribble (1908-1985)**
a prolific English writer who served
in the Press and Censorship Division of the
Ministry of Information, London 1940-45.

On Wednesday, 11 February 1942 33-year-old Lieutenant Commander Eugene Esmonde commanding 825 Squadron, Fleet Air Arm went to Buckingham Palace to receive from the King the DSO he had been awarded for his part

UNTERNEHMEN 'DONNERKEIL-ZERBERUS'

in the *Bismarck* operation. Esmonde had been one of the last to leave *Ark Royal* on 13 November 1941 during the return to Gibraltar when she was torpedoed by *U-81* and sank in tow within sight of her base. After leaving the *Ark*, 825 Squadron had re-formed at Lee-on-Solent in Hampshire. Later the squadron was reduced to six Swordfish, with a complement of seven pilots, each with an observer and telegraphist-air-gunner assigned. At the beginning of February 1942, the Squadron had expected to be sent to escort one of the new escort carriers from the United States and in the throes of 'working up' but rumours persisted about the anticipated breakout of the battleships *Scharnhorst* and *Gneisenau* and the heavy cruiser *Prinz Eugen,* which had been holed up in Brest since their arrival on 22 March 1941 following the success of Operation 'Berlin' in the Atlantic.

On 4 February 825 Squadron moved from Lee-on-Solent to RAF Manston near Ramsgate, Kent and they were put on full alert. On 5 February de-coded German Engima intercepts revealed that Vice-Admiral Otto Ciliax, the 'Type Commander, Battleships' (*Befehlshaber der Schlachtschiffe*) had joined *Scharnhorst* sheltering at Brest. Hitler had ordered the return of the *Scharnhorst* and *Gneisenau* and *Prinz Eugen* to return to Germany so that they could be used to interdict Allied convoys to the Soviet Union, as well as to strengthen the defences of Norway. For surprise and air cover by the Luftwaffe the Führer insisted that the ships would make the voyage via the English Channel, a shorter route than a long detour around the British Isles.

In April 1941 the Admiralty had developed Operation 'Fuller' for combined operations between the Royal Navy and the RAF to attack the ships at Brest should they try and sail up the English Channel by night to return to their home bases at Wilhelmshaven and Kiel. Confident that with radar and air patrols, any dash up the Channel could be easily discovered, the operation would combine the 32 Motor Torpedo Boats at Dover and Ramsgate that would attack with a Motor Gun Boat (MGB) escort from 3700 metres. Following up would be Swordfish torpedo bombers with fighter escort, plus Beaufort torpedo bombers and the coastal guns at Dover whilst the ships were in range. Bomber command would then attack any damaged ship that had been slowed or stopped. Once out of the Dover Strait, six Royal Navy destroyers would make torpedo attacks and the RAF would continue to bomb and lay mines in the fleet's path.

On 8 February, reconnaissance showed the German battleships were still in dock at Brest but another two destroyers had arrived. Enigma decrypts were also reporting that the Germans were minesweeping a route up the English Channel. For weeks Motor Torpedo Boats stationed at Dover and the six torpedo-carrying Swordfish aircraft had been practising converging attacks on both sides of ships' bows with flares from the aircraft lighting the way but by 10 February the Admiralty decided that the emergency was nearly over and had removed most of the MTBs, leaving just six boats under the charge of Lieutenant Commander Nigel Pumphrey. At South Foreland on the Kent coast Second Lieutenant Hagger had been rehearsing with the 49.2-inch guns in his battery. So persistent were the rumours, that officers not wishing to miss their first opportunity to fire their guns in anger cancelled their leave.

On the 11th the Swordfish crews of 825 Squadron were stood down from their 5-minute standby as there appeared to be no real threat. HMS *Sealion*, the only modern Royal Navy submarine that was in home waters, and stationed close to Brest to monitor the German ships, moved away at 2135 hours to surface and recharge her batteries and the watch was abandoned for the night. At 1200 hours, Vice-Admiral Ciliax had ordered the battle fleet to prepare to depart Brest at 1930 hours. At 1400 hours the German weather service reported that a warm front was approaching the British Isles, which meant low cloud and poor visibility in the Channel.

Some of the RAF officers, together with the Fleet Air Arm flying crews, meanwhile, had arranged a small party to celebrate Esmonde's DSO decoration that evening, though his senior observer, 30-year-old Lieutenant William Henry Williams, took the opportunity to visit his mother and family who had been evacuated from their Leigh-on-Sea home to Ruskin Manor at Denmark Hill in London. When he received a telegram recalling him to RAF Manston an air raid was in progress and no public transport was running. Jack Hulbert, a well-known variety artist who was a war reserve policeman and as such had a petrol ration, was visiting a friend who had also been evacuated to Ruskin Manor. When he understood just how important it was for Williams to return to RAF Manston, he readily agreed to drive him there. The party did not go on late, as they had to be standing by their aircraft at 4 o'clock the next morning for the routine pre-dawn alert.

At Brest the German battle fleet had begun to prepare for departure as ordered by Vice-Admiral Ciliax, but the deadline coincided with a raid that night by 18 Wellingtons and eight Stirlings, the first bombs falling just as the *Scharnhorst*, *Gneisenau* and *Prinz Eugen* were casting off and the destroyer

UNTERNEHMEN 'DONNERKEIL-ZERBERUS'

escort had already formed up at the entrance to the harbour. The ships were ordered back to their berths until the bombers had left. At 2115 hours, a post reconnaissance flight over the port by a Lockheed Hudson revealed that the ships were still in harbour, but the fleet was casting off. The replacement Hudson reconnaissance from St. Eval was delayed due to engine problems and so the ships moved out unobserved, eventually forming up in the roadstead outside Brest at 2245 hours, over an hour behind schedule. A Resistance agent in Brest was unable to signal the departure because of the jamming of wireless signals by the Germans.

In the event the Kriegsmarine's Unternehmen 'Zerberus' (Operation Cerberus - 'The Channel Dash') was the largest fleet the Germans ever assembled. The *Scharnhorst*, *Prinz Eugen* and *Gneisenau*, escorted by more than thirty destroyers, flagships, torpedo-boats, 'E-boats' and minesweepers, formed up outside Brest and at midnight the fleet prepared to enter the English Channel, expecting to reach it by 0125 hours the next day,[38] before heading for Norway protected by a flotilla of torpedo boats and a strong air umbrella provided by General der Jagdflieger Adolf Galland in 'Donnerkeil' ('Thunderbolt'), code-name for the air superiority operation. The fighters flew at masthead-height to avoid detection by the British radar network. Liaison officers were present on all three ships.

At 0400 hours on 12 February 825 Squadron were brought to routine alert, standing by their aircraft ready for take-off at a time before dawn that the Admiralty believed the Germans would use to slip through the straits. At 0835 hours as dawn broke, the high alert of the British forces was cancelled by Admiral Ramsey who was at that time unaware that the enemy fleet was passing Cherbourg and 825 Squadron was stood down as the freezing snow swirled over Manston, scattering its icy dust on the six Swordfish, which stood alone in a corner of the dispersal area. Meanwhile, Second Lieutenant Hagger was organising yet another practise drill session. At 1000 hours 22-year-old Sub Lieutenant Brian Westland Rose and his observer, 20-year-old Sub Lieutenant Edgar Frederick Lee took off from Manston on a practice torpedo run in Pegwell Bay. Born on 13 May 1921 in Perth, Scotland, Rose had excelled at athletics, boxing, cricket and football at Elizabeth College, Guernsey from 1933 to 1939 and had performed in the Shakespearian

---

38. See, *Channel Dash – The Bravest of the Brave* (History of Manston Airfield, 12 February 2022).

THE AIR WAR AT SEA IN THE SECOND WORLD WAR

Society's production of 'Macbeth'. By 1941 the Old Elizabethan had become a Leading Naval Airman in the RNVR. Sixteen minutes after Rose had taken off, British radar finally confirmed a large fleet of vessels and aircraft support in the English Channel but due to the reduced alert, the report was to only slowly make its way to Royal Navy headquarters and the enemy fleet continued unopposed.

At 1016 hours, the radar station at Swingate near Dover began to plot three big 'blips', indicating ships 56 miles distant in the direction of Boulogne. The size of the 'blips' and the estimated distance indicated they were much bigger than anything ever before seen. At the same time, other radar stations began picking up constant circular plots, which they identified as patrolling German E-boats. But they were in fact Galland's fighter umbrella circling over the German battleships. The Swingate radar station commander, 31-year-old Flight Lieutenant Gerald Kidd, a solicitor in civilian life, suddenly asked, 'Are these the *Scharnhorst* and the *Gneisenau*?' When Kidd tried to telephone a warning to Dover Castle, the GPO line was defective. Further attempts to call on the scrambler proved equally frustrating. Later investigation of the defective telephone revealed that both the GPO and the secret scrambler were plugged into the same line.

At 1030 hours two pairs of Spitfires took off, ten minutes apart. The first pair were from RAF Hawkinge with Squadron Leader 'Bobby' Oxspring, the CO of 91 Squadron and Sergeant Roland 'Bee' Beamont; the second from RAF Kenley with Group Captain Victor Beamish of the North Weald Wing and Squadron Leader Finlay Boyd. Both pairs found the fleet but radio silence as part of Operation 'Fuller' dictated that they had to wait to report the sightings back at base. On the bridge of the *Scharnhorst*, Admiral Ciliax watched the wave-hopping Spitfires and said to Kapitän Kurt Hoffmann, 'This is the start of it. We are now discovered. The attack will come at any minute.' As they were now out of the narrow mine-free lane, Ciliax ordered the battleships to increase speed to thirty knots. Mist and low cloud came drifting down over the Channel. It was bitterly cold and driving rain began to fall as the German gunners waited for the British attack. It did not come.[39]

Beamish and Boyd spotted two Bf 109s and attacked, finding themselves over a German flotilla of two big ships, a destroyer screen and an outer ring of E-boats. After being dived on by around 12 German fighters and attacked by

---

39. See *The Channel Dash*, Key Aero Forum.

UNTERNEHMEN 'DONNERKEIL-ZERBERUS'

anti-aircraft fire from the ships, they returned to Kenley, flying just above the waves. At 1050 hours Oxspring and Beaumont reported. Even then, it was not until the Kenley report was received at 1111 hours that Admiral Ramsey was informed.

Out to sea there was a thick fog and all the coastal observers could see as they strained through their binoculars was swirling mist. Understandable then, that when radar signals showed the German fleet to be in the Channel, the command post at Dover Castle was thrown into a state of uproar. In the middle of the confusion sat Brigadier Cecil Whitfield Raw studying the first radar reports. With the German ships only 32,000 yards away, as commander of the coastal artillery, he realised that the only weapons he could engage were Hagger's at South Foreland. He gave the signal to sound action stations, but Hagger assumed that like so many previous alerts, this one was a false alarm and instructed his gunners to resume their practice drill session and then picked up the telephone to query the order with his battery commander, Major Guy Huddlestone. He received a sharp reply: "This is the real thing, take post!"

The news was flashed to Dover Naval Command and Operation 'Fuller', the Admiralty and Air Ministry plan for a combined operation aimed at preventing the battle-cruisers from escaping unscathed, was put into action. But by 10 February the Admiralty had removed most of the MTBs, leaving only six boats under the charge of Lieutenant Commander Nigel Pumphrey. These were at once dispatched from Dover to attack the enemy formation. Visibility on the morning of 12 February just before noon was poor, varying three to five miles, with low clouds and at no time were the enemy ships visible from the English coast. At 1120 hours the German ships reduced speed to pass a British minefield but had resumed full speed by 1140 hours when the telephone rang at Lee-on-Solent. Wing Commander Constable-Roberts, RAF Liaison Officer at Dover Castle HQ, confirmed that at 1109 an enemy squadron consisting of the *Scharnhorst*, *Prinz Eugen* and the *Gneisenau*, escorted by destroyers, torpedo-boats, E-boats and minesweepers, had been sighted by a Spitfire off Boulogne approaching the Straits of Dover from the west.

At 1210 hours radar showed the battleships to be 27,000 yards away approaching Cape Griz Nez travelling at an estimated speed of 22 knots, but in reality, it was nearer 30 knots. Brigadier Cecil Whitfield Raw gave the order to fire at 1219 hours. Major Huddlestone's guns erupted; the two heavy armour piercing shells would take almost a minute to reach their target. Huddlestone, who tried to catch a glimpse of the ships from his observation post, could only see mist. Without observation of the 'fall of shot' there could be no accurate correction of aim. Were they on target? No one knew. What's more, no one had ever fired these guns on radar alone; the radar blips showed that the early salvoes fell well short. Twice Brigadier Raw ordered them to add another 1,000 yards to the range, but not one shell fell close enough to the Germans to cause any damage.

Nigel Pumphrey was in his office at Dover making out reports when the telephone rang. It was Captain Day, naval chief of staff to Admiral Bertram Ramsey at Dover Castle, who asked briskly: "How soon can you get going? The German battle cruisers are off Boulogne!" Pumphrey didn't need telling twice, he slammed down the receiver and dashed into the operations room to order his MTBs to be manned, in fact, only five set out to intercept the Germans. Because Pumphrey's own boat was under repair, he took another.

As they raced towards the smoke, made by the German E-boats screen it suddenly cleared and Pumphrey and Lieutenant Arnold Foster in the two leading boats had a clear view of the great grey ships streaking through the straits in patches of hazy sunshine.

The Germans were about five miles ahead with half a dozen destroyers astern and air cover totalling a massive 256 aircraft. The largest air umbrella ever assembled was now circling above them, but between Pumphrey and the German ships were the E-boats, much bigger and faster than his MTBs, with 20 mm cannon against his machine guns. Suddenly their shells smashed into the hull of Pumphrey's boat and his engine died, letting the bows down into the water. As Pumphrey fought with the controls, the remaining four boats slowed to maintain formation, then Pumphrey's engine spluttered to life again, and he turned to drive his small flotilla through the E-boat screen, running the gauntlet of their heavy fire with his quarry still 4,000 yards away. Pumphrey's intention was to reduce the range to 2,000 yards, a dangerous decision which could result in the loss of all his craft, but as he charged through the screen the matter was taken out of his hands and his starboard engine failed and his speed immediately fell to 16 knots. There was only one this to do, to press ahead until the E-boat fire became too much and then to fire his torpedoes from a range of not much short of 4,000 yards.

Luckily the sea was too rough for the E-boats to fire accurately and Pumphrey chugged on. When German fighter aircraft began attacking the

UNTERNEHMEN 'DONNERKEIL-ZERBERUS'

MTBs Pumphrey ordered the others to split up and make individual attacks. If he could just keep afloat until the battleship came abreast of him, he could fire his torpedoes from about two miles.

Finally, the battleships came into his sight and Pumphrey pointed his boat's nose ready to launch his weapons, but warning shouts from his gunners alerted him to two E-boats which had raced up to within 800 yards and begun firing. As his gunners returned fire Pumphrey operated the lever and his two torpedoes splashed into the sea. Shortly afterwards he realised his torpedoes had missed. There was nothing more he could do but to swing his boat away from the battle and head for the British coast. The rest of his MTBs fared little better, twisting and turning to avoid the swarms of enemy fighters diving at them. They launched their torpedoes from a range of 3,500 yards but the *Scharnhorst* had plenty of time to take avoiding action and their attacks came to nothing. A German destroyer suddenly appeared through the smoke and against such odds, the MTBs were forced to scatter. By 1300 the ships had cleared the Strait of Dover.[40]

Admiral Ramsey realised that the only means now left to him was to attack the convoy with the six Swordfish of 825 Squadron at Manston. But how could he send them out in daylight against the ferocious firepower of the German battleships and accompanying heavy fighter escort? It would be certain death. Ramsey telephoned the First Sea Lord, Sir Dudley Pound, in Whitehall and pleaded with him not to be asked to send these 18 men on such a suicidal mission. Pound replied: 'The navy will attack the enemy whenever and wherever he is to be found.' Lieutenant Commander Esmonde had volunteered to lead his meagre force against the German ships should there be a need for such a strike force and his request was granted, with the promise that every possible means of support would be given.

After a false alarm during the early hours, Esmonde addressed his crews in a clipped voice: 'The balloon's gone up. Get ready.' The crews, who arrived during a blizzard, were placed at five minutes readiness. At this point Esmonde was expecting to make a night attack and arrangements had been made for RAF fighters to accompany the Swordfish as flare droppers. He received a telephone call from 11 Fighter Group, saying, 'We intend putting in the Biggin Hill Wing of three squadrons as top cover with the Hornchurch Wing of two squadrons as close escort to beat up the "flak" ships for you.

---

40. Cited on *WW2 People's War website* by Ted Powell.

Both Wings have been told to rendezvous over Manston. What time should they be there?'

Esmonde glanced at his watch and said: 'Tell them to be here by 1225 hours. Get the fighters to us on time – for the love of God.' Constable-Roberts telephoned Esmonde again to stress that the Swordfish must go only if he was satisfied that the fighter cover was adequate. Both the RAF and RN officers on the spot felt that even with a heavy fighter escort, few Swordfish crews would return from this operation.

The maintenance ratings arrived by road and first had to dig their aircraft out of the snowdrifts and then service them, running the engines up at intervals to keep them warm and ready for action. One gunner, although a sick man, serviced the torpedoes night and day until he collapsed.

Brian Rose and 'Fred' Lee were returning to the mess after their practice flight when a lorry carrying the rest of the Squadron's officers came past. Someone shouted a warning to them that action was imminent. It was just after noon. Rose and Lee ran back to the crew room and put their flying kit back on. Esmonde entered the room and said: 'The *Scharnhorst*, *Gneisenau* and *Prinz Eugen* have had the cheek to put their noses into the Channel and we're going out to deal with them. Fly at 50 feet, loose line astern, individual attacks, and find your own way home. We shall have fighter protection.'

Because of the extreme need for secrecy, Esmonde had committed the orders to paper, which having been read by his officers was then burned. Three replacement Swordfish were to be collected from storage at Campbeltown in Scotland and 22-year-old Petty Officer William Johnson 'Clints' Clinton was detailed to visit to check-out polar diagrams for the replacement aircraft.[41] He had arranged a date with his fiancée in London for that particular weekend, and because Chief Petty Officer Les Sayer's wife was living in Scotland, he willingly agreed to swap duties. Sayer had previously flown with pilot 'Percy' Gick in the attack led by Esmonde against the *Bismarck*. Clinton became Senior TAG and so it was his lot to accompany the CO. As there were seven pilots and only six aircraft, the two most junior pilots, 20-year-old Sub Lieutenant Peter Bligh and Sub Lieutenant Bennet tossed a coin to decide

---

41. Clinton's pilot on the *Bismarck* operation was Sub Lt Alexander James Houston RNVR and Sub Lt John Robert Geater RNVR the observer. Houston's crew failed to find the *Bismarck*.

UNTERNEHMEN 'DONNERKEIL-ZERBERUS'

who should fly. Peter Bligh called tails and would fly whilst Bennet stayed on the ground.

Once the order was given, Esmonde called his five pilots together and told them to be in readiness for a strike at any moment. Six aircraft were prepared and armed with torpedoes. Esmonde asked Constable-Roberts, 'Where's Jerry? What's his speed?' The reply was, 'About ten miles north east of the Straits, sailing at 21 knots.' Esmonde was promised an escort of five squadrons of Spitfires - three for close escort and two for diversionary attacks but 11 Group had stated that it would be a 'rush' to get them to Manston by the required hour of 1225. Between 1200 and 1215 Biggin Hill and Hornchurch both passed word to Manston that their squadrons would be a few minutes late. The controller of Hornchurch spoke personally to Esmonde, who replied that whatever happened he must leave at 1225. Constable-Roberts asked Esmonde, 'Are you satisfied with fighter escort? If so, Admiral Ramsay says it's OK to go'. Then adding in a quieter voice, 'Best of luck old boy.'

It was 1215 hours as the six crews climbed into their six Swordfish. It was at this point that a runner came with a message from the Control Room, 'Dover says the enemy's speed now estimated 27 knots Sir'. This was three to four knots faster than previously estimated. It now made a quick take-off vital. Message acknowledged, the crews were ready for take-off. It was a desperate attempt to intercept and delay the enemy ships until other measures could be taken. Wing Commander 'Tom' Gleave the Manston station commander stood alone on the snow-covered airfield giving a farewell salute to the 18 heroic young men. In biplanes only capable of flying 90 knots due to the weight of their torpedoes, they were on their way to attack two mighty battleships and a heavy cruiser, escorted by seven large destroyers, flagships and four E-boats. And all were supported by the largest Luftwaffe air cover ever put up. 'They were the finest bunch I have ever seen,' said Gleave, who watched them take off. 'They came out of the mess grinning and went across to the six Swordfish. They knew that they were going to face death. But they waved, climbed into the planes and took off. It was real heroism.'

It was exactly 1225 when Eugene Esmonde waved his arm to signal the pilots behind him to take off. One by one the six torpedo-laden Swordfish taxied along Manston's frozen grass runway and took off into the wintry sky. As the Swordfish circled the airfield levelling off at 1,550 ft, they set course for Ramsgate to await fighter escort.

THE AIR WAR AT SEA IN THE SECOND WORLD WAR

Esmonde had as his crew Lieutenant Bill Williams and Petty Officer Clinton, his telegraphist air gunner.[42] Taking up position immediately behind the CO's Swordfish was Sub Lieutenant Brian Rose with Sub Lieutenant Edgar Frederick Lee as observer and 22-year-old Leading Airman Ambrose Laurence 'Ginger' Johnson DSM as his TAG. Thirdly came Sub Lieutenant Charles Major 'Pat' Kingsmill with Sub Lieutenant Reginald McCartney 'Mac' Samples as his observer[43] and Naval Airman 1st Class Donald Arthur Bunce as his TAG. These three Swordfish formed the first vic formation. Behind them, leading the second vic, was 27-year-old Lieutenant John Chute Thompson with 21-year-old Sub Lieutenant Robert Laurens Parkinson as observer and 26-year-old Leading Airman Ernest Tapping as his TAG. On one side of these three aircraft was positioned Sub Lieutenant Cecil Ralph Wood with 22-year-old Sub Lieutenant Eric Herbert Fuller-Wright as his observer and 30-year-old Leading Airman Henry Thomas Albert Wheeler as his TAG. On the other side was Sub Lieutenant Peter Bligh with Sub Lieutenant William Beynon as observer and 22-year-old Leading Airman William Grenville Smith as his TAG.

The weather was thickening up but there was not a fighter to be seen in the sky let alone the promised five Spitfire squadrons. Passing under an evil looking black cumulus cloud, the Swordfish reached Ramsgate and began to circle around the east coast of Kent at 1,500 ft waiting for their vital Spitfire escort to arrive. The weather was thickening up and there was not a fighter to be seen in the sky. Finally, at 1228, three minutes late on rendezvous, ten Spitfires of 72 Squadron led by Squadron Leader Brian Kingcombe appeared. After two more minutes orbiting, Esmonde decided, that in view of the failure of the other squadrons to arrive he could wait no longer and Operation 'Fuller' must proceed without further delay. He waved his arm and the six Swordfish dived down to 50 ft above sea level to head out to sea. Unfortunately, 401 Squadron RCAF and 124 Squadrons at Biggin Hill arrived over Manston 15 minutes late and missed the rendezvous. Realizing that they were behind schedule these two squadrons avoided Manston and flew straight out across the south coast at Deal. Failing to find the Swordfish

---

42. On the strike against the *Bismarck* his observer had been Lieutenant Colin Croft Ennever and his TAG was Pilot Officer Stanley Edgar Parker.
43. On the *Bismarck* strike, Sub Lieutenant Leslie Bailey RNVR had been MacLean's observer.

UNTERNEHMEN 'DONNERKEIL-ZERBERUS'

on their way to the attack, they turned back to Manston and seeing no sign of Swordfish, proceeded out to sea once again. They would arrive over the German vessels only a few minutes after the Swordfish had delivered their attack - too late to help but nevertheless taking on the Luftwaffe fighters.

The situation now facing 825 Squadron was completely different from the night attack originally envisaged. Seeing no Swordfish, 72 Squadron set off in an easterly direction and soon became embroiled in combat with Bf 109s and Focke Wulf 190 fighters. Within minutes the Spitfires were approaching the main Luftwaffe screen and as they flew through layers of cloud, they met German fighters at all levels. As soon as the Spitfires broke up one wave of attacking aircraft, another flight of Messerschmitts dived to attack the Swordfish. The Luftwaffe contributed five Jagdgeschwaden (Wings) to the operation. Every Luftwaffe sortie had been meticulously timed to allow the fighters exactly 30 minutes over the ships, enough to maintain cover and allow the relieved units to refuel and rearm and return to start the cycle again. However, the relieving sortie arrived after only 20 minutes which reduced the actual fighter cover to 32 fighters for half of the operation.

Squadron Leader Brian Kingcombe noticed more than 20 Focke Wulf 190s circling to make a mass dive on the Swordfish and rushed in to scatter them, suddenly all ten Spitfires were enveloped in a whirling battle with JG 26 led by Gruppenkommandeur Gerhard Schöpfel. The slow flying Swordfish forced the German pilots to lower their undercarriages to prevent overshooting them.

Meanwhile, Nos. 64 and 41 Squadrons from Hornchurch arrived over Manston at 1245 hours. They set off in the direction of Calais and were engaged by stragglers from Oberstleutnant Walter Oesau's Jagdgeschwader 2 'Richthofen' staffels.

The Swordfish formation set off east of Ramsgate hugging the waves. The German ships were calculated to be around 23 miles off Ramsgate and heading at speed towards safety. At their basic speed of 85-90 knots, it would take the Swordfish 15 minutes' flying to reach and attack them. As the gallant six flew away from the coast, Spitfires of 72 Squadron went up to 2,000 ft and slightly ahead of their charges. One of their problems was to keep visual contact with the Swordfish. This meant keeping the throttle to the minimum and flying in a weaving pattern.

At about ten miles out, the six Swordfish ran into Messerschmitt Bf 109s of Jagdgeschwader 2. The Spitfires descended from above and began to beat

THE AIR WAR AT SEA IN THE SECOND WORLD WAR

off the enemy aircraft towards Ramsgate. This first clash with the air cover to the German Fleet was brief. Facing overwhelming odds, the Spitfires were soon back giving cover to the Swordfish.

At 1250 hours Esmonde and his crews had the first daunting sight of their prime targets a mile and a half away, an awesome array of large battleships, sleek destroyers, numerous flak ships, with E-boats darting along the sides of the great naval procession steaming in line ahead, with *Prinz Eugen* leading, followed by *Scharnhorst* and *Gneisenau*; they were almost through the Straits. Aboard the *Prinz Eugen* the anti-aircraft gunnery officer, Lieutenant Commander Paul Schmalenbach heard one of his lookouts cry the warning: 'Enemy planes at the sea level'. He realised he faced the greatest danger of all, a suicide attack. When the Swordfish were 2,000 yards away every gun in the German fleet burst into a flickering flame; everything from the 4-inch to the multiple barrelled guns spewed forth a deadly hail of gold tracer shells and white stars of bursting flak filled the skies up around the Swordfish, who flew on unswervingly. In a rare moment of cooperation between the Kriegsmarine and the Luftwaffe, the sky over the fleet was covered from 50 ft to 2,000 ft by a vast armada of aircraft. From just above sea level to 2,000 ft, the whole sky swarmed with Luftwaffe fighters. In addition to Jagdgeschwader 2 there were the Focke Wulf 190s from Major Gerhard Schopfel's Jagdgeschwader 26 'Schlageter' in almost full strength.

The Swordfish went into the attack over the destroyer screen at only fifty feet, facing a barrage of gunfire. As they closed towards the capital ships, they were again met by intense anti-aircraft fire. As the ships' gunfire died, attacks from the Bf 109s on the Swordfish began, followed by the Fw 190s. Spitfires continued their dog fights as one by one the Swordfish flew on to press home their attack on the capital ships with a great and gallant effort. Pilots came under enemy fire, fighting to keep control of their Swordfish, often being directed by their observers and with air gunners fighting to defend the aircraft.

Esmonde was holding his course steady for the *Prinz Eugen* for the others, who were following while Petty Officer Clinton continually fired his machine gun at the diving Luftwaffe fighters. Esmonde kept going, though he knew that at any moment his aircraft would be shot to pieces above the waves. The German destroyers were furiously making smoke, but Esmonde went across the billowing cloud of oily murk towards his target. Tracer from the destroyers smacked into the cockpit as some Fw 190s joined the attack. Frail

UNTERNEHMEN 'DONNERKEIL-ZERBERUS'

and slow, the Swordfish forced German pilots to lower their undercarriages to prevent overshooting the biplanes. They dived onto the Swordfish and their cannon shells tore large holes in the fabric of the wings and the fuselage. It was a miracle they kept flying.

Vice Admiral Otto Ciliax on the bridge of the *Scharnhorst* watching the old 'Stringbags' with their open cockpits, carrying torpedoes lumbering towards them, remarked to Kapitän Kurt Hoffmann 'the British are now throwing in their mothball navy' and added that the Swordfish 'were doing well to get their torpedoes away'. Tracer bullets set fire to Esmonde's tailplane, at which point Clinton was seen by Spitfire pilot, Flight Lieutenant Michael Crombie to climb out of his cockpit and crawl along the back of the fuselage to the tail where he beat out the flames with his hands. By the time that Clinton had eased himself back to his cockpit they were over the outer screen of the flak ships and now faced the German battleships' main 11-inch guns. Belching smoke and flames they laid down a barrage which sent spray splashing over the low flying, now limping Swordfish. A shell ricocheted off the water in front of Esmonde's Swordfish, blowing off his lower port wing and causing him to steer an erratic course The gallant 'Stringbag' shuddered and dipped but somehow stayed in the air. Esmonde, now bleeding from head wounds, clung to the controls and made for the *Prinz Eugen*. Behind him lay the bodies of Clinton and Lieutenant Williams, both killed in the last attack by the Fw 190. In a final desperate attempt, Esmonde pulled up and released his torpedo just before gunfire from a FW 190 ripped off the top of the mainplane of his aircraft in a red flash and he went straight down into the sea. The bodies of his air-gunner and observer were flung clear and later were picked up by searching British craft. As the wreckage splashed into the sea, lookouts aboard the *Prinz Eugen* reported the track of the torpedo and Kapitän Brinkman ordered 'Port 15' and easily avoided it.

As the Swordfish following Esmonde's, at about 50 yards astern, piloted by Sub Lieutenant Brian Rose, lined up for the attack, Sub Lieutenant Fred Lee saw Esmonde going down. Rose followed, his Swordfish being savagely attacked by Bf 109s and FW 190s. Lee constantly told Rose exactly when to take avoiding action through the Gosport tube shouting 'Now Brian, now!' unaware that the tube had been severed by gun fire and that his instructions were not being heard. Rose, hit in the back by splinters from a cannon shell that struck the bulkhead behind his seat, almost flew into the sea but managed to hold on to the controls while Lee kept talking to him and guided him to the point of torpedo release but he was too busy shouting directions to notice when the torpedo was released. After that the fighters lost interest and Rose climbed to 1,200 ft. The main petrol tank had been holed on the final torpedo run in (which was completed on the 12-gallon emergency gravity tank which would allow them ten to 12 minutes flying time). The engine began to splutter and it was obvious that the English coast could not be reached and so they decided to head for some Motor Torpedo Boats, but the engine cut out four miles away from them. As they were losing height Rose tried to pass round the stern of the *Gneisenau*, but he flew right as they swerved away from the barrage of anti-aircraft fire and glided the aircraft down towards the sea and pancaked about half a mile from *Prinz Eugen*.

Lee released the dinghy and then tried to free 'Ginger' Johnson, who had slumped down over his gun but could not and he had to leave him. He had been mortally wounded when the cannon shell had hit them. The Swordfish sank taking the body of Leading Airman Johnson with it, as he was still attached by his 'G strap'. The dinghy automatically inflated and was washed from the aircraft. Brian Rose, despite his left arm being useless, managed to recover it and get it upright. Lee held the dinghy while Rose got into it. He then returned to try again to free the TAG but this was impossible and the wreckage sank. There was no doubt that Johnson was dead; he had been killed much earlier in the action.

The sea was choppy and the dinghy soon filled with seawater. They tried bailing it out with their flying helmets, but with little success. Then from their emergency gear they took out the marine distress signals and the aluminium dust-markers. The dust formed a silver pool around the dinghy and could be seen at a distance. But they flung the dust to windward and it blew back on them, so that they looked like a couple of shining tin soldiers. However, they could use the empty tins for baling out the dinghy, and when it was dry, they fired the distress signals. Two MTBs then closed in on the dinghy. By then they had been in the water for an hour and a half but Fred Lee never lost heart, tending and encouraging Rose, who was suffering severely from his wounds, and both he and Lee were numb with the cold. They were taken to Ramsgate where they received medical treatment and were thawed out after their harrowing experience. Brian Rose was then admitted to Chatham where he was hospitalised for treatment to the severe back injuries he had sustained during the attack.

When Sub Lieutenant 'Pat' Kingsmill in the third Swordfish had started to go into attack, fighters came screaming at him and ships threw up a barrage

UNTERNEHMEN 'DONNERKEIL-ZERBERUS'

of flak. He flew on relentlessly as 'Don' Bunce, standing up, firing his Vickers gun, continued to engage enemy fighters. Throughout the action his coolness was unshaken and he is believed to have shot down one of the attackers. After several bursts he looked down to where his seat should have been, only to see a gaping hole. Shells and bullets ripped through the wings, setting the upper wing on fire and almost three quarters of the fuselage was full of holes and tears but amazingly the Swordfish kept flying. Enemy shells sliced the top off two or three cylinders which reduced the engine power. A cannon shell hit the fuselage behind the pilot and exploded wounding Kingsmill and 'Mac' Samples. Kingsmill recalled: 'The tracers came floating gently towards us and then whizzed past. There were more and more large splotches in the sea as aircraft and ships fired at us and their shells burst into the waves. We were really in it, when suddenly I felt a sharp pain in my shoulder and my foot went squelchy. Oddly enough I didn't feel any more pain and I managed to keep control of the plane. Mac had been hit in the legs at this point but luckily Don Bunce was unhurt.' Mac Samples felt a sudden burning sensation in his leg and when he looked down at his black flying boots, he was astonished to see that in one there was a neat pattern which looked like button holes. He felt no pain but whilst gazing at his leg that had been riddled with holes, he did not notice that Kingsmill had dropped his torpedo, aimed at the *Prinz Eugen*, from about 2,000 yards. Bunce saw that the observer was covered in blood, but as he was continuing to shout orders to Kingsmill to dodge the attacking aircraft, he continued firing his Vickers gun.

Suddenly, through the mist, 'Mac' Samples caught a glimpse of the *Prinz Eugen*. The Swordfish chugged along at 50 ft above sea level, but Kingsmill could not at first get lined up properly. He then turned back to make another run in, against the intense flak sent up from the destroyer screen. As he once again flew towards *Prinz Eugen,* they continued to fire everything that they could at him. 'Mac' Samples did not notice that his pilot had dropped his torpedo aimed at *Prinz Eugen* from 2,000 yards. After releasing his torpedo Kingsmill turned the Swordfish with difficulty. With 'Mac' Samples guiding him though, he managed to keep airborne until his engine finally cut out and the Swordfish crashed on the water a few hundred yards from some British Motor Torpedo Boats. Kingsmill did a flat turn and he pulled the stick back to bring the nose up to keep flying but with the fabric of the wings tattered with holes the aircraft could not maintain height. As it was sinking towards the water the engine burst into flames and the port wing caught fire. 'Don'

THE AIR WAR AT SEA IN THE SECOND WORLD WAR

Bunce continued firing as 'Pat' Kingsmill tried to shout to 'Mac' Samples through the Gosport tube but it had been shattered. Despite his wounds Samples managed to climb towards the pilot and shout in his ear, 'We'll never make it; try to ditch near those friendly MTBs', pointing towards the craft of Lieutenant Commander Nigel Pumphrey that were still in the area. Before easing gently into the sea Kingsmill gave everyone watching a spontaneous fireworks display as the distress signal cartridge pyrotechnics detonated. The Swordfish was fired on by some E-boats before Kingsmill and 'Don' Bunce, who were badly injured and 'Mac' Samples took to the icy wintry water, their dinghy having been destroyed by fire. Samples was lucky to survive the ditching, as in his weak state he found his harness difficult to release and was almost drowned.

Kingsmill had seen the second vic of Swordfish led by Lieutenant John Chute Thompson approaching the *Prinz Eugen* at a height of about 100 ft, all the while taking violent evasive action, but proceeding steadily towards the German capital ships. Kingsmill, being unable to gain height passed underneath them never to see them again. According to German sources, almost immediately after that the Swordfish were massacred by Focke Wulf 190s of Jagdgeschwader 26. Thompson's Swordfish limped on, the fabric of the wings and fuselage now tattered and Sub Lieutenant Robert Laurens Parkinson and Leading Airman Ernest Tapping wounded and dying. They maintained a steady course and flew into the red and orange wall of exploding shells. One after another, these three young aircrew, and their fellow men in the other two Swordfish, Sub Lieutenants Cecil Ralph Wood and Eric Herbert Fuller-Wright and Leading Aircraftsman Henry Thomas Albert Wheeler and Sub Lieutenants Peter Bligh and William Beynon and Leading Airman William Grenville Smith, were all killed. Of these nine, only the body of Grenville Smith was recovered.

As he watched the 'Stringbags' torn to matchwood and strips of fluttering canvas and the smoking wrecks falling into the sea, Kapitän Kurt Hoffmann of the *Scharnhorst* exclaimed: 'Poor fellows, they are so very slow, it is nothing but suicide for them to fly against these big ships.'

The heroic incredible Swordfish attack was over. There were only five survivors out of the 18 who had flown into the hail of fire, all six Swordfish being lost.

It was now the turn of the Beauforts to attack but only three squadrons were made available by Coastal Command for the operation and they were

UNTERNEHMEN 'DONNERKEIL-ZERBERUS'

short of torpedoes.[44] At 1130 very few of the Beauforts were within range of the German ships. 86 Squadron and part of 217 Squadron were at St. Eval in Cornwall; the remainder of 217 (seven aircraft) was at Thorney Island near Portsmouth and 42 Squadron, after flying down from Leuchars was delayed by snow on airfields and was late arriving at Coltishall near Norwich.[45] At Thorney Island two of the Beauforts were armed with bombs, which had to be changed to torpedoes and a third developed a technical fault. Only four of the Beauforts thus took off at 1325 and when they did so they were 20 minutes late on planned rendezvous with their fighter cover at Manston. To make up for this delay the Beauforts were ordered to proceed independently to the targets but the message was not received and they therefore proceeded to Manston, where they circled for several minutes but were unable to make radio contact with their Spitfire escort circling the airfield because of differences in radio frequencies. Exasperated, two of the leading Beaufort crews set off for the French coast, found nothing and returned to Manston. (They set off again later, picked up the *Scharnhorst* off the Dutch coast and with the aid of their ASV radar delivered their attacks at 1710 and 1800. But these were as unsuccessful as all the rest.) Meanwhile the two other Beauforts had already landed at Manston, learned the location of their target and set off towards the Belgian coast. At 1540 at about the same time as the ineffective attack by the destroyers, the two Beauforts braved intense flak from the enemy ships and launched their torpedoes from a thousand yards' range at the *Prinz Eugen*. Both missed.[46]

After the abject failure of Operation 'Fuller', Admiral Sir Bertram Ramsay, from his Dover Castle Headquarters signalled the Admiralty: 'In my opinion the gallant sortie of these six Swordfish constitutes one of the finest

---

44. At a time when a major enemy naval operation was expected, 57 Beauforts had been diverted to other theatres and a further two squadrons had been withdrawn to convert to Hampdens while another Beaufort squadron was in the midst of a transfer to the Middle East.
45. Despite having found no sign of the escort they were expecting they at once headed for the enemy fleet but only came across four minesweepers. One pilot caught sight of what he took to be a big ship but by then his aircraft was so damaged that he was unable to release his torpedo. Two of the Beauforts, victims of flak or the dangerous flying conditions, failed to return.
46. Royal Air Force 1939-45 Vol 1. *The Fight at Odds* by Denis Richards (HMSO, 1974).

exhibitions of self-sacrifice and devotion that the war has yet witnessed.' Another member of the Admiralty said that 'Being familiar with the details of the heroic and dramatic torpedo attack of Eugene Esmonde and his men we can only make a deep bow for such gallantry.'

There was admiration too from the Germans. Wilhelm Wolf aboard the *Scharnhorst* said 'What a heroic stage for them to meet their end. Behind them their homeland, which they had just left, with their hearts steeled to their purpose, still in view.' Vice Admiral Otto Ciliax, writing in his diary next day, said: 'The attack of a handful of ancient planes, piloted by men whose bravery surpasses any other action by either side that day.' Helmuth Giessler, Navigating Officer on board *Scharnhorst*, wrote: 'Such bravery was devoted and incredible. One was privileged to witness it… They knowingly and ungrudgingly gave their all to their country and went to their doom without hesitation.'

Wing Commander Tom Gleave the Commanding Officer of RAF Manston said: 'Those Swordfish crews were courage personified…' The Victoria Cross was awarded posthumously to Lieutenant Commander Eugene Esmonde on his recommendation; probably the only time in the history of the Victoria Cross that a RAF officer has recommended a Royal Navy officer for the award. The recommendation went through the RAF High Command before being passed onto the Admiralty for their action. It would be the only Victoria Cross awarded to the Fleet Air Arm during World War II.

Esmonde's body was recovered from the River Medway at Gillingham, Kent, having drifted from near Calais and he was buried on 30 April at Woodlands Cemetery in Gillingham.[47] Of the five survivors, only Observer 'Fred' Lee was not wounded although the wound suffered by 'Don' Bunce was slight. Having made his report to the naval authorities, Lee apologised

---

47. William Henry Williams lies in a shared grave at Aylesham Cemetery in Kent with his brother Stanley who died on 29 December 1947 aged 33 as a result of war service in the RAF. The body of Pilot Officer William Johnson Clinton was returned to his home in Ruislip, Middlesex, where he was buried with full military honours in St. Martin's Church Cemetery. Grenville Smith was found on Upchurch Marshes, close to Gillingham. Naval authorities would not allow his widow to have his body for burial at his home town of Poplar, East London, and he was buried at a private ceremony in the same Woodlands Cemetery Naval Reservation, 40 yards away from his commanding officer.

UNTERNEHMEN 'DONNERKEIL-ZERBERUS'

for having to hurry away, but as he explained, he was now acting senior officer of the little squadron.

Pat Kingsmill and 'Mac' Samples had serious leg injuries. Brian Rose had back injuries but after some months was fit for duty.[48] The surviving officers were each made a Companion of the DSO and 'Don' Bunce received a CGM. The others who lost their lives were awarded a posthumous Mention in Dispatches. Sub Lieutenants 'Fred' Lee, Brian Rose, 'Pat' Kingsmill and 'Mac' Samples were decorated with the Distinguished Service Order, an unusual occurrence for such junior officers to receive this senior award. 'Don' Bunce, the sole surviving non-commissioned airman, received the Conspicuous Gallantry Medal. This again was a relatively rare award. (Seventy-two were awarded in World War II, of which only two were members of the Fleet Air Arm.)

Under contemporary rules governing awards and decorations within the British Armed Services, only two gallantry awards could be recommended and awarded posthumously - the Victoria Cross and a Mentioned in Despatches. Accordingly, in strict adherence to the book, each of the remaining 12 men who gave their lives so bravely in this action was merely listed as 'Mentioned in Despatches'.

In Britain the *Daily Mail* put a brave face on the disastrous venture, reporting that 'This is an episode of which Britons can be rightly proud. In planes which, against the German protecting aircraft, were as slow as a cart horse compared with a motorcar, 18 men of the Fleet Air Arm flew over the Channel. Crippled and ablaze before they got within range, they kept on, delivered their attacks - and died!' Others were less complimentary. 'Vice Admiral Ciliax has succeeded where the Duke of Medina Sidonia failed', said the *Times*: 'Nothing more mortifying to the pride of sea-power in Home Waters has happened since the 17th century.' On 16 February Francis McMurtrie, *Daily Telegraph* Naval Correspondent, reported that an

---

48. On 8 October 1944, while awaiting posting as a Deck Landing Control Officer or BATS to an aircraft carrier Lieutenant Rose died piloting a Barracuda III, in an accident at Macrihanish. He had volunteered to deliver the aircraft to Northern Ireland but en route he encountered undercarriage problems on approach to Abbotsinch, near Glasgow. Turning tightly at 300 ft on his 2nd circuit the aircraft spun and crashed into a stubble field and he was fatally injured. He is buried in Paisley Cemetery in Scotland.

THE AIR WAR AT SEA IN THE SECOND WORLD WAR

Official Enquiry was to be held in order to answer the important questions raised into the escape from Brest of the *Scharnhorst, Gneisenau* and *Prinz Eugen*. Suffice it to say, that despite the many reasons advanced at the time, the squadron of enemy ships was allowed to proceed up the Channel in daylight for nearly 13 hours without being reported. Fire from British coastal artillery batteries and MTB attacks and torpedoes fired from five Royal Navy destroyers and subsequent air attacks by Beauforts had no more success than the 'Stringbags' or the heavy bombers,[49] which attacked later in three waves. Earlier in the day Bomber Command had suggested that instead of wasting effort on bombing attacks that could not possibly succeed, mines should be laid ahead of the ships but the Air Ministry, after consulting with the Admiralty, had decided that the operation should be carried out as planned.[50]

At 1431 hours *Scharnhorst* did strike a mine as Bristol Beauforts from Thorney Island attacked but without success. At 1530 hours the Harwich destroyers located the enemy ships but were unable to close. Shortly afterwards high-level bombers and Beauforts at Leuchars in Scotland arrived. There was a mêlée as they attacked but the ships were not hit. Late that evening both *Scharnhorst* and *Gneisenau* were slowed down after striking mines laid by 5 Group Hampdens or Manchesters in the Frisian Islands during recent nights. *Scharnhorst*'s speed was reduced to 12 knots and was shipping a thousand tons of water but both ships safely reached home waters. *Prinz*

---

49. 92 Wellingtons, 64 Hampdens, 37 Blenheims, 15 Manchesters, 13 Halifaxes, 11 Stirlings and 10 Bostons of 2 Group. The first Bomber Command aircraft were airborne at 1330 hours and 242 sorties were flown by the squadrons before dark. It was the largest Bomber Command daylight operation of the war to date. Most of the bombers were unable to find the German ships in the poor weather conditions and, of those aircraft which did bomb, no hits were scored. Ten Hampdens, four Wellingtons and a Blenheim FTR. The RAF also lost 20 fighters, 14 pilots killed and three captured. Only eight of the RAF fighters were shot down by the Luftwaffe. A further eight were shot down by AAA fire, two collided and two were lost to unknown causes. Ten of the fighters were Spitfires, six were Hawker Hurricanes and four were Westland Whirlwinds. RAF Fighters claimed 16 Bf 109s destroyed and 13 damaged. Four FW 190s were also claimed destroyed and six damaged. Actual German losses amounted to seventeen fighters, along with five Do 217s.
50. *Operation Cerebus: The Channel Dash* by Ralph Barker (Purnell's History of the Second World War Vol.3).

UNTERNEHMEN 'DONNERKEIL-ZERBERUS'

Eugen arrived in Brünsbuttel on the morning of 13 February, completely undamaged but suffering the only casualty in all three big ships, killed by aircraft gunfire.

Ciliax sent a signal to Generaladmiral Alfred Saalwächter in Paris on 13 February, 'It is my duty to inform you that Unternehmen 'Zerberus' has been successfully completed.' Even so, some high-ranking German officers were not satisfied. Admiral Raeder, summing up the operation, said that the German navy 'in winning a tactical victory had suffered a strategic defeat'.

This was borne out shortly thereafter. On 23 February the *Prinz Eugen* was torpedoed off Norway by the British submarine *Trident* and after being repaired, spent the rest of the war in the Baltic; the *Gneisenau* went into dry dock and was bombed on the night of 26/27 February and never ventured to sea again and the *Scharnhorst*, out of action for the next eight months, was sunk during the Battle of the North Cape on 26 December 1943 by the battleship *Duke of York* and her escorts.

'The greatest flight of the old "Stringbags"', wrote Leonard Gribble 'resulted in a wordy war in the British Press, which proclaimed the aircraft obsolescent. With a top speed of only 150 mph [reduced to 107 mph when encumbered with a torpedo and long-range fuel tanks], they had been doomed to disaster, but they were a forlorn hope and the 18 young men of the Fleet Air Arm who flew in them knew they were going into the teeth of destruction.

'But three years later the old "Stringbags" were still in service and on a memorable day in January 1945 when the weather in North-West Europe was too bad for all other Allied aircraft, an official communiqué announced that one British plane took the air on a reconnaissance patrol from a base in Belgium. That plane was an open-cockpit Swordfish, flown by a Fleet Air Arm crew temporarily attached to Coastal Command.

'The Stringbags, in at the beginning of hostilities, were seeing the war through to its close.'[51]

---

51. *See* also, *The Channel Dash Heroes* by Ted Powell and J. C. Burnhams article in the *RNCC March 1991 edition of the Naval Historical Review.*

Chapter 6

Sink The *Tirpitz*!
9 March 1942 – 29 August 1944

> *The destruction or even the crippling of this ship is the greatest event at sea at the present time. No other target is comparable to it. The entire naval situation throughout the world would be altered.*
>
> **Winston Churchill,**
> **writing on 25 January 1942.**

Tirpitz was the second *Bismarck* class battleship that was built for the Kriegsmarine. Her keel was laid on 2 November 1936 at the Kriegsmarinewerft in Wilhelmshaven. The battleship was launched on 1 April 1939. With a length of 823 ft, *Tirpitz* weighed over 50,000 tons when fully loaded. The steel in the hull was 12 inches thick. *Tirpitz* had eight 15-inch guns, some of the biggest naval guns ever built. The vessel had a crew of more than 2,600, including 100 officers. With a speed of 30 knots, *Tirpitz* was twice as fast as the Hurtigruten coastal express ships, which were faster than any of the Allied warships. After the *Tirpitz* had been commissioned on 25 February 1941, a period of sea trials and training of the 2,065 crew members began in the Baltic. Adolf Hitler paid a visit to the two *Bismarck* class vessels *Bismarck* and *Tirpitz* in Gdynia. Even before the new vessel was commissioned, 15 air raids with Hampden and Wellington bombers were launched on the 'Lonely Queen of the North', as the Norwegians called her, while berthed in the final assembly dock in Wilhelmshaven. These raids caused minor damage to the battleship and final assembly of the *Tirpitz* was only slightly delayed. After commissioning her commander, Kapitän-zur-See Friedrich Karl Topp, and prior to her sea trials, the *Tirpitz* was targeted twice by British air raids which also had little effect.

In September 1941, her sea trials were temporarily suspended as *Tirpitz* joined the Baltenflotte, the German Baltic Fleet which consisted of the heavy

SINK THE *TIRPITZ*!

cruiser *Admiral Scheer*, three light cruisers, a number of destroyers and two flotillas of minesweepers as well as the *Tirpitz*. The squadron was to prevent the Soviet Baltic Fleet from breaking out of its base in Kronstadt near Leningrad. To this end, the German squadron patrolled off the Aland Islands between 23 and 26 September. After it dawned on the Germans the Soviet fleet was not going to come out, the Baltic Fleet was disbanded and *Tirpitz* resumed her trials. During this period, the primary and secondary armament of *Tirpitz* was extensively tested and target practice was conducted. For these exercises, the aged battleship *Hessen* was used as a radio-controlled target vessel.

On 13 November 1941 Grossadmiral Erich Raeder, Commander-in-Chief of the German navy suggested dispatching the *Tirpitz* to occupied Norway in order to pose as a 'Fleet in Being', a move that would also enable the battleship to attack Allied convoys sailing to and from the Soviet Union. This in turn would discourage the British Home Fleet from making a possible invasion in Norway. Hitler agreed to Raeder's proposal as he had forbidden *Tirpitz* to venture out into the open sea after the loss of the *Bismarck*. At Kiel *Tirpitz* was given more 20 mm anti-aircraft guns and her 10.5 cm guns could also be used in an anti-aircraft role with a wider field of fire. Two four-barrelled torpedo tubes were also installed. On 10 January 1942 Topp declared his ship ready for action and two days later *Tirpitz* sailed through the Nord-Ost Sea canal from Kiel to Wilhelmshaven, arriving on the 14th and with four destroyers to escort her to Norway. On 14 January at 2300 hours, the five German battleships sailed for Trondheim. British military intelligence had deciphered the German Enigma codes but the RAF could not intervene because of adverse weather conditions. On 16 January *Tirpitz* was spotted in Trondheim by RAF reconnaissance aircraft leaving for Fjaettenfjorden near Trondheim to the north. The fjord is three quarters of a mile wide with steep cliffs on three sides and *Tirpitz* was berthed on the north shore below a steep cliff. The ship was well camouflaged and was protected from attack by anti-submarine nets and protective booms in the water as well as anti-aircraft and searchlight positions on the surrounding cliffs.

Operation 'Oiled', the first aerial attack on the *Tirpitz* in Norway by RAF Bomber Command took place on the night of 30/31 January 1942 when seven Stirlings of 15 and 149 Squadrons and eight Halifax bombers – four from 10 Squadron and five from 76 Squadron – took off from RAF Lossiemouth in Scotland at 0030 hours and 0204 hours respectively but weather conditions were not good with cloud from sea level to 20,000 ft and this and the camouflage made finding the battleship difficult. One of the Stirlings reported having seen the mast tops of *Tirpitz*, but was unable to gain sufficient height in order to drop its bomb load. All four of the 10 Squadron Halifaxes had to return before reaching the target due to lack of fuel. The five 76 Squadron Halifaxes reached the target area, but weather conditions prevented them from locating the target. All aircraft returned to base with the exception of one 76 Squadron Halifax which ditched in the North Sea just off the coast from Aberdeen. The crew were all uninjured and were rescued by the Aberdeen lifeboat.

Between 5 and 9 March 1942 *Tirpitz* took part in Unternehmen 'Sportpalast' (Operation 'Sports Palace'). The intention was an attack on the Allied convoy PQ-12, on its way from Iceland to Murmansk in the Soviet Union and convoy QP-8 on the return voyage. The battleship set sail on 5 March from Fjaettenfjorden escorted by three destroyers under overall command of squadron commander Rear Admiral Ciliax. As the British were aware of the plans for the attack, they ordered the convoy to change course. *Tirpitz* and three destroyers detached themselves and searched two areas separately. On 7 March the German destroyers spotted the Russian merchantman *Izhora* of QP-8 which had fallen behind and sank her. Subsequently they retreated to base in Trondheim for lack of fuel. *Tirpitz* vainly searched for merchantmen for three days. Operation Sportpalast' was aborted and *Tirpitz* steamed towards the Lofoten, an island group west of Narvik. Just before the battleship had reached the cover of the Vestfjorden near Bogen, between the Norwegian mainland and the Lofoten, she was attacked by 12 Fairey Albacore torpedo bombers from the *Victorious* in the early morning of 9 March. *Tirpitz* had launched two of her Arado spotter-planes to search for the enemy aircraft. During a dog fight, one of the British planes was damaged. Two Albacores were shot down by anti-aircraft fire from the *Tirpitz* during the failed attempt. *Tirpitz* successfully evaded all the torpedoes fired and on 13 March she safely returned to the Fjaettenfjorden. On 30 March 33 Halifax bombers attacked the battleship. They scored no hits and five aircraft were shot down.

By the end of March 1942, the only dry dock on the Atlantic coast large enough to accommodate the *Tirpitz*, at Sainte-Nazaire, was destroyed as a precautionary during Operation 'Chariot' when the obsolescent destroyer HMS *Campbeltown* was rammed into the lock gates to explode later. The

SINK THE *TIRPITZ*!

German warships in Norway suffered from a chronic shortage of fuel and it took three months before they were ready for action against the Allied convoys.[52] Over these three months, *Tirpitz* was attacked three times by Halifax and Lancaster bombers but owing to bad weather, all three attacks failed. During the three attacks against *Tirpitz* in the spring of 1942 13 aircraft from Bomber Command were lost with the loss of 60 lives. One Coastal Command Beaufighter was lost with the loss of two men and three PRU Spitfires with the loss of two pilots. A total of 64 RAF airmen lost their lives between January and April 1942 attempting to sink *Tirpitz*,

The next target for the German was convoy PQ-17 which had been under way from Iceland to the Soviet Union since 27 June. The convoy was escorted by the British battle cruiser *Duke of York*, the new American carrier USS *Washington*, HMS *Victorious* and a number of destroyers. In Unternehmen 'Rösselsprung' (Operation 'Knight's Move'), *Tirpitz*, the heavy cruiser *Admiral Hipper*, five destroyers and two torpedo boats left Fjaettenfjorden and the heavy cruisers *Lützow* and *Admiral Scheer* left Bogenfjorden near Narvik along with six destroyers in an attempt at sinking Allied merchantmen. On 1 July *Tirpitz* and her escort left in the direction of Convoy PQ 17 which was spotted northwest of Norway after leaving Iceland on 27 June bound for the Soviet Union. Shortly after *Tirpitz* left Norway, the Soviet submarine *K-21* fired two or four torpedoes at the ship, all of which missed. (The Soviets claimed two hits on the battleship.) *Lützow* and three destroyers were damaged however by collisions with cliffs that did not show on German sea charts and they had to return to Vestfjorden. Swedish intelligence had meanwhile reported the departure of the *Tirpitz* to the Admiralty, which considered the threat so severe and ordered the convoy to scatter and proceed to Murmansk on its own. Aware that they had been detected, Unternehmen 'Rösselsprung' was aborted and the attack left to U-boats and the Luftwaffe. The Admiralty's decision to scatter ended in catastrophe. Between 2 and 5 July, 21 out of a total of 34 vessels in convoy PQ-17 were sunk by U-boats and the Luftwaffe. Only eleven made port. Prime Minister Winston Churchill called the event,

---

52. The actions of *Tirpitz* and her escorting destroyers in March 1942 used up 8,230 metric tons of fuel oil, which greatly reduced the available fuel supply. It took the Germans three months to replenish the fuel spent in the attempt to intercept two Allied convoys which left Iceland on 27 June bound for the Soviet Union.

'one of the most melancholy naval episodes in the whole of the war'. *Tirpitz* arrived in Bogenfjorden on 6 July.

On 23 October 1942 *Tirpitz* returned to the Fjaettenfjorden for maintenance. Hitler had not allowed the battleship to make the perilous passage to a port in Germany and Trondheim was the only base in Norway with enough technical personnel at its disposal. The defence of the mooring place in the fjord was expanded by a number of anti-aircraft batteries and a double steel net against torpedoes. British forces and the Norwegian resistance attempted to attack the battleship using Chariots or human torpedoes in Operation 'Title' but it failed because the fishing vessel *Arthur*, used by the Norwegian resistance to tow the Chariots, lost them because of bad weather. On 28 December maintenance work was completed and *Tirpitz* set sail for some trial runs.

On 21 February 1943 Kapitän-zur-See Hans Meyer took over command of the battleship from Friedrich Karl Topp. Five days' later the *Scharnhorst* arrived to reinforce the German battle fleet in Norway. After the heavy losses suffered by convoy PQ-17, the Allies had suspended the convoys to the Soviet Union so Grossadmiral Karl Dönitz the new *Oberbefehlshaber der Kriegsmarine* had the German warships perform exercises from Kåfjorden, a tributary of the Alta fjord in the extreme north of Norway. Between 6 and 9 September *Tirpitz* and *Scharnhorst* launched an attack on the mining communities on Svalbard (Spitsbergen), a group of Norwegian islands in the north Atlantic, in concert with Unternehmen 'Sizilien'. German troops came ashore on the main island where the British had a weather station and a refuelling facility for ships. The German troops, tasked with the destruction of the enemy installations were covered by the *Tirpitz* and *Scharnhorst*. They in turn were protected by ten destroyers. *Tirpitz* fired 52 38cm rounds and 82 15cm rounds at the British positions. Following the raid, the German vessels returned to Norwegian ports and *Tirpitz* lay camouflaged in Altenfjorden.

Winston Churchill considered the sinking of the *Tirpitz* as a major priority and attacks grew in intensity. Operation 'Source' was launched between the 20 and 22 September in an attack by ten X-craft midget submarines, each equipped with two mines of 2,200 lbs each, against the *Scharnhorst*, *Tirpitz* and *Lützow* berthed in Altenfjorden. Towed to Norway by submarines, only three of the X-craft were able to penetrate the torpedo barrier surrounding the *Tirpitz*. The other midgets were either lost or had to return empty-handed. Two X-craft succeeded in placing their charges beneath the *Tirpitz*

SINK THE *TIRPITZ*!

and two massive explosions lifted the battleship almost 3 ft out of the water. The damage caused was so severe that the Admiralty estimated that it would be at least six months before the battleship was repaired. X-6 was spotted and scuttled by her own crew. The four crewmembers were picked up by a lifeboat and taken aboard the *Tirpitz*.

On 26 December 1943 the *Scharnhorst* was lost during the battle of the North Cape. The *Lützow* and the destroyers were recalled to Germany to be deployed elsewhere. *Tirpitz*, with the maintenance vessel *Neumark* moored alongside, remained in Altenfjorden. During the night of 10/11 February 1944 she was attacked by 15 Soviet bombers which scored just one near miss that did not inflict any lasting damage. At the end of March when the departure of the *Neumark* was noticed, it was assumed correctly that *Tirpitz* was at anchor again in the Altenfjorden after repairs to the damage caused in the attack by British midget submarines in September 1943 were complete; it would only be a matter of months before the *Tirpitz* would be seaworthy again.

On 3 April Operation 'Tungsten', probably the most carefully planned, briefed and rehearsed strike operation undertaken by the Fleet Air Arm during the war was put into action. A dummy range was built on Loch Erriboll in Caithness and the Fairey Barracuda dive-bombers of No. 8 Torpedo Bomber Reconnaissance Wing and 52 TBR Wing from *Furious* and *Victorious* respectively, rehearsed the attack with their supporting fighters. The last occasion was on 28 March with less than a week to go before the strike by four squadrons (42 aircraft) of Barracudas from *Victorious* and *Furious* and three auxiliary carriers: *Emperor*, *Pursuer* and *Searcher* went ahead. *Anson*, *Sheffield*, *Jamaica* and *Royalist* made up the heavy cover; the whole screened by a dozen destroyers. Eighteen Seafires on *Furious* would carry out CAP to protect the fleet during the strike. Swordfish and Wildcat IVs on the anti-submarine warfare carrier *Fencer* would provide anti-submarine support. In order that the Wings which had rehearsed together should strike together, the Fleet carriers exchanged a Barracuda squadron apiece before the force sailed.

For the strike itself there would be a close escort of 60 aircraft from four squadrons of Wildcat Vs and two squadrons of Hellcats, some of which would also carry out flak suppression and top cover provided by 28 Corsairs, 14 each from 1834 Squadron and 1836 Squadron. The former was commanded by Lieutenant Commander Philip Noel Charlton RN (who was known as 'Fearless Freddy', likely due to a 1943 incident at Macrihanish, Scotland when he suffered burns pulling a pilot and observer from their Swordfish after it crashed and burst into flames. 1836 Squadron was commanded by Lieutenant Commander Christopher Charles Tomkinson RNVR.[53]

Anchorage at Kåfjorden was heavily defended by *Tirpitz*'s main battery of eight 15-inch guns, each capable of firing 1,750lb shells; 12 5.9-inch guns in its secondary batteries; and 16 4-inch heavy anti-aircraft guns. Additionally, nine single and nine quadruple 20mm flak guns had recently been installed on top of the existing gun turrets. Each gun was capable of about 8,500 rounds per minute. She was also very well protected with 12½-inch thick side armour plating. Also, there were several anti-aircraft warships and a system of smoke generators capable of hiding *Tirpitz* from aircraft located around the fjord.

After a full dress-rehearsal on 28 March, the Home Fleet's Second Battle Squadron sailed from Scapa Flow in the Orkneys in two formations on the 30th, under the command of Sir Henry Moore, with the C-in-C Home Fleet, Admiral Sir Bruce Fraser in *Duke Of York*. *Furious* and the escort carriers headed for the launch position direct, while the battleships and *Victorious* provided distant heavy cover for the Northern Russian convoy JW 58. The two forces joined up on the afternoon of 2 April at a point about 220 nautical miles northwest of Altenfjorden and in the early hours of 3 April they reached the flying-off position, 120 miles north-west of Kåfjorden, 80 miles from the main entrance to Altenfjorden.

The strike began at between 0415 and 0423 hours. Eleven Corsairs and 21 Barracudas of 827 and 830 Squadrons in No. 8 TBR Wing took off from the *Victorious* and were closely followed by the second wave of 21 Barracudas of 829 and 830 Squadrons in No. 52 TBR Wing on *Furious*. Twenty-three-year-old Lieutenant Philip 'Bud' Abbott, one of the Barracuda pilots in the second wave, had, in the past two years, flown many types of aircraft - mostly the Swordfish - on routine, uneventful anti-submarine patrol in the North Sea and the Atlantic. 'We called them "Stringbags" since it seemed they were tied up mostly with haywire. It was an old-school biplane, fixed undercart, no hood, no canopy, open air, no radio. Quite a neat, light little plane; it tottled along, not very fast.'

Born on 26 January 1921 in Southend-on-Sea, 'Bud's' father was a policeman and he had four siblings. In the early days of the Second World

---

53. In July 1944 *Victorious* transferred to the Far East, and the squadron attacked the Nicobar Islands and, on 24 January 1945, the important Palembang oil refineries as part of Operation 'Meridian'. Tomkinson was killed leading his squadron against airfields on Okinawa on 26 March 1945. He was 28 years old.

SINK THE *TIRPITZ*!

War, 'Bud' worked as an insurance clerk, commuting to London each day on the steam train. He joined the Royal Navy in 1941, at the age of 20. After the Swordfish he went on to a more advanced biplane, the Fairey Albacore. 'It had a sliding canopy, so we were inside - out of the weather! Our planes were called TBR: Torpedo-Bomber-Reconnaissance. But reconnaissance was our principal duty. Later on, we developed sonar to locate enemy submarines, but to begin with, we just kept our eyes open.

'We would not fly Stringbags this time - for this mission we were to fly Fairey Barracudas. The Barracuda was a dive bomber, as well as a torpedo bomber and a reconnaissance plane. It was an interesting, but a frustrating plane. It was okay, but it was only okay. Nothing you would brag about in the officers' canteen. It was a flying three-seater abortion really. Way underpowered, with that Merlin 32 engine. On paper, the damned thing was supposed to make 240 mph, but in practice you could only cruise at 160-170 knots (184-195 mph) ...maybe 200 mph - downhill, with a following wind, yes?'

This poem describes the pilots' sentiments on the Barracuda:

> *My skipper done tol' me*
> *When I was in Stringbags*
> *My skipper done tol' me*
> *Son, that Barra's a bastard*
> *She looks like a sleek job*
> *But when the mods are done,*
> *That Barra's a bastard*
> *She's a dirty old bitch*
> *She'll give you the twitch*
> *And the blues in the night.*
> *Hear that Merlin moaning,*
> *Hear that airframe groaning,*
> *See the struts abending*
> *See the tail plane rending*
> *Whoo-ee Whoo-ee*
> *A dirty old bitch*
> *She'll give you the twitch -*
> *And the blues in the night.*
>
> The Barracuda Blues Song
> (*sung to* The Blues in the Night)

THE AIR WAR AT SEA IN THE SECOND WORLD WAR

'I'd been stationed on the *Victorious* but Petty Officer Gallimore and Sub-Lieutenant Peck and I were temporarily switched to the *Furious*. The squadrons were split between the two ships so we could all take off simultaneously. I went over with the rest of my squadron to the *Furious*. The *Furious* was a weird ship, the oldest aircraft carrier afloat at that time. She was laid out in 1915, but she wasn't originally designed as an aircraft carrier - she was refit in the 1920s! And her deck always rolled to and fro, like a bloody logging truck!

'And I understand that the officers and crew of the *Tirpitz* were all just moping there in this idiot fjord, doing nothing, and thoroughly bored. They would be anxious to get some action.'

In an account to the BBC after the raid, 42-year-old Commander Anthony Martin Kimmins, who had served during the First World War as a midshipman and in the newly created aviation branch before a skiing accident, which damaged his spine, put an end to his career in operational flying,[54] said: 'There was little sleep in those carriers the night before the attack, for we were now in the danger period as we steamed close into enemy waters. Look-outs and guns' crews, only their eyes visible through their scarves and balaclava helmets, were constantly on the job. Supply and Damage Control parties never left their posts. Down in the huge hangars there was feverish activity. On one side were the long lines of Merlin-engine Fairey Barracudas - the new Fleet Air Arm torpedo-bombers which were being tried out in action for the first time. With their wings folded back over their bodies they looked rather like enormous beetles. And on the other side were the American Corsairs with their wings folded vertically and almost touching overhead at the tips. While mechanics swarmed over their aircraft making final adjustments, great yellow bombs were being wheeled down the narrow gangways, loaded up and fused.

'At first light, at exactly the prearranged minute, Commander Flying shouted the welcome order "Start up!" The words were hardly out of his mouth before there was a roar of engines. By now the carriers and the escorting ships were all heeling over and swinging into wind. A final nod from the captain, a signal from Commander Flying, the Flight Deck officer raised his green flag, the engines started to rev up, the flag dropped and the

---

54. On the outbreak of the Second World War he had re-joined the Navy, serving in the Fleet Air Arm in Intelligence and the Admiralty and as Chief of Naval Information to the Pacific Fleet. He retired as a captain in 1945.

SINK THE *TIRPITZ*!

first aircraft was roaring away over the bow. One after the other they followed in rapid succession and nearby you could see the same thing going on. More Barracudas, Seafires, Corsairs, Wildcats and Hellcats. In a few minutes the sky was full of them and as the sun started to rise and the clouds turned pink at the edges, they formed up in their squadrons.'

'Some of those fighters, especially those beautiful gull-winged Corsairs, flew off the carriers like a damned rocket', Abbott said. 'Quite impressive. While us, the underpowered heavily-laden bombers, were crowded to the far aft of the flight deck.

'The first wave flew off at the break of dawn and got through to the target without any problems. They weren't expected. They dropped their bombs and flew back to the carriers. Got through unscathed, with no casualties. But there was an hour's lapse between waves. It took time to raise the next round of Barracudas up to the deck, fuelled and armed. We hoped to hell we could gun the engine hard enough to make enough speed to actually catch the air and take flight when we roared off the edge of the ship's bow!'

'It wasn't long before the mountains in the coastline showed up ahead', continues Commander Kimmins. 'As they gained height and crossed the coast the sun was rising to their left, shining across the snow-covered mountains, throwing shadows in the gorges and against the snow-covered trees in the Valleys and lighting up the deep blue of the calm fjord. Down to the left were two or three enemy ships, but these took no visible interest in the proceedings. Everything seemed calm and peaceful, but I'll bet that down below the wires were humming and that up at the far end of the fjord alarm bells were ringing, fat-headed Huns were falling out of bed, rubbing their eyes and cursing the British as they threw on some clothes and stumbled out to their cold action stations.'

Though visibility was 'excellent' 9/10ths snow cover on the ground made it difficult to see the aircraft below. After 65 minutes flying, the Corsairs' long-range tanks were jettisoned between Altafjorden and Langfjorden (literally 'The Long Fjord'). As the target came into view a German smoke-screen was beginning to form and as the bombers began their dives from 8,000 ft, the Corsairs ranged over Langfjorden and Kåfjorden while the close-escort Martlets and Hellcats attacked the flak guns. The *Tirpitz* seemed to be caught unawares and the Barracudas scored several hits on the battleship. At 0600, about half an hour after the first wave attack, the Corsairs set course for *Victorious*. All the strike aircraft, except for one Barracuda, which was shot down, were safely recovered aboard the carriers. The longest of the Corsair sorties lasted two hours 30 minutes.

'By now the strike was passing its next landmark, a huge glacier on the top of a mountain', recalled Kimmins. 'Soon they were crossing the final ridge and sighted a flak ship on the far side of the fjord. She immediately opened up, but raggedly and without great effect. And then, as they crossed over the final ridge, they had a thrill which none of those aircrews will ever forget. There, nestling under the sheer mountains in a fjord not much wider than the Thames at London lays one of the largest battleships in the world - the *Tirpitz*. A motor-boat alongside raced off at full speed and I don't blame him. Up till then the strike had kept dead radio silence, but now as they arrived in position everyone gave an instinctive start as a sudden rasping noise hit them in the ears. The leader had switched on. And then a shout - "All fighters anti-flak - leader over.' And with that shout things really happened. Hellcats and Wildcats literally fell out of the sky. As the Barracudas hurtled down, they could see the fighters strafing the surrounding gun positions and whistling across the *Tirpitz*, with the tracers from their bullets bouncing off her deck. Green and red tracer came shooting up, but the fighters had entirely disorganized her AA fire and the Barracudas were able to take perfect aim. Down they went with their eyes glued to her funnel - 6,000 - 5,000 - 4,000 ft. They went down so fast that anything loose shot up to the roof of the cockpits.

'Now the leader was at the right height and he let go. The first three bombs went whistling down, exploding bang on the bridge; the nerve-centre of the ship. The other pilots - diving from either side - were close on his tail. One extra-large bomb, bursting through the armour-plate amidships, went off with a terrific explosion between decks. The huge ship shuddered, her stern whipping up and down and sending waves across the fjord. It was only 60 seconds - one minute - from the first bomb to the last. There was no sign of life from the hutments close to her berth. No doubt these housed many of the repair workers. Six months' work was going west in 60 seconds.'

Despite the difference in speed, the escort of 80 plus Corsairs from *Victorious*, Hellcats from *Emperor* and Wildcat IVs and Vs from *Pursuer*, *Searcher* and *Fencer* formed up with the 40 plus Barracudas without difficulty. The formation headed for the target, climbing to 15,000 ft. Hellcats and Wildcats meanwhile, made their attacks on the battleship's gun crews and flak defences ashore. Though visibility was 'excellent' 9/10ths snow cover

SINK THE *TIRPITZ*!

on the ground made it difficult to see the aircraft below. After 65 minutes flying, the Corsairs' long-range tanks were jettisoned between Kåfjorden and Langfjorden.

The *Tirpitz* seemed to be caught unawares and the Barracudas of No.8 TBR Wing scored several hits on the battleship. Meanwhile, the Corsairs ranged over the two fjords while the close-escort Wildcats and Hellcats attacked the flak guns. At 0600, about half an hour after the first wave attack, the Corsairs set course for *Victorious*. Thirty minutes' later the Barracudas of No. 52 TBR Wing attacked.

'So, there we were', recalled 'Bud' Abbott, 'Petty Officer Gallimore and Sub-Lieutenant Peck and me, crammed into our Barracuda. We flew in for the coast, barely 50 ft above the waters to avoid German radar. The *Tirpitz* was 120 miles from our fleet and when we reached the Norwegian coastline, we all climbed steeply to about 9,000 ft altitude and flew inland between the mountains. It was a bright, clear day at the end of winter. The mountains were gleaming white with snow and the delightful scenery was very impressive.'

The breath-taking beauty of the Norwegian wilderness was forgotten, though, as the Barracuda crews neared their target. As the strike force reached the *Tirpitz* the mighty ship was getting underway and a smoke-screen was beginning to form.

'And now', continues Commander Tony Kimmins, 'as the first strike weaved away and made off down the valleys with fires raging in the *Tirpitz* and the artificial smoke cover belching out from all around her, they saw above them the second strike - which had been ranged in the carriers the moment the first had taken off - now coming in from the sea.

'This second strike had, if anything, a more difficult task than the first. Admittedly the artificial smoke and the smoke from the first strike's explosions helped to guide them to the target, but by the time they got over the whole fjord was almost completely obscured with a strong box barrage above the smoke. But luckily - at the critical moment - the smoke cleared over the *Tirpitz* and with a shout of joy they roared down, carrying out similar tactics.'

'During our run on the *Tirpitz*', recalled Abbott, 'we fortunately didn't have to dive bomb. We came in at a reasonable angle - not like a bloody Stuka!'

The Barracudas gradually reduced height to 10,000 ft and began their final dives from 7,500 to 8,000 ft.

'Again, there were many hits', recalled Commander Kimmins. 'One heavy bomb in particular was seen to crash from the upper deck and explode with a sheet of flame that reached above the topmast. By the time the last pilot dived the AA fire had ceased. And so a few hectic minutes over the target and the brilliant dash of those Fleet Air Arm crews had been the highlight in a naval operation which had left the *Tirpitz* crippled.'

'Bud' Abbott concurs: 'The first wave had inflicted significant damage on the *Tirpitz*. They landed several bombs on the ship's main deck, and caused all sorts of ruckus – but none of the big 1,600 lb armour-piercing bombs managed to pierce the lower armour in the hull! The first bomber pilots had dropped their ordnance at too low an altitude for the penetration to be effective. And the Germans were spitting mad and had had a good hour to prepare themselves for any follow-up attacks. So, we finally rounded the last turn at the far end of Kåfjorden and actually saw the *Tirpitz* anchored in harbour. There she was!

'We were immediately met with a heavy barrage of anti-aircraft fire, and dozens of Luftwaffe interceptors raced at us out of the sun! Our particular squadron, I think there were nine of us, peeled off from the main flight and began our attack run. We could see the ship, but much of it was clouded in by an artificial fog, created by the shore-mounted German smokescreen generators. Down in this fjord, this deep hole, if you will, and difficult to see! But each Barracuda had three 500 lb bombs, and we had to deliver them. So down we dived, our Barracuda shuddering through the explosions of the incoming anti-aircraft shells. Difficult to keep aiming straight. Our escort fighters were dog-fighting like mad with the Messerschmitts in the skies above us, and other fighters were below us, strafing the *Tirpitz*'s deck and attacking the anti-aircraft batteries on shore. We dropped our bombs, made our strike, and then banked off hard. We flew away as fast and low as we could get, racing back to the carriers. It all happened so very fast. Our squadrons got out of the skirmish quite lucky, actually. We only lost nine airmen and four aircraft, all told. It could have been a heck of a lot worse, but the *Tirpitz*'s smokescreen actually worked double-duty in our favour. The German anti-aircraft gunners couldn't see us and were all firing blind into the sky.'

Altogether, the Barracudas were believed to have hit the *Tirpitz* with three 1,600 lb armour-piercing, eight 500 lb semi-armour piercing, five 500 lb MC (Medium Capacity) and one 600 lb anti-submarine bomb and a near miss with bombs of 1,600 and 500 lbs. In addition to the extensive damage to the superstructure and fire-control systems, the two wave attacks killed 122 sailors and wounded 316 more. A supply ship, *C. A. Larsen*, was severely damaged by bombs and two other German ships damaged to a lesser extent.

'After the attack', wrote 'Bud' Abbott, 'the weather suddenly became quite cloudy. It was now difficult to find our ship and we were still over enemy territory. No one knew if the Luftwaffe would chase us down. And we were flying under complete radio silence. Radio communication was absolutely forbidden on this operation. We're up there in the clouds and the carrier was somewhere down underneath the clouds. Some of the pilots couldn't find our ships and had to ditch in the North Sea and make their way back to the Norwegian shore, where they had to surrender to the rather unsympathetic German troops. But we managed to locate the *Furious*. Our approach to landing back on the carrier deck was to come in high, just above the stall, as opposed to the American method where they bore in just above the waves. The stern of the carrier would be heaving up and down in the choppy seas, as much as 30 ft of movement high and low. You ran the risk of simply crashing hard and flat into the ass-end of the carrier if you didn't have your wits about you. We came in high at full throttle, just above the stall, and came down almost in the centre of the deck, where there was a minimum of movement, and you hope to hell your braking hooks would catch the deck cables. You were a nervous wreck!

'We killed 123 crew and wounded another 329 of them, including her commander, Hans Meyer. But that was part of it. It was war. It was a shame, really, to have such a magnificent ship destroyed. It was the idiocy of war. It would be wonderful to see such a fine piece of naval history sitting pretty in some maritime museum.'[55]

Ten direct hits on the *Tirpitz* were from height insufficient to penetrate the decks but the *Tirpitz* was put out of action for three months, during which the weather and enemy interception prevented any more attacks on the battleship. Two 15cm turrets were destroyed and the two remaining spotter planes burned to ashes in their storage spaces. Two thousand tons of water leaked through buckled frame beams but her decks had not been penetrated

---

55. The foregoing is based on an interview with 'Bud' Abbott in 2016 by Cranbrook, Canada career journalist Elinor Florence plus a newspaper article written for *The Cranbrook Townsman* by freelance writer Ferdy Belland of Cranbrook, B.C. You may read more about Elinor on her website at www.elinorflorence.com. Bud Abbott passed away in Cranbrook, British Columbia on 30 January 2019, just four days after his 98th birthday

THE AIR WAR AT SEA IN THE SECOND WORLD WAR

and the vessel was still operational. Karl Dönitz ordered the *Tirpitz* to be repaired again as he needed the vessel as a threat to the Arctic convoys which had been resumed by the Allies.

All the strike aircraft, except for two Barracudas that were shot down by flak – one crashing into a hillside after releasing its bomb load and the other shot down in flames as it pulled out of its dive – and one that was lost on take-off, and a Hellcat that was forced to ditch alongside a destroyer, were safely recovered aboard the carriers. One of the returning Corsairs missed the arrestor wire on *Victorious* and crashed on its nose about 25-30 ft beyond the second barrier. Incredibly, no one was hurt.

The slight losses were undoubtedly due to the efficient support given by the strafing Hellcats and Wildcats, which put the target's flak directors out of action and shot up the flak positions ashore immediately before the dive bombers entered their dives. In the absence of strong enemy fighter opposition, the flak suppression role increasingly became the prime employment of the carrier fighters in all future operations against the *Tirpitz* off the Norwegian coast.

After the attack, additional radar stations and observation posts were established and the number of smoke generators was increased. *Tirpitz*'s air defences were strengthened by fitting her with additional 20 mm cannons, modifying the 5.9 inch guns so they could be used to attack aircraft, and supplying anti-aircraft shells for her 380 mm (15 inch) main guns. The Luftwaffe had few fighters stationed at airfields near Kåfjorden and their operations were restricted by a lack of fuel.

Over the following three months the weather and enemy interception prevented any more attacks on the *Tirpitz*. In April Operation 'Planet' was to be launched with 40 Fairey Barracudas and 40 escorting fighters and the Home Fleet sailed from its base at Scapa Flow in the Orkney Islands on the 21st. This operation involved the same aircraft carriers as had taken part in 'Tungsten' apart from the substitution of the escort carrier HMS *Fencer* with her sister ship *Striker*. The fleet reached the position where its aircraft were to be flown off three days later, but the raid was cancelled when Allied agents near Kåfjorden reported bad weather over the target area. The fleet then sailed south, and attacked a German convoy near Bodø, sinking three merchant ships for the loss of six aircraft. The same situation occurred in Operation 'Brawn' on 15 May, when 27 Barracudas escorted by 28 Corsairs with four Seafires and four Martlets were flown from *Victorious* and *Furious*

SINK THE *TIRPITZ*!

but 10/10ths cloud at 1,000 ft in the target area forced a recall while the aircraft were en route. And on 28 May weather conditions were so bad that the aircraft could not even take off from the carriers and Operation 'Tiger Claw' was aborted. Instead, the carriers sailed south in search of German convoys. In a raid conducted on 1 June, the carriers' aircraft sank four merchant vessels near Ålesund. No further attacks were attempted during June as the ships of the Home Fleet were needed to support the Normandy landings that month.

Despite the lack of success, the Admiralty and Admiral Sir Henry Moore, who had assumed command of the Home Fleet on 14 June, remained committed to attempting further carrier raids against *Tirpitz*. During June the Admiralty received a series of intelligence reports indicating that repairs to *Tirpitz* were generally progressing well and the battleship would soon be ready to put to sea. In late June, after Allied spies spotted *Tirpitz* conducting steaming trials in Kåfjorden and reported that she was capable of sailing at up to 20 knots and could rotate her main gun turrets, the Admiralty directed that another carrier raid be conducted against Kåfjorden during mid-July before the resumption of the Arctic convoys, which had been suspended since April 1944 to free up ships for the invasion of France. As *Victorious* had been redeployed to the Indian Ocean in June, Operation 'Mascot' was duly mounted on 17 July using the recently commissioned *Indefatigable* and *Formidable* and *Furious*. *Formidable* embarked No. 8 Torpedo Bomber Reconnaissance Wing, whose 827 and 830 Naval Air Squadrons each operated a dozen Barracudas, as well as 1841 NAS, which was equipped with 18 Corsairs. *Indefatigable* carried No. 9 TBR Wing, which was also equipped with 24 Barracudas split between 820 and 826 Naval Air Squadrons, as well as the Seafire-equipped 894 NAS and 1770 NAS with 12 Fairey Firefly fighters. *Furious* did not embark any Barracudas and instead operated 20 Grumman F6F Hellcat fighters of 1840 NAS, three Seafires assigned to 880 NAS and three Fairey Swordfish anti-submarine aircraft on 842 NAS. The carriers were escorted by the battleship HMS *Duke of York*, four cruisers and 12 destroyers. Admiral Moore commanded the force from *Duke of York* and the carrier group was led by Rear Admiral Rhoderick McGrigor on *Indefatigable*.

The carriers began launching their aircraft shortly after midnight on 17 July. Forty-eight fighters, including 18 Corsairs of 1841 Squadron, escorted 44 Barracudas of No. 8 Torpedo Bomber Reconnaissance Wing's aircraft which would attack before those of No. 9 TBRW. All but two of the dive bombers carried 1,600 lb armour-piercing bombs; the other aircraft

THE AIR WAR AT SEA IN THE SECOND WORLD WAR

each carried three 500 lb bombs. Twelve of the Corsairs carried cameras to photograph the bombing attacks and the other six were to be used in flak suppression duties, providing no enemy fighters were encountered. Twenty Hellcats and 12 Fireflies operated by 1840 and 1770 Naval Air Squadrons respectively were also given the task of suppressing anti-aircraft guns.

After forming up, the bombers and fighters began their flight to Kåfjorden at 0135, flying at 50 ft above the sea to evade German radar until they reached a point ten minutes flying time from the Norwegian coast, at which time the Barracudas climbed to 9,000 ft and the fighters to higher altitudes. The weather was fine throughout the flight, but clouds were sighted as the aircraft neared the target area. The strike force was detected by the German radar stations when it reached a point 43 miles from Kåfjorden at 0200 and German forces began jamming the radios as the aircraft came within ten miles of the Norwegian coastline.

After the last attack, additional radar stations and observation posts were established and the number of smoke generators located around the *Tirpitz* was increased. The improved defences in place by the time of 'Mascot' included a cliff-top observation post near Kåfjorden, which was capable of directing the battleship's anti-aircraft guns if necessary. *Tirpitz*'s air defences were also strengthened during the period she was under repair by fitting additional 20 mm cannons, modifying the 150 mm guns so they could be used to attack aircraft and supplying anti-aircraft shells for her 15-inch main guns.

After the attack was detected on the enhanced Funkmess Ortung (FuMO) 26 radar equipment, it had taken four minutes to pass a warning to *Tirpitz* and by 0213 the defenders were able to fill Kåfjorden with smoke, obscuring the *Tirpitz*. The battleship and anti-aircraft batteries located on the shore began firing a barrage towards the attackers at 0219. The smokescreen frustrated the British attack, as the crews of only two of the Barracudas and a pair of fighters managed to spot *Tirpitz* during the raid. The Hellcats and Fireflies were first to attack and strafed anti-aircraft positions as well as a destroyer and a small patrol craft, which was forced aground and later declared a total loss. Due to the thick smoke, the fighter pilots were only able to locate targets by aiming at the sources of tracer gunfire. As they arrived over Kåfjorden the 37 Barracudas were targeted by heavy, but inaccurate, anti-aircraft gunfire and those attempting to attack the battleship were forced to aim at her gun flashes. These bombing attacks took 25 minutes to complete; seven near misses were achieved but no damage was inflicted on *Tirpitz*. One Barracuda

SINK THE *TIRPITZ*!

attacked an anti-aircraft battery, another attempted to bomb a destroyer and a third scored a near miss on the tanker *Nordmark*. Three of the remaining four Barracudas did not find any targets and jettisoned their bombs into the sea; the fourth was unable to drop its bombs due to a faulty release mechanism.

A Corsair in 1841 Squadron flown by the senior pilot, Sub Lieutenant H. S. Mattholie RN was escorting the Barracuda flown by the No. 8 TBR Wing leader, Lieutenant Commander Roy Sydney Baker-Falkner RN when the weather worsened and they became separated. Baker-Falkner, his observer, Lieutenant G. N. Micklem and his air gunner, Pilot Officer A. H. Kimberley, were lost at sea. Mattholie crash-landed in Norway and was subsequently taken prisoner. (His successor as senior pilot was Lieutenant Robert Hampton Gray RCNVR, who was later to posthumously earn the Victoria Cross in the Pacific.) A damaged Barracuda was also forced to ditch near *Indefatigable* and its crew were rescued by the destroyer HMS *Verulam*. Several other Barracudas and five Hellcats were damaged during the raid and returned to their carriers. One of the damaged Hellcats was later written off after being judged beyond repair.

The second strike, which had been scheduled to take-off from 0800, was cancelled two minutes before the aircraft were to begin launching when fog threatened and the British fleet turned south to return to Scapa Flow. As well as the German forces located near Kåfjorden, a patrol line of 12 submarines designated Wolfpack or Group 'Trutz' ('Defiance') was also assigned the task of intercepting any carrier forces that ventured into the Norwegian Sea. Swordfish and Seafire aircraft flew anti-submarine patrols over the Home Fleet throughout the morning's operations. While Kåfjorden was under attack, the commander of the German submarines ordered the Wolfpack to take up new positions to the south-east of Jan Mayen and intercept the warships as they returned to Scapa Flow. The Admiralty had anticipated this redeployment, and maritime patrol aircraft from 18 Group RAF were directed to sweep the Home Fleet's route back to its base.

At 2148, a Consolidated B-24 Liberator on 86 Squadron from Tain in Ross-shire detected and sank *U-347* with all 49 hands. Eight minutes' later a 210 Squadron PBY Catalina piloted by 24-year-old Flying Officer John Alexander Cruickshank spotted *U-361* on the surface. Cruickshank attacked the U-boat, flying his Catalina through a hail of flak. His first pass was unsuccessful, as his depth charges did not release. He brought the aircraft around for a second pass, this time straddling the U-boat and sinking it. All

52-crew perished. The submarine's anti-aircraft guns damaged the Catalina, killing the navigator and seriously wounding Cruickshank and less seriously wounding second pilot Flight Sergeant Jack Garnett as well as injuring the two other crewmen. Cruickshank was hit in 72 places, with two serious wounds to his lungs and ten penetrating wounds to his lower limbs. Despite this, he refused medical attention until he was sure that the appropriate radio signals had been sent and the aircraft was on course for its home base. Even then, he refused morphine, aware that it would cloud his judgement. Flying through the night, it took the damaged Catalina five and a half hours to return to Sullom Voe, with Garnett at the controls and Cruickshank lapsing in and out of consciousness in the back. Cruickshank then returned to the cockpit and took command of the aircraft again. Deciding that the light and the sea conditions for a water landing were too risky for the inexperienced Garnett to put the aircraft down safely, he kept the flying boat in the air circling for an extra hour until he considered it safer, when they landed the Catalina on the water and taxied to an area where it could be safely beached.

When the RAF medical officer boarded the aircraft, he discovered Cruickshank had lost a great deal of blood, and had to give him a transfusion before he was stable enough to be transferred to hospital. John Cruickshank's injuries were such that he never flew in command of an aircraft again. For his actions in sinking the U-boat and saving his crew he received the Victoria Cross while Jack Garnett received the DFM. That night the Home Fleet sailed through the gap in the German patrol line that had been opened by the sinking of the two U-boats.[56]

---

56. Attacks on the Wolfpack continued for the next six days. On the evening of 18 July *U-968*, one of four boats that had sailed from Narvik, was attacked twice by Liberators; she shot down the first attacker but was damaged by the second and had to return to port. U-716 also suffered severe damage from a Liberator attack at 1915 and at about 2300 the U-boat was seriously damaged by a Short Sunderland but also survived. Three other U-boats were attacked on 20 July but only one suffered any damage. The commander of U-boats in the Norway area now decided to dissolve Group 'Trutz' as it was too vulnerable to air attack; all but four of the surviving submarines returned to port and the remaining boats were ordered to sail north so that they were out of range of the British aircraft. The final attack on the U-boats was made on 23 July when a Sunderland on 330 Squadron damaged *U-992* near Vestfjord.

SINK THE *TIRPITZ*!

The failure of Operation 'Mascot' convinced the commander of the Home Fleet, Admiral Sir Henry Moore, that the Fleet Air Arm's main strike aircraft, the Fairey Barracuda dive bomber, was not suited to operations against Kåfjorden. The dive bombers' slow speed gave the defenders of Kåfjorden enough time to cover *Tirpitz* in a smoke screen between the time incoming raids were detected and their arrival over the target area. Moore concluded therefore that further attacks using these aircraft would be futile. However, First Sea Lord Andrew Cunningham judged that repeatedly striking Kåfjorden with Barracudas over a 48-hour period might increase the period the battleship was out of service and harm her crew's morale, wear down the German defences and exhaust the supply of fuel for *Tirpitz*'s protective smoke generators. The commander of the Home Fleet, Vice Admiral Bruce Fraser, initially resisted Cunningham's order on the grounds that further carrier raids on Kåfjorden were unlikely to be successful as *Tirpitz*'s defences would have been reinforced and weather conditions were likely to be worse than those encountered during 'Tungsten'. Following an argument with Cunningham, Fraser eventually agreed to attack Kåfjorden again. Consideration was also given to flying fast and long-ranged de Havilland Mosquito bombers off the carriers in an attempt to achieve surprise, but none of these land-based aircraft could be spared from supporting the Allied bombing of Germany.

Despite his misgivings, Moore agreed to make another attempt to strike *Tirpitz*, which on 31 July and 1 August went through exercises on the northern Arctic Sea with five destroyers on what was to be her last exercise. As proposed by the Admiralty, Moore's plans for Operation 'Goodwood I, II, III and IV', the new attack on Kåfjorden, involved the Home Fleet's aircraft attacking the region on four separate days: 22nd, 23rd, 24th and 29th August using the largest group of Fleet Air Arm aircraft assembled up to that point in the war. Their main striking element was the 35 Barracudas assigned to 820, 826, 827, and 828 Naval Air Squadrons which operated from the three fleet carriers. *Indefatigable* carried 12 Barracudas and *Formidable*, 24 Barracudas. A total of 48 Seafires were assigned to 801, 880, 887 and 894 Squadrons on board *Indefatigable* (16 Seafires) and *Furious* (24 Seafires). In addition, *Indefatigable* carried 12 Fairey Firefly and a dozen Hellcat fighters of 1770 and 1840 Squadrons respectively. Concerned by the possibility of heavy fighter opposition, a second force comprised the auxiliary carriers HMS *Nabob* and *Trumpeter*, cruiser HMS *Kent* and a group of frigates. The two escort carriers embarked a total of 20 Grumman TBF Avengers (which had responsibility for the mine-dropping element of 'Goodwood') and eight Grumman F4F Wildcat fighters; these aircraft were split between 846 Squadron on board *Trumpeter* (eight Avengers and six Martlets) and 852 Squadron on *Nabob* (12 Avengers and four Martlets).

In the run up to 'Goodwood' the Home Fleet's aviation squadrons carried out training exercises using a target range at Loch Eriboll in northern Scotland. The terrain in this area is comparable to that around Kåfjorden and the loch had also been used for this purpose as part of the preparations for 'Tungsten'. A new element of the plans for 'Goodwood' was a decision to use Fleet Air Arm aircraft to drop mines near *Tirpitz* and the entrance to Kåfjorden. The mines dropped near the battleship were to be fitted with time-delay fuses and it was hoped that the explosions of these devices would cause *Tirpitz*'s captain to try to move the warship into safer waters and pass through the minefield at the fjord's entrance.

While the fighter aircraft involved in the previous raids had used only their machine guns to strafe German defences in order to reduce the threat they posed to the Barracudas, it was decided to use some of these aircraft as dive bombers on the operation. Though expected to fly mainly top-cover escort duty, the two units of 6 Naval Fighter Wing which contributed 30 Corsairs on *Indefatigable* (18 Corsairs of 1841 Squadron) and *Formidable* (12 Corsairs of 1842 Squadron) and a single squadron of Grumman F6F Hellcats received training in dive-bombing tactics during the period between 'Mascot' and 'Goodwood' in case dive-bombing should be needed.

This news had earlier alarmed pilots like 21-year-old Christopher Cartledge on 1842 Squadron, commanded by Lieutenant Commander Tony McDonald Garland RNVR and which had officially formed at Brunswick in April with 18 Corsair IIIs. 'We spent two months working up the squadron', he recalled, 'and by June we were ready to complete our preparations by a trip down to Norfolk, Virginia where we achieved the standard three successful landings on a US carrier. This new and powerful fighter aircraft was immediately distinguishable by its cranked "gull" wings. From head on, with its radial engine, it had an aggressive appearance, but was fast and nimble, its long and horizontal nose giving it an unmistakable profile. It was faster than the Hurricane on which I had trained and was very responsive and manoeuvrable, with formidable fire power. For a crisis it could go into water injection mode for those extra knots, the water tank giving ten minutes of boost. It was particularly tricky to deck-land due to its long, straight nose, which blotted out the pilot's vision ahead when the aircraft was adopting the landing position with flaps down. The final approach had to be made while still turning in order to keep the deck and batsman in sight, straightening out at the last moment before touchdown. Of the 18 pilots in the squadron photo at Brunswick only nine would survive the war. Total squadron losses were 14. Tragically, half these losses were non-operational and could, to some extent, have been caused by the Corsair's long, level nose, which restricted the pilot's view ahead.

'In June coming back to the UK on HMS *Rajah* we were based briefly at RNAS Eglinton (where we lost Sub Lieutenant William Derek Wheway who dived out of cloud vertically into the ground at Doungbrewer Farm, a mile west of the airfield, before being embarked from Stretton on to HMS *Formidable* in the Irish Sea in August. We were on our way to the Arctic to attack the *Tirpitz*, which was sheltering in the Altenfjorden. Little did we know that some of us were to be used as dive-bombers. Corsair Squadrons 1841 and 1842 were on board, plus 848 Avenger Squadron. Stopping briefly at Scapa Flow, we sailed northwards carrying out flying exercises whenever weather permitted. Those who had volunteered for dive-bombing, of which I was one, were given practice on towed targets. We lost another pilot in an air collision, the younger brother of our own ship's surgeon. As we neared the Arctic, we ran into the roughest seas I had so far experienced. There was no possibility of flying. The huge seas were throwing the ship in all directions and breaking over the flight deck, drenching the lashed down aircraft with salty water.'[57]

On 18 August the battleship HMS *Duke of York* with the fleet aircraft carriers, *Furious*, *Formidable* and *Indefatigable* as well as two cruisers and 14 destroyers sailed for Norway. A pair of fleet oilers escorted by four corvettes sailed separately to support the two attack groups. The timing of the operation was set to allow the Home Fleet to also protect Convoy JW 59, which had departed from Scotland on 15 August bound for the Soviet Union. After an uneventful journey north, the attack forces arrived off Norway on 20 August. The first attack against Kåfjorden had been planned to take place on 21 August, but as the fleet drew nearer the target the weather conditions were considered unsuitable for flying operations and Moore decided upon a 24-hour postponement. While flying conditions were poor due to low cloud, Moore's decision to attack was arrived at because some of his ships were starting to run low on fuel and would soon need to move away from

---

57. *My War*, an unpublished memoir by Chris Cartledge.

THE AIR WAR AT SEA IN THE SECOND WORLD WAR

Norway to refuel. At 1100 a force comprising 32 Barracudas, 24 Corsairs, eleven Fireflies, nine Hellcats and eight Seafires was launched from the three fleet carriers. No Avengers were dispatched as the cloudy conditions were unsuitable for their task. Because few mines were available and the Avengers could not safely land while still carrying these weapons, the mine-dropping element of the plan would fail if the aircraft were unable to locate *Tirpitz* and had to dump their loads into the sea.

As the strike force neared the coast, heavy cloud was sighted covering the hills near Kåfjorden. Because the clouds prevented accurate bombing, the 31 Barracudas and Corsairs in *Formidable* were forced to turn back 15 miles short of the Norwegian coast without attacking and leaving just eight Fireflies and nine bomb-armed Hellcats from *Indefatigable*, approaching the fjord below the cloud base to make a surprise attack at 1249. *Tirpitz* was not obscured by smoke and the Fireflies began the attack by strafing anti-aircraft guns on and around the battleship. Two minutes later the Hellcats attacked with 500 lb bombs but did not achieve any hits. As the strike force returned to the carriers it destroyed two of *Tirpitz*'s seaplanes in Bukta harbour and badly damaged the submarine *U-965* at Hammerfest. At Ingøy, north of Hammerfest, three Hellcats strafed a German radar station. The attack set the station's buildings ablaze and damaged the aerials. The eight Seafires made diversionary attacks on the Banak area and a nearby seaplane base, destroying five German seaplanes. Three British aircraft were lost on 22 August; one Hellcat and a Seafire were shot down and one of the Barracudas was forced to ditch into the sea during its return flight.

After the strike force was recovered, much of the Home Fleet sailed away from the Norwegian coast to refuel. A group comprising *Formidable*, *Furious*, two cruisers and several destroyers set a course for the two fleet oilers and the escort carrier group withdrew so that the carriers could refuel their escorts. At 1725 *Nabob* was struck by a torpedo fired from *U-354*. The carrier suffered serious damage and 21 fatalities but was able to continue limited flight operations. Despite a hole eleven yards square below the waterline aft *Nabob* managed to reach Scapa Flow under her own steam that evening, escorted by *Trumpeter*, a cruiser and several destroyers.[58] Shortly afterwards *U-354* torpedoed the frigate HMS *Bickerton* as she searched for *Nabob*'s

---

58. *Nabob* was assessed as being beyond economical repair and was scrapped at the end of the war.

attacker, wrecking her stern and the frigate was scuttled at around 2030.[59] (Shortly after the attacks on *Nabob* and *Bickerton*, Seafires from 894 Naval Air Squadron shot down two German Blohm & Voss BV 138 reconnaissance aircraft.) *Formidable* and *Furious* covered their withdrawal; during this period *Furious* also refuelled from the Home Fleet's tankers. The departure of both escort carriers meant that the mine-dropping component of Operation 'Goodwood' had to be cancelled.

During the evening of 22 August, eight Fireflies and six bomb-armed Hellcats from *Indefatigable* arrived over Kåfjorden at 1910 hours undetected and the Fireflies' strafing attacks on German gun positions killed one member of *Tirpitz*'s crew and wounded ten. However, the Hellcats' bombs failed to inflict any damage on the battleship. The British fighters also attacked German ships and radar stations on their return flight, damaging two tankers, a supply ship and a patrol boat. No British aircraft were lost during this raid.

Fog caused the cancellation of the *Indefatigable*'s flying operations on 23 August, including a planned diversionary attack against German shipping in Langfjorden. The other two carriers and their escorts re-joined Moore and *Indefatigable* off Norway during the morning of 24 August. While conditions that day were initially foggy, the weather cleared enough in the afternoon to permit a strike against Kåfjorden. The attacking force comprised 33 Barracudas carrying 1,600 lb armour-piercing bombs, 24 Corsairs (including five armed with a 1,000 lb bomb), ten Hellcats, ten Fireflies and eight Seafires. In an attempt to achieve surprise, the aircraft flew off from the carriers from a point further to the south of those used in previous raids. The strike aircraft then flew parallel to the coast, before making landfall and approaching Kåfjorden from the south. A German radar station detected the force at 1541 and immediately alerted *Tirpitz*.

At 1600 the British attack began with strikes on German gun positions by the Hellcats and Fireflies, flying five minutes ahead of the Barracudas and 24 Corsairs of 1841 and 1842 Squadrons in *Formidable*. *Tirpitz*'s protective smokescreen was not fully in place at the start of the raid, but by the time the Barracudas and their escort arrived she was completely covered by smoke. As a result, the bombers had to blind bomb the ship, releasing their weapons from altitudes between 5,000 and 4,000 ft. Chris Cartledge wrote: 'These included

---

59. Only three days later *U-354* was sunk off Bear Island by Swordfish operating from the escort carrier *Vindex* which was escorting Convoy JW 59.

THE AIR WAR AT SEA IN THE SECOND WORLD WAR

some dare-devil attacks led by a New Zealander, Lieutenant Commander Archibald 'Arch' Richardson RNZVR [a 27-year-old Hellcat pilot on 1840 Squadron in *Indefatigable*][60] and Major Vernon Beauclerk George Cheesman (known throughout the Navy as 'Cheese') [a Royal Marines Firefly pilot], who screamed low over the *Tirpitz* attempting to lob their bombs down the funnels.'

A hail of flak and shell hit Richardson's Hellcat and it is thought that he climbed steeply to escape but clipped the top of a hill on Sakkobadne Mountain above the fjord and crashed. It was his third mission of the war. 'Arch' was considered for the posthumous award of the Victoria Cross for his part in the attack; but eventually received a Mention in Despatches. Two bombs hit *Tirpitz*. The first was a 500 lb bomb dropped by a Hellcat that exploded on the roof of her 'Bruno' main gun turret. The explosion destroyed the quadruple 20 mm anti-aircraft gun mount located on top of the turret, but did not cause any significant damage to the turret itself. The second bomb to strike the ship was a 1,600 lb armour-piercing weapon which hit just forward of the bridge and penetrated two decks, killing a sailor in a radio room and lodging near an electrical switch room. This bomb failed to explode and German bomb disposal experts later determined that it had been only partially filled with explosives. Had it exploded it would have caused 'immeasurable' damage.

British fighters also attacked other German ships and facilities in the Kåfjorden area, damaging two patrol boats, a minesweeper and a radar station, as well as destroying an ammunition dump and three guns of an anti-aircraft battery. *Tirpitz*'s last remaining Arado Ar 196 seaplane was attacked in Bukta harbour and damaged beyond repair. Two Hellcats and three Corsairs were shot down by anti-aircraft fire as the Corsairs traversed Kåfjorden to strafe the 88mm flak gun positions and a fourth Corsair ditched close to *Formidable* on the return flight. Later, a Barracuda pilot Sub Lieutenant R. Fulton praised the Corsair pilots for their 'sheer cold-blooded gallantry'.

---

60. Born in Gisborne, Archibald Ronald Richardson, like other New Zealanders opted for service with the Fleet Air Arm. Within the strongly escorted carrier attack force, there were about 60 Kiwis, including Barracuda aircrew of Nos. 827 and 830 Squadrons as well as the Hellcat pilots on 1840 Squadron. The crew of HMS *Indefatigable* never forgot Acting Lieutenant Commander Richardson. After the war, the fleet carrier visited New Zealand and made a special visit to Gisborne, where crew flew a large formation of Seafires, Fireflies and Avengers over the town in remembrance of their lost pilot.

SINK THE *TIRPITZ*!

Eight men on *Tirpitz* were killed and 18 men wounded. Casualties among the anti-aircraft units stationed around Kåfjorden were heavy.

At 1930 hours on 24 August, a pair of Fireflies conducted a photo-reconnaissance sortie over Kåfjorden to gather intelligence on the results of the attack; their presence caused the Germans to generate a smoke screen over the fjord and fire an intensive anti-aircraft barrage. The German command at Kåfjorden judged that the attacks on 24 August had been 'undoubtedly the heaviest and most determined so far' and requested that fighter units be transferred from northern Finland to bolster the area's defences. Due to the other demands on Germany's fighter force at this time, the request was turned down on 26 August by the Luftwaffe's headquarters.

On 25 August *Indefatigable* and *Formidable* and two cruisers and seven destroyers refuelled from their oilers. Both of the cruisers later detached from the force and returned to Scapa Flow. *Duke of York*, *Furious*, a cruiser and five destroyers also sailed to the Faroe Islands to load supplies. As the *Furious* was judged to be no longer capable of combat operations, she proceeded from the Faroe Islands to Scapa Flow with the cruiser and several destroyers. Before leaving the fleet, she transferred two Barracudas and two Hellcats to *Indefatigable*. On 29 August *Duke of York* and the remaining destroyers re-joined the main body of the Home Fleet off north Norway. During this period maintenance personnel worked to repair aircraft which had been damaged during the 24 August attacks. Convoy JW 59 completed its journey on 25 August with most of its ships docking at Kola in northern Russia. The convoy had been repeatedly attacked by U-boats from 20 to 24 August and its escorts and aircraft claimed two U-boats. All of the merchant vessels arrived safely, with the only Allied loss being the sloop HMS *Kite* which was torpedoed and sunk by *U-344* on 21 August.

Gales and fog prevented more British attacks between 25 and 28 August. Then, at 1530 hours on 29 August 'Goodwood IV' began when two Corsairs from *Formidable*, each carrying a 1,000 lb bomb apiece and three Hellcat fighter-bombers joined 26 Barracudas in attacks on *Tirpitz*. Fifteen more Corsairs and ten Fireflies flying as close escort were used on flak suppression. Seven Seafires also conducted a diversionary raid on Hammerfest. In an attempt to give the bombers accurate aiming points once the artificial smokescreen was generated around *Tirpitz*, four of the Hellcats were armed with target indicator bombs.

The strike failed to achieve surprise. Enemy radar stations had been tracking the Home Fleet's routine anti-submarine and fighter patrols and the Seafires were detected at 1640 when they were 54 miles from Kåfjorden and the smoke generators around the fjord were activated and the defenders went to their battle positions. The arrival of the main body of aircraft was delayed by stronger than expected winds and a navigational error and they did not reach the target area until 1725. By this time *Tirpitz* was covered in a very thick smokescreen and none of the British airmen sighted the ship. The Barracudas and Corsairs were forced to blind-bomb Kåfjorden. While no hits were achieved, six members of the battleship's crew were wounded by bomb fragments from near misses. Ships and gun positions were once again strafed by the fighters, but no significant damage was inflicted. Heavy anti-aircraft gunfire from *Tirpitz*, which was directed by a party of observers stationed on a mountain near Kåfjorden, shot down a Firefly and one of the Corsair dive-bombers.

Christopher Cartledge, the other Corsair dive bomber pilot, recalled: 'We were told that a 1,000lb bomb would be fastened under the port wing, the central fuselage position being taken up by the extra fuel tank. We were advised to trim the aircraft to give maximum lift to the port wing in the hope that this would compensate for the bomb. We would only find out when the aircraft left the flight deck on take-off! It was a fine and beautiful morning and we approached the islands and main coast line as low as possible to avoid radar detection knowing the Germans would operate a smoke screen as soon as they received warning. We climbed as we hit the coast and gained height for the dive-bombing.

'The view over the mountains and fjords on this brilliant morning was breath-taking and I could see the whole party of Avengers and the escorting Corsairs of 1841 and 1842 Squadrons. As we approached the *Tirpitz*, the white puffs of AA shells started to burst around us and I lost my No.2, Sub Lieutenant [John Howard] French RNVR. The smoke screen was already across the fjord, but leaving the huge outline of the *Tirpitz* just visible through it. I turned and as I dived, saw one bomb explode close to the outline of the battleship. I released my bomb and pulled away hard, partially blacking out. There was a lot of flak blazing away in all directions. I turned and fired into one of the gunnery positions and then broke away at low level along the fjord. Cruising along just above the water I was admiring the scenery when bullets kicked up the water just in front of me. My Corsair responded well to some violent turns and twists and I escaped. Several pilots did not return however, two of whom were from 1842 Squadron. Whilst waiting his turn to land, one pilot ran out of fuel and ditched alongside the fleet. He was quickly picked up from the icy water. Very few of our aircraft returned unscathed, causing the maintenance crews a busy time patching up the bullet holes. Although immediate observation was made impossible by the smoke, we learned as we withdrew southwards that the *Tirpitz*, such a menace to Atlantic shipping, was disabled but not sunk. At least it was put out of action until it could be finished off by RAF Lancasters operating from Russia.

'It had been a gallant operation and had served its purpose of preventing the German battleship from sailing out of the fjord on further deadly missions. Major Cheesman was awarded a DSO and later, Sub Lieutenant French and Lieutenant Commander Richardson a posthumous MiD, for their exceptional bravery and determination in the attacks. There were also 12 DSCS and a DSM awarded to other squadron commanders and flight leaders of which I was privileged to be one, which I took as recognition of the gallantry of all the aircrew involved.'

Of the 52 tons of bombs dropped, several near misses and just two hits were claimed. Apart from the single Corsair lost, a Firefly was shot down over Kåfjord and later two Barracudas had to pushed over the side of their carrier after crash landings. The losses took the total Fleet Air Arm casualties to 40 airmen killed and seventeen aircraft destroyed.

Following the raid, the Home Fleet sailed west to cover Convoy RA 59A which had sailed from northern Russia on 28 August bound for Britain. Due to fuel shortages, *Indefatigable* and three destroyers detached later that day to return to Scapa Flow and *Formidable* with two destroyers followed 24 hours later. *Duke of York* and six destroyers remained on station in the Arctic Sea until 1100 on 1 September when the convoy was judged to be safe from attack.

In the wake of 'Goodwood' the results were analysed. They made for pretty grim reading. The degree of surprise achieved by the April strike was never repeated. It had been the most costly Fleet Air Arm operation of the war. During four separate attacks the aircraft of the Royal Navy scored only two hits and a small number of near misses. One of the 1,000 AP bombs that had 'possibly' hit the *Tirpitz* had been dropped by one of the Corsair fighter-bombers. It was learned from decoded 'Ultra' signals that *Tirpitz* had not sustained any significant damage but publicly the Royal Navy claimed to have damaged or sunk 19 German warships during the attacks on Kåfjorden, but did not report damage to *Tirpitz*. Royal Navy planners were now of the opinion that further Fleet Air Arm operations against Kåfjorden would be futile. They accepted that the enemy was now able to cover *Tirpitz* in smoke before Barracudas could reach the battleship. They were too slow and could not carry bombs large enough to inflict heavy damage. Moreover, there was a growing urgency to transfer carriers to the Pacific to strengthen Britain's contribution to the war against Japan and it was suggested that future carrier attacks on *Tirpitz* should be carried out either by 'Mosquitoes, or as many Hellcats and Corsair fighter-bombers as possible with suitable anti-flak support provided these can be adapted to carry 1,600lb bombs.'

In fact, *Tirpitz* was later moved south to Tromsø for repairs and the RAF now assumed all the attacks on the *Tirpitz* as the British carriers were badly needed elsewhere to protect troop transports in particular. *Victorious* and *Formidable* headed for Scapa Flow and later they both left home waters to join the British Eastern Fleet.

In October 1944 when the German occupying forces were in the process of retreating from Finnmark, *Tirpitz* was moved south to Håkøybotn near Tromsø to function as a floating fortress at the new front line. It was there that the battleship, on 12 November 1944, was finally capsized by 12,000 lb 'Tallboy' bombs dropped by Lancasters of Nos. 9 and 617 Squadrons and sank in only 11 minutes. Between 950 and 1,200 men died. Two hundred men were saved from the ship.[61]

---

61. On 28 January 1945 Swordfish of 813 Squadron in *Campania* carried out a night shipping strike on Vågsö. The only shipping there was trawlers and three of these were sunk in the moonlight augmented by flares, with anti-submarine rockets. This was the only night strike by an escort carrier group, *Premier* and *Nairana* flying covering sorties and the lack of success was typical of the difficulties encountered in finding suitable targets in these waters. The final Fleet Air Arm strike of the European War was a brilliantly executed attack on a U-boat depot ship at Kilbotn, near Harstad on 4 May. In a carefully planned and co-ordinated strike, 44 Avengers and Wildcats from *Queen*, *Trumpeter* and *Searcher* sank the 5,000-ton depot ship *Black Watch*, *U-711* alongside and an 860-ton merchant ship. *Trumpeter*'s experienced 846 Squadron was responsible for the sinking of the depot ship and U-boat, while *Queen*'s 853 sank the motor vessel. Flak suppression by the Wildcats of all three escort carriers was so effective that only one aircraft of each type was lost, in spite of intense ground-fire. After this operation, on 4 May, the force moved south to cover the Allied occupation of Denmark, where fighter and anti-submarine patrols were provided until 8 May 1954. *Carrier Operations in World War II: Vol 1. The Royal Navy* by J. D. Brown (Ian Allan 1968).

Chapter 7

Hunting the Hunters

Catapult Armed Merchantmen or CAMs for short were merchant navy ships fitted with catapults from which fighters, often Hawker Hurricanes ('Hurricats'), could be launched in an effort to combat German aircraft intent on sinking the merchantmen or other ships. The CAMs were equipped with a single fighter aircraft and had no flight deck, instead being fitted with a catapult consisting of a girder framework and a trolley, connected by wire ropes and pulleys to the ram of a cylinder. The cylinder was connected by a pipe to the chamber in which the charge was exploded, causing the ram to push the aircraft forward with sufficient velocity to make it airborne at the end of its run. Pilots had to ditch their aircraft in the sea after each sortie and await rescue. The merchantmen CAMs, as opposed to the Fighter Catapult Ships (FCS), were allocated 50 Hurricanes with specially trained RAF crews. In spite of heavy losses and wastage of aircraft, the catapult ships remained in service until 1943 when large numbers of decked escort carriers became available.

When Flying Officer Alastair James Hay, who was born in Johannesburg on 13 September 1921, volunteered to fly with convoys as a catafighter on a Cam-ship - that is, a catapult-armed merchantman - he knew he was not inviting himself to join a picnic. But when he discovered that he had been selected to join a Russia-bound convoy he was certain of one thing - he would see action. Actually, he saw more than a single man's share, even on a Russian convoy.

The convoy left Britain in the spring of 1942 with supplies vitally needed by the hard-pressed Soviet armies and when German reconnaissance aircraft spotted it the order was given to the Luftwaffe: 'Stop the convoy getting through. Sink it.' For the Luftwaffe it must be said they did their best to carry out the command. Heinkel torpedo-carrying aircraft and Ju 88 dive-bombers again and again swept in over the columns of ships and did their low-level best to break up the formations.

It was on the evening of 25 May that the first desperate attack was made by the Luftwaffe, in the steely glow of a sub-Arctic twilight. That attack was merely an overture to a great onslaught that was kept up for five nerve-racking and soul-searing days.

Only the brilliant defence put up by the airmen and seamen - Merchant Navy and Royal Navy alike - of the convoy prevented the Luftwaffe from obeying its instructions. The German pilots and air-crews had to fly through an exploding screen of steel if they wished to lay their torpedoes or aim their bombs with any accuracy and beyond the flak flew the lone catafighters, grim challengers whose purpose it was to break up enemy formations before they could strike in effective force.

Barely a year before joining the convoy Flying Officer Hay had received his commission in the Royal Air Force Voluntary Reserve, in which he had enlisted in 1940. He had trained specially for catafighter work and knew that he travelled with the convoy for only one really desperate battle with the Luftwaffe, for once he was launched over the icy Arctic seas his Hurricane could be written off as lost. It would go down under the waves. With luck he himself might be able to bail out into his dinghy and with very much more luck he would be picked up by an escort vessel. But for him there would only be that one desperate fight and it would be made at a moment when the convoy was in supreme danger and when the odds against the South African fighter were considerable.

The moment of supreme danger arrived at the height of the pitched convoy battle. A close formation of six Heinkel 111s and 115s appeared in the grey sky, making straight for the port bow of the convoy, while a similar formation appeared on the starboard bow. The German tactics were clear. The bombers were to lay a broad lethal arrow of torpedoes. Once it was put down nothing could save the convoy. It could turn neither to starboard nor port and there would be no time to perform a complicated manoeuvre, for the torpedoes would be travelling too fast. The only way to save the convoy was to prevent the arrow from being laid.

An order was flashed to the ship [the British steamship SS *Empire Lawrence*] in which Hay sailed [on 27 May 1942 when the CAM ship formed

HUNTING THE HUNTERS

part of the PQ16 convoy to Murmansk and was east of Bear Island - the southernmost island of the Norwegian Svalbard Archipelago]. He climbed into the cockpit of his Hurricane, there was a loud explosion behind him and he was catapulted along his ramp and flung into the cold, thin air. His objective was the six Heinkel [He.111s and He.115 seaplanes] coming in on the port bow. He climbed steeply, swung about and dived straight at the bomber formation. As he came among them his guns were blazing. The Heinkels broke under the fury of his attack and the one chance the Germans had of synchronizing their arrow attack was lost.

But having broken up the formation, Hay next turned to fight. Alone he had to run into a powerful cross-fire from the German air-gunners, but he was there because he was prepared to take on dangerous odds. He went straight for one Heinkel, swept through its fire and punched lead into its tanks until it went toppling down in flames. Bullets came at him from other directions and his Hurricane was badly holed, but he turned on another bomber and his fire-power was too much for it. The German pilot turned tail and took his aircraft limping away.

From the decks of the ships maintaining station in the convoy a rousing cheer rose from the witnesses of Hay's clever counter-attack. The seamen, forgetting the danger that still menaced them, stared at the tiny Hurricane, weaving and twisting like a gull in the sky and making rings round the cumbersome Heinkels. They saw the other Heinkels turn and retreat and they saw Hay's Hurricane, with petrol-tank dry, turn over on its back and plummet towards the waves. For a moment they held their breath and then another cheer rang out as a parachute was seen to open. The man who had saved the convoy from certain destruction was drifting down to the water, far from the ships he had fought to protect.

An escort ship swung round and raced towards the spot where Hay would come down. It reached him fortunately before the bitter chill of the Arctic waters could freeze the blood in his veins. He was picked up and smothered in warm blankets.

The Germans claimed to have sunk 18 ships of that convoy, besides damaging many others. But when the ships arrived at their destination in North Russia the Admiralty were able to state officially that the enemy's claims represented an exaggeration of 175 per cent.

When Flying Officer Hay got back to England it was to learn that his gallantry had earned him the Distinguished Flying Cross.

THE AIR WAR AT SEA IN THE SECOND WORLD WAR

An Arctic Catafighter by Leonard Gribble. (Hay was picked up by HMS *Volunteer* after having been in the icy water, thankfully, for only ten minutes and a message was sent to *Empire Lawrence*, stating that 'Your pilot is safe. He is having a bullet removed from his thigh.')

Hay attended the SATS *General Botha* from 1937-38. After leaving the SATS, he had joined the Union Castle Company, in which he remained until 1940, when he enlisted in the RAF. The captain of HMS *Volunteer*, who came to Hay's rescue was not only a fellow South African but also himself an ex-SATS *General Botha* cadet, namely Lieutenant-Commander Arthur Shubrook Pomeroy, Royal Navy (who had attended the *"General Botha"* from 1927-1929). Pomeroy was to write of this episode in the 'Old Boy Association' newsletter, May 2005, Part Two:

'On the Roll of Honour Board in the General Botha is the name of A.J. Hay DFC. Let me tell you how I met him in the Arctic. Our station was on the port bow of the leading ship of the port column, the *Lawrence*, which was fully loaded with explosives and ammunition. Mounted on her forecastle was a catapult with a Hurricane fighter aircraft piloted by Alastair Hay. On the first day of intense bombing, he was shot off into the air to engage single-handed the squadrons of Heinkel 111 and Junkers 88s. Eventually, wounded, he had to bail out, as there was no carrier to land on. I lowered a boat to pick him up, and just as the boat's falls were hooked on again for hoisting, two torpedo-bombers came at us low down from the North. With the boat still only a few inches out of the water and my hair standing on end, I ordered 'Full Ahead' and 'Hard-a-Starboard' to steady course to comb the tracks of the torpedoes, which we could see, one on each quarter. This took us on an exact collision course with the *Empire Lawrence*. There was just time to alter to port ahead of the port torpedo, and then both of them struck her and she disintegrated in an immense explosion, just a grating and a few bits of wood left floating. The gallant Alastair was killed later, but I had him safe on board this time.'

On 18 August 1944 Hay was serving on 182 Squadron in North West Europe flying a Typhoon 1b (JP427) when he was shot down and killed by flak near Orbec in the Falaise area. He lies buried in Ste-Desir War Cemetery in France. On a voyage from Reykjavik to Murmansk on 27 May 1942 the *Empire Lawrence* was bombed by He 111 and Ju 88 aircraft and sank off the North Cape.

'Before Brest fell and Brittany was liberated there was a stretch of the French Biscayan coast known to Coastal Command sub-hunting pilots

HUNTING THE HUNTERS

as 'Pockley's Corner'. It was that part of the coast where U-boat pack commanders from bases such as Brest and Lorient made rendezvous before proceeding into the Atlantic sea-lanes to attack Allied shipping. There, over the wild waves of Biscay, Flight Lieutenant Harold Graham Pockley of Randwick, New South Wales won fame, made Coastal Command history and earned a bar to his DFC. Pockley, the skipper of a Sunderland flying-boat of 10 Squadron RAAF, flew a thousand hours on operational flights in 'R for Robert'. Half that time was spent in active opposition to the enemy, who came to dread the persistent attentions of the man known among his fellows as 'the U-boat magnet.' The name was not bestowed lightly. Pockley's luck on patrol was phenomenal. Where other men spent months on dreary, un-enlivened patrols he encountered a continuous series of spirited actions against Coastal Commands' chief enemy before 'D-Day'. He seemed to find the elusive undersea enemy by some uncanny instinct. Over a long period he sighted more U-boats than any other Coastal Command captain engaged in the Battle of the Bay. Within the space of a few months his log-book recorded two U-boats destroyed and three others damaged, an R-boat sunk and two German merchantmen of 6,000 tons each severely damaged.

'Once he caught an Italian submarine on the surface and characteristically dived at it. The four-engined Sunderland, controlled by his skill, hurtled seaward at an angle more suitable to a Stuka dive-bomber than a giant flying-boat. But Pockley knew exactly what he was doing and it was no part of his intention to have the U-boat commander give the order to crash-dive while the Sunderland planed down gracefully in a series of wide circles. Pockley believed that, in the air just as much as on the ground, the shortest distance between two points is a straight line. He flew whenever he could in a straight line. On this occasion his steep dive over the Italian submarine caught the crew unawares. Before the U-boat could be steered clear of Pockley's line of flight his bombs were crashing down and they straddled the steel hull of the undersea pirate in a long line of detonations. The submarine's engines must have been damaged, for even after this successful attack the Australian airmen observed no attempt on the part of the Italians to submerge. Back flew Pockley, giving his air-gunners a chance to spray the U-boat's deck and conning-tower. But the underwater ship was well armed and this time Pockley, in pressing home his attack, had to fly through a curtain of flak. The Sunderland was hit repeatedly as Pockley skimmed his wing-floats low over the conning-tower, but fortunately the flying-boat sustained no structural damage. Their task completed, the U-boat left wallowing on the surface, Pockley and his crew made off, handing over the attack to another Sunderland which had been radioed to continue where Pockley left off. The attack was continued not only by another Sunderland, but also by a Polish Wellington, which gave the steel pirate its coup de grace.

'On my first operational flight I sank an R-boat' [recalled Pockley]. 'They are small motor launches used for various jobs - escort duty and mine-laying. This one was about 78 ft long. We were right down in the corner of the Bay of Biscay, patrolling not far from the French coast. We were nearing the end of our patrol. There were some Spanish trawlers about which we inspected very carefully. We saw this boat about five to eight miles away. He looked innocent enough until he started turning and twisting so we dived past him at a respectable distance to inspect him and through the glasses we identified him as a German naval craft. He clapped on all speed and so did we. He didn't get much of a chance to fire at us. We climbed up to attack.

'It was my first action. My hair was standing on end, but it's always like that. Every time I sight the enemy, I have a feeling that I've nearly trodden on a snake. You're going to get him and kill him, but meanwhile you've got to step back from the danger. We climbed up ready to attack and positioned ourselves. I took over the controls then and he was so agile that the only way to attack him was to dive-bomb him. We did this. We dived twice and machine-gunned him heavily. They seemed to be too disorganized to return the fire effectively. Then we did two dive-bombing attacks and released a stick of bombs, pulling out fairly low and going at a terrific speed and we could see him lifted clean out of the water by the explosions and he fell back into the water pretty badly battered. The tail gunner called out, 'Tell the captain we've blown hell out of him.' We attacked again. When the spray cleared away from the second attack - almost a direct hit - we saw them throwing lifeboats and dinghies overboard and abandoning ship. We ceased fire then and watched the boat listing heavily to port and sinking by the stern, while about half a dozen survivors were swimming away as rapidly as possible.

'I had it in mind to go down and rescue the survivors, but at this stage enemy fighters appeared on the scene and I had to take avoiding action. By the time I got clear our petrol supply was so low that all we could do was to set course for home. We were all very excited about our first action, but by

HUNTING THE HUNTERS

the time the day was over we were so tired that all we could do was to turn in and go to bed. It's always like that when you have an action.

'As a matter of fact, between the middle of March and the end of October we've had a rather lively time – much more so than most of the crews. Besides our first R-boat, we managed to sink two submarines and damage three others and damage two merchant ships; we've also been involved in a number of air actions. I have known of crews that have gone out for a year and not even seen a U-boat, so we've been rather lucky. Our first U-boat we didn't even see. We were patrolling in the Bay of Biscay when I saw a trail of oil bubbles two or three miles away. It was about 100 yards long, so he hadn't very long submerged. We weren't sure at first if it was a U-boat, but we examined it very closely and found it was moving at a U-boat's usual speed under water.

'We didn't know how far down the U-boat was. We attacked with depth charges. Now there was no doubt at all in our minds about its being a U-boat, because a great flood of oil came up and spread in a widening pool and later fairly big air bubbles came up in the middle of the oil.

'We were wildly excited now, because we had apparently damaged him to some degree and although the trail of oil moved on and changed direction sharply, we were sure the damage was real. We followed him for some time, making careful measurements as to speed so that we could make our next attack as accurate as possible. We followed him for six miles before we attacked again. Again, he altered course and a huge quantity of oil came up, spreading in a widening patch and some minutes later still more air bubbles, quite large ones, rose to the surface. We were out of bombs by this time, but another aircraft was sent out to relieve us and we signalled to them giving them every possible detail to help with their attack. We just had time to see them attack before we had to turn for home as our petrol was getting low. We couldn't stay long enough to see the results of their attack, but we know that, between us, we maintained contact until after dark and he must have been rather crippled by then because my relief aircraft reported that his speed was reduced and his course was very erratic. On the way back I couldn't help feeling sorry for the crew of the U-boat, being hammered again and again and not knowing when or where the assault was coming from.

'The first U-boat that we knew for certain that we had sunk was in the Mediterranean when I was operating from Gibraltar [on 28 May 1942], shortly after the other action. We were out on patrol to cover an area where a U-boat had been attacked the previous day. There was a dead flat calm.

THE AIR WAR AT SEA IN THE SECOND WORLD WAR

We sighted a big [600-850 ton] Italian U-boat dead ahead cruising fast on the surface. I immediately dived at maximum speed. There was the mad moment of feverish activity that always follows my sounding the submarine attack alarm, which blares throughout the aircraft and startles everybody into action. Everyone jumps to their routine job at action stations. An extraordinary number of things get done in a surprisingly few seconds. We dived at maximum speed to get him before he crash-dived. When we were about half a mile away, he showed no signs of crash-diving, so we thought we'd taken him by surprise, coming dead astern. But suddenly there was a bright flash and a loud explosion as a big shell burst dead ahead of us. We got a terrific surprise and pulled away into a steep climbing turn which shot us up about 2,000 ft, with flak and machine-gun bullets bursting all round us and sometimes hitting us. My tail gunner was so furious that, unconsciously taking up his microphone, he reeled off a string of good Australian abuse in such a loud voice that I had to stop him because he was monopolizing the wire without realizing it. We circled the submarine and studied every detail of its construction, especially the placing of the guns, so as to plan an attack which would be as safe as possible.

'We attacked him with bombs and machine-gunned him heavily, but he turned sharply to port and we missed him. We were under machine-gun fire throughout the attack. Our port bomb racks were not working, but during the action and while we were under fire, my armourer, LAC 'Bob' Scott, with the help of some of the crew, carried the bombs from the port racks to those on the starboard side, which were now empty, so that we could make another attack.'

Scott said later: 'After we broke off the first attack, it was discovered that only four depth charges had dropped from the starboard bomb racks, the port rack still having its full load because of a faulty circuit. Another attack run was executed with all air gunners concentrating on 'knocking out' the U-boat gun crews. During this second bombing run, again the depth charges failed to drop from the port bomb racks. After a conference, it was decided to attempt a bomb change over from the unserviceable racks to the good racks. With the help of another crew member and while the skipper kept the U-boat under close observation, we succeeded in about an hour. A final attack was set up and through very heavy and accurate hostile gunfire the skipper pressed home the attack, dropping our aircraft to a height of about 50 ft over the top of the boat before releasing the four remaining depth charges which resulted in maiming the boat.

HUNTING THE HUNTERS

'The final attack was so low we could see the upturned faces of the boat crew. As this particular action had lasted five hours, our aircraft was very low on fuel and we had to break off the engagement. A coded radio message was sent to Gibraltar and three Hudsons were dispatched to finish the job.'

'We made a second attack', continues Pockley, 'but the U-boat's fire forced us to turn aside before we could drop any bombs: however, my gunners poured a hail of accurate fire at point-blank range into the U-boat's conning tower, which was very crowded. Finally, we attacked him with our remaining bombs, diving very low over him, in spite of his accurate fire. A stick of bombs fell diagonally across him and plumb centre. That stopped him all right and he lay with no movement for some minutes while we machine-gunned him heavily. We had to return to base, but we know that the U-boat never got home. Our Sunderland was fairly badly shot up, but none of us had a scratch. Scott well deserved the DFM that he got for this action. In fact, the whole crew were simply marvellous.

'I said that we've been lucky in our boat because we've seen a lot of action. As a matter of fact, I think that about 35 per cent of our patrols have involved us in some action or other. We're rather disappointed if we have an uneventful patrol. We feel reluctant to leave the patrol area unless we've seen something of the enemy. I was trying to think what the feeling was like when it suddenly occurred to me that it's like going fishing. If the fish aren't biting you want to stop on and on until you get some sort of a catch and that's just how all of us feel. All my crew are as keen as mustard and they really are disappointed when we have a quiet patrol.

'The way I look at it is this. The U-boats are certain to be there somewhere and it's a battle of wits between them and us. If we are more cunning and keen-eyed than the U-boat crew, we will see them first and be able to attack. If they see us, they can get away, so if we let the boredom of uneventful patrols make us relax and spoil our enthusiasm, we simply won't get the results so we've given a lot of thought to working out a technique by which we keep an efficient look-out and use the sun and cloud cover to our own advantage. But the technique is no good unless the crew are keen and my crew are. You can't stop studying antisubmarine warfare. The whole of my crew eat, drink, sleep and dream U-boats and I believe that's been the chief thing in getting our bag.

'Now with surface ships it's different. They can't crash-dive, but their fire is more deadly than that of a U-boat, so we have to use different methods.

THE AIR WAR AT SEA IN THE SECOND WORLD WAR

The two ships we damaged were a naval supply vessel of 6,000 tons and a merchant vessel converted into a flak ship. We attacked these, making our dive from a height of several thousand feet and we managed to score hits and near misses on each before leaving them. When we attacked the naval supply-vessel we saw his bows lift clean out of the water. We couldn't stop to see the final result as our engines were damaged by his fire, but his speed was considerably reduced and it was obvious that he had fairly severe damage below the water-line. By the way, before we attacked him, he tried to trick us. When we had sighted him first about 12 miles away there was a U-boat alongside which dived immediately and disappeared. As we came closer, the ship ran up the British red ensign and put out in various conspicuous places RAF roundels or rings. Pretending to be bluffed we flew round in a friendly fashion while we made a careful inspection of the ship and at the same time kept a look-out for any signs of the U-boat. Just when we had made sure of our quarry we went straight into the attack and caught him napping through his own bluff.

'The most exciting time we have had was when we sank our second U-boat. We saw him a long way off and were able to stalk him through the clouds. In the last stage of our attack there was a small cloud between us and him, so we used it as a protection and dived through it to come out a mile and a half from him and take him so completely by surprise that he couldn't crash-dive in time to avoid my attack. In fact, I was able to turn away and wait until he was about to disappear under the surface. Then I released my bombs right across his bows. I knew we'd got him, because I could see every inch of the U-boat under the surface and we all saw him run into the bombs as they exploded, just as we got clear. We circled the position and after the commotion from the bombs had subsided, huge streams of air bubbles arose, seedling on the surface like an immense kettle boiling furiously and this went on for some minutes. Large quantities of thick oil covered the area. The U-boat must have gone straight to the bottom. We knew that we had hit him with several bombs.

'The mine just sits there, waiting patiently.'

'Every now and then you may have heard a little phrase at the end of the Air Ministry's communiqués: 'Mines were laid in enemy waters.'

'It may be that you haven't taken a great deal of notice of those few rather colourless words. All the same, they describe one of the most useful parts of the work being done by our bombers today.

HUNTING THE HUNTERS

'I was taking part in this work the other night in one of our bombers. We droned away for those enemy waters in which our dangerous seed was to be sown. A mine is really a sort of delayed-action bomb dropped into the water. You see it flop out of the aircraft and go sailing down on its parachute. It sinks into the water very quietly; no flame, no flash, and no leaping debris such as a big bomb may make. The mine just sits there waiting, very, very patiently. It may wait for only a few hours. It may wait months. But if during all that time a ship comes anywhere near it, the mine will get it. Just think what it means to the enemy, that night after night British aircraft buzz round that long coastline from Narvik to Bordeaux, along which must go his vital convoys carrying the slave-produced goods of occupied Europe.

'The convoys must hug the shores, or else our bombers, motor torpedo boats, or submarines will get them. But along the shore in the shallow waters the mine-layers have been at work the night before. It was a dirty night on which we went, with cloud down to within a few hundred feet above the sea. We flew above it. Up there it was a lovely starlit evening with a young moon hanging in the light western sky. The trouble with flying above cloud like that is, of course, that you may not be able to tell where you are. And your mine must be dropped just where you want it. However, for us that night the question largely solved itself. As soon as we reckoned that we were off the enemy coast we began to see searchlights and flak. Those of our crew who had been in these parts a good many times before had little difficulty in placing themselves. Soon we found a flak barrage going up to port as well as to starboard. That told us definitely where we were. Down through the cloud we went, lower and lower; the altimeter seemed to be trying to knock its bottom out. At last, we came out of the greyness and then just a few feet below, was the sea, rough and brown and cold and too near for comfort. Back we went into cloud.

'Bomb doors open.'

'Clonk.'

'Mine gone.'

'Bomb doors shut.'

'On the way home I thought, 'Well, it's there. Probably, of course, the enemy knows these channels are now dangerous. But that means that all his convoys will have to put into port. For days, probably, a fleet of mine-sweepers will have to come out seeking for what we have dropped. Maybe they won't find it. Maybe our mine will be detected and swept up. But then, just as the channels are clear again, the next dark night they will hear the drone of our bombers.

'They will wonder if all these channels aren't dangerous again. And maybe they will be, or maybe somewhere else will be. Then they will have to decide whether to send the convoys through and risk half a dozen laden ships going to the bottom, or start their sweeping all over again.

'For this is one of the great advantages of this new method of dropping mines from aircraft. If you think of it, a minelayer or a submarine cannot revisit a minefield once it has been laid for if it did it would probably be blown up on its own mines. But an aircraft can come back and back, keeping up the supply as it were, relaying just as the sweeping is done. Aircraft mining is a good example of the intimate co-operation between the Navy and the Air Force. The whole thing is planned at the Admiralty as part of our general programme of mining, by all sorts of agencies. We of the Air Force are the delivery agents as it were. Every now and then they tell us about the results. Information seeping through from Europe tells us of new wrecks along the coast, convoys held up, supplies dislocated, ships diverted to mine-sweeping.

'So when you next hear that, 'Mines were laid in enemy waters,' feel a little pleased that something very awkward and unpleasant and something which he simply cannot stop, is being done to the enemy.'

The U-Boat Magnet and the Sunderland's mixed bag by Leonard Gribble. Pockley flew his last operation on 10 Squadron on 12 November 1942 before being posted to 41 Squadron RAAF in Australia flying regular supply operations to New Guinea to resupply the ground forces in the Papua and New Guinea campaigns. Squadron Leader Pockley was posted to command the newly formed 200 Flight (Special Duties) at Leyburn airfield near Toowoomba in February 1945. The squadron was formed to support M and Z Special units operating in the Netherlands East Indies and Borneo. He was reported MIA flying a Liberator on 25 March after failing to return from a successful operation to insert personnel and supplies into the jungles of Sarawak.

The following is the story of how the courageous crew of an Australian heavy cruiser saved nine men of an RAF Sunderland from the sea on Tuesday, 29 October 1940, related by 18-year-old Midshipman Mackenzie J. Gregory on HMAS *Australia* and Pilot Officer Peter Hermann Neugebauer, the third

HUNTING THE HUNTERS

pilot of the Sunderland on 204 Squadron, which had left its base at Oban, Scotland at 1700 on Monday evening, despatched to escort a convoy. The poor visibility prevented them from finding their convoy and the weather became too bad to enable Canadian Flight Lieutenant S. R. Gibbs and crew to obtain a D/F bearing of their base, the high winds caused more petrol to be used than normal. At 0700 the next morning they ran out of petrol and were forced to attempt a landing in the Atlantic Ocean. It was a magnificent feat of airmanship for the pilot to put down his flying boat into this raging sea without capsizing it...

'We had arrived on the Clyde at Greenock, Scotland, only three days earlier', 'Mac' Gregory recalled, 'after passage from Gibraltar. What a contrast we found the weather from our recent time in the tropics, cold bleak days and even colder nights, and rough Atlantic Ocean weather to cope with at sea. We had been ordered to sea to join a search for a German merchant raider, reported to be operating against our shipping. As Tuesday dawned, we learned about a Coastal Command Sunderland flying boat that had to make a forced landing in the Atlantic west of the Hebrides. Our task was to try and locate this stricken Royal Air Force plane and save her crew. There was a gale blowing in earnest, the barometer had fallen and was still going down; visibility was poor and finding this Sunderland in such adverse conditions appeared difficult, if not unlikely. The ship was running with an extremely rough sea, rolling heavily from port to starboard, and then all over again.

'Just after noon we received a message from the flying boat: 'Hurry up.... am breaking up'.

'During the afternoon watch, the flying boat kept up transmitting on her radio, so that we could use our directional finding equipment to locate her and then run down this D/F bearing. The weather was awful and as we approached closer to her estimated position we made smoke at intervals, hoping her crew might spot us.

'Visibility was now very low, and we had increased speed to 26 knots in an attempt to arrive before it was too late, but the ship was making very heavy weather of the prevailing conditions.

'By now, a huge sea was running, and our heavy cruiser, when picked up on the crest of each wave, was literally surfing down into the next trough, with the wind now blowing at gale force. When surfing, the ship picked up several extra knots over her speed of 26 knots, and we actually touched 30 knots on the speed indicator.

THE AIR WAR AT SEA IN THE SECOND WORLD WAR

'At 1435 the Sunderland hove into view right ahead, her tail only occasionally visible above the huge waves, a crewmember constantly operating a flashing light to guide us. When but a half a mile from the flying boat, one of the floats dropped off. A moment later, an enormous wave picked up the Sunderland and flipped it completely over on its back. We could only see one crewmember perched on the upturned boat.

'We now approached from upwind, allowing the gale force winds to drift us down onto the site of the wreckage. Ropes had been prepared over our starboard side; scrambling nets and jumping ladders were also in place over the starboard side.

'We suddenly sighted a group of airmen in the water with life jackets on, the ship drifted down to them and ropes were passed. However, the rough and icy Atlantic was not going to give up this group easily. The conditions prevented the airmen from securing a rope around themselves. They were just too exhausted to tie a knot. Salvation was at hand, but were the elements going to win this struggle after all? *Australia* was rolling heavily. One minute the starboard side would be feet under water and then a heavy roll would reverse to port and the starboard side would be well clear of the water. Given the wind force and the state of the sea, the only way to pluck our survivors from the clutches of the Atlantic was to send several officers and sailors over the side with bowlines to secure to each airman. These volunteers were led and encouraged by the ship's executive officer, Commander J. M. ('Jamie' or 'Black Jack') Armstrong RAN. One by one the airmen had to be hauled on board, with the ship rolling heavily, the airmen's waterlogged gear making each rescue a long and difficult task.

'Persistence and sheer bravery from those over the side securing each airman finally triumphed. Nine of the crew of 13 were finally on board, suffering from exposure and seasickness, but they were now safe and would all be fine after time spent in our sick bay.

'The remaining four airmen drifted out of reach, just clear of *Australia*'s bow and could not be reached. I was up in the bows with a team of seamen, trying to reach this group with heaving lines, but the force of the wind made this task impossible to cast a line. It merely blew back into one's face before achieving its objective, to reach the doomed four.

'It was total frustration. They were only several yards away but we could not reach the group; no boat could have survived in these seas.

'The Sunderland had survived seven and a half hours in a howling Atlantic gale before their luck ran out, and the boat was overturned. The airmen were all seasick and very weak from their ordeal. While there was joy on the faces of those we rescued, we experienced anger and sadness at having to leave the remaining four airmen to face a certain death.

'At 1725 after many hours taken up in this rescue operation, we were forced to abandon our task, we altered course to the South, and proceeded at only nine knots into the face of this storm.'

Pilot Officer Peter Hermann Neugebauer, the Third pilot of the Sunderland recalled: 'The odds were so heavy against us that it is a miracle we were not all written off. The crew was a fairly mixed crowd. The captain and second pilot were Canadian. I was from Cape Town. The rest hailed from the Empire and the home country. I suppose superstitious people might deduce something from the fact that we numbered 13, but that didn't worry us as it is quite a normal number in a Sunderland. Incidentally, it was my first operational trip and the navigator's, too.

'We had been flying through the night for over nine hours on our patrol when we set course back for the coast of Scotland, several hundred miles away. The weather was absolutely filthy with wind, rain and mist; visibility, which matters most in the air, was practically nil. In fact, conditions were so bad that even the wireless wouldn't function because of atmospheric interference. I put the earphones on once or twice and the noise might have been an echo of what was going on outside - a rushing sound like a close-up of a mighty waterfall.

'We did our best to navigate back to our base without wireless help. We climbed to 5,000 ft, where we got a bit of icing-up and came down low when we calculated we should be near home. There was nothing in sight but sea and we knew we were well and truly lost.

'Petrol was getting very low. We had enough left for only about another 15 minutes flying, so the captain, a flight lieutenant with the DFC, decided to try and alight while he could still use his engines. The closer we came to the sea, the worse it looked. The waves were simply enormous. It is one of the most difficult operations in flying to land a boat successfully with anything of a sea running. If you get even a wing-tip float stove in you're finished, because she loses trim and the wing goes in.

'Down we came towards the dark sea. Our normal landing speed is about 100 knots. The captain brought her in at 50 knots to try and save the hull and with the terrific wind our ground speed was probably not more than 20 knots. We held our breath as we touched down, but nothing came adrift. It was a really wonderful landing in almost insuperable difficulties.

'Now we were tossing up and down on the huge waves, with the engines stopped and the wind whistling past like a tornado. It was still dark. The wireless operators, who had been trying ceaselessly to get into touch with the base, were tapping out messages. We learned later that these had been received and a directional bearing obtained from them which resulted eventually in our rescue.

'The motion was so violent that we were all sick except the chief air-gunner [Charles Leslie Gough], a man of Malvern. He took long spells at the controls, using the ailerons to save the aircraft from buffeting as much as possible, while the rest of us got the dinghies prepared.

'As time went by, the wind and sea were rising. It didn't seem possible for conditions to get any worse, but they did! We'd had nothing to eat for 12 hours or so and anyway it was impossible to keep anything down. I ate an orange, but it was no good.

'When daylight came, we received a wireless message that help was on the way. A ship was expected to reach us about 2.30 in the afternoon. The waiting hours were pretty anxious ones, but at 2.45 we saw her smoke. It was a beautiful sight. In driving, drizzling rain we let off distress signals. She turned towards us and stood off a bit to make rescue preparations.

'Then something happened that we had all been dreading. An enormous wave got us. I can see it coming now. The gunner was still at the controls and he shouted, 'Look what's coming!' As it swept past us, the control column hit him in the stomach and then went loose. Our port wing-tip and float had carried away. It was amazing that the thing hadn't happened before. The fact that we had floated securely in that sea for eight and three-quarter hours is the finest tribute possible to our captain's landing and the stout build of a Sunderland.

'But now the boat was going. She heeled to port and we scrambled out on top. If it hadn't been so serious, it would have been funny to see us all throwing our heavy flying clothing into the sea - boots, parachute harness, overalls, etc. One chap held up his wool-lined boots, shook his head sadly and dropped them gently into the sea.

'The chief air-gunner climbed out on the starboard wing to try and balance the aircraft. He slipped on a patch of oil and fell into the water. Then things happened rather quickly.

HUNTING THE HUNTERS

'We threw him ropes. The Sunderland started to turn over. I found myself in the water and tried to undo one of the dinghies. The mooring ropes got round my neck and I thought I was going to he drowned underneath.

'Our rescue ship saw what was happening to the Sunderland and steamed to windward giving us the shelter of her lee. We were in a bunch in the sea, supported by our Mae West lifejackets and swam and paddled towards the warship. From her deck, someone flung a lifebelt towards me. On it was painted HMAS *Australia*. The crew threw out ropes and scrambling nets for us to climb up.

'In a few minutes some of the *Australia*'s crew themselves were in the water with us, helping to get us aboard. I learned later that the ship's captain was among them. They assisted us to ropes, but we were paralysed with cold and could hardly hold them. Even if you'd got a rope round our arm, you were in the water one moment and pulled high out of it the next by the movement of the ship. There was always the danger of being crushed against the ship's side. Several chaps climbed partly up the rope ladders and fell back into the sea. I'm sorry to say that four of our number disappeared in those dreadful few moments and were not seen again. Without the very gallant help of the Australians, I don't think any of us would have reached the deck.

'Somehow I got on the wrong side of one of the scrambling nets and was in imminent danger of being slapped against the ship's plates. But a sailor got hold of me through the net and held on. Someone let down a bowline, which I got beneath my arms with the sailor's help and the next minute I was going up to the rails like a lift. I remember noticing, half dazed, that my watch glass was cracked and muttering, 'Damn, I've broken the glass!'

'They wanted to carry me below, but with a sort of muzzy stubbornness, I insisted on walking. Of course, I had to be supported on both sides and the officers laughingly humoured me. The nine of us who had been saved were put in the sick bay with warm blankets, hot bottles and drinks to thaw us out. We must have been in the water round about 30 minutes and some of us didn't stop shivering for two hours. Meantime, the search went on for the missing four, but without success.

'At last, we turned for the land, leaving the Sunderland floating upside down, hull awash. The seas were by then about 50 ft high and the wind was so strong that it was right off the ship's indicator, gusting at well over 100 mph.

The captain, when he had dried and changed, came down and told us it was the worst storm he had seen in his life.

'The crew, nearly all Australians, couldn't have been kinder to us during our two days' voyage to port. We parted from them regretfully – but it felt grand to be ashore again.'[62]

---

62. Pilot Officer J. M. Ennis, the second pilot, who became a Flight Lieutenant, later captained another Sunderland (T9041), which ditched in the South Atlantic while escorting Convoy OS.31 on 28 June 1942. He was picked up two days later by HMS *Velox*. Another survivor, Sergeant H. W. Taylor was a member on the crew of Sunderland N9023 which flew into a mountain near Fragjadalsfjall, Iceland on 23 April 1941 when ten of the 13 crew were injured. Taylor died from his injuries just after he had been rescued.

Chapter 8

Pearl Harbor and the US Pacific Fleet

From our end of the peninsula we could see the old battlewagon Utah *as it turned on its side in the murky water. Everywhere we looked there was smoke and fire. The odor of burning oil hung over the Harbor. All these unbelievable sights and sounds and smells stunned my senses. I remember the worried expression on my dad's face as he surveyed the chaos around us and yelled, 'Get in the car! We've got to get away from the harbor!'*

Dorinda Makanaonalani, *Pearl Harbor Child – From Attack To Peace*, **Sunday morning, 7 December 1941.**

At 0702 hours on Sunday, 7 December 1941 two US Army privates manning their British radarscope at a mobile radar site at Opana Point on Oahu's north coast in the Hawaiian Islands discovered an unusually large 'blip' 136 miles to the north and closing. The officer on watch in the control centre, however, dismissed the incoming planes picked up by the radar as the expected 12 unarmed B-17Ds of the 7th Bomb Group and four B-17Cs and two B-17Es of the 88th Reconnaissance Squadron, all of which were en route to the island of Mindanao in the Philippines from Hamilton Field, California inbound that morning for Hickam Field, the AAF bomber base on the island. Meanwhile, 200 miles north of Oahu, Japanese Vice Admiral Chūichi Nagumo's First Air Fleet or Kido Butai (striking force) aboard the aircraft carriers *Akagi, Kaga, Sōryū, Hiryū, Shōkaku* and *Zuikaku* had launched 183 aircraft at 0550 hours in the pre-dawn darkness. Fuchida Mitsuo, who led the first wave was responsible for the coordination of the entire aerial attack.

THE AIR WAR AT SEA IN THE SECOND WORLD WAR

A second strike consisting of 54 Nakajima B5N 'Kate' torpedo bombers, 80 Aichi D3A 'Val' dive bombers and 36 Mitsubishi A6M5 'Zero' fighters[63] led by Lieutenant Commander Shigekazu Shimazaki of the *Zuikaku* was launched an hour later.

US Navy cryptanalysts having broken the Japanese 'Purple Code', the United States of America was aware that the Japanese were planning an attack in the Pacific (on a location the Japanese code-named 'AF'). The attack location and time were confirmed when the American base at Midway sent out a false message that it was short of fresh water. Japan then sent a message that 'AF' was short of fresh water, confirming that the location for the attack was the base at Midway. Station 'Hypo' (where the cryptanalysts were based in Hawaii) was also able to give the order of battle of the Imperial Japanese Navy. It was expected therefore that the first bombs would fall on the Philippines or Malaya. However, the target for the 51 'Vals', 89 'Kates' and 43 'Zeros' of the first wave and those of the second wave was not the Philippines or Malaya but the US Pacific Fleet at Pearl Harbor and the army and AAC bases and US Naval Aviation facilities at Kaneohe Bay and Ewa Mooring Mast Field. At 0616 hours, the Japanese aircraft droned undetected toward Oahu while, 250 miles due west, the USS *Enterprise* with Task Force 8, under Vice Admiral William F. 'Bull' Halsey Jr., was returning to Pearl after ferrying 12 F4F Wildcats of VMF-211 to Wake Island. Fortunately, none of the three carriers operating at Pearl Harbor were in port when the Japanese attacked. *Lexington* too was at sea after having delivered fighters to Midway and *Saratoga* was at San Diego.

Between 0615 and 0629, *Enterprise* launched 18 two-seat carrier-based Douglas SB2C Dauntless dive bombers. The nine two-plane sections were to search ahead of the carrier to a distance of 150 miles and then proceed to NAS Pearl Harbor. Task Force 8, which had been operating on a war footing since it had departed Pearl on 28 November, was to make port that afternoon. At 0630, the general stores issue ship *Antares* summoned the destroyer *Ward*, on harbour-entrance patrol, to investigate what appeared to be a small submarine 1,500 yards off *Antares*' starboard quarter. In the sky were three

---

63. Aichi D3A2 ('Val') dive bomber; Nakajima B5N2 ('Kate') torpedo bomber; Mitsubishi A6M2 Zero-Sen ('Zeke') fighter, which could also perform in the fighter-bomber role.

PEARL HARBOR AND THE US PACIFIC FLEET

PBY-5 Catalinas armed with depth charges on patrol in Fleet Operating Areas off Oahu with orders to bomb any submarine seen.

On the *Enterprise*, Admiral Halsey was having breakfast with his flag secretary, Lieutenant Doug Moulton, when the telephone rang. Moulton answered and reported that there had been an air raid on Pearl Harbor! Within minutes, all hands were at General Quarters and Lieutenant (jg or Junior Grade) Francis 'Fritz' Hebel, the VF leader, Lieutenant (jg) Eric Allen and Ensigns James G. Daniels and J. C. Kelley of Fighting Squadron 6 (VF-6) were running to their stubby Grumman F4F Wildcats waiting on deck ready to launch for the first Combat Air Patrol (CAP) of the Second World War. Ensign (later Captain) James Daniels, who was born in Kansas City in 1915, had joined Fighting Squadron 6 attached to Air Group 6 in *Enterprise* in San Diego, California just before she departed to be the flagship of Admiral 'Bull' Halsey. They arrived in Hawaii in late September 1939 and were based ashore operating out of Ford Island. The runway then was only 3,500 ft in the middle of Pearl Harbor. The standard operating procedure was that, if the carrier was in port, the air group would be shore-based and would fly from Ford Island to carry out gunnery or bombing exercises. Daniels' war actually started on 28 November 1941, when VF-6 was ordered to fly out to *Enterprise* for air operations. He was then married, living in Manoa Valley, so his wife Helen took him down to Pearl Harbor's landing 'Charlie'. They said their good-byes and her husband reported to VF-6 across the field and prepared to fly out to *Enterprise* sometime that morning.

Daniels recalls: 'The ship had gotten underway at 0600 and about 1000 we flew out to join her. She was operating an area off the south-west coast of Oahu. Normal procedure was to land the fighter squadron first - we called it a 'run through' the deck. Since we hadn't flown aboard for perhaps three or four months, it was wise to refresh our procedures. After the initial landing, we'd launch immediately and then fly around and make a second landing. Two such landings would qualify us for the next six months for our carrier landing requirements. On this particular Monday morning, we landed our F4F Wildcats aboard and were immediately struck below. No 'run through' this time. We taxied onto number 1 elevator and were dropped down to the hangar deck and run aft on the hangar deck until it was full. We didn't understand this unusual procedure! It became apparent moments later when VMF-211 flew their Wildcats aboard. This Marine Corps squadron was based at Ewa, a small airfield that was there long before Barber's Point was built. Our first supposition was that VMF-211 was getting carrier refreshed and then would turn around and fly back to Ewa. The Marine pilots also thought this because none of them had brought any baggage. They didn't even have a toothbrush or a change of shirts - nothing.

'So we got all our other aircraft aboard and the ship turned and headed west. Later that morning, we finally found out that we were taking VMF-211 to Wake Island. As we steamed west, we received orders from Halsey's staff for our squadron to give VMF-211 all the help we possibly could. Some of their guns were in bad shape, so we re-gunned their planes as necessary. We also took their two or three older planes and gave them the best planes we had. As we approached Wake Island, our Air Group Commander, Howard L. 'Brigham' Young in an SBD with one wingman and a second SBD, took off about 100 miles distance away from Wake as navigators for the marines. During our transit to Wake, whenever the weather was permissible, VF-6 flew combat air patrol over the ship in four-hour flights in four-plane sections from daylight to dark. When the Air Group Commander and his wingman landed back aboard, *Enterprise* turned back toward Pearl Harbor. We were scheduled to arrive there early on Saturday, 6 December. As we were passing south of Midway, we ran into some very heavy weather and the destroyers were taking a beating. They were taking green water over their bows, so Admiral Halsey ordered the Task Group to slow down so that the 'small boys' wouldn't have such a bad time. By slowing down, we were late arriving at Pearl Harbor.'

'Early on the morning of 7 December, we launched a partial air group. Some of our SBDs carried staff officers in the rear seat instead of our enlisted gunners because they had business to attend to at Ford Island to prepare for the ship's entry - such as the Supply Officer who was making arrangements for food and ammunition to the waiting dock side when the ship tied up. While the group of SBDs led by Group Commander Young was in the landing pattern at Ford Island about 8.00 am, the Japanese had already begun their attack on Pearl Harbor.

A 'Zero' attacked Lieutenant Commander 'Brig' Young's SBD and his wingman, Ensign Perry L. Teaff, near Ewa. They evaded the 'Zero' and flew through friendly anti-aircraft fire before putting down on Ford Island where Young and his passenger, Lieutenant Commander Bromfield B. Nichol, Halsey's tactical officer, headed by car and boat for the Submarine Base and the HQ of Admiral Husband E. Kimmel, C-in-C US Pacific Fleet.

PEARL HARBOR AND THE US PACIFIC FLEET

Two other SBDs flown by Lieutenant Clarence Dickinson and Ensign John R. McCarthy engaged the 'Zeros'. Born in Jacksonville, Florida on 1 December 1912, Clarence Earle Dickinson, Jr. was from Raleigh, having been raised at Wrightsville Beach and Wilmington. He graduated from the US Naval Academy at Annapolis, Class of 1934. During pre-flight checks of the SBD-3, Radioman 1st Class William Cicero Miller had stood on Dickinson's wing adjusting his radio cord while he had a word with the Lieutenant. Born on 19 July 1919, Miller was the second of five children. He told Dickinson that this four-year hitch was up in a few days and he was going home to marry his sweetheart. 'But,' he told Dickinson, 'there is something funny about it. Mr. Dickinson, out of the 21 of us fellows who went through radio school together, I'm the only who hasn't crashed in the water. I hope you won't get me wet today, sir!'

Dickinson replied, 'Miller, next Saturday, we all go home for five months, so this will probably be our last flight together. Just stick with me and the first thing you know, we'll be on the Ford Island runway. That's all we have to do is get by this morning's flight.'

After they were airborne 'Zeros' dived out of the smoke cloud and attacked Dickinson's and 'Mac' McCarthy's SBDs. Dickinson later recounted: 'A glance to the right at McCarthy's plane was almost like seeing Miller and myself in a mirror - there they were, in yellow rubber life jackets and parachute harnesses and almost faceless behind black goggles and radio gear fixed on white helmets. Mac's gunner [Earl E. Howell], like mine, was on his seat in his cockpit, alert to swing his twin machine guns on the ring of steel track that encircled him. Things began happening in split-second sequences. Two fighters popped out of the smoke cloud in a dive and made a run on us. 'Mac' dipped his plane under me to get on my left side, so as to give his gunner an easier shot. But the bullets they were shooting at me were passing beneath my plane. Unlucky Mac ran right into them. I put my plane into a left-hand turn to give my gunner a better shot and saw 'Mac's plane below, smoking and losing altitude. Then it burst into yellow flame. The fighter who had got 'Mac' zipped past me to the left and I rolled to get a shot at him with my fixed guns. As he pulled up in front of me and to the left, I saw painted on his fuselage a tell-tale insigne, a disk suggesting, with its white background, a big fried egg with a red yolk. For the first time I confirmed what my common sense had told me; these were Jap fighters - 'Zeros'. I missed him, I'm afraid.

THE AIR WAR AT SEA IN THE SECOND WORLD WAR

'Those 'Zeros' had so much more speed than I did that they could afford to go rapidly out of range before turning to swoop back after McCarthy. Four or five more 'Zeros' dived out of the smoke cloud and sat on my tail. Miller was firing away and was giving me a running report on what was happening behind me. 'In a calm voice, Miller said, 'Mr. Dickinson, I have been hit once, but I think I have got one of them.' He had, all right. I looked back and saw with immense satisfaction that one of the 'Zeros' was falling in flames. [This made Miller the first American flyer to shoot down a Japanese plane in aerial combat in the Second World War.] In that interval, watching the 'Jap' go down, I saw McCarthy's flaming plane again, making a slow turn to the right. Then I saw Mac's parachute open, just above the ground. As he jumped, he was thrown against the tail surface of his plane and his leg was broken. But he landed safely.' Earl Howell was killed.

'Jap fighters were behind us again. There were five, I should say, the nearest less than 100 ft away. They were putting bullets into the tail of my plane, but I was causing them to miss a lot by making hard turns. They were having a field day - no formation whatever, all of them in a scramble to get me, each one wildly eager for the credit. One or more of them got on the target with cannon. They were using explosive and incendiary bullets that clattered on my metal wing like hail on a tin roof. I was fascinated by a line of big holes creeping across my wing, closer and closer. A tongue of yellow flame spurted from the gasoline tank in my left wing and began spreading.

'Are you all right, Miller?' I yelled. 'Mr. Dickinson, I've expended all six cans of ammunition,' he replied. Then he screamed. It was as if he opened his lungs wide and just let go. I have never heard any comparable human sound. It was a shriek of agony. When I called again, there was no reply. I'm sure poor Miller was already dead.

'I was alone and in a sweet fix. I had to go from a left-hand into a right-hand turn because the fast Japanese fighters had pulled up ahead of me on the left. I was still surprised at the amazing manoeuvrability of those 'Zeros'. I kicked my right rudder and tried to put my right wing down, but the plane did not respond. The controls had been shot away. With the left wing down and the right rudder on and only 800 or 900 ft altitude, I went into a spin.

'I yelled again for Miller on the long chance that he was still alive. Still no reply. Then I started to get out. It was my first jump, but I found myself behaving as if I were using a check-off list. I was automatically responding to training. I remember that I started to unbutton my radio cord with my right hand and unbuckle my belt with my left. But I couldn't unfasten my radio cord with one hand. So, using both hands, I broke it. Then I unbuckled my belt, pulled my feet underneath me, put my hands on the sides of the cockpit, leaned out on the right-hand side and shoved clear. The rush of wind was peeling my goggles off. I had shoved out on the right side, because that was the inside of the spin. Then I was tumbling over in the air, grabbing and feeling for the rip cord's handle. Pulling it, I flung my arm wide. There was a savage jerk. From where I dangled, my eyes followed the shroud lines up to what I felt was the most beautiful sight I had ever seen - the stiff-bellied shape of my white silk parachute.'

Dickinson landed near Ewa airfield and proceeded to the naval air station at Ford Island where he was immediately assigned to a 175-mile aerial search operation at sea, his recent ordeal not reported to his superiors.

Ensign Walter M. Willis was also shot down by Japanese fighters and he and his gunner were killed. Lieutenant (jg) Frank A. Patriarca was also attacked. He searched in vain for the *Enterprise* and later landed at Burns Field on Kauai. Ensign Fred T. Weber had become separated from his section leader, Ensign Manuel Gonzalez during their search and Gonzalez found himself alone against six 'Vals' from *Shōkaku* and *Zuikaku*. At 0645 hours in the radio room aboard the *Enterprise* was heard 'Don't shoot! This is an American plane!' Then there was an anguished scream. Gonzalez and his gunner were never heard again.

Ensign John H. L. Vogt and his radio-gunner RM3C Sidney Pierce collided with a 'Val' passing Ewa on return to its carrier. Vogt and Pierce bailed out but both were killed when their parachutes did not open fully and they slammed into some trees. Ensign Edward T. Deacon and his radioman, RM3C Audrey G. Coslett, were shot down by gunners at Fort Weaver and the Fleet Machine Gun School and ditched off Hickam. Both men were picked up by an army crash boat.

Ensign Wilbur E. Roberts' SBD was hit also, but he managed to land at Hickam safely. Six other SBDs, knowing that without armour or self-sealing fuel tanks they stood little chance against the Japanese aircraft, circled between Ewa and Barbers Point at 400-500 ft and watched the enemy aircraft 3,500 above them. Around noon, nine SBDs took off from Oahu and flew 175 miles out to search and attack any Japanese forces encountered. This and another search by 31 TBDs, SBDs and F4Fs led by Lieutenant Commander Eugene E. Lindsey launched from *Enterprise* late the same afternoon proved equally futile. Ensign Perry L. Teaff in his SBD remained with his group for over three hours despite an overheating engine and when he tried to land, found it difficult to lower the landing gear. His courage in continuing the search when there was little chance of success earned him the Navy Cross. After being shot at by friendly gunners, two of the SBDs had to land at Kaneohe, which had parked vehicles on the runway in a vain attempt to make it unusable![64]

"On the *Enterprise'*, continues James Daniels, 'the skipper of VF-6, Lieutenant Commander Clarence Wade McClusky was scheduling normal combat Air Patrols (unaware of the attack) to protect a very vulnerable carrier as she closed the channel while entering port. This was routine. I was scheduled for the second launch of four VF-CAP at nine o'clock. The first early CAP was airborne at the time the Japanese were attacking Pearl Harbor and exactly at the moment our air group was approaching for a landing at Ford Island. We didn't know it then, neither did the Japanese, but here was an American carrier only 150 miles from Pearl - fortunately, to the south-west - with its air group absent, except for a few VF-6 aircraft. Had they known this, certainly the 'Big E' would have been discovered and sunk. It was about this stage of our early morning operations that the Japanese attack on Pearl became known to us. Normal flight procedures called flight quarters about 30 minutes before launch. Pilots reported to the ready room to complete navigation, find out what the code words for the day were and then manned our planes, started engines and got launched.'

'However, on this particular morning for VF-6's second flight, we got no warning. Flight quarters were sounded on the PA system, followed immediately by 'Pilots, man your planes.'

'What the hell was going on? We ran to our ready room, grabbed navigation boards - we had no idea where we were going or what the mission was. I manned my plane - which was parked number two on the flight-deck - and found that its engine was already turning up. That had never happened before. Nobody started my airplane except me. The young plane captain, about 18-years-old, said, 'Mr Daniels, they told me to start the airplane. They told me!' I said, 'All right, don't worry about it. Is it all right?' He said, 'Yes, Sir, the plane checks out.'

---

64. See *This Is No Drill* by Robert J. Cressman and J. Michael Wenger, *Challenge Magazine's Second World War Special* (Vol. 1, No. 1, 1994).

PEARL HARBOR AND THE US PACIFIC FLEET

'We had no time to really warm up our engines. As we taxied into position, one of the plane handlers held up a little blackboard. On it was written: *Japs attack Pearl Harbor. No shit.*'

'And with that, the launching officer dropped his hand – not even giving a "turn up" signal – he just launched us. As I left the deck, I charged my guns and the four of us rendezvoused, while our earlier CAP came on in to land.

'We shifted our radios from the *Enterprise* tower frequency to the local radio station KGMB in Honolulu – or maybe it was KGU – where we heard such reports such as "all truckers report to such and such", 'Red Cross workers report to your posts." It was utter chaos on both military and civilian communication frequencies! But we did get some fragmentary feedback, such as "All ships at Pearl Harbor have been sunk, there are no survivors and tens of thousands of people have been killed." It was utter, utter chaos.

'Meantime, we were receiving partial and sometimes contradictory instructions. My flight was ordered to land aboard about noon, so another VF flight was launched to relieve us. When we landed, we found out what had happened to Air Group 6 as it landed at Ford Island. Pilots like Manny Gonzales in our Scouting Squadron and others were dead. And I remember the last thing we heard from Manny Gonzales was, 'Don't shoot! I am an American.' I had heard that before I landed.

'We got a bite of lunch and went back to the ready room to man the planes when needed. In the middle of the afternoon, word was received aboard that our search planes had found the Japanese fleet some 250 miles south-south-west of Kauai. (How wrong that was!) Admiral Halsey planned to launch all available torpedo planes and a group of SBDs and scouts rigged to lay smoke screens so the torpedo planes could make an attack. VF-6 would provide a six-plane fighter escort. As the skipper, Wade McClusky was already airborne leading a flight. He was not aware that VF-6 was to provide escort with all available pilots and planes.

'About 4:00 that afternoon, we were launched for about an hour and a half flight to the south to hunt for the Japanese fleet. The torpedo planes were very, very slow because they were so heavily loaded, full of both fuel and torpedoes. The scouting aircraft were rigged with two large smoke tanks (modified fuel tanks) for laying smoke screens and we fighters were, by necessity, weaving back and forth over the top of this very slow-flying task unit. We got to where the enemy was supposed to be – but they weren't there.

THE AIR WAR AT SEA IN THE SECOND WORLD WAR

'The skipper of Torpedo Six and the leader of the torpedo planes, Lieutenant Commander 'Gene' Lindsey, made a turn toward the west where he thought the Japanese might be. Then, as his planes were getting short of fuel, he let it be known that he was heading us back to *Enterprise*. We were all flying in radio silence and now it was getting dark. We were flying without lights and our six fighters were in an echelon of echelons to the right, stepped up one behind the other. The instrument panel lights in the cockpits were red - we could see them and the exhaust manifold in each fighter, which was glowing white hot. We were using those two reference points in order to fly as a unit, stay in position and not get lost.

'As we neared where our Carrier Task Force should be, 'Fritz' Hebel had done a tremendous job in navigation. He got us back to the ship and told us to look down. Even though there were no ships' lights, we could see the wakes of the four destroyers and the *Enterprise* with their white wakes bubbling up behind them. We made one circle around the Task Force, but instead of landing, the ship told us to fly on to Ford Island. They gave us a coded message - no actual course of direction - just ordered us to return to Ford Island. Hebel had done such a fine job to even locate the carrier force, because we had neither radar, nor direction finding equipment help from the ship (the *Enterprise* had turned it off because they were afraid the Japs might home in on it). He took a heading for Pearl.

'So we dead-reckoned our way to the Hawaiian Islands from the south.

'I probably had as much or more experience flying around the islands than the other VF pilots in this particular group. When we saw the fires that we thought were cane fields burning on Kauai, I told Hebel that we should head south-east to Oahu. 'Fritz' had done another splendid job of navigation and had hit Oahu right on the nose at Barber's Point. But as we went on I looked back after we got into the Molokai Channel and for some reason or other Diamond Head Light had not been turned off. Every other light on Oahu was blacked out except this one glaring searchlight at Diamond Head. We turned back and 'Fritz' asked us how much gas we had and all of us indicated we were nearly empty. We made a 180-degree turn and came back to the entrance of Pearl Harbor Channel. We could see the landing floodlights at Ford Island at that time. I'm not sure how *Enterprise* got word to Ford Island tower that we were coming, though the tower could not tell anybody else we were coming in because the tower radio was only on the one very low ground-to-air frequency. The Ford tower had no contact with any ground stations or any gun control stations or anyone else. All they could do was talk to the pilots coming in from the carrier.

'At the time we arrived, Lieutenant Commander 'Brig' Young was in the tower and we were given instructions to make a standard carrier approach and land. We got in landing configuration and the first four planes cranked their wheels down, made their break, turned on their running lights and as the first plane 'broke' leaving two planes - Eric Allen's and mine - just above them to make another circle and then come in and land.

'As the first four planes broke to land, all hell broke loose on Ford Island. Every gun on every ship, every gun at Hickam, every gun at Fort Shafter, all the guns at the ammunition depot in West Loch, the USS *Nevada* - aground off Hospital Point, the USS *Utah* - every gun, including individuals with .45s - everything around Pearl Harbor opened up on us. Hebel got through the stuff and flew up to Wheeler Field. Very low on gas, he lowered his wheels and made an approach at Wheeler. They obviously didn't know what was going on, but since everyone at Ford Island and Pearl Harbor was shooting, they figured that we were enemy planes, so everybody at Wheeler opened up on poor 'Fritz'. He tried to evade, but with his wheels down, he crashed on the far side of the field across the road and put his head through the gun sight. His wingman, Ensign Herb Menges, crashed and burned in Pearl City. Number 3, Ensign Gayle L. Herman, took a 5-inch shell from one of the ship's guns through his engine. He was so low that the shell didn't have time to arm and was therefore a 'dud,' but it did tear his engine apart. He crashed on the little golf course at the end of Ford Island. He lived. In fact, he grabbed his parachute and walked back to our hangar, where he later saved my neck.

'Dave' Flynn got through the flak only to have his engine run out of gas over Barbers Point. 'Dave' bailed out and broke a leg landing in the Keawi trees and coral. The army found him and got him to a hospital. Our squadron was not notified until ten days later that he was even alive!

'That left me and Lieutenant (jg) Eric Allen, my wingman, still in the air. Eric was a Naval Academy graduate. I'll never forget his beautiful tenor voice. He bailed out right over the Ford tower when his engine quit, very close to Battleship Row and our own gunners who put a .50 calibre hole through his chest killed him. He died in the oil and muck of Pearl Harbor about 0200 that morning! How terrible! I did a split 'S' from about 1,500 ft past the floodlights and flew on into the dark, turning off my running lights.

THE AIR WAR AT SEA IN THE SECOND WORLD WAR

'When I settled down a little bit, I knew I was nearly out of fuel and I didn't know how long I could stay in the air, so I called the tower. This was the first communications since the gunnery show started. I called the tower and 'Brig' Young came on the air and said, 'Who are you?' and I gave him my side number. I said, 'I'm 6 Fox 5' and he asked, 'What is your name?' Then I became cosy because I didn't really know who I was talking to. I didn't know whether the Japanese were in the tower or what – but 'Brig' was my former CO and my daughter's godfather – so we knew each other pretty well. So I said, 'Who are you?' And he answered that he was the Air Group Commander and again asked, 'Who are you?' I answered, 'I'm your godchild's father – what's my middle name?' He came back right away with my middle name, which for the record is 'Ganson,' so there wasn't a Jap in the world who would know my middle name. He then asked me what his nickname was and I replied, 'Brig' – so we established our private code and he told me to come in low and fast. I cranked my wheels down. I didn't know how much fuel I had because my gauge still read empty. Twenty-two turns later, my wheels were down and locked.

'The Wildcats had spring-loaded flaps and they wouldn't come down until the speed dropped below 130 knots. I was doing about 150 to 180, so I just hit the flap handle and made my approach into Ford. The next time I looked up, I could see the foretop of the *Nevada* right in front of me. I dropped my left wing and went around her bow and made a right turn into Ford Island.' Again, everything with guns began shooting – the *Nevada*, all ships in Pearl Harbor, West Loch, the Ammunition Depot – everything! The tracers were going over my head like a tepee. I touched down at the end of the runway, much too fast for the flaps to work, but they did come down toward the end of the run-out. I rolled into the area at the end of the runway where the little golf course was (where Herman had landed) and they had 50-gallon drums and trucks and everything else to keep parachuters from landing. I ran into an area off the runway, ground looped, but didn't even drag a wing-tip, taxied back up to our hangar on the north side of the field, where we had left one fighter aircraft to have an engine change while we were taking the marines to Wake.

'As I taxied up to my normal parking spot, there was a marine in a sandbag revetment with a .50-calibre gun on a tripod who started to shoot at me, his bullets went right over the top of my head. I could see the tracers coming right at me, but missing. Thank God for Gayle Herman who, as I've related, had earlier crashed on the field. He saw the guy shooting at me and hit him over the head with a gun butt and silenced him. I then taxied up the line and cut my engine and Gayle climbed up on my wing and he was crying, 'My God, 'Jim', you're alive!' I said, 'Gayle, what's happened?' We were nearly incoherent, both of us. I turned the plane over to our maintenance team and told them I didn't know what condition my plane was in but we would probably need it as soon as possible, if it was flyable. The next morning, I found there was one .30-calibre bullet hole outboard in my right wing, about 2 ft outboard from the cockpit. It had done no damage, missing both hydraulic lines. The crew chief put two 2-inch-square blind rivet patches, one on the upper part of the wing and one on the lower part of the wing and the plane were ready the next day.[7]

'Gayle said we were supposed to report to 'Brig' Young in the tower. He had a jeep, so we crossed the field and went up into the tower where I told CAG [Commander Air Group] what I knew. And he told me what he knew, which was six had gotten their tails shot off pretty badly. We had lost five airplanes that night and three very fine pilots were dead. I was the only pilot to get a plane down safely and get down alive at the same time.

'Brig' said, 'We're going to have to go back to *Enterprise* in the morning and I want you and Gayle to have your planes ready. You, Gayle, can take the one with the engine change and Jim you take your plane if it's flyable. I have to debrief Admiral Halsey personally.' Then he said, 'In the meantime, I have a set of quarters that have been vacated. We'll stay there tonight.' We went over to these quarters and he said, 'I think I know where the guy kept his liquor and I think both of you need a shot of whiskey,' which we didn't turn down.

'We went to the quarters where I was going to bunk - it was all blacked out. Of course, Helen, my wife, had no idea where I was, whether I was alive or not. There was a telephone on my bedside table and I asked 'Brig' if it could be used to call Helen in Manoa. 'Brig' said, 'Impossible, as all the phones are out. Only official lines are open.' I said, 'OK', so as I sat there and looked at that damn phone, I thought, 'What the hell; give it a chance.' So I picked up the phone, got a dial tone and dialled my wife's number, which I'll never forget - 98114 - and she answered the phone on the bedside table in our home in Manoa Valley. We talked for a long time. I gave her what information I had, that the *Enterprise* had not been sunk as reported and that I was going back to the ship the next morning.'

THE AIR WAR AT SEA IN THE SECOND WORLD WAR

Twenty-two-year-old Richard M. 'Ricky' Dolim was at work on the overhead crane in the foundry at Pearl Harbor when the first bomb went off. His father Augustine also worked in the naval dockyards, but on Sundays, he would take his fishing boat out of Kewalo Basin. Normally, his youngest son Abe would be with him but on this particular Sunday, the 19-year-old attended 7 o'clock mass and returned to the family home in Kimuki where the front porch looked down towards Pearl. When he returned home, 'Abe' for some reason turned around and looked out. He saw white puffs over Pearl and was surprised. 'What were the navy doing having gun practice on Sunday?' While Abe Dolim watched the whole attack from the front porch, his older brother 'Ricky' was in the thick of it.

'The first explosion shook like crazy. I hollered down to the lead man, 'What the heck's going on?' I was in this overhead crane, about 30 ft off the floor. We had a big, wide-open door at the end of the shop and being that you're in the crane, you couldn't look up because you were up against the bulkhead. The crane was shaking and I hollered at 'Charlie', so he walked down to the big door and looked up. He yelled back, 'Ah, just manoeuvres.' We had been having a lot of that stuff the past year or so. Just then, they must have hit the *Oklahoma* or *Arizona* or something, because boy, I'm telling you, the crane really shook. I climbed out of the cab and came down the ladder. I wanted to see these manoeuvres because they must have been really good.

'I ran down to the end of the shop to the doors and looked up. I couldn't believe my eyes. These airplanes were going after the *Cassin* and the *Downes* and the *Pennsylvania* and when one of them banked I saw the big red moons on it. I just couldn't believe it. Then I saw another one bank and I could see the tracer bullets it was firing. It was real bullets. I hollered words that I can't use right now.

'I ran the whole length of the shop yelling, 'It's the real thing.' Everybody ran behind me and we ran across the street, through the Pattern Shop, picking up some pattern makers working there. Right behind the shop was this big, old lumber pile – two by fours, two by twelves and stacked about 3 ft off the ground. We dived under there. We stayed there – under the woodpile – scared as hell. From our vantage point under the pile, we could see more airplanes living. Nobody was firing back at the planes at that point. Boy, were we scared. After a while, a truck full of marines came driving through that lumberyard and rounded us all out from under that woodpile. They handed each of us rifles, gas masks and tin helmets. No ammunition. We questioned that and they said, 'Don't worry. If they attack, we'll issue ammunition. You guys are going to have to help us defend this place.'

'And then we saw the *Oklahoma*. We didn't know it was the *Oklahoma* until somebody told us. It was in the middle of the harbour and it was over on its side. We were only about 200 yards from where the *Pennsylvania*, *Cassin* and the *Downes* were in dry dock. The *Pennsylvania* didn't look like it was badly damaged, but the *Cassin* and the *Downes* were on fire. Behind there, they had a marine way, a track that runs down into the water. There, in that floating dry dock was the *Shaw*, a four-stacker destroyer and it was really burning. I mean, they really blasted it. And that was a good-sized marine way. It could handle a destroyer. The *Helena* and the *Honolulu* were tied up side by side on 1010 dry dock. *Helena* was on the outside and it was going down, they were pumping water from it. They hit the *Honolulu* too but mostly with bombs, because they couldn't get to it with torpedoes. It was havoc; we were all scared; we didn't know what to do.

'We were ordered back to our shops to await further orders. A truck would come by and load a bunch of us guys on it. They trucked a lot of sand in and they dumped it on the docks. We were given shovels and they said, 'Shovel.' Because they couldn't put the fires out on the *Cassin* and *Downes* with water, they wanted us to shovel sand on them from the docks. You had to be pretty good to heave a shovel full of sand from the dock and hit the boat. The best way to have put the fire out was to flood the dry dock, but the *Pennsylvania* was also in there and they were repairing the four shafts on it, so they had pulled the propellers off and pulled the shafts out. That left four big cavities back there that they just couldn't plug up. Finally, the sand wasn't working and the fires became very dangerous, so they flooded the dry dock and sunk the *Pennsylvania* putting the fires out on the *Cassin* and *Downes*.

'We were walking up and down that dock, trying to help. They were pulling bodies out of the water and laying them on 1010 dry dock, which was the longest dock in the world at one time. And, so help me God, I remember four rows of bodies. They would cover them up with canvas. Some of the guys, when they pulled them out, they would be missing an arm. It was terrible. One particular scene I will never forget. I saw a sailor that was pinned up against the bulkhead by a boiler. A bomb exploded and blew this boiler off its mounting and pinned this sailor up against the bulkhead. It took three days to get him out of there. And the boiler was hot. The stench was terrible. I became a pretty mature 22-year-old after that.'

THE AIR WAR AT SEA IN THE SECOND WORLD WAR

That night, as he went to bed only 100 yards away from where the *Arizona* was blowing up, James Daniels heard her shells keep on 'cooking off'.

'Sometime during the night, one of them cooked off – boom, boom, boom – and a piece of shrapnel went through the side of the wall, through the headboard and fell down at the foot of my bed. That was my third escape of the day and they still hadn't gotten me!

'The next morning, we got a little breakfast and then took off on schedule. By this time, communications had been established with *Enterprise*. They knew we were coming, so the ship had to re-spot the flight-deck to make room to take us aboard. We landed safely and, of course, 'Brig' went right up to Admiral Halsey on the Flag Bridge and made his report.

'That was the beginning of my war!'[65]

Of the 94 ships of the US Pacific Fleet within Pearl Harbor at the time of the attack, 18 (including eight battleships and three cruisers) were damaged and sunk. The *Oklahoma*, *Arizona* and *Utah*, which had been demilitarised and was classified as a target ship, were irretrievably lost. Fifteen of the damaged ships – the destroyers *Cassin*, *Downes* and the *Shaw* and the battleships *Pennsylvania*, *West Virginia*, *California*, *Nevada*, *Maryland* and the *Tennessee* were subsequently repaired and returned to duty as were the minelayer *Oglala*, the seaplane tender *Curtiss*, the repair ship *Vestal* and the naval tug *Sotoyomo*. (In total, 159 US Navy ships were assigned to the Pacific Fleet, 29 having been transferred to the Atlantic Fleet in May 1941; 224 ships were assigned to the Atlantic Fleet.) A total of 2,665 sailors, soldiers and airmen were killed or listed as missing and another 1,800 were wounded and badly injured. Ten ships were at sea within a ten-mile radius of Pearl Harbor during the attack and were safe. Twelve undamaged warships put to sea during and immediately after the attack to hunt for the Japanese fleet. More than 75 per cent of the Hawaiian Air Force was destroyed, the US Army lost 96 aircraft and 128 were damaged and the US Navy and Marines, 92 aircraft lost and 31 damaged. Twenty-nine Japanese aircraft (nine 'Zeke' fighters, five 'Kate' torpedo bombers and 15 'Val' dive bombers) failed to

---

65. Jim Daniels took part in the first offensive on the Marshall Islands in February 1942 where he shot down his first e/a. He flew 55 combat missions in the Pacific. Ordered to LSO (Landing Signals Officer) training, he returned to *Enterprise* as Air Group 10's LSO. During the Korean War, he became Carrier Air Task Group 2 aboard *Essex*, flying 60 missions in jets.

PEARL HARBOR AND THE US PACIFIC FLEET

return to Nagumo's First Air Fleet. One Japanese submarine and six Midget two-man submarines were lost or sunk and 163 men were killed or declared missing in action.

Some measure of revenge for the Japanese attack on Pearl Harbor came in April 1942. In January, Captain Francis S. Low, Admiral King's operations officer, had conceived the idea of flying army B-25B bombers off the deck of an aircraft carrier as a means for raiding Tokyo. Admiral King found the idea interesting and directed his air operations officer, Captain Donald B. Duncan, to work out the details in coordination with the army air force. Lieutenant Colonel James H. Doolittle was selected to lead the raid under Admiral Halsey's operational command. A conventional carrier-borne attack had been ruled out due to the fact that the Japanese were capable of operating shore-based aircraft well beyond carrier strike range and that a line of early-warning picket boats was known to be patrolling the waters at least 500 miles off the Japanese home islands. B-25s could be launched at 500 miles from Tokyo. On 18 April, 16 B-25Bs led by Doolittle took off from the *Hornet*'s flight-deck and carried out a bombing raid on Tokyo, Kobe, Yokohama and Nagoya. All the Mitchells were lost as they tried to find safe landing fields in China, but of the 50 aircrew who bailed out over China, 49 survived. From the aircraft that crash-landed along the coast, the Chinese rescued ten more. The Japanese executed eight men and the others were imprisoned, one to die a PoW. Damage at the targets was minimal but the morale boost was immense.

Chapter 9

Attack On Davao

The squat shapes of the Dornier Do 24 flying boats were hardly visible against the night sky as they droned through the early hours of 23 December 1941. The flying boats of the Royal Netherlands Navy had been briefed to attack Japanese warships at Davao in the Philippines in an attempt to protect Dutch territory in Indonesia. Flying in two groups of three were flying boats X-26, X-27 and X-30 in the first group, followed by X-11, X-12 and X-25. They had taken off at 2 am, the first group from New Guinea and the second from Tondano, Celebes and were bound for their first full-scale attack in the Pacific War. The Dutch had had their eyes on the Japanese long before Pearl Harbor and after there was no doubt about the intentions of the Japs the Dornier flying boats attacked every Japanese vessel they saw. One Dornier had already been lost in this fashion.

The Dutch had always been well aware of the importance of marine reconnaissance in the Dutch East Indies and for many years this had been carried out using Dornier Wal flying boats, some of them ordered from the German government and some built under licence by Aviolanda. But it soon became obvious that a more modern aircraft would be needed and some rough plans were drawn up by the Dutch Navy. These were seen, one day, by a Dornier representative visiting workshops at Morokrembangan, near Surabaya. He asked what the aircraft was and when told that the Dutch would like something of that type for use in the Indies, he took the sketch back to Germany with him. The result was the three-engined Dornier Do 24K which, naturally enough was ordered by the Royal Netherlands Navy.

ATTACK ON DAVAO

The German invasion of the Netherlands on 10 May 1940 rapidly overwhelmed Dutch resistance and The Netherlands Naval Aviation Service (Marineluchtvaartdienst, MLD) aircraft were redeployed to France before the Dutch formally surrendered on 15 May. Shortly after, the MLD was ordered to Britain, where Dutch personnel formed 320 Squadron, RAF Coastal Command in June 1940. A second squadron, 321 Squadron, was also formed, but later merged with 320 Squadron. Other MLD personnel served on MAC ships in the Fleet Air Arm's 860 and 861 Naval Air Squadrons, flying the Fairey Swordfish.

At this time efforts were made to strengthen the MLD in the Dutch East Indies. When the war with Japan began in December 1941, the MLD numbered 130 aircraft; mainly 37 Dornier Do 24 K-1 flying boats and 36 PBY-5 Catalina flying boats. The major base was at Naval Air Station Morokrembangan near Soerabaja in eastern Java. The MLD had secondary bases as well as seaplane tenders that enabled it to spread out and cover the entire Netherlands East Indies. It was organized into 18 squadrons (GVT, Groep Vliegtuigen) of about three aircraft each to provide reconnaissance, anti-submarine patrols and convoy escort in support of Dutch forces.

The first engagement between Dutch and Japanese forces of the Pacific War occurred on 13 December 1941 when Dornier X-22 shot down a Mitsubishi G3M 'Nell' bomber with its 20mm cannon. December 16th saw what may have been the first ever dogfight between two flying boats, Dornier X-30 versus a Kawanishi H6K 'Mavis'. The X-30 hit the 'Mavis' starboard inboard engine, but return fire knocked out the X-30's centre engine and its electrics. The crippled X-30 then successfully withdrew. On 17 December, off the coast of Miri, Borneo, X-32 sank a Japanese destroyer, DD *Shinonome*, with the loss of all 228 on board.

The Japanese invasion of Davao and on Jolo on the island of Mindanao in the Sulu Archipelago on 19 December 1941 was one in a series of advance landings made by Imperial Japanese forces as the first step in their invasion of the Philippines. The purpose was to cut off the possibility of reinforcements reaching Luzon from the south and to complete the encirclement of American forces there, with the secondary purpose of establishing a base from which the

Imperial Japanese 16th Army could launch an invasion of British North Borneo and the Netherlands Indies. The first invasion of the Philippines was at Bataan Island on 8 December 1941. This was followed by Vigan, Aparri, Legaspi, Davao and Jolo over the next few days. Davao City is the economic centre of southern Mindanao and before the start of the war was the hub of Japanese settlement and economic activity in the Philippines. For the invasion of Davao, Major General Shizuo Sakaguchi Imperial Japanese Army's 56th Division organized two detachments totalling 5,000 men. The Miura Detachment, led by Lieutenant Colonel Toshio Miura consisted of the 1st Battalion of the 33rd Infantry Regiment and the Sakaguchi Detachment, led by Sakaguchi himself, consisted of the 146th Infantry Regiment, as well as an armoured and an artillery battalion. Whereas the Imperial Japanese 14th Army was in charge of the invasion of the Philippines, Sakaguchi's forces were under the Imperial Japanese 16th Army and were scheduled to continue to advance south to Tarakan in the Netherlands Indies via Jolo in the Sulu islands after Davao was secured. For the Jolo portion of the mission, Sakaguchi was to be assisted by the Kure SNLF (Special Naval Landing Force), who has just completed their mission to secure Legaspi.

The area of Davao was in theory defended by 2,000 men of the Philippine Commonwealth Army's 101st Infantry Regiment, let by Lieutenant Colonel Roger B. Hilsman. As with other units in the Philippine Army, the force was only partially trained and suffered from a serious shortage of equipment.

Davao was of concern to the Imperial Japanese Navy, as it had an American naval base in Malalag Bay and was only 500 miles from Palau, the major Japanese military centre in the western Pacific. However, at the start of the war, only the small seaplane tender USS *William B. Preston*, with three operational Consolidated PBY Catalinas was in the harbour. From February to November 1941, while the US Asiatic Fleet continued its preparations and some fleet units, including the majority of the destroyers, were sent south, the *William B. Preston* was maintained in readiness in the Philippines for any eventuality. She tended PBYs and occasionally acted as target tug for fleet manoeuvres in the southern islands in the Philippine archipelago. After an overhaul at the Cavite Navy Yard in November, the ship departed the Manila area on 1 December, bound for the south-eastern coast of Mindanao. Upon her arrival in Davao Gulf, she dropped anchor in Malalag Bay, where she was joined by a group of PBYs of the newly formed Patrol Wing 10 which soon commenced patrols. The PBYs reconnoitred several small bays and inlets, looking out for suspicious shipping or for any signs of strange activity.

ATTACK ON DAVAO

Shortly after 0300 on 8 December, the *William B. Preston* picked up the following radio message: *Japan has commenced hostilities. Govern yourselves accordingly.* Soon after the receipt of the notification of war, all three PBYs were readied for operations. Two remained behind while the rest flew off on their first war patrols over the Celebes Sea. The ship, meanwhile, shifted anchorage away from the two moored Catalinas to lessen the chance of one bomb damaging both ship and planes in one fell swoop. Bluejackets on *William B. Preston* belted ammunition for the ship's anti-aircraft defence of four .50-calibre water-cooled Browning machine guns and took down the awnings which had shielded the crew from the tropical sun. Around 0800, the ship's commanding officer, Lieutenant Commander Etheridge Grant, went forward to check the progress of the preparations to slip the anchor chain (should that become necessary). Suddenly a lookout called out, 'Aircraft!' The Japanese launched an attack on Davao with 13 'Val' dive bombers and nine 'Claude' fighters[66] from the aircraft carrier *Ryūjō*, while the destroyers *Hayashio*, *Kuroshio*, *Oyashio* and *Natsushio* made a high-speed run for the entrance to Davao harbour to catch any escaping vessels. Grant sprinted to the bridge as the attacking Japanese aircraft swept around the narrow neck of the land shielding Malalag Bay from the broad Gulf of Davao. The raid was somewhat of a fiasco, as the Japanese pilots did not even recognize the *William B. Preston* as a warship and only managed to destroy the two PBYs riding at their mooring buoys. They sank into the waters of the bay as the survivors, carrying one dead and one wounded comrade with them, swam for shore. Meanwhile, the *William B. Preston* lowered a boat to pick up survivors while she got underway for the open sea. Slipping her anchor chain, the ship zigzagged across the bay as the 'Claudes' and 'Vals' attacked the fleeing tender. Evading the bombs, the ship managed to emerge from the attack unscathed and returned to the bay to pick up her boat and the survivors from the two lost Catalinas.

Later that day, upon receipt of orders dispatching her to Moro Gulf, *William B. Preston* got underway to establish another advance base for PBYs at Polloc Bay. Arriving off the mouth of Moro Bay in the afternoon, the ship lay to until the following morning, 9 December, when she entered the bay. An explosion ahead of the ship sent the American bluejackets to their

---

66. Aichi D3A Type 99 carrier-borne dive bomber and the Mitsubishi A5M (Navy Type 96), the world's first monoplane shipboard fighter to enter service.

general quarters stations before it was discovered that the local fishermen were just out dynamiting for their catch. A PBY was awaiting her arrival and she commenced tending operations. Three more Catalinas and two Vought OS2U Kingfisher catapult-launched observation floatplanes from the seaplane tender *Heron* arrived later in the afternoon. After being informed that Japanese troops had landed north of Gagayan and were marching overland to Polloc, the ship prepared to get underway and dispatched the PBYs on patrol over the Celebes Sea. Leaving word that the planes were to rendezvous with the ship at Tutu Bay, Jolo, *William B. Preston* got underway on 10 December. The *William B. Preston* arrived at Tutu Bay later that day and found the PBYs awaiting her, after having found no trace of enemy activity during their patrol sweeps.

Next day, the US aircraft were again sent out on patrols while the ship upped anchor and proceeded for Tawi Tawi, receiving word en route that the PBYs were to return to Lake Lanao in Mindanao and the OS2Us were to rendezvous with the ship at Tawi Tawi. Although she had never hoisted aboard any aircraft before, *William B. Preston*'s bluejackets rigged up a crude cradle between the two 50-foot motor-boats aft and provided padding for the Kingfisher's centre float with mattresses and life jackets. One OS2U was taken aboard and berthed in this fashion while the other was towed astern. Smooth seas and a 15-knot pace facilitated the towing operation, and the two Kingfishers arrived safely at Tarakan, Borneo. Met by two Dutch destroyers the *William B. Preston* made port at Tarakanbut and was soon underway again, this time for Balikpapan, Borneo, joining five ships from the Asiatic Fleet Two hours after arrival, the *William B. Preston* received orders to accompany the small fleet to Makassar and got underway on 13 December. The ship arrived at Sourabaya, Java, shortly before Christmas.[67]

The Japanese invasion force under the overall command of Admiral Raizo Tanaka departed Palau on 17 December in five transports, escorted by the light cruiser *Jintsu* and six destroyers (*Amatsukaze, Hatsukaze, Kuroshio, Oyashio, Hayashio* and *Natsushio*), with the aircraft carrier *Ryūjō* and the seaplane carrier *Chitose* and the cruisers *Nachi, Haguro* and *Myōkō* providing distant cover. On the afternoon of 19 December *Ryūjō* launched aircraft to

---

67. *Dictionary of American Naval Fighting Ships Vol. VIII*, James L. Mooney, Editor, Naval Historical Center Dept of the Navy Washington: 1981.

ATTACK ON DAVAO

destroy the radio station at Cape San Augustin and the *Chitose* launched reconnaissance aircraft, which flew over Davao.

The Japanese transports arrived at Davao by midnight and landing commenced from 0400 hours, with the Miura Detachment landing to the north and the Sakaguchi Detachment landing to the southwest of the city. The only opposition was a single machine gun squad, which attacked the Miura Detachment before it was destroyed by a direct hit by a shell fired from a Japanese destroyer. However, since the Miura Detachment suffered casualties, Major General Shizuo Sakaguchi was forced to commit reserve forces he was holding back for the Jolo portion of the operation. By 1030 Colonel Roger Hilsman pulled his men out of the city northwest into the hills.[68] By 1500 hours the city and airfield were in Japanese hands and by evening a seaplane base was established to the south of the urban area.

On 20 December, as Sakaguchi was reorganizing his forces into nine transports for the landing on Jolo Island, he was attacked by a force of nine USAAF Boeing B-17 Flying Fortress bombers which had launched from Darwin, Australia. Visibility was poor and the bombers caused little damage.

It was not until the night of 23 December that any organised attack by the Royal Netherlands Navy was planned. This was the mission of the six flying boats on their way to Davao. In the lead was X-27 as the six aircraft flew at 13,000 ft over a changing cloudscape. Suddenly the clouds increased in size and X-27 found herself cut off from the other flying boats. It was not until 5 am that the clouds began thinning and when the captain of the X-27 looked about him he could only see one other flying boat. Away in the distance a few fires could be seen against the dim morning light. It was Davao and it seemed as if the Americans had already visited the town. Down below were Japanese cruisers, a destroyer and a tanker together with several merchant ships. It seemed as if the excitement was about to begin - and it did!

Anti-aircraft fire came leaping up at the two flying boats and X-27 was hit in the starboard engine which spewed oil and ground to a stop. At the same time the captain noticed that the three aircraft in the second group

---

68. Two weeks into the conflict, newspaper reports described Colonel Hilsman as still holding Davao. Later reports reflected his retreat to Malaybalay after facing overwhelming Japanese forces, followed by another move onto the island of Negros after which he was captured by the Japanese once all the islands were surrendered during 1942.

had caught up with him and he altered course slightly to make way for them. As he did this, he heard the rear gunner signalling 'J' – the sign that he had spotted enemy fighter aircraft.

By now heading straight for Davao, X-27 was losing speed steadily and was unable to keep up with the other flying boats. As they flew over the Japanese shipping the crew saw a tanker on fire while a cruiser which had been refuelling was desperately trying to get away from the flames. It was good to know that the other Dorniers had been doing their work well. But two Japanese catapult fighters had materialised and one repeatedly attacked the flying boat while the other took station 2–3,000 ft below. X-27's captain took what little evasive action he could with his missing engine while the gunners fired resolutely at the fighter. Then a terrific explosion seemed to rent the aircraft amidships. It did not sound like fighter fire, nor yet flak. The commander went back to find out what had happened. As he did so a large piece of shrapnel embedded itself into the aircraft a few inches from his back. The cause of the explosion was discovered when a gunner revealed that an ammunition pan had been incorrectly fitted and had discharged all its shots in one explosion. Meanwhile the rear gun seemed to have been silenced. A few seconds later the rear gunner was seen crawling forward with bullet wounds in his right leg and blood pouring from his stomach. He reported that his gun was severely damaged.

Despite these repeated attacks X-27 kept flying. The pilot had only one idea in mind and that was to get to Davao. Fuel from punctured fuel tanks was swilling around the fuselage as he saw X-30, way ahead, make its attack and then he, too, began his run in over some barracks just as the centre gunner was able to dispose of the troublesome Japanese fighter. The bombs went down and the crew were treated to the gratifying spectacle of a huge fire developing where their bombs had hit. The attack had been successful but there was little opportunity for rejoicing over their part in the raid.

The starboard engine had fallen completely away and the two remaining engines refused to develop full power. All petrol tanks except one had been holed and the fuel awash in the fuselage presented an ever-present danger of fire. It was hopeless trying to maintain height. They had been at 10,000 ft when they attacked and by this time were down to 7,000 ft. A few minutes after the attack the centre gunner came forward to say that there were only 22 gallons of usable fuel left – hardly enough to carry the flying boat half-way back to Davao. Then a sergeant came forward with the idea that they should

Douglas TBD-1 Devastator torpedo plane assigned to Torpedo Squadron VT-6 from the USS *Enterprise* flies over Wake Island during the raid on 24 February 1942.

Dormer Do 24 flying boat X-13 of the Netherlands Naval Aviation Service (Marineluchtvaartdienst, MLD). The first engagement between Dutch and Japanese forces of the Pacific War occurred on 13th December 1941 when Dornier X-22 shot down a Mitsubishi G3M 'Nell' bomber with its 20mm cannon. X-13 was lost near Roti on 7 February 1942.

A mushroom cloud rises from the USS *Lexington* on 8 May 1942 probably from the detonation of torpedo warheads stowed in the starboard side of the hangar, aft, that followed an explosion amidships and the crew began abandoning ship at 1707 hours. Some 216 crewmen were killed and 2,735 were evacuated.

Zuikaku crewmen service aircraft on the flight deck on 5 May 1942 before the Battle of the Coral Sea.

Bombing Squadron Five (VB-5) SBD-3 Dauntless scout bombers spotted forward on the flight deck of the USS *Yorktown* during operations in the Coral Sea in April 1942. The battle was a strategic victory for the United States. The Japanese invasion fleet turned back, saving the region that a Japanese air base at Port Moresby would have dominated. The *Yorktown* is hit on the port side, amidships, by a Type 91 aerial torpedo during the mid-afternoon attack on 6 June 1942 by planes from the carrier *Hiryū* during the Battle of Midway. The crippled but still-floating carrier was finally sunk by two torpedoes from Japanese submarine I-168 after she had been taken in tow.

USS *Wasp* entering Hampton Roads 26 May 1942.

Lieutenant Commander Lance E. "Lem" Massey seated in his TBD Devastator at Pearl Harbor on 24 May 1942. He was killed while leading VT-3 during the Battle of Midway on 4 June that same year.

Captain Richard Eugene Fleming of Marine Scout Bombing Squadron 241 who was killed during the Battle of Midway on 4 June 1942 during an attack on the Japanese heavy cruiser *Mikuma*. The posthumous award of the Medal of Honor was bestowed on the brave Vought SB2U Vindicator dive bomber pilot for his heroism and self sacrifice.

SBD-3 Dauntless bombers of VS-8 over the burning and sinking Japanese cruiser *Mikuma* on 6 June 1942.

A SBD Dauntless passing beached Japanese transports burning on Guadalcanal on 16 November 1942 during the Battle for the Solomons.

SBD-3 Dauntless, F-4F-4 Wildcat and Grumman TBF-1 Avengers preparing to take off from the USS *Enterprise*, northeast of Nouméa, New Caledonia on 2 May 1943.

Crash landing of a Grumman F6F-3 Hellcat of Fighting Squadron 2 (VF-2) aboard the USS *Enterprise*, into the carrier's port side 20mm gun gallery on 10 November 1943. Lieutenant Walter L. Chewning, Jr. USNR, the Catapult Officer, is seen climbing up the plane's side to assist the pilot from the burning aircraft. The pilot, Ensign Byron M. Johnson, escaped without significant injury. *Enterprise* was then en route to support the Gilberts Operation.

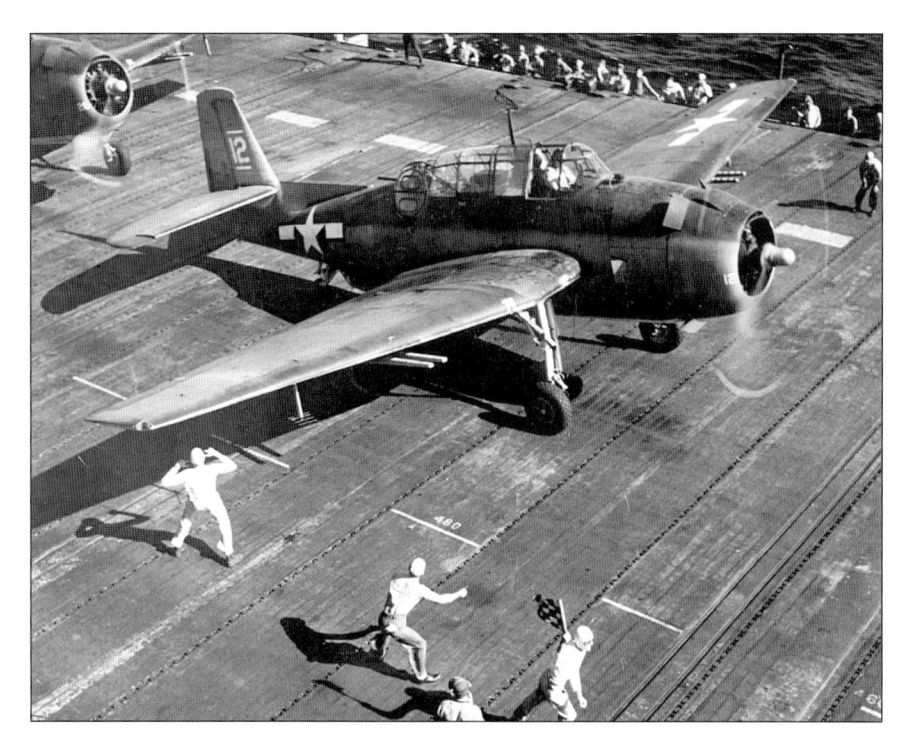

Grumman Avenger of Torpedo Squadron (VT) 8 on 10 June 1944 poised for launch from *Bunker Hill* for a strike against Saipan. Note the rocket rails under the wings.

USS *Bunker Hill* is near missed by a Jap bomber on 19 June 1944 during the Battle of Philippine Sea.

Operations in the Philippine Sea in late 44 with Air Group (CVG) 11 on deck of the USS *Hornet*. F6F Hellcats of Fighting Squadron 11 warming up are followed by Avengers of Torpedo Squadron 11 (wings folded back) and SB2C Helldivers of Bomb Squadron 11 (wings folded up).

Kamikaze attack on USS *Intrepid* off Luzon in the Philippines on 25 November 1944. For over three hours and under constant threat of further air attack, her sailors struggled to bring roaring gasoline fires under control. Remaining on her station to recover her aloft aircraft, the battered *Intrepid* withdrew on 26 November for repairs. Arriving at San Francisco on 30 December, the *Intrepid* was repaired, modernized and re-joined the fight on 15 February 1945. Some 59 enlisted men and six officers were killed or listed as missing as a result of the attack.

Kamikaze strike on the USS *Essex* off Luzon on 25 November 1944.

FAA Fairey Firefly over *Indefatigable*.

A FAA Grumman Avenger being armed on HMS *Indomitable* during Operation 'Meridian'. Meridian I', the first strike on Japanese oil refineries on Sumatra, was originally scheduled to take place on the 22nd. However, a prolonged tropical storm of high winds and driving rain on the night of 21st/22nd January and again on the night of 22/23rd each time caused a 24-hour delay.

Oil installations burning on Palembang following a strike by FAA aircraft.

Supermarine Seafire hits the barrier on HMS *Indefatigable* after returning from a strike on the Japanese oil refinery at Pangkalan Brandan, Sumatra in January 1945.

FAA Avengers over Palembang.

Left: Pladjoe refinery on the north bank of the Komerine on fire during the attack on the night of Tuesday 23rd/Wednesday, 24 January 1945.

Below: HMS *Illustrious* entering the Captain Cook Graving Dock in Sydney on 11 February 1945.

Lieutenant Walter 'Wally' Thomas Stradwick a FAA Corsair pilot who was the first British aviator killed over Japan in the war, on 18 July 1945.

Ensign Kiyoshi Ogawa hit Bunker Hill on 11 May 1945. Op Kikusui.

HMS *Formidable*, which was hit by a Kamikaze off Okinawa on 4 May 1945, killing 2 officers and 6 ratings and wounding 55 other crewmen.

A Seafire crash lands during 'Meridian' on 17 June 1945.

USS *Bunker Hill* which was hit by two Kamikazes in 30 seconds on 11 May 1945 off Kyushu during the Battle of Okinawa. Of the 2,600 ship's company, 389 personnel were killed or officially listed as missing and 264 were wounded.

The damage to the deck of the USS *Bunker Hill* after a kamikaze-attack on 11 May 1945.

Surrender of Japan, 2 September 1945: US Navy carrier planes fly in formation over the US and British fleets in Tokyo Bay during surrender ceremonies. The battleship USS *Missouri*, where the ceremonies took place, is at left. The light cruiser USS *Detroit* is in the right distance. Aircraft include Grumman TBM Avenger, Grumman F6F Hellcat, Curtiss SB2C Helldiver and Vought F4U Corsair types.

Aircraft fly in formation over the USS *Missouri* during the Jap surrender ceremony, Tokyo Bay 2 Sept 1945

ATTACK ON DAVAO

try and pump some of the loose fuel back into the one usable tank. The crew set to work and succeeded in pumping a considerable quantity of fuel back into the tank.

The commander, taking no unnecessary chances, had already transmitted the message that he was desperately short of fuel in the hopes that X-30 was not so far ahead that she could not hear. There was no acknowledgement of his message. It seemed as if X-27 was out on its own as it flew along the coast. They passed a convoy of two Japanese warships with three merchant ships but luckily no anti-aircraft fire was put up.

From time to time the engines stopped completely and when they had reached Tinanca Point they were down to 1,500 ft. A brisk wind had sprung up from the north-east and the sea was turning decidedly choppy. X-27 managed to get past the Kawio Islands, by which time it was down to only 60 ft, with no hope of ever climbing again. Then the engines stopped yet again. This time there was nothing the pilot could do to keep the flying boat out of the sea. It hit the water hard, bounced twice with bone-shaking jars and then settled into the water. The crew moved up to the front of the flying boat and did their best to make the wounded gunner comfortable. Still hoping that his radio message had been heard by X-30, the commander decided to wait in the aircraft for one hour in the hope that the other flying boat would return. To delay longer would be dangerous because of the Japanese convoy they had passed before ditching. This was steadily bearing down on them.

Only three-quarters of an hour had passed when the commander gave the order for the dinghy to be launched. He had noticed that the flying boat was drifting towards the convoy and this had cut down the time he had reckoned to spend on board the aircraft. Most of the crew were already in the dinghy and were preparing to get the wounded gunner on board when they heard the sound of aero-engines. Sure enough, it was X-30 but the flying boat passed by to starboard and, apparently did not see the stranded aircraft. Taking a Very pistol, the commander fired a low-trajectory shot, anxious not to catch the attention of the Japanese convoy. X-30 then turned, made a quick circuit of the ditched flying boat and came in for a tricky tail-wind landing on a rough sea. With the crew of X-27 safely on-board, X-30 made a successful take-off and 20 minutes later touched down at Tahuna.

Once back at their respective bases the crews of the flying boats were able to piece together the full story of the raid. X-30 had made a successful attack as the crew of X-27 had witnessed. The gunners had also claimed a Japanese fighter shot down on the way home. X-26, the other aircraft which should have attacked in the first group with X-27, had eventually found Davao beach where the pilot made an unsuccessful attack on a light cruiser.

The Jolo invasion force departed Davao on 23 December, reaching its destination the following afternoon. Jolo, the capital of the former Sultanate of Sulu, was defended by only 300 members of the Philippine Constabulary. The Japanese landed on the morning of 25 December with no resistance. The advance landings by the Japanese in southern Mindanao and the Sulu Island had little to no impact on the overall campaign in the Philippines, but placed the Japanese in a good position for the planned invasion of Borneo and the Netherlands East Indies in early 1942.[69]

The MLD fought about 95 combat actions before it was forced to evacuate to Ceylon and Australia. They lost 95 per cent of their aircraft and half of their personnel. On 3 March 1942 nine MLD Dornier and Catalina flying boats were destroyed in the Japanese air attack on Broome in Australia. About 58 MLD personnel were killed, wounded, or missing. The Dutch forces in Indonesia capitulated on 8 March. On 1 July in Ceylon, 321 Squadron was re-formed under the command of Willem van Prooijen with MLD Catalinas. The PBYs in Australia were transferred to Ceylon and the surviving Dorniers were sold to the Australian government. The flight school was relocated to the United States.

---

69. See the story by B. van der Klaauw based on the official report by the Commander of Dornier X-21, which appeared in *RAF Flying Review*, XVI. No.9.

Chapter 10

Battle of the Coral Sea (4–8 May 1942)

In the Pacific five naval battles would be fought between the aircraft carriers of Japan and the United States. Critically, four naval battles involving the US Navy and the Imperial Japanese Navy would occur within a six-month period during 1942 and their outcome would affect the whole course of the war. But for six months following Pearl Harbor, America and her allies were powerless to stop the Japanese advance, which overran critical islands like the Philippines, East Indies, Guam and Wake. To turn the tide, the United States needed to recapture these islands and others under Japanese control.

On 23 December 1941, the Japanese attacked Wake Island in force and captured the atoll. Vice Admiral William S. Pye, by then the acting Commander in Chief, Pacific Fleet decided not to risk his carriers even though Fleet Intelligence estimated that at least two Japanese carriers and battleships and heavy cruisers were in the vicinity of Wake Island. Pye recalled Task Force 14, commanded by Rear Admiral Frank Jack Fletcher aboard *Saratoga* and Task Force 11 commanded by Vice Admiral Wilson Brown on *Lexington* to Pearl Harbor. On 31 December Admiral Chester W. Nimitz, who took formal command of the Pacific Fleet at Pearl Harbor, began rebuilding his forces for the strike back across the Pacific.[70] Nimitz could immediately call upon three aircraft carriers: the *Saratoga*, *Lexington* and *Enterprise*. The *Lexington* and the *Saratoga* had been commissioned in 1927 and were laid down originally as battle cruisers but completed as carriers by a provision of the Washington

---

70. Admiral Ernest J. King became the new Commander-in-Chief, United States Fleet, in Washington DC.

THE AIR WAR AT SEA IN THE SECOND WORLD WAR

Naval Treaty of 1922, which specified limits on naval armaments that would have resulted in both ships having to be scrapped. At 36,000 tons, they were the largest carriers operated by the US during the war. The three carriers, or flattops as they are known in navy parlance, together with five others, *Langley*, *Ranger*, *Wasp*, *Hornet* and *Yorktown*, would form the backbone of the Pacific Fleet from 1941 to 1945. (On 11 January 1942, *Saratoga* was torpedoed by the Japanese submarine I-6 near Johnson Island and had to return to the West Coast for repairs. The carrier remained out of action until April and Nimitz would have to make do with only three fleet carriers.)

After the expiration of the Washington Treaty and its limits, *Hornet* (and *Essex*) were authorised in the Naval Expansion Act of 1938. In order to expedite construction, *Hornet* was laid down in late September 1939 as a full-scale repeat of *Yorktown*'s proven design. *Ranger* was commissioned in 1934 as the first American ship designed and built from the keel up as an aircraft carrier. At 13,800 tons, she represented the smaller carrier school of thought within Naval Aviation in the 1920s.[71] *Yorktown* had been the fourth carrier to join the Pacific Fleet after being transferred from the Atlantic shortly after Pearl Harbor.

At the end of January 1942, Admiral Halsey's TF 8 and Fletcher's TF 17 prepared to go on the offensive. Halsey's targets were the seaplane bases at Wotje and Maloelap in the eastern Marshalls and Japanese shipping and aircraft at Kwajalein Atoll while Fletcher's were Makin in the northern Gilberts and Jaluit and Mili in the southern Marshalls.

The two task forces approached their respective targets from the direction of Samoa and split off on the evening of 31 January to launch their air strikes before sunrise on 1 February. Halsey took *Enterprise* within 40 miles of Wotje before launching his air strikes. The first attack, principally against the air base at Roi-Namur Island on the north end of the lagoon at Kwajalein and Kwajalein Island on the southern end, was by 37 Douglas SBD-2 dive bombers and nine Douglas TBD-1 Devastator torpedo bombers of Torpedo 6 led by 'Brig' Young, the *Enterprise* air group commander. On the way in, Young's force had difficulty identifying their targets in the early morning mist and surprise was lost. Four Dauntlesses were shot down in the attack on the airfield but the rest of the force returned with claims of two ships sunk and having caused damage to at least seven others. Eighteen Japanese aircraft

---

71. *Prologue To War. Target: Japan, Challenge Magazine, Second World War Special* (Vol. 1, No. 1, 1994).

BATTLE OF THE CORAL SEA

were destroyed or badly damaged and the area commander, Rear Admiral Yashiro was killed.

F4Fs and later SBDs, which had returned from the raid on Kwajalein, hit Taroa airfield on Maloelap Atoll. Lieutenant (jg) Wilmer E. Rawie became the first US Navy fighter pilot in the Second World War to shoot down an enemy aircraft when he destroyed a 'Zero'. Wotje too was attacked initially by F4Fs, each carrying 100 lb bombs and gunfire from Rear Admiral Raymond A. Spruance's cruisers and destroyers. At around midday, 'Brig' Young led another force of eight Dauntlesses and nine TBDs carrying bombs against Wotje and the seaplane base suffered substantial damage. Bad weather, especially over Jaluit, hampered the strikes by TF 17 and Commander Curtis S. Smiley, *Yorktown*'s air group commander, lost seventeen Dauntlesses and eleven Devastators while damage was only inflicted on two Japanese ships in Jaluit harbour. Results of the attacks on Makin and Mili were also poor. One Japanese four-engined flying boat that attacked the task force was shot down by *Yorktown*'s F4Fs. Given the weather conditions and the high losses, all further strikes were cancelled. Among the lessons learned from these early skirmishes was that American carriers would have to embark more than one squadron of F4F-3 Wildcats because not only would they have to escort the bombers and fly CAP, but additionally they would be required to carry out attacks on enemy shipping and targets ashore.

A typical air group consisted of 18 Wildcats, 36 SBD Dauntlesses and 18 TBD Devastators, or 72 aircraft. The SBD, which equipped both the scout and bomber units, was considered obsolete, but the prolonged development of its intended successor, the Curtiss SB2C Helldiver, which did not finally enter service until the end of 1943, saw the Dauntless enjoy a long and successful career, which was unsurpassed by any other dive bomber in the world. Designed in 1934, the TBD-1 was the first all-metal monoplane carrier aircraft in the US Navy when it joined the fleet in 1937, but by modern standards, it was too slow, had a poor rate of climb and its range was limited. It also carried a very unreliable torpedo, the Bliss-Leavitt Mk.13, whose pre-war development had suffered badly because of lack of funding and limited testing. This torpedo could be dropped only at a height of 100 ft or less if it was not to break up on impact, porpoise, or dive to the bottom. It was also slow, left a visible wake and could be avoided with ease.

The attacks made by TF 8 and TF 17 in the Marshalls and Gilberts were mounted as a diversion for the operation to attack Wake Island.

THE AIR WAR AT SEA IN THE SECOND WORLD WAR

Admiral Halsey's TF 8 had left Pearl Harbor on 14 February and ten days later *Enterprise* dispatched 36 bombers and six fighters against the island. Destruction, which was only limited, included the sinking of one enemy patrol boat and several Kawanishi flying boats. Following the raid, Halsey retired north-eastward to refuel and then sailed westward to attack Marcus Island. No Japanese aircraft attempted to intercept but one SBD was shot down by anti-aircraft fire. TF 8 then headed for Pearl Harbor, arriving there on 10 March. It would be nearly another month before Halsey again put to sea.

By now, the Japanese threat to Nouméa on New Caledonia and Port Moresby was very real and it was feared also that the enemy could use Rabaul, 3,000 miles from Pearl Harbor, as a base for further Japanese expansion operations in the Pacific, so Admiral King instructed Vice Admiral Wilson Brown commanding TF 11 on *Lexington* to carry out a carrier strike on Rabaul. It was a risky enterprise. Refuelling the task force so far from home could only be undertaken by the slow-moving fleet oilers that would be vulnerable to submarine attack and battle repairs were practically impossible in the South Pacific, while the charts of the waters around New Guinea, New Britain, New Ireland and the Solomons were years out of date. Finally, the task force could expect to see Japanese search aircraft of the 24th Air Flotilla up to 600 miles from their base on Rabaul. Brown hoped that he could avoid detection and launch his strike 125 miles off Rabaul, but on 20 February, *Lexington*'s radar detected a Japanese floatplane only 43 miles from the task force while still only 450 miles east of Rabaul. *Lexington*'s F4F CAP shot down the enemy floatplane and a second Japanese aircraft but at least one other flying boat escaped and the defences were alerted.

A short while later nine Mitsubishi G4M 'Betty' twin-engined bombers attacked TF 11. F4Fs, however, intercepted them and shot down all the raiders, with no damage caused to the task force. When eight more 'Bettys' attacked, these too were dealt with by the Wildcats. Lieutenant Commander Edward L. 'Butch' O'Hare single-handedly destroyed three and seriously damaged two more in six minutes. One of the crippled 'Bettys' attempted to crash dive on the 'Lady Lex', but splashed 1,500 yards off the carrier's port bow. In all, 15 'Bettys' and two Mavis flying boats were destroyed, while VF-3 from the *Lexington* led by Lieutenant Commander John S. 'Jimmy' Thach lost two Wildcats with one pilot killed and another wounded. The enemy losses delayed the planned Japanese landings at Lae and Salamaua on

BATTLE OF THE CORAL SEA

the north coast of New Guinea for five days, when replacement aircraft were redeployed to the south-west Pacific. 'Butch' O'Hare was officially credited with five Japanese aircraft destroyed on 20 February and was later awarded the Medal of Honor. O'Hare, now commanding the 'Big E's CVG-6, was killed on the night of 26 November 1943 when he hit the water while taking evasive action after being fired on by a TBM Avenger.

The next attack on Rabaul, scheduled for early March, would require two carriers and *Lexington* and *Yorktown* were duly selected, but Japanese landings on 8 March on the north coast of New Guinea resulted in a change of target for Task Forces 11 and 17. On 10 March the carriers closed to within 45 miles of the Papuan shoreline before launching 18 F4Fs, 61 SBDs and 25 TBDs in a raid on the airstrip at Lae and Salamaua harbour. (A reconnaissance the day before had revealed that the towering Owen Stanley Mountains, which form the spine of New Guinea's Papuan Peninsula, could be crossed using a 7,500-foot-high mountain pass that was generally free of mist between 0700 and 1100 hours. The single TBD squadron (Torpedo 2 from *Lexington*) carrying torpedoes were able to take advantage of a fortuitous updraft to clear the mountains.) The American pilots found few Japanese aircraft on the airstrip at Lae, but there were 16 ships in the Lae-Salamaua area. Due mainly to the combination of surprise and lack of fighter cover, three transports were sunk and six other ships (including a light cruiser and two destroyers) were damaged and caused almost 400 enemy casualties, all for the loss of one Dauntless to anti-aircraft fire.

Despite these setbacks, by mid-April 1942 the Japanese were well on the way to total domination in the New Guinea/New Britain/Solomon Islands area of the South Pacific. The decision was taken to send a Japanese seaborne task force to take Tulagi in the Solomons and Port Moresby in New Guinea with the intention of cutting the America-Australia supply route and at the same time establishing a base for the invasion of Australia itself. The main Japanese task force assembled at Truk in the Carolines and on 30 April sailed south towards Rabaul at the northernmost tip of New Britain, where Vice Admiral Shigeyoshi Inouye was assembling five separate naval forces to carry out his invasion plans. In addition, he could call upon over 140 land-based fighters and bombers.

As the Japanese made their preparations for the invasion of Port Moresby and the occupation of Tulagi, the US Navy, forewarned by signals intelligence of the impending operation, made their dispositions to counter it. On 1 May two carrier task forces, TF 17, built around USS *Yorktown* (Rear Admiral Frank Jack Fletcher), with three heavy cruisers and six destroyers (one escorting an oiler) and Task Force 11 consisting of USS *Lexington* (Rear Admiral Aubrey B. Fitch), two heavy cruisers and seven destroyers rendezvoused off Espiritu Santo. From Sydney TF 44, consisting of the heavy cruiser HMAS *Australia* and the light cruiser HMAS *Hobart*, under the command of Rear Admiral John Gregory Crace RN, departed Sydney (eventually to join the carriers on 4 May).[72] The cruiser USS *Chicago* and the destroyer USS *Perkins*, also part of TF 44, came up from Nouméa. On 2 May the two task forces separated when Fletcher, leaving Fitch replenishing, steamed north-west to a reach a position 550 miles south of Guadalcanal by dawn on the 3rd.

Ranged against them were Rear Admiral Takeo Takagi's main strike force, comprising the aircraft carriers *Zuikaku* and *Shōkaku*, two cruisers and a screen of destroyers. The carriers between them had on board 42 A6M5 'Zero' fighters, 42 'Kate' torpedo bombers and 41 'Val' dive bombers. The US Navy outnumbered the Japanese in dive bombers, but more importantly, American carriers were equipped with radar and many of the *Yorktown*'s aircraft carried IFF (Identification, Friend or Foe) equipment, two innovations the Japanese carriers lacked.

The Port Moresby invasion force consisted of five navy and six army transports plus a number of other vessels and a destroyer escort. The Japanese strike force sailed from Truk on a course well to the east of the Solomons in order to avoid American reconnaissance aircraft for as long as possible.

On 3 May, under cover from the *Shōhō*'s group, Inouye ordered a small strategic strike force under Rear Admiral Shima to attack and occupy Tulagi.

---

72. Crace was an admiral in the Royal Navy and he commanded Task Force 44 consisting of the heavy cruiser HMAS *Australia* and the light cruiser HMAS *Hobart* and a destroyer escort. On 1 May TF 44 departed Sydney under orders to join the US carriers. After refuelling from HMAS *Kurumba* in Hervey Bay the two cruisers proceeded east, joining the US force on 4 May. On that day a concentration of transports and warships was sighted at Rabaul by Australian-based aerial reconnaissance and *Shoho* was seen 40 miles south of Bougainville. The 5th May was spent refuelling, and on the 6th, the entire force was amalgamated as TF 17. Crace, with *Australia*, *Hobart*, the heavy cruiser USS *Chicago* and the destroyers USS *Perkins* and *Walke*, commanded the Support Group, designated Task Group 17.3.

BATTLE OF THE CORAL SEA

By 1100 hours, the island was under Japanese domination and a seaplane base with six A6M2-N floatplane fighters was established on the island. The Japanese carrier striking force remained north of Rabaul. Fletcher heard of the occupation of Tulagi that evening. He detached his oiler and its escorting destroyer and proceeded north at high speed.

Task Force 17 reached a position 110 miles south of Tulagi on the morning of 4 May and at 0630 launched a strike comprising 12 TBD torpedo bombers and 28 SBD dive bombers from *Yorktown* to attack Tulagi. At 0630 hours the first aerial strike force consisting of 12 Devastators of VT-5 (Torpedo) and 28 Dauntless dive bombers of VS-5 (Scout) and VB-5 (bomber) headed for Tulagi. Bad visibility shielded the aircraft until they were 20 miles from the island, which was just as well because the crews could only rely on their own machine-guns for protection; all 18 Wildcat fighters of VF-42 (Fighting Squadron 42) were required for combat air patrol over the carrier.

The attack went in between 0815 and 0830, catching the Japanese by surprise. The two Dauntless squadrons and one Devastator squadron made their attacks on shipping and land targets on Tulagi. Each squadron attacked targets independently, as was the practice of the time. Altogether, two air strikes succeeded in sinking two small minesweepers, while the destroyer *Kikuzuki* was damaged beyond repair and a patrol craft was badly damaged for the loss of one Devastator. Minor damage was inflicted on a minelayer and supplies on the beach. The torpedo bombers sank the minesweeper *Tama Maru*. A second strike destroyed five of the six aircraft based there and a third sank four landing barges. A third attack by 21 Dauntlesses dive-bombed landing barges but they succeeded in sinking only four. Three aircraft from the second strike were lost, the others suffering no casualties. The most successful action was the destruction of five Kawanishi H6K 'Mavis' flying boats. By 1632 hours, the last of the returning bombers was safely back on the carrier deck of the *Yorktown*. Two Grumman F4F-3 Wildcat fighters, which had strayed off course on the return to the carrier, had crash-landed on Guadalcanal, but their pilots were picked up later and returned to the ship.

Generally, bombing results had been poor and the Devastator had proved most unsatisfactory. The Dauntless strikes had fared little better considering the high number of bombs dropped, but crews were jubilant, believing they had sunk two destroyers, one freighter and four gunboats among others. The strikes gave a valuable edge to the *Yorktown*'s Air Group's efficiency, which had been built up over nine weeks of intensive training. Realising that the Japanese would now be aware that there was at least one American carrier in the offing, Fletcher quickly retired southwards through the night to re-join TF 11 at dawn on 5 May in a position some 400 miles south of Tulagi. This force had been joined by TF 44 the previous day. The Allied force spent the day replenishing. Meanwhile, the Japanese Carrier Strike Force had moved rapidly down the eastern flank of the Solomons and by midday on the 5th they were to the east of San Christobal Island, covering what they anticipated to be the US carriers' line of retreat. Traditionally the American carrier task forces had rapidly cleared the area after a raid. Admiral Takagi's force turned west and passed north of Rennell Island. Allied reconnaissance aircraft failed to find the strike force in the prevailing bad weather.

At 0930 hours on 6 May, Takagi turned south. Throughout that day the opposing forces remained in ignorance of each other's whereabouts. The Japanese carriers rounded San Christobal and steamed westwards to a position 100 miles south of Guadalcanal and then turned south to avoid precipitating a night battle. They flew no searches that day, leaving reconnaissance to the long-range aircraft of the 25th Air Flotilla based mainly at Rabaul. The American carriers remained roughly in the same area all day waiting to find better weather for the next day's operations. At one stage the fleets were only 80 miles apart.

Meanwhile, the Port Moresby invasion force, commanded by Rear Admiral Kajioka, was underway from Rabaul and was moving south and by nightfall of the 6th was just north of the Louisiades. Its covering force, the small carrier *Shōhō* and her accompanying cruisers, had refuelled after covering the Tulagi landing. Kajioka in his flagship, *Yubari*, rendezvoused with Rear Admiral Marushige's support group off Buin, Bougainville and moved south-westwards towards the Jomard Passage. During the day USAAF B-17Es from Australia spotted the *Shōhō* operating in support of the invasion force but no immediate action could be taken. At noon, a H6K flying boat sighted and reported the position of the *Lexington* and the *Yorktown*, but the report was not passed on to the Japanese carrier commander for 18 hours. The H6K was shot down by Wildcats of VF-42. During the evening of 6 May, in squally weather, the opposing US and Japanese task forces were only 70 miles apart but neither force was aware of the other. As the American and Japanese fleets played cat and mouse during the night, both forces changed course and the gap between them widened again. When enough

BATTLE OF THE CORAL SEA

information became available to make the Japanese intentions apparent, Fletcher, having amalgamated his three task forces to form the single TF 17, steamed westwards through the night in preparation for launching search flights at dawn. The fleet tanker *Neosho* and her escorting destroyer *Sims* were left to steam southwards to a new refuelling position.

Both the Japanese and US carrier forces launched searches at dawn on 7 May and Fletcher turned TF 17 to the north. At 0645 he detached Crace's Support Group (now redesignated TG 17.3 and comprising the *Australia* and *Hobart*, USS *Chicago* and the US destroyers *Perkins*, *Wallke* and *Farragut*) to the north-west, towards New Guinea to close the southern exit of Jomard Passage. It was late on 5 May that enough information had been gathered and assessed to make clear the Japanese intention to move south through the Jomard Passage. Crace's mission was to prevent any Japanese force debouching from the Jomard Passage into the Coral Sea.

After being detached by Fletcher on the morning of 7 May Crace proceeded at 25 knots to take up a blocking position south of Jomard Passage. At 1447, when the force was 70 miles south of Deboyne Island, aircraft were engaged ineffectively at long range. At 1506 a dozen G3M torpedo bombers made a determined attack on the force. Dropping their torpedoes at a range of between 1,000–1,500 metres the aircraft came onto strafe the ships. The torpedoes were narrowly avoided by skilful handling of the cruisers. Five bombers were claimed shot down. Immediately following this attack, the *Australia* was subjected to an accurate level bombing attack by 19 aircraft, which was avoided by skilful ship handling. A few minutes later three American high-level bombers bombed the ships with no result.

Crace was uncertain about what was occurring at that stage as he had received no situation reports from Fletcher, although intercepts of Australian reconnaissance reports and from US aircraft radios gave some indication of the carrier battle in progress on the 8th. That evening, the *Hobart*, short of fuel was detached to Brisbane as was the *Walke*, which had engine defects. The remainder of Task Group TF 17.3 remained on patrol until 0100 on the 10th and then proceeded to Australia, arriving at Sydney Harbour on the 11th, where the ships refuelled again from the *Kurumba*. Although Task Force 17.3 had not gone into action against the Port Moresby Landing Force its presence, combined with bombing attacks from shore-based aircraft, was important in influencing the decision by the Japanese Commander-in-Chief to turn back the landing force early on 7 May – thereby achieving the Allies' strategic objective for the battle.[73]

Meanwhile, Fletcher's Task Force 17 had held a steady westward course 225 miles south of Rennell Island. At first light, he sent off two reconnaissance aircraft to try and locate the Japanese carriers. At this time, the Port Moresby invasion force was just off the Louisiade Archipelago. At 0815, 225 miles to the north-west one of the American reconnaissance aircraft reported seeing 'two carriers and four heavy cruisers'. Their position was radioed to the *Yorktown*. Although the search aircraft had actually discovered and mistakenly identified Rear Admiral Aritomo Gotō's covering force bound for Deboyne Island, en route to their target Fletcher, believing it to be the main force, ordered a strike. Further to the east the searches launched by the Japanese Carrier Striking Force were successful in sighting the *Neosho* and *Sims* at about 0830. They were mistakenly reported as a carrier and light cruiser. After two unsuccessful level bombing attacks by B5Ns the two ships were attacked by 36 D3A dive bombers at noon. The *Sims* was sunk and the *Neosho* heavily damaged but remained afloat until discovered and sunk by friendly forces on 11 May. While these strikes were airborne Admiral Takagi received his first intelligence of the position of the American carriers. To his chagrin he was unable to launch a strike until late that afternoon. The Japanese pilots missed TF 17 and on the return flight they were intercepted by American fighters and badly mauled. Further heavy loss resulted from their inability to find their carriers in the dark and only four aircraft landed of the 27 despatched.

At 0926 *Lexington* launched 28 SBDs, 12 TBDs and ten F4F-3 fighters. Twenty minutes later the *Yorktown* launched 23 SBDs, ten TBDs and eight F4Fs, which left 47 for combat patrol. The Dauntless scouts soon returned, however and it soon became apparent that the ships they sought were in fact two heavy cruisers and two destroyers, the error having been made during encoding. Nevertheless, Fletcher allowed the strike to continue in the hope that a more profitable target would present itself. It did. Shortly after 1100 hours Lieutenant Commander Weldon L. Hamilton, who was leading one of *Lexington*'s Dauntless squadrons, spotted the *Shōhō* with some cruisers and destroyers near Misima Island in the Louisiades. The *Shōhō* was only 35 miles south-east of the original target location, so it was an easy matter to redirect the air groups to the new target. The two air groups overwhelmed

---

73. *Battle of the Coral Sea, 4-8 May 1942* by Ric Pelvin, Australian War Memorial.

BATTLE OF THE CORAL SEA

the Japanese defences, even though four cruisers and a destroyer protected the *Shōhō*.

Commander William Bowen Ault, *Lexington*'s Air Group Commander, led the first attack and succeeded in knocking five aircraft over the carrier's side. His attack was followed at intervals shortly after by successive waves of Hamilton's ten Dauntlesses, the *Lexington*'s Devastator torpedo squadron and the *Yorktown*'s Dauntless attack group, all of which scored 13 bomb and seven torpedo strikes (and a crashed SBD) on the carrier, leaving it on fire and listing. The *Shōhō* sank shortly after 1135 hours with 638 of the 800-complement going down with the carrier. Six American aircraft were shot down. Lieutenant Commander Robert Dixon, leading *Lexington*'s other Dauntless squadron, radioed his ship and said, 'Scratch one flat-top!'

By now the Port Moresby landing force, aware of Crace's blocking force and having been bombed by land-based aircraft, had turned back permanently and the strategic objective of the Allies had been achieved.

The loss of the *Shōhō* deprived Inouye's invasion force of air cover and he was forced to delay north of the Louisiades until the Jomard Passage had been cleared. Early in the afternoon, Rear Admiral Crace's force was attacked in strength by successive waves of shore-based torpedo bombers, but the Japanese crews failed to sink any of the Allied ships. *Shōkaku* and *Zuikaku*, meanwhile, had been kept unnecessarily busy launching 60 sorties, which resulted in the sinking of the oil tanker USS *Neosho* and the destroyer *Sims* after the ships had been mistaken in earlier reports for a carrier and a cruiser. Realising the error, 12 D3A 'Val' dive bombers and 15 B5N 'Kate' torpedo bombers were launched just before 1630 hours from *Shōkaku* and *Zuikaku* with orders to attack Fletcher's carriers if they managed to locate them. The weather worsened during the afternoon and prevented any patrols from taking off from the American carriers. Fletcher had to rely on reports from shore-based aircraft such as the B-17Es. The Japanese were even further hampered in their search mission. They had no radar, so the attacking aircraft could only search the area where they estimated the American carriers to be. It proved fruitless, although they were closer to the American task force than they realised. The Japanese attack force was picked up on American radar and a combat patrol of F3F Wildcats of VF-3 from the *Lexington* was vectored to engage them. The Wildcats shot down nine bombers while the 'Vals' accounted for the loss of two fighters, which tried to dogfight with the dive bombers.

THE AIR WAR AT SEA IN THE SECOND WORLD WAR

Nearing nightfall, the Japanese crews finally gave up their search. They dropped their torpedoes into the sea and began the flight back to their carriers. At 1900 hours three Japanese planes were spotted blinking in Morse code on Aldis lamps on *Yorktown*'s starboard beam. They managed to get clean away, but 20 minutes later three more attempted to join the *Yorktown*'s landing circuit and one was shot down. A further eleven bombers failed to land back on their carriers and crashed into the sea in darkness. Only six of the original 27 managed to return safely to their carriers. Inouye's invasion plans were now in tatters. With the *Shōhō* sunk and his path through the Jomard Passage into the Coral Sea blocked by Crace's cruisers, the Port Moresby invasion force remained north of the Louisiades until it was ordered to withdraw. Fletcher's and Takagi's carrier forces remained to fight it out alone like two colossi until one emerged victorious. During the night of 7 May, the two task forces sailed further away from one another, neither admiral daring to risk a night attack.

Next morning, brilliant sunshine replaced the previous day's murk over Fletcher's task force but the Japanese task force was covered by a low overcast. At 0600 hours, the Japanese, who had steamed southwards during the night, launched searches to cover a south-east to south-west arc. Fifty-one strike aircraft and 18 fighters were ranged in readiness. At 0625 18 SBD reconnaissance planes from the *Lexington* set out on an all-round search to find the elusive Japanese fleet. The two carrier groups were each detected at approximately the same time.

At 0815 hours and most out of fuel, one of the Dauntless dived through thick cloud and squalls and the excited radio-navigator exclaimed, 'Ships at two o'clock!' The pilot dived for a closer look and the aircraft was rocked immediately by an explosion as a shell from one of the ships exploded near the port wing-tip. The pilot pulled up on the stick and headed for the safety of the clouds, while his radio-navigator sent a Morse code message back to the US task force pinpointing the Japanese task force's position, 175 miles to the north-east of Fletcher's position. Fighters and bombers aboard the *Lexington* and *Yorktown* were prepared for take-off from the rolling carrier decks. At around 0850 hours, the *Yorktown* group of 24 Dauntless dive bombers with two Wildcats and nine Devastators with four Wildcats were flown off her deck and they turned on course to their target.

Aboard the 'Lady Lex', Fitch ordered off his aircraft starting at 0900 hours. Twenty-four Dauntlesses, 12 Devastators and ten Wildcats got airborne and

BATTLE OF THE CORAL SEA

they proceeded independently of the *Yorktown* strike force of 24 bombers and nine torpedo bombers and six fighters to their target. By 0925 hours, all the American aircraft had left the decks of the two American carriers. Meanwhile, in the same period, the Japanese had launched a strike force of 51 bombers and 18 fighters for a concerted attack on the American carriers. The opposing Japanese and American pilots passed each other en route to their targets, oblivious of one another, high in the sky above the Coral Sea. At 1032 hours, *Yorktown*'s Dauntless pilots spotted the Japanese ships first. As the American aircraft approached, the two carriers separated, with *Zuikaku* disappearing into a squall. The *Shōkaku*, however, turned into the wind and began to launch aircraft.

Down below, the Americans could make out the *Shōkaku* and *Zuikaku* eight miles apart, heading for their own carriers protected by two cruisers and several destroyers. The Dauntless crews hid in low cloud and rain while they waited for the slower Devastators to arrive. The *Shōkaku* emerged from the squally overcast and at 1057 hours, the American bombers attacked. The Dauntless crews from the *Yorktown* made their attacks but only two bombs hit the *Shōkaku*. The Devastators launched their torpedoes from too far out and they either missed or failed to explode and the Japanese carrier took violent evasive action to miss them. Japanese fighters rose up to attack as the Dauntlesses went in with their bombs and they shot down three American aircraft. One bomb, which had hit the *Shōkaku*, exploded and a gasoline fire started up and the aero-engine repair workshop was wrecked and a second bomb damaged the flight-deck preventing the launch of any further aircraft, though not recoveries, for an hour.

The *Lexington*'s group did less damage. Many were unable to find the target and only eleven TBDs, four SBDs and six F4Fs attacked. They scored only one bomb hit. The 22 Dauntless dive bombers from the *Lexington* failed to find the enemy in the expected location and, low on fuel, they were forced to break off, leaving only four Dauntless scouts, eleven Devastators and six F4F Wildcats to continue the search. They soon sighted the enemy carriers, but patrolling 'Zeros' intercepted the strike while it was still 15 miles out. They succeeded in driving off the Wildcat escorts but the low-flying Devastators managed to launch their torpedoes.

Despite claims to the contrary, none of the torpedoes found their mark, but a bomb dropped by a Dauntless hit the *Shōkaku* and caused more damage. The attack cost the Americans five bombers and one fighter and had almost been in vain. The small carrier was burning but none of the bombs had hit below the waterline. Most of her aircraft were transferred to the *Zuikaku*, which had briefly emerged from the murk only to slip back into it again before the American aircraft could draw a bead. At 1300 hours the *Shōkaku* left the battle zone with 108 dead strewn on her decks and limped home to Truk.

Meanwhile, the American battle fleet had been discovered at 1055 hours bathed in bright sunlight and with little fighter cover. The incoming raid by 35 'Val' dive bombers, 18 B5N 'Kate' torpedo bombers and 18 'Zero' fighters was detected on the radar screens 68 miles from the *Lexington*, which was charged with overall fighter direction, but the fighter defences had been badly positioned to meet the attack. Low on fuel, a dozen Wildcats on combat air patrol at 10,000 ft were forced to circle the ships, unable to climb at full power or zoom off into the distance and intercept the dive bombers flying at 18,000 ft. Only three fighter pilots spotted the Japanese strike force before the attack began. Twelve Dauntless SBDs, their pilots schooled to expect the Japanese attack at low level (which was the tactic adopted by the US Navy torpedo squadrons) had been positioned three miles outside the destroyer screen at 2,000 ft on anti-submarine or reconnaissance patrols. The 'Kates' and their 'Zero' escorts flew over the SBDs at 6,000 ft and only dropped down to low level after clearing the destroyer screen. Even so, the SBDs (and two F4Fs which had been launched in time) defended magnificently, shooting down two Kates' before torpedo release and destroying two more B5Ns, a 'Val' and two 'Zeros' for the loss of four SBDs. Larger and less manoeuvrable than the *Yorktown*, the *Lexington* was pinned by a well-coordinated attack by six aircraft, three converging from either bow. At 1120 hours she was hit twice on the port side, forward and amidships. Dive-bombing was less successful, only two light bombs hitting the ship although near misses buckled her hull plates.

The *Yorktown* twisted and turned as bombs rained down from the bellies of the 'Vals' while the 'Kates' launched eight torpedoes against her port quarter. Only violent evasive action ensured that all of them missed the huge carrier. Five minutes later, at 1123 hours, the carrier came under attack from the 'Vals'. An 800lb bomb went right through the flight-deck and exploded three decks below, killing 66 sailors. A fire broke out and thick black smoke poured through a hole in the deck, but the fires below were quickly brought under control and *Yorktown* remained afloat.

The Japanese bombers fanned out and made a low-level torpedo attack on the *Lexington*, attacking both bows at once from barely a thousand yards out and at heights ranging between 50 and 200 ft. The carriers sustained two hits and water flooded the three boiler rooms. At the same time, Aichi 'Vals' dive-bombed the carrier from 17,000 ft, scoring two hits. Listing heavily, the *Lexington* limped away. The jubilant Japanese pilots broke off the attack and returned to their carriers, having hit both the American carriers. However, the carriers remained operational and returning aircrews were still able to land on the 'Lady Lex'. Fletcher still had 37 attack aircraft and 12 fighters left. Most of the Japanese returned to the crippled *Shōkaku* and had to ditch. Only nine aircraft were left operational.

In total, the Japanese had lost 80 aircraft and approximately 900 men, while the Americans had lost 66 aircraft and 543 men. The greatest loss occurred later in the day. At first it was thought that *Lexington* was not grievously damaged. Counter-flooding had corrected the list caused by the torpedo damage and three fires were burning which could normally have been brought under control. Unfortunately, the damage from the near misses had so distorted her hull that the lifts were stuck in the 'up' position and her aviation gasoline tanks were leaking. Escaping fuel vapour built up inside the *Lexington* and at 1247 hours was ignited by a still-running motor generator; a great internal explosion rocked the ship. A second major explosion occurred at 1445 hours and the fires soon got out of control. At 1710 hours the inferno forced the abandonment of the ship and her crew was taken aboard the *Yorktown*. At 1956 hours the destroyer *Phelps* put five torpedoes into her and the 'Lady Lex' sank beneath the waves. Two hundred and 16 of her crew were lost.[74]

Both forces were now too battered to continue the fight. The *Zuikaku* escorted her damaged sister back to Japan. In the course of the voyage

---

74. Four Medals of Honor were awarded at Coral Sea: Lieutenant John J. Powers (*Yorktown*, VB-5) for actions while attacking *Shōhō* on 7 May at Tulagi and on 8 May while attacking *Shōkaku* (KIA); Lieutenant Milton E. Ricketts (*Yorktown*), engineering repair party, on 8 May (KIA); Lieutenant William E. Hall (*Lexington*, VS-2) for his attack on *Shoho* on 7th May and interception of Japanese torpedo planes (too few available fighter aircraft forced the use of dive/scout bombers as low-level interceptors) on 8th May (survived); Chief Water Tender Oscar V. Peterson (*Neosho*) for his heroism in the ship's engineering spaces on 7 May (died of wounds).

THE AIR WAR AT SEA IN THE SECOND WORLD WAR

the *Shōkaku* came close to capsizing in a gale. Fletcher retired to the New Hebrides and then to Pearl Harbor, arriving on 27 May.

The Battle of the Coral Sea was unique in that it was the first sea battle in which the opposing ships neither engaged nor even saw each other. America is generally adjudged to have emerged victorious, not only because Japan was forced to cancel the amphibious invasion of Port Moresby in favour of a much more difficult overland campaign, but also because of significant losses to the Japanese fleet, which she could ill-afford for campaigns to come. Apart from the loss of the small carrier *Shōhō* and the destroyer *Kikuzuki*, the damage to the *Shōkaku* and the *Zuikaku* and their air groups meant that both were unable to take part in the Battle of Midway a month later.

The American post-mortem, meanwhile, revealed that not enough Wildcats were embarked; when the *Yorktown* sailed to Pearl Harbor and, incredibly, was ready for sea again after just three days undergoing repairs in port, its fighter complement was increased from 18 to 27. The aircraft were new type F4F-4s that were among the first of the newer types to reach the US Navy. The F4F-4, which had arrived in Hawaii just too late for service aboard *Lexington* and *Yorktown* in the Battle of the Coral Sea, was produced with folding wings for greater accommodation aboard the carriers and fitted with six machine-guns instead of four. The Devastators, which had proved totally unsuitable for modern combat operations, remained aboard only because there was no time to embark the new Grumman TBF-1 Avengers. The *Yorktown* was needed for immediate action to the north because, even as the Battle of the Coral Sea was being fought, Fleet Admiral Isoroku Yamamoto, the architect of the attack on Pearl Harbor and his staff officers in Japan were planning an even bigger operation, the seizure of Midway Island and the occupation of Kiska and Attu in the Aleutians. Yamamoto would then use Midway as a base for further raids on the Hawaiian Islands and for the destruction of what remained of the US Pacific Fleet.

Chapter 11

The Battle of Midway (4–7 June 1942)

A look-out screamed: 'Hell-Divers!' I looked up to see three black enemy planes plummeting towards our ship. Some of our machineguns managed to fire a few frantic bursts at them, but it was too late. The plump silhouettes of the American Dauntless dive-bombers quickly grew larger and then a number of black objects suddenly floated eerily from their wings.
Fuchida Mitsuo (3 December 1902 – 30 May 1976) who is perhaps best known for leading the first wave of air attacks on Pearl Harbor on 7 December 1941.

Isoroku Yamamoto hoped to surprise the Americans and take Midway Island, 1,300 miles north-west of Oahu with little difficulty. Its capture would give a wider defence perimeter and prevent further American air raids on the Home Islands. Lieutenant Jimmy Doolittle's strike on Tokyo with 16 B-25 Mitchells operating from the carrier *Hornet* on 18 April 1942 had been a small beginning but had proved most embarrassing for the Japanese military. However, American intelligence services had broken the Japanese code and Admiral Chester Nimitz and his staff were well aware of the Japanese strength and intent long before their plan was put into effect. This information was absolutely invaluable to the Americans because it allowed Nimitz to make best use of his meagre resources in the Pacific and he could plan his defence of Midway safe in the knowledge that he need not spread his limited resources too thinly. Yamamoto's battle strategy was complex. The Japanese architect of the raid on Pearl Harbor decided on a strong diversionary strike on the westernmost Aleutian chain lying off Alaska, which would be occupied to deter the Americans from sending reinforcements south into the Pacific. Although it was only a diversionary force, Yamamoto knew he had to include enough important vessels, such as the fleet carrier *Jun'yō* and the light

THE AIR WAR AT SEA IN THE SECOND WORLD WAR

carrier *Ryūjō*, which would have been invaluable at Midway, to persuade the Americans to split their defensive forces.

Vice Admiral Chūichi Nagumo's 1st Carrier Striking Force aimed at Midway was composed of four carriers: the *Akagi, Kaga, Hiryū* and *Sōryū*, as well as the light carrier *Hoshō*. The Japanese could also call upon an impressive number of battleships, destroyers and other craft. The light carrier *Zuihō* was part of a central covering force, which could be diverted to help in the Aleutians or Midway depending on how the battles developed.

The Americans could immediately call upon only two carriers, the *Hornet* and the *Enterprise*, which had taken part in the Tokyo raid. Fortunately, the repair crews at Pearl Harbor managed to perform miracles and got the badly damaged *Yorktown* ready for sea again after her heavy involvement in the Battle of the Coral Sea. Her air group was a combination of her own and the survivors from the late lamented *Lexington*. The battle-hardened pilots and crews provided the US task force with the experience that fliers on the *Hornet* and *Enterprise* generally lacked.

On 30 May Admiral Jack Fletcher took *Yorktown* north-westwards to join the two cruisers and five destroyers, which formed the remainder of Task Force 17. The *Yorktown* rendezvoused with Task Force 16, whose flagship was the *Enterprise*, commanded by Admiral Raymond Spruance. While Nimitz was thus able to call upon a third, highly valuable flat-top, Admiral Chuichi Nagumo could only ponder the loss of the *Zuikaku* during the Coral Sea battle and the badly damaged *Shōkaku*, which could not be repaired in time to join the battle fleet heading for Midway. Even so, the Japanese naval forces closing in on Midway from two directions were formidable.

Nimitz's defence plan was announced to his senior officers on 27 May, two days after the first of two Japanese task forces sailed for the Aleutians. On Midway ground forces worked tirelessly and without sleep to turn the island into a fortress while the airborne elements were brought up to strength.[75]

---

75. The defence of the island was entrusted mainly to the US Marine Corps' MAG 22 (Marine Aircraft Group 22) whose seven F4F-3 Wildcats and 21 obsolete Brewster F2A-3 Buffaloes were led by Major Floyd B. Parks. Major Lofton R. Henderson commanded MAG 22's 17 Vought SB2U-3 Vindicators – or 'Wind Indicators' as the US Marines sardonically referred to them – and 19 Douglas SBD-2 Dauntless dive bombers. In addition, USAAF B-17E Flying Fortresses of the 26th, 31st, 72nd and 431st Bomb Squadrons in the 11th Bomb Group and a few B-26 Marauders in the 22nd and 38th Bomb Groups and USMC Avengers helped swell the defences.

THE BATTLE OF MIDWAY

Meanwhile, Nagumo's 1st Carrier Striking Force and the main body led by Yamamoto in the massive battleship *Yamato* approached the island from the north-west, while the Occupation Force, commanded by Vice Admiral Kondo and consisting of the Second Fleet Covering Group and an additional three groups comprising Transport (under Tanaka), Support (commanded by Vice Admiral Takeo Kurita) and Minesweeping, headed for Midway further to the south.

For three days, 31 May to 3 June two Aichi ET3A 'Jake' reconnaissance floatplanes searched in vain for the American task forces, but on 3 June, a PBY Catalina about 700 miles west of Midway sighted ships of the Japanese fleet. It was assumed the force was the main Japanese task force and a bombing strike was ordered. At 1230 hours, nine B-17Es of the 11th Bomb Group led by Lieutenant Colonel Walter C. Sweeney, which had arrived at Midway from Hawaii on 29 May, took off in search of the Japanese invasion fleet. Despite returning with claims that they had hit two battleships or heavy cruisers and two transports, it was later confirmed that the enemy force was in fact the Midway Occupational Force and the 'battleships' and 'cruisers' were in reality tankers and transports. No hits were scored on the ships until four Catalinas from Midway discovered them in bright moonlight in the early dawn of 4 June and torpedoed a tanker.

Meanwhile, at 0415 hours 15 B-17Es cleared Midway Island and assembled in the vicinity of Kure Island to attack the same fleet they had bombed the previous afternoon, but word was received that another enemy task force, complete with carriers, was approaching Midway and was now only about 145 miles away. At 0430 hours, Lieutenant Joichi Tomonaga's strike force of 36 'Kate' torpedo bombers carrying 1,770 lb bombs, 36 Aichi 'Val' dive bombers and 36 'Zero' fighters took off from Nagumo's carriers and headed for Midway Island. The softening-up operation of the American bastion, if successful, was to be followed two days later by an amphibious invasion force. At the same time, ten Dauntless scout dive bombers were flown off the *Yorktown* and they began a search mission in a wide arc to the north of the island. Six Japanese reconnaissance aircraft were also launched, although the second of two Jake floatplanes launched from the cruiser *Tone* was delayed until 0500 hours, when a troublesome catapult was finally repaired. As luck would have it, his search sector corresponded with the American task force's location. The breathing space afforded the American ships would prove significant. With the decks of the Japanese carriers *Akagi* and *Kaga* clear, the second wave of 'Kates', armed with torpedoes this time, were hoisted up on deck ready for a follow-up raid on any American shipping that might be uncovered by the first wave.

At 0534 hours a Navy Catalina reconnaissance flying boat flown by Lieutenants Howard Ady and William Chase radioed Midway with the news that the Japanese carrier fleet had been sighted. *Yorktown*, only 250 miles to the east, was tuned to Midway's radio frequency and intercepted the message. Rear Admiral Fletcher recalled the Dauntless scouts and dispatched Rear Admiral Spruance on the *Enterprise* with *Hornet* and the rest of Task Force 16 to attack the Japanese carriers. At 0553 hours, the radar operators on Midway picked up Tomonaga's strike force of 108 aircraft and the island's defence forces quickly got airborne. Midway was mainly defended by the obsolete Brewster F2A-3 Buffaloes of VMF-221, which had arrived on the island on Christmas Day 1941. The B-17s and flying boats which were already in the air were told to stay away as the 21 Buffaloes and seven Wildcat fighters set off in two groups to attack the incoming Japanese forces. Major Parks' group of seven Buffaloes and five Wildcats intercepted the enemy while Major Kirk Armistead's group was further westward where another strike was expected. The American fighters intercepted the bombers, shot down four and damaged a few others before Tomonaga's escort of 36 'Zeros' intervened. Although two 'Zeros' were shot down in successive dogfights, the superior Japanese force soon completely overwhelmed Parks' outnumbered group. Vicious dogfights continued until almost all over the island Armistead's fighters joined in the one-sided battle. It was too late. Although they fought valiantly, the nimble 'Zeros' hopelessly outclassed the Marine Corps' fighters.[76]

Six new Grumman TBF-1 Avenger torpedo bombers of VT-8 commanded by Lieutenant Langdon K. Fieberling and four Army Air Corps' B-26 Marauders led by Captain James F. Collins, which had also taken off from Midway, fared almost as badly. One of the Avenger pilots was 25-year-old

---

76. Altogether, 13 Buffaloes and three Wildcats were lost in the engagements and seven others were damaged beyond repair. Of the 27 fighters that had engaged the Japanese, one F2A developed engine trouble and had to abort, only three survived intact. Major Parks was among the 16 pilots killed. Three Japanese aircraft shot down by anti-aircraft fire over the island was small consolation.

THE BATTLE OF MIDWAY

Ensign Albert Earnest from Richmond, Virginia. He first spotted what looked like a single transport about 15 miles distant and then his turret gunner, Jay Manning, called and told him that they were being attacked by fighters as 20 'Zeros' already on patrol dived on the torpedo bombers from upwards of 3,000 ft. Seventeen-year-old radioman Harry Ferrier, who had lied about his age when he had joined up five days after his 16th birthday, immediately manned the .30-calibre machine-gun, which fired aft, under the tail of the TBM. Earnest looked ahead and made out the whole Japanese force in front of them. In just a matter of a few seconds, he saw 'two carriers and quite a few other ships'. His Avenger was the first to reach the Japanese fleet and the Marauders and TBMs bored in at low level for their attacks. Incredibly, Earnest's Avenger was still in one piece but a shell fragment came through the canopy and went right through the right strap of his helmet into his cheek just below his jawbone. There was blood all over the cockpit but Earnest kept going. Manning had fired just two bursts of .50-calibre before his guns fell silent. It was obvious to young Harry Ferrier kneeling at his gun that Manning was dead because, when he looked back behind his shoulder, he saw that the turret had stowed itself and that he was hanging dead in the harness.

The TBM's hydraulics were shot out and then Ferrier was hit by a bullet that grazed his left wrist. A split second later, he felt a stunning blow on the head before losing consciousness. The Avenger was damaged further when a bullet hit the right elevator, which severed the control cables and threatened to nose the TBM into the sea but Earnest was determined to drop his torpedo at the nearest ship before he hit the water. Using his rudder and aileron, Earnest broke formation and swung the Avenger left toward a cruiser and released the torpedo with the electrical system before pulling the emergency release as a backup. The TBM did not hit the sea. When he was about ready to hit the water, Earnest rolled the elevator tab wheel back, causing the torpedo bomber to lurch upwards the instant before impact. He kept the TBM level only a few feet off the water and skirted behind the Japanese cruiser he had just aimed his torpedo at. All the torpedoes missed their targets.

The enemy fighters were unable to prevent the torpedoes from being launched, but when the unprotected bombers turned away after launching, they were easy prey. Machine-gun fire from the 'Zeros' and intense anti-aircraft fire from the ships destroyed seven aircraft and badly damaged three others. Earnest's TBM and two B-26s were the only aircraft to crash-land back on Midway. Earnest finally put down on one wheel on the third attempt and the wing dropped down, hit the runway, spun around and the TBM 'parked itself off the runway very nicely'.[77]

Lieutenant Joichi Tomonaga, who commanded the air assault on Midway, radioed Admiral Chūichi Nagumo that despite heavy damage a second strike was required to put Midway out of action. Nagumo agreed with him, his decision influenced by the succession of enemy torpedo attacks on his carriers. At 0715 hours he ordered the 'Kates' to be re-armed with bombs, a procedure which involved bringing the torpedo bombers back below decks and re-arming them. The time taken would have severe consequences for the Japanese; particularly in view of the signal he received 13 minutes later from the *Tone*'s 'Jake' floatplane, which had spotted 'what appear to be ten enemy surface ships' 240 miles from Midway. Nagumo agonised, wasting a precious 15 minutes weighing up the information before finally ordering that the re-arming of the 'Kates' be stopped and that all aircraft be prepared to attack the US task force. He was only stopped when the Jake floatplane confirmed at 0809 hours that there were no carriers in the US formation, only cruisers and destroyers. Nagumo knew these posed no immediate threat to his carriers because they were well out of range. However, he had more immediate problems to think about when 16 SBD dive bombers of Marine Scout Bombing Squadron VMSB-241 and 15 Flying Fortresses of the 11th Bomb Group appeared overhead at heights ranging to 20,000 ft, followed by eleven Marine Corps' obsolete Vought SB2U Vindicator scout bombers led by Major Benjamin W. Norris.

The carriers circled under broken cloud and the Marine Corps and Fortress crews had to search for them. The Fortresses spotted the first carrier, which was seen to break cloud cover, but despite claims to the contrary, no hits were scored on the enemy fleet. Despite the number of American attacks, they were too uncoordinated and widespread to be effective and no bombs or torpedoes hit the Japanese fleet.

The *Enterprise*'s 14 TBDs in VT-6 led by Lieutenant Commander Eugene E. Lindsey flew on to their targets alone while the ten Wildcats in VF-6 commanded by Lieutenant James S. Gray followed, 36 F4F-3s remaining behind to take it in turns to patrol over the task force. The *Hornet*'s ten

---

77. See *Only One Returned* by Adam Makos, *Ghost Wings*, Issue 8 (summer/fall 2002).

THE BATTLE OF MIDWAY

Wildcats in VF-8, led by Lieutenant Commander Samuel G. Mitchell, failed to make contact with Lieutenant Commander John Charles Waldron's 15 Devastators in VT-8. They tacked on to the 35 Dauntlesses divided into Bombing Squadron 8, led by Lieutenant Commander Robert R. Johnson and Scouting Squadron 8, commanded by Lieutenant Commander 'Walt' Rodee, leaving Waldron's torpedo bombers to fly on alone. The Devastators took up station alone, flying along at wave-top height while the protective screen of F3F-3 Wildcat fighters and trailing Dauntless dive bombers were stacked up to 19,000 ft. In the lead was Commander Stanhope Cotton Ring, *Hornet*'s Air Group Commander.

Eight Dauntlesses were shot down by intense anti-aircraft fire from the ships and by the defending 'Zeros'. Major Lofton Henderson, commanding officer of VMSB-241 was among the dead, the first Marine aviator to perish during the battle. The Vindicators, which were last in, were forced off their targets by the 'Zeros', which by now had expended almost all their ammunition. Even so, they managed to shoot down two of the Marine Corps' SB2Us.

Meanwhile, Nagumo's repeated insistence that the pilot of the *Tone* floatplane should positively identify the enemy ships he was shadowing finally had some effect. At 0820 hours, the pilot of the *Tone* floatplane chillingly reported to Nagumo that one of the American ships 'appeared' to be a carrier. Nagumo did not want to risk his air task force and instead of proceeding to attack Midway with the second wave, he abandoned it. He could not attack the American task force either because his remaining torpedo-carrying aircraft would have to be brought up from below deck. Ten minutes later, the same floatplane reported the sighting of two more cruisers. Nagumo wanted to attack the American ships immediately but most of his bombers were improperly armed for such a strike and his 'Zero' fighters were low on fuel and ammunition after engaging the Marine Corps attacks and would be unable to escort the bombers. Before he could order the fighters to be re-armed and refuelled, Tomonaga's strike force returned to the carriers and Nagumo ordered that all aircraft which would have made up the second wave were to be kept below deck so that Tomonaga's air group could be recovered. The first wave survivors, which amounted to 36 'Vals' and 54 'Kates', were re-armed with torpedoes and refuelled aboard the four Japanese carriers. It was at this moment that Nagumo was informed by his vessels to the south that a very large formation of American aircraft was approaching the task force. Spruance had taken advantage of Nagumo's problems in recovering the first wave and had dispatched his air groups.

In the time since take-off from the American carriers Nagumo's task force had changed course to the north-east. The four air groups therefore arrived at the anticipated position and found no carriers. The *Hornet*'s dive bombers decided to search south, but finding nothing and getting low on fuel, many of the Dauntlesses were forced to land back on *Hornet* or refuel at Midway. Unfortunately, the Wildcats burned up fuel far quicker and all ten were forced to ditch in the sea.

At 0910 hours Gray's fighters spotted the enemy ships but they did not wish to break radio silence and failed to inform the other squadrons. The much lower-flying torpedo bombers sighted smoke on the horizon, turned north and found the Japanese carriers just after 0930 hours. Waldron could not afford to waste precious fuel waiting for the fighter support and he must have known it was now a suicidal mission as he turned the formation into their attack positions and prepared to launch torpedoes from a height of just 300 ft. Meanwhile, Gray's Wildcats remained on station 6,000 ft above them waiting for the prearranged call for assistance from 'Gene' Lindsey, not realising that the Devastators below belonged to Waldron's torpedo squadron. Upward of 50 'Zeros' attacked the 15 Devastators and wreaked havoc. One after the other of Waldron's torpedo bombers were blasted out of the sky by the Japanese fighters and supporting fire from the ships in the Japanese task force. Waldron and 29 of the 30 men of his squadron perished But by tying up the 'Zeros' in defending their carriers against the torpedoes, the attack allowed dive bombers from *Enterprise* to mortally damage three of the Japanese carriers.

Only 25-year-old Ensign George H. Gay of Waco, Texas who piloted the last plane in the formation, remained alive. He had heeded the words of his commander, who, before the raid, had urged, 'I want each of us to do his utmost to destroy our enemies. If there is only one plane left to make a final run in, I want that man to go in and get a hit.' With his single fixed .30 calibre machine gun, Gay fired at anything that flew in front of him and managed to hit and damage one 'Zero' until the gun jammed. Suddenly Gay felt something hit his left arm and found blood on his hand. Squeezing a dark lump on his arm a spent Japanese machine gun round popped out. Moments later something hit the back of his left hand, disabling his use of it. Then his gunner, Aviation Radioman Third Class Robert K. Huntington of Los Angeles, California

THE BATTLE OF MIDWAY

called over the intercom that he was hit and then the radio went silent; Gay was on his own. He managed to get his torpedo away before he skimmed over the bow of the carrier and crashed into the sea. Gay miraculously emerged as his aircraft began to sink with his dead gunner aboard. He swam away from the wreckage as 'Zeros' circled overhead. Luckily, his rubber seat cushion floated clear and Gay grabbed it. He bobbed in the sea clutching it until dusk when he finally inflated his dinghy without fear of being strafed by the 'Zeros'. Later, he reported having thought to himself during his ordeal: 'It's the end of the world and I have a grandstand seat.' A PBY Catalina picked up Gay the following day after 30 hours in the water.

Twenty minutes later, Lindsey's 14 Devastators arrived. Without fighter support now that VF-6 had left the target area, they singled out the *Kaga* and began their attack on the starboard side. Quite by chance, the *Yorktown*'s air group appeared on the scene and flew in on the port side at the same instant proposing to attack the *Sōryū*. The air group consisted of 12 TBD Devastators, commanded by Lieutenant Commander Lance E. 'Lem' Massey of Watertown, New York, six Wildcats of Fighting Squadron 3, led by Lieutenant Commander 'Jimmie' Thach and seventeen Dauntlesses split into two groups led by the CO, Lieutenant Commander Maxwell F. Leslie commanding VB-3 and Lieutenant Wallace C. Short. The latter had received the Navy Cross for his action on 10 March when attacks were made on Japanese forces near Salamaua and Lae, New Guinea. Short had pressed home, in the face of heavy anti-aircraft fire, a vigorous and determined dive bombing attack on three aircraft tenders or transports and obtained a direct hit on one of the enemy vessels. Leslie's and Short's groups' arrival would draw some of the 'Zeros' away from the *Enterprise*'s Devastators, but even so, eleven of the torpedo bombers, including Lindsey's, were shot down in a hail of gunfire.

Following the Japanese destroyer *Arashi* that had been counterattacking USS *Nautilus*, Leslie and Lieutenant Commander Wade McClusky from *Enterprise* managed to arrive above the Japanese task force at the precise moment its combat air patrol had been drawn down to the deck to repel *Yorktown*'s torpedo bombers. This was the moment of the First Air Fleet's maximum vulnerability. With the 'Zeros' too low to be effective, the SBDs of McClusky's VB-3 of 20 dive bombers and 'Max' Leslie's squadron of seventeen dive bombers screamed down in a near-vertical dive in three waves, through the fortuitous clear air to unload their 1,000 lb bombs on the enemy carriers, their hangar decks cluttered with confused ranks of recovered and warming up aircraft massed on the carrier deck, snaking fuel hoses and stacks of munitions from the various rearmament operations. Leslie himself did not have a bomb as it was accidentally released via a faulty electrical arming switch. Nevertheless, he also dived with the rest of the SBDs, strafing carrier decks. After their attack on *Sōryū* Leslie and his wingman Lieutenant (jg) P. A. Holmberg ditched near USS *Astoria* due to fuel exhaustion, after *Yorktown* was under attack when they returned. Leslie, Holmberg and their gunners were rescued by one of the cruiser's whaleboats.

Three bombs dropped on *Sōryū* found their mark, including one that penetrated to the hangar deck and exploded. The other two bombs exploded among the aircraft ranged on deck and caused mayhem among the crews.

'Lem' Massey's Devastators had closed in on the Japanese carriers, protected only by 'Jimmie' Thach's six fighters. The small strike force penetrated to within only three miles of the Japanese carriers before shellfire from one of them alerted the 'Zeros', which were still busy dealing with the remnants of VT-6. The Wildcats were outnumbered and out-manoeuvred as about 40 defending 'Zero' fighters soon overwhelmed them. Nine A6Ms from *Hiryū* fought with the F4Fs, shooting one down and badly damaging two others, which were forced to break off. Thach and his two remaining wingmen, greatly outnumbered, were unable to help the TBD crews directly, but they drew some of the 'Zeros' away before they too were forced to break off and return to the *Yorktown*.

The cumbersome Devastators, meanwhile, came under a fusillade of fire from the ships and were cut to pieces as they split into two sections. Massey's TBD was hit, burst into flames and careered into the sea. In the confusion, five Devastator crews who managed to get their torpedoes away aimed them at any target which presented itself before they were blasted out of the sky. Altogether, ten of Massey's Devastators were shot down and once again none of the torpedoes had found its mark, although two torpedoes passed within only 50 yards of *Kaga*. All 12 pilots of Torpedo Squadron 3 received the Navy Cross.

Lieutenant Clarence Earle Dickinson, who had been shot down on Pearl Harbor Day, who was now Executive Officer of VS-6 on the *Enterprise* recalled: 'I think everybody with a few rare exceptions made determined attacks, it was just that unfortunately the torpedo planes were slow, which was their biggest failing. They never could really get in position; when they

THE BATTLE OF MIDWAY

tried to get into position to make coordinated attacks from each of the bows, that is left and right, they simply were shot down one by one. But the fact that they kept going on in, I would have expected it of them, I think everybody would have done that. I think the thoughts were that whatever happens they would go in until the last man was gone. They were that kind of people.

'I was one of the few individuals that had access to those magic dispatches on the carrier because I was in essence the group operations officer and therefore the predictor for the dive bombers and scouts, so I was well aware personally of the numbers and I think that in general the information was available to all of the air group as to what was there. Halsey told us a certain amount what ships we were up against, so I don't think there were any illusions.'

The Devastators' suicidal attacks had not been in vain, however. Their action had kept the defending 'Zeros' occupied at low level so that when the SBD Dauntlesses did appear high overhead the Japanese fleet, seventeen 'Zeros' that still had enough fuel were unable to gain enough altitude in time to intercept the SBDs before they began their dive-bombing. Lieutenant Commander Clarence W. McClusky the *Enterprise* Air Group Commander led his attack with 33 Dauntless dive bombers from VB-6 and VS-6. There was no time for them to form up because of the need to bomb the Japanese carriers before they got their own aircraft away. VB-6's Dauntless scout bombers led by 32-year-old Lieutenant Richard Halsey Best became separated with the unexpected arrival of McCluskey's bombers. Splitting his force, Best led the 1st Division of three SBDs from the southwest against *Akagi*. The 2nd Division (VS-6) led by Lieutenant Wilmer E. Gallaher flew on alone heading for the *Kaga*. The rest of the air groups aboard the *Enterprise* and *Hornet* followed at intervals, but even using double launching methods, getting the large formations airborne took about an hour to complete. The time lag between take-offs and a build-up of layers of broken cloud en route scattered the formation and ruled out effective fighter protection for the slow-flying Devastators.

Three of McClusky's SBDs peeled off and aimed their 1,000 lb bombs at Nagumo's mighty flagship crowded with aircraft far below. At 1026 the first bomb, dropped by Lieutenant Edwin John Kroeger, missed. The second bomb, aimed by Ensign Frederick Thomas Weber, landed in the sea, near the stern, the force wave of which jammed the *Akagi*'s rudder. The last bomb was dropped by 'Dick' Best, who, seeing *Akagi*'s yellow flight deck emblazoned with a large red circle, dropped his 1,000-pounder from 2,500 ft, scoring a hit amidships, opposite the bridge and just behind the aircraft lift. It ripped through to the hangar below where it exploded among stored torpedoes. This was followed in succession by hits from his two wingmen. The second bomb exploded among the 18 'Kates' and the deck erupted into a blazing inferno. Other explosions went on for some time as petrol tanks, bombs and torpedoes were enveloped in the conflagration.

McClusky's remaining Dauntlesses concentrated their attacks on the *Kaga*, which received four direct hits, including one that exploded a petrol tanker near the bridge. The petrol ignited and a searing burst of flames burned everyone on the bridge, including the captain, to death. The other three bombs hit the aircraft ranged for take-off on the carrier deck and they were quickly enveloped in an inferno. Wilmer Gallaher turned the nose of his Dauntless dive-bomber down toward the *Kaga* heading into the wind so his dive was coming downwind into a carrier that was on a steady course heading into the wind. 'My dive was awfully steep,' said Gallaher. 'I put my bombsight on the red rising sun up on the bow of the carrier and I came down as low as I dared and let the thing go. It was a perfect situation for a dive-bombing attack. Of course, the SBD was a wonderful dive-bombing airplane anyway. The planes on the *Kaga* were already armed and they were ready to take off. All the planes were armed; they had bombs on them and they were all gassed up. It was like diving on to a group of planes that were ready to take off.'

Gallaher, who had always chided any pilot who dared to pull up and watch their bomb explode could not resist the temptation himself and he pulled up and watched it hit the *Kaga*. His radioman, said 'god damn; that was a beaut cap'n'. The memory of Pearl Harbor, which he had witnessed, flashed across his mind. As the carrier blew up, he exulted: '*Arizona*, I remember you!'

'After we pulled away', said Gallaher, 'there were other hits on the ship, too. They had one explosion that must have sent the flames and smoke up at least 2,000 ft in the air. There was just a terrible explosion on the ship. As I was retiring, I thought there were two other carriers that were aflame and burning, too.'

In just five minutes, *Enterprise*'s VS-6 and Bombing Squadron Six destroyed two Japanese fleet carriers. Although the *Akagi* and the *Kaga* continued to remain afloat, as did *Sōryū*, the raging fires could not be extinguished and all three carriers were finally abandoned and sunk by

THE BATTLE OF MIDWAY

Japanese or American torpedoes. *Kaga* was abandoned at 1700 and sank at 1925. *Akagi* was abandoned just after *Kaga* went down and was scuttled before dawn on 5 June. Seven Dauntlesses had been shot down in dogfights while eight 'Zeros' were shot down. Eleven SBDs from the *Enterprise* were forced to ditch after running out of fuel on the return flight to the carrier. 'Dick' Best landed back with only 30 gallons of fuel to spare. He reported to Admiral Raymond A. Spruance that three carriers were burning but a fourth (*Hiryū*, which was ten miles to the north of the other three carriers after becoming separated from the main Japanese force) had not been touched.

The *Hiryū* became a haven for 23 'Zeros', which were diverted from the damaged carriers. Its total complement of about 40 'Zeros', 18 'Vals' and ten 'Kates' now posed a threat to American carriers like the *Yorktown*. A Yokosuka D4Y-1C 'Judy' reconnaissance aircraft from *Sōryū* located the American task force and, alone with fake floatplanes, shadowed the carrier's every move. Admiral 'Jack' Fletcher, meanwhile, had ordered ten SBDs aloft to search for the Japanese carrier while 12 Wildcats took off and flew a defensive patrol. At around 1100 hours, *Hiryū* launched 18 'Vals' with mixed bomb loads and six 'Zeros' led by the wily veteran Lieutenant Michio Kobayashi. Shortly before noon, the radar operators on the *Yorktown* picked up the specks of the Japanese air striking force 46 miles west of them and heading their way behind the returning Dauntlesses.

The Wildcats intercepted the Japanese formation about 15 miles out at 10,000 ft and shot down seven 'Vals' and four 'Zeros'. The surviving 'Vals' broke away from the engagement and dived on the *Yorktown*. Six 'Vals' were shot down, including two by anti-aircraft fire from the American cruisers. The 13th victim, who fell to the anti-aircraft guns, succeeded in lobbing a bomb onto the flight-deck before it broke up and the explosion started a fire in the hangar below. A second bomb caused extensive damage to the ship's insides and knocked out most of the boilers so that the carrier's speed was severely reduced and then finally halted. A third bomb, which penetrated to the fourth deck, caused a serious fire, which threatened to engulf the forward petrol tanks and ammunition stores. Despite severe losses and damage to her decks, the crew of the *Yorktown* managed to dampen down the raging fires and soon the ship was underway again. The Wildcats were refuelled and re-armed aboard *Enterprise* and were almost ready when a second wave of ten 'Kate' torpedo bombers and six 'Zeros' led by Lieutenant Joichi Tomonaga, who had led the first attack on Midway, appeared on radar 40 miles distant.

THE AIR WAR AT SEA IN THE SECOND WORLD WAR

Only four Wildcats got airborne to join with six already in the air when the Japanese arrived in the area. The F4F pilots screamed into the attack, trying to get at the 'Kates', but the 'Zero' pilots, who lost three of their number, fended them off. Four Wildcats fell to the 'Zero' guns. The 'Kates' flew ruggedly on, despite the curtain of withering fire put up by the cruisers and the gunners aboard the *Yorktown* and attacked the cruiser from four angles. Five of the torpedo bombers were shot down, but the survivors, who launched four of their deadly torpedoes from only 500 yards, scored two hits below the waterline. The ship's fuel tanks were sliced open and the lower decks flooded. *Yorktown* began listing badly and the order was given to abandon ship.

The remaining five battered but jubilant 'Kate' crews zoomed off back to the *Hiryū*, unaware that the same fate was about to befall their carrier that had escaped being hit that morning. Now only five 'Kates', four 'Vals' and about 25 'Zeros' remained of the carrier's original 63 aircraft. Soon after they had been recovered, the *Hiryū* came under a surprise attack by 14 Dauntlesses of VS-6 from the *Enterprise* led by Lieutenant Wilmer E. Gallaher and ten more from VB-6 led by Lieutenant 'Dick' Best, which had been transferred from the *Yorktown* after that carrier had been damaged in the Japanese attack.

During pre-flight Best had become sick when he checked his oxygen levels and inhaled gas fumes but he cleared his senses well enough to participate in the attack. Close behind were 16 Dauntlesses from the *Hornet*. Thirteen 'Zeros' on patrol intercepted the SBDs and one of the leading dive bombers was shot down during its dive with two more falling after bomb release. Despite the attacks, Gallaher's dive bombers and Best's succeeded in getting hits on the *Hiryū*, which caused uncontrollable fires and destruction. 'The *Hiryū* made this 180° turn from under me', Gallaher said many years later, 'and I tried to toss the bomb on board and my number two man who followed me, he missed too astern. But the third plane caught up with him and got a hit.'

'Dick Best's gunner, James Francis Murray saw the flash of their bomb through the smoke as it struck amidships forward of the island.

'*Hiryū* threw everything she had at us', recalled Best. 'I never tried to look where my bomb hit: she was shooting, the battleships were shooting and the 'Zeros' were swarming around. I dropped all the way to the deck to get out of there.' After returning to the *Enterprise*, he began coughing up blood and developed a fever. He was transferred to the hospital in Pearl Harbor, where

THE BATTLE OF MIDWAY

X-rays showed cloudy spots on his lungs. While flying the first mission that morning, a faulty oxygen canister had created gases that turned to caustic soda. He had breathed in the soda to clear it out and the caustic soda had activated latent tuberculosis. He never flew again.[78]

Beginning at 1022, the two squadrons of the *Enterprise* air group split up with the intention of sending one squadron each to attack *Kaga* and *Akagi*. Lieutenant Clarence Dickinson recalled: 'As we went out and couldn't find the Japanese carrier fleet, our group commander turned north and the air group who was from the *Hornet* turned south towards Midway. Commander 'Stan' Ring did and they never found anything. [On returning to the *Hornet* Commander Ring found only 18 Dauntlesses had made it back; 15 of the 17 dive bombers landed on Midway and later were able to return to action. Of his 60 planes dispatched, in the confusion of the early hours of the Battle of Midway, 45 never saw the Japanese armada and many ran out of fuel and crashed into the sea. As well as the 15 torpedo bombers lost, ten fighters and two dive bombers were lost. The two Dauntless pilots and 29 of the 30 pilots and radio operators of the torpedo bombers died. Ring was shaken at the realization of such losses.]

'As we turned north', continues Dickinson, 'within a few minutes, the group commander picked up a single destroyer who had been left behind by the Japanese to keep an American submarine down that had been spotted. Figuring that the destroyer was headed back to the Japanese fleet, McClusky turned to that course, followed the destroyer and went on past it. We were up at about 24,000 ft and suddenly we broke out into the clear and there were four Japanese carriers and everything. And we knew we had them by the balls.

'We started our approach, pushing over and going down about 19,000 to 20,000 ft, picking up speed and got in position to attack. We were coming down in all directions on the port side of a carrier. I recognized her as the *Kaga*; and she was enormous. At that time the group commander gave orders to 'Dick' Best and Bombing 6 to take one of the carriers and told Earl Gallaher to take the other one. At the same time, to the northeast, one of the other squadrons from the *Yorktown* came in and spotted one of the carriers [*Sōryū*] and as a great coincidence dived within 15 to 20 seconds of the same time that our two squadrons dived. The target was utterly satisfying ... I saw a bomb

---

78. After undergoing 32 months of treatment Best retired from the Navy in 1944 with a 100 per cent disability. Between ages 32 and 42 Best spent four years in and out in the hospital recovering from tuberculosis. He died aged 91 in November 2001.

hit just behind where I was aiming ... I saw the deck rippling and curling back in all directions exposing a great section of the hangar below ... My 500 lb bomb hit right abreast of the carrier's island. The two 100 lb bombs struck in the forward area of the parked planes ...' [*Kaga* sustained four or five direct hits, which caused heavy damage and started multiple fires. One of the bombs landed near the bridge, killing Captain Jisaku Okada and most of the ship's senior officers.] As I pulled out there were three carriers burning and the fourth carrier was off to the northwest, high-tailing it back under the clouds.

'At the time you know you never think too much about getting killed, but I think most of us at that time felt that this was probably going to be it. When you figured that we brought back out of our air group only 16 pilots plus three that were later picked up, we were pretty near right.

'I reckon there were probably more hits on Japanese aircraft claimed than actually were hit, but I think I got a hit alright. I got one of the Japanese planes as he flew underneath me and pulled ahead of me and he didn't see me, so I, after deliberation, because I knew if I missed him, he was gonna be mad and would come up after me. I just put the nose down and shot him up the rear; then he went into the water.

'We all could see the carriers burning. We knew that this was the whole heart of the enemy fleet. Three of those four Japanese carriers were burning. I think everybody was jubilant. Then the problem was to get home because down low the air was full of Japanese fighters and destroyers. We were down to around 300 or 400 ft and all of the destroyers were shooting at us. You just had to bore out and get out of the ring of ships and get back on home. Some made it and some didn't. A lot went into the water and were never picked up, but that's another story. As we came on back, we were running out of gas and when I was about five miles from the *Enterprise* I ran out of gas, so I put the plane down. The sea was quite calm, three or four good waves and landed the plane ahead of a destroyer and it turned out that this was the destroyer *Phelps* that I had been on for a couple of years back in the late thirties.'[79]

---

79. Ensign J. R. 'Mac' McCarthy who like Dickinson, was shot down on Pearl Harbor Day, was also rescued. Six of the VS-6 pilots were never seen again. When Lieutenant Dickinson's Second Gold Star was presented in 1942, he became the first person in history to receive three Navy Crosses, a distinction he gained simultaneously with fellow pilot Lieutenant Noel A. M. Gayler. Clarence Dickinson retired as a US Navy Rear Admiral.

THE BATTLE OF MIDWAY

A miscommunication had caused both of the Dauntless squadrons to dive at *Kaga*. *Hornet*'s SBDs arrived to find the *Hiryū* burning fiercely. Recognizing the error, Lieutenant 'Dick' Best and his two wingmen were able to pull out of their dives and, after judging that *Kaga* was doomed, headed north to attack *Akagi*.

Lieutenant Joichi Tomonaga flew the last strike from *Hiryū* after the three other carriers of the First Air Fleet had been bombed by Dauntlesses. On a one-way mission because of damage to his aircraft and lack of fuel, he successfully dropped his torpedo but was shot down by Lieutenant Commander 'Jimmie' Thach of Fighting Squadron 3 on the *Yorktown*. His body was never found; he was symbolically interred in Yasukuni Jinja (Shrine).

Some USAAF B-17Es en route to Midway from Oahu also joined in the attack on the *Hiryū* but their bombs missed. The surviving 'Zero' pilots made a few passes at the Fortresses before ditching in the sea to be picked up by ships of the task force. That evening, 13 bombers of VMSB-241, now led by Major Benjamin Norris, took off from Midway but failed to find the *Hiryū* and returned guided by the fires still raging on the island. Major Norris failed to return after crashing into the sea. The *Hiryū* was finally abandoned the next morning and finished off by Japanese torpedoes.

To all intents and purposes, the Battle of Midway was over. However, Yamamoto, believing the Americans to have only one carrier in the vicinity of Midway, proposed to move his main body up to replace the now almost non-existent Striking Force and recall the Aleutian task force to join him in a joint attack on the island. It was only after pilots returning to the *Hiryū* late on 4 June reported the existence of the other American carriers that Isoroku Yamamoto ordered his invasion force, in the early hours of 5 June, to withdraw.[80]

The Americans, unaware of the true situation aboard the Japanese flagship and knowing the lack of experience their pilots had in flying at night, waited until dawn of 5 June before getting their aircraft into the air. By then the Japanese main body had retreated well to the west and the 58 Dauntlesses, which were sent to look for the enemy force returned empty-handed. Later,

---

80. Admiral Isoroku Yamamoto, C-in-C Combined Fleet, who was responsible for planning the attack on Pearl Harbor and later Midway was ambushed and killed by P-38 Lightnings while flying from Rabaul to Bougainville on 18 April 1943.

however, a dozen dive bombers succeeded in crippling the heavy cruisers *Mogami* and *Mikuma* after they had collided while taking avoiding action after sighting an American submarine.

On the night of 4 June, when the Marine Scout Bombing Squadron 241 Squadron Commander lost his way and became separated from the others, Captain Richard Eugene Fleming brought his Vought SB2U Vindicator dive bomber in for a safe landing at its base despite hazardous weather conditions and total darkness. When his squadron Commander was shot down during the initial attack upon the enemy carriers, Fleming led the remainder of the second division with such fearless determination that he dived his own plane to the perilously low altitude of 400 ft before releasing his bomb. Although his aircraft was riddled by 179 hits in the blistering hail of fire that burst upon him from Japanese fighters and anti-aircraft batteries, he pulled out and only suffered two minor wounds. The following day, after less than four hours sleep, Fleming led his squadron in a coordinated glide-bombing and dive-bombing assault upon the *Mikuma*. Despite being hit and his aircraft set on fire, he grimly pressed home his attack to an altitude of 500 ft, released his bomb to score a near-miss on the stern of the heavy cruiser and then crashed into the sea in flames. No bombs hit the *Mikuma* but the cruiser's after-turret and petrol fumes sucked into the engine-room ignited and exploded, killing the entire engine-room crew. Captain Fleming was posthumously awarded the Medal of Honor for his heroism.

A further attack by dive bombers sunk the *Mikuma* but the *Mogami* managed to limp home to Truk. The crippled but still-floating *Yorktown* was not as fortunate, finally being sunk by two torpedoes from a Japanese submarine on 7 June after she had been taken in tow.

The Battle of Midway proved to be the decisive turning point in the Pacific War. Although Japanese fighters had scored an impressive victory over the American aviation units, which lost 85 out of 195 aircraft, a large part of the elite in Japanese naval aviation had also perished. The loss of her carriers meant Japan would never again dictate events in the Pacific. Her shipyards could not hope to replace the carriers lost in action at Coral Sea and Midway, while in America US shipyards were already building fleet carriers in large numbers and factories were turning out more powerful aircraft to put aboard them. Midway marked the beginning of the way back for the Americans who would see the liberation of the central Pacific and the final destruction of the Japanese home islands.

Chapter 12

The Battle for the Solomons (August – November 1942)

Guns charged and ring sights glowing, our four Corsairs float like hawks over enemy-held land. Below us are the jungle hills of New Ireland; ahead, the purple volcanoes of Rabaul. Elsewhere, our eyes see a wilderness of cloud, sky and blue Pacific water.

We are cruising at 8,000 ft on a marine patrol to cover the morning's strike to make sure that 'Zeros' don't interfere with American bombing crews. Our planes are from VMF 223, based on a rolled-coral strip in the Green Islands - 200 miles east of New Guinea - 4° south of the equator.

This is my first combat mission and therefore unlike all other flights. My senses are peeled of the calluses formed by everyday routine. They awoke this morning with new awareness, crying out that I'll go forth to kill and to run the risk of death; that, like man of primitive times, I'm both the hunter and the hunted. Inside this sun-browned skin that covers me, civilized perception and barbaric instinct are melting into some not-yet-tested-out alloy. Ever since my ears heard the noises of daybreak, all things around me - the air I breathe, the ground I walk on, the very trees of the jungle - seem to have taken on new qualities of beauty and of danger...

The Lone Eagle Flies Again: Thoughts Of A Combat Pilot by Colonel Charles A. Lindbergh, Civilian Technical Representative. In 1944 Lindbergh was able to visit the Pacific Theater of Operations as a Corsair technical rep. Lindbergh left for the Pacific on 24 April 1944, flying to Hawaii in a Navy C-47. From there he moved through Midway, Palmyra and Funa Futi to Espiritu Santo, visiting and flying with Corsair equipped squadrons. After two weeks he moved on through Guadalcanal (Koli) and Bougainville to Green Island. On 22 May Lindbergh flew his first combat mission, escorting TBFs to Rabaul with a Marine Corsair squadron and strafing assigned ground targets before starting home. Before returning to Guadalcanal on 10 June he had flown 13 missions to Northern Solomon and Rabaul targets from Green and Emirau islands.

In August 1942 the US Navy began the bold struggle for supremacy of the sea around Guadalcanal, a humid, jungle-covered, hilly tropical island in a remote group known as the Solomons, which lie on the north-eastern approaches to Australia and which occupied a key strategic position early in 1942. If the Solomons fell into Japanese hands they could be used as a base to cut through the sea supply routes between America and Australia and if seized by the Americans, they could ultimately be used as a springboard for operations against the Japanese in the South Pacific. On 7 August 1942, Allied forces, predominantly US Marines, landed on Guadalcanal, Tulagi and Florida in the southern Solomon Islands, with the objective of denying their use by the Japanese to threaten Allied supply and communication routes between the United States, Australia and New Zealand. The Allies also intended to use Guadalcanal and Tulagi as bases in supporting a campaign to eventually capture or neutralize the major Japanese base at Rabaul on New Britain.

The Japanese defenders, who had occupied those islands since May 1942, were outnumbered and overwhelmed by the Allies, who captured Tulagi and Florida, as well as an airfield that had been under construction on Guadalcanal by the Japanese. It was later named Henderson Field in honour of Major Lofton Henderson who was killed during the Battle of Midway while leading his squadron into action. The airfield would soon become the focus of months of fighting during the Guadalcanal Campaign, as it enabled US airpower to hinder the Japanese attempts at resupplying their troops. The Japanese made several attempts to retake Henderson Field, resulting in continuous, almost daily air battles for the Tainan Kōkūtai.

Surprised by the Allied offensive, the Japanese made several attempts between August and November to retake Henderson Field. Meanwhile, on 23 August an attempt was made by the Imperial Japanese Navy ships at night to deliver personnel, supplies and equipment to their forces operating in and

THE BATTLE FOR THE SOLOMONS

around New Guinea and the Solomon Islands. Originally called 'The Cactus Express', a phrase coined by Allied forces on Guadalcanal who used the code name 'Cactus' for the island, American newspapers had begun referring to it as the 'Tokyo Express', apparently in order to preserve operational security for the code word and Allied forces also began to use the phrase. The operation involved loading personnel or supplies aboard fast warships (mainly destroyers), later submarines and using the warships' speed to deliver the personnel or supplies to the desired location and return to the originating base all within one night so that US aircraft could not intercept them by day. The sea passage to Guadalcanal took 'The Tokyo Express' through New Georgia Sound or 'The Slot' as it was known in Allied circles due to its geographical shape and the amount of warship traffic that traversed it; which in this instance was supported by the aircraft carriers, *Shōkaku*, *Zuikaku* and the light carrier *Ryūjō*.[81]

Vice-Admiral 'Jack' Fletcher's TF 61, patrolling to the east of the Solomon Islands sighted the Japanese fleet, which reversed course and avoided the American strike aircraft. On 24 August, US carriers finally caught up with the *Ryūjō*, which was sailing ahead of the main Japanese fleet, when it was sighted by a Catalina flying boat. An armed reconnaissance of 29 SBDs and TBF Avengers was flown off from *Enterprise* and at 1345 hours, this was followed by a strike force of 30 SBDs and eight Avengers from the *Saratoga*. *Ryūjō* launched her aircraft to attack Henderson Field. Just as the American strike flew off, scout planes sighted the *Shōkaku* and *Zuikaku*, who had also launched a massive striking force. An attempt to divert the SBDs and Avengers to the new target failed, but the *Ryūjō* was sent to the bottom by a combination of 1,000 lb bombs and a torpedo. Only a few aircraft from the *Enterprise* attacked the *Shōkaku*. *Enterprise* was hit three times on the

---

81. During the 'First Battle of Savo Island' or in Japanese sources, the 'First Battle of the Solomon Sea' on 8/9 August, a Japanese cruiser force had advanced down 'The Slot' to attack the American transports unloading off Guadalcanal and its Allied screening force. The Allied screen consisted of eight cruisers and 15 destroyers under the Royal Navy's Rear Admiral Victor Crutchley VC, but only five cruisers and seven destroyers were involved in the battle. It became known colloquially as 'The Battle of the Five Sitting Ducks' by Guadalcanal veterans, after the five US cruisers that attempted to intervene were disabled. One destroyer was also damaged before the Japanese retired.

flight-deck by bombs dropped by a force of 30 'Val' dive bombers, which arrived undetected at 18,000 ft over the flat-top. *Enterprise* was hit three times by bombs dropped by the 'Vals' but though two of the bombs penetrated to lower decks before exploding, the carrier was able to continue recovering her aircraft. Later, her steering gear broke down and *Enterprise* was immobilised at the very moment the second Japanese strike wave appeared on the radar screen, but fortunately, they were unable to find the stricken carrier.

On 11 and 12 October 1942 the Japanese navy suffered another defeat when, off Cape Esperance on the northernmost point on Guadalcanal, in the Solomon Islands a US supply convoy sailed for the island, escorted by a cruiser squadron which was also to ambush any Japanese forces moving down 'The Slot'. A junior officer on the *Helena* that detected the Japanese at a range of 14 miles on radar later wrote that 'Cape Esperance was a three-sided battle in which chance was the major winner.' Two Japanese ships were severely damaged and after the force turned and retreated a destroyer was also sunk.

Between 24 and 26 October, Japan was to fare far worse at the Battle of Santa Cruz, a volcanic group of islands in the Solomons, 345 miles east of Guadalcanal in the fourth carrier battle of the Pacific campaign. It began after the Japanese Combined Fleet moved to the north of Guadalcanal, ready to fly aircraft to Henderson Field as soon as it was captured. As in the battles of the Coral Sea, Midway and the Eastern Solomons, both the battle fleets were rarely in sight or gun range of each other. Instead, almost all attacks by both adversaries were carried out by carrier- or land-based aircraft.

TF 16 (*Enterprise*) re-joined TF 17 (*Hornet*) and was ordered to intercept any Japanese forces approaching Guadalcanal. On the 25th the day broke in fair weather over the two US fleets with a light south-westerly breeze through columns of cumulus cloud in the blue tropical sky with occasional local rainstorms. At noon, Catalina flying boats sighted two of the Japanese carriers, but an American strike failed to make contact. On the 26th, just north of the Santa Cruz Islands, as the Japanese ground offensive on Guadalcanal was under way in the Battle for Henderson Field, the Japanese fleet was again sighted. The *Enterprise* launched 16 SBD dive bombers each with a 500 lb bomb to make an armed reconnaissance. At 0658 hours, the *Shōkaku*, *Zuikaku* and *Zuihō* launched 64 aircraft, including 21 Aichi D3A2 dive bombers, 20 Nakajima B5N2 torpedo bombers, 21 A6M3 Zero fighters and two Nakajima B5N2 contact aircraft in a first strike. As a second striking

THE BATTLE FOR THE SOLOMONS

force was being ranged up, two of the *Enterprise*'s SBD-3s Dauntless scout aircraft arrived and dived on the *Zuihō*. Lieutenant Commander Stockton Birney Strong and Ensign 'Chuck' Irvine attacked *Zuihō* and hit the carrier with two bombs that exploded on the flight-deck, punching a huge, jagged hole and preventing the carrier's flight deck from being able to land aircraft.

At 0810 *Shōkaku* launched a second wave of strike aircraft, consisting of 19 dive bombers and five 'Zeros' and *Zuikaku* launched 16 torpedo bombers and four 'Zeros' at 0840 so that by 0910 the Japanese had 110 aircraft en route to attack the US carriers. Between 0730 and 0815 hours, *Enterprise* and *Hornet* launched three small strike forces. The first group consisted of 15 SBD Dauntless dive bombers, six TBF-1 Avenger torpedo bombers and eight F4F Wildcat fighters led by Lieutenant Commander William J. 'Gus' Widhelm from *Hornet*. The second group comprised three SBDs, nine TBFs and eight Wildcats from *Enterprise*. A third group included nine SBDs, ten TBFs and seven F4Fs from *Hornet*. At 0840, the opposing aircraft strike formations passed within sight of each other. Nine 'Zeros' from Zuihō surprised and attacked the *Enterprise* group, attacking the climbing aircraft from out of the sun. Four 'Zeros', three Wildcats and two TBFs were shot down, with another two TBFs and a Wildcat forced by heavy damage to return to *Enterprise*.

The remaining 'Zeros', having exhausted their ammunition, withdrew from the action. The dive bombers in the first group made their attacks without fighter escort and 12 'Zeros' shot down two SBDs (including Widhelm's, although he survived) and forced two more to abort. The remaining eleven SBDs began their attack dives on *Shōkaku*, hitting her with three to six bombs, wrecking her flight deck and causing serious damage to the interior of the ship. The final SBD lost track of *Shōkaku* and instead dropped its bomb near the destroyer *Teruzuki*, causing minor damage. The six TBFs in the first strike force, having become separated from their strike group, did not find the Japanese carriers and eventually turned back towards *Hornet*. On the way back, they attacked the heavy cruiser *Tone*, missing with all their torpedoes. The TBFs of the second attack formation from *Enterprise* failed to find the enemy's carriers and instead attacked the heavy cruiser *Suzuya* but caused no damage. At around the same time nine SBDs from the third attack formation from *Hornet* attacked the Japanese heavy cruiser *Chikuma*, hitting her with two 1,000 lb bombs and causing heavy damage. The three *Enterprise* SBDs then arrived and also attacked *Chikuma*, causing more damage with one bomb hit and two near-misses. Finally, the nine TBFs from the third strike group arrived and attacked the smoking *Chikuma*, scoring one more hit. Chikuma, escorted by two destroyers, withdrew from the battle and headed towards Truk for repairs.

Meanwhile, *Shōkaku* and *Zuikaku* had launched their second strike. At 0852 the Japanese strike force commander sighted the *Hornet* task force (the *Enterprise* task force was hidden by a rain squall) and deployed his aircraft for attack. At 0855 the American carriers detected the approaching Japanese aircraft on radar at about 40 miles distant and began to vector the 37 Wildcats of their CAP to engage the incoming enemy aircraft. However, communication problems, mistakes by the American fighter control directors and primitive control procedures prevented all but a few of the US fighters from engaging the Japanese aircraft before they began their attacks on *Hornet*. Although the US CAP was able to shoot down several dive bombers, most of the Japanese aircraft commenced their attacks relatively untouched by US fighters.

At 0909 hours the anti-aircraft guns of *Hornet* and her escorting warships opened fire as the 20 untouched Japanese torpedo planes and remaining 16 dive bombers commenced their attacks on the carrier. At 0912 a dive bomber placed its 551 lb semi-armour-piercing bomb dead centre on *Hornet*'s flight deck, across from the island, which penetrated three decks before exploding, killing 60 men. Moments later, a 534 lb 'land' bomb struck the flight deck, detonating on impact and creating an 11 ft hole and killing 30 men. Then a third bomb hit *Hornet* near where the first bomb hit, penetrating three decks before exploding, causing severe damage but no loss of life. At the same time as the dive bombers were attacking, the 20 torpedo bombers were also approaching *Hornet* from two different directions. Despite suffering heavy losses from anti-aircraft fire, the torpedo planes planted two torpedoes into *Hornet*'s side between 0913 and 0917, knocking out her engines. As *Hornet* came to a stop, at 0914 a damaged Japanese dive bomber set on fire by *Hornet*'s anti-aircraft guns approached and purposely crashed into the carrier's side, starting a fire near the ship's main supply of aviation fuel, killing seven men and spreading burning aviation fuel over the signal deck.

At 0920, the surviving Japanese aircraft departed, leaving *Hornet* dead in the water and burning. Twenty-five Japanese and six American aircraft were destroyed in this attack. With the assistance of fire hoses from three escorting destroyers, the fires on *Hornet* were under control by 1000 hours. Wounded

THE BATTLE FOR THE SOLOMONS

personnel were evacuated from the carrier and an attempt was made by the heavy cruiser USS *Northampton* to tow *Hornet* away from the battle area. However, the effort to rig the towline took some time and more attack waves of Japanese aircraft were inbound. The US destroyers USS *Mustin* and *Anderson* attempted to scuttle *Hornet* with multiple torpedoes and over 400 shells, but she still remained afloat. With advancing Japanese naval forces only 20 minutes away, the two destroyers abandoned *Hornet*'s burning hulk at 2040. The Japanese destroyers *Makigumo* and *Akigumo* then finished *Hornet* with four 24-inch torpedoes. At 0135 on 27 October, she finally sank.

Meanwhile, American dive bombers seriously damaged the *Shōkaku*. The second Japanese strike concentrated on the *Enterprise*, her flight deck full and fuel-depleted aircraft having to ditch in the sea. From 0930 hours, LSO (Landing Signals Officer) 'Jim' Daniels (a former Wildcat pilot who had been aloft on 7 December 1941 during the attack on Pearl Harbor) had helped get 47 (some badly shot-up) F4Fs and SBDs down in 43 minutes (one every 55 seconds) under harrowing conditions without a mishap. Senior LSO Robin Lindsey took over for the last 30 or so with no barriers to catch them in the event of a crash. At 1222 hours, Lindsey gave Vejtasa a 'high dip' - drop the nose slightly, then recover - and then slashed his paddles down in the cut signal to 'Swede' Vejtasa. [82] Vejtasa responded as ordered. He recalled, 'I was looking right at the ramp,' the aft end of the flight deck. He chopped the throttle, dropped the Grumman's stout airframe onto the deck and caught the one wire. In the nearby catwalks, sailors applauded and cheered a virtuoso performance by two accomplished professionals. 'Swede' Vejtasa shut down his engine, climbed out and warmly shook hands with his friend Robin Lindsey, the best 'waver' in the business.

Daniels left the LSO platform to go below deck. In the hangar he discovered the 'unbelievable horror' wrought by the second Japanese bomb hit. All around lay the dead and dying. One sailor in particular he never forgot. 'I recognized a fo'castle bos'n with only one arm and no legs and fingers that seemed to dig into the steel deck, slowly and painfully pull himself to an opening on the starboard over the side. One of the corpsmen spoke to me thinking that I might make a move to help and cautioned me to just let him

---

82. See *The First Team* and *the Guadalcanal Campaign: Naval Fighter Combat from August to November 1942* by John B. Lundstrom (Naval Institute Press, Maryland, 1994).

alone and let him pull himself over the side. He would die anyway. In a very few minutes, he made his last trip off the 'E'.' (The fo'castle bos'n was among the 240 killed aboard the ships of TF 61 during the battle.)[83]

Enterprise succeeded in only shooting down two of the 19 dive bombers as they began their dives on the carrier. Attacking through the intense anti-aircraft fire put up by *Enterprise* and her escorting warships, the Japanese bombers hit the carrier with two 551lb bombs and scored a near-miss with another. The bombs killed 44 men and wounded 75 and caused heavy damage to the carrier, including jamming her forward elevator in the 'up' position. Twelve of the 19 Japanese bombers were lost in this attack. Fortunately, *Enterprise*'s speed and manoeuvrability were unaffected. Twenty minutes later, the 16 torpedo planes from *Zuikaku* arrived and split up to attack *Enterprise*. One group of torpedo bombers was attacked by two CAP Wildcats which shot down three of them and damaged a fourth. On fire, the fourth damaged aircraft deliberately crashed into the destroyer *Smith*, setting the ship on fire and killing 57 of her crew. The torpedo carried by this aircraft detonated shortly after impact, causing more damage. The remaining 16 torpedo planes attacked *Enterprise*, *South Dakota* and cruiser *Portland*, but all of their torpedoes missed or failed, causing no damage. Nine of the torpedo aircraft were lost in this attack. After suppressing most of the onboard fires, *Enterprise* reopened her flight deck to begin landing returning aircraft from the morning strikes on the Japanese force. However, only a few aircraft landed before the next wave of Japanese strike aircraft arrived and began their attacks, forcing *Enterprise* to suspend landing operations. *Enterprise* and her task force would be forced to retreat as soon as they were able.

Between 1140 and 1400, the two undamaged Japanese carriers, *Zuikaku* and *Jun'yō*, recovered the few aircraft that returned from the morning strikes on *Hornet* and *Enterprise* and prepared follow-up strikes. Between 0905 and 0914, Jun'yō had arrived within 320 miles of the US carriers and launched a strike of seventeen dive bombers and a dozen 'Zeros'. Then *Jun'yō* readied follow-up strikes and at 1121 the dive bombers from *Jun'yō* dived on the *Enterprise* task force. They scored one near miss on *Enterprise*, causing more

---

83. In the summer of 1952 Commander 'Jim' Daniels was in command of ATG-2 aboard the *Essex* and Commander Vejtasa was air boss. See *'Air Task Group Two: Ready When Needed'* by Barrett Tillman. (*The Hook: Journal of Carrier Aviation*, Summer, 1989).

THE BATTLE FOR THE SOLOMONS

damage and one hit the *South Dakota* and light cruiser *San Juan*, causing moderate damage to both ships. *Enterprise* recovered 57 of its 73 airborne aircraft as she retreated. The remaining US aircraft ditched in the ocean; their aircrews being rescued by escorting warships. Eleven of the seventeen Japanese dive bombers were destroyed in the attack. Lieutenant Commander Okumiya Masatake, *Jun'yō*'s air staff officer, described the return of the carrier's first strike groups: 'We searched the sky with apprehension. There were only a few planes in the air in comparison with the numbers launched several hours before... The planes lurched and staggered onto the deck, every single fighter and bomber bullet holed ... As the pilots climbed wearily from their cramped cockpits, they told of unbelievable opposition, of skies choked with anti-aircraft shell bursts and tracers.'

Only one of *Jun'yō*'s bomber leaders returned from the first strike and upon landing he appeared 'so shaken that at times he could not speak coherently'. At 1306, Junyō launched her second strike of seven torpedo planes and eight 'Zeros' and *Zuikaku* launched her third strike of seven torpedo planes, two dive bombers and five 'Zeros'. At 1535, *Junyō* launched the last Japanese strike force of the day, consisting of four bombers and six Zeros. The third strike from *Zuikaku* attacked *Hornet* during this time, hitting the sinking ship with one more bomb. All of *Hornet*'s crewmen were off by 1627. The last Japanese strike of the day when they found her burning hulk dropped one more bomb on the sinking carrier at 1720. The third Japanese strike failed to achieve any results and the American forces then withdrew.

Santa Cruz was a tactical victory and a short-term strategic victory for the Japanese in terms of ships sunk and damaged (the *Hornet* and the destroyer *Porter* had been sunk and damage caused to *Enterprise*, the light cruiser *San Juan*, the destroyer *Smith* and the battleship *South Dakota*). After Santa Cruz not a single US carrier remained operational. *Enterprise* received temporary repairs at Nouméa on New Caledonia and, although not fully restored, returned to the southern Solomons area just two weeks later to support Allied forces during the naval battle of Guadalcanal where she played an important role in what was the decisive naval engagement in the overall campaign for Guadalcanal when her aircraft sank several Japanese warships and troop transports during the naval skirmishes around Henderson Field.

But if Santa Cruz was a Japanese victory that victory cost Japan her last best hope to win the war. Admiral Nagumo was relieved of command shortly after the battle and reassigned to shore duty in Japan. He acknowledged that the victory was incomplete. And Japan's loss of many irreplaceable veteran aircrews proved to be a long-term strategic advantage for the Allies. At least 409 of the 765 elite Japanese carrier aviators who had participated in the attack on Pearl Harbor were dead. In addition to losing 99 aircraft of the 203 involved in the battle, they lost 148 pilots and aircrew members including two dive bomber group leaders, three torpedo squadron leaders and 18 other section or flight leaders. Forty-nine per cent of the Japanese torpedo bomber aircrews involved in the battle were killed along with 39 per cent of the dive bomber crews and 20 per cent of the fighter pilots. The Japanese lost more aircrew at Santa Cruz than they had lost in each of the three previous carrier battles at Coral Sea (90), Midway (110) and Eastern Solomons (61).

American pilots and aircrew losses in the battle were relatively low (26) and quickly replaced. Eighty-one of the 175 US aircraft at the start of the battle were lost, of which 33 were fighters, 28 were dive-bombers and 20 were torpedo bombers. The undamaged *Zuikaku* and *Jun'yō* were forced to return to Japan because of the loss of trained aircrew to man their air groups. Although the Japanese carriers returned to Truk by the summer of 1943, they played no further offensive role in the Solomon Islands campaign. Five Japanese carriers had been completed in 1941 and six more in 1942, but the losses in the Coral Sea, Midway and the Bismarcks had taken a heavy toll and Japan's one-time ascendancy in carriers was in decline. In spring 1943 she still possessed eleven carriers, but only one fleet carrier was really ready for sea. The others were either damaged or were, in reality, light carriers or converted merchantmen. In stark contrast, in December 1942 the first of the new Essex-class fleet carriers[84] was commissioned and the second followed in April 1943 while another 22 were in various stages of planning or construction.

Three major land battles, seven large naval battles, including two carrier battles and almost daily aerial battles, ended with the decisive naval battle of Guadalcanal in early November 1942, with the defeat of the last Japanese attempt to bombard Henderson Field from the sea and to land enough troops

---

84. *Essex* incorporated the most important lessons learned by the US Navy about aircraft carriers. Her 27,000-ton design became the standard to which all American carriers commissioned during the war were built but her keel was not laid down until April 1941 and she was not commissioned until 31 December 1942.

THE BATTLE FOR THE SOLOMONS

to retake it. In December the Japanese abandoned their efforts to retake Guadalcanal and by 7 February 1943 after six months of fierce resistance against occupying US Marines they had evacuated their remaining forces from Cape Esperance. With Japanese reinforcements and supplies cut off by the US Navy, retreat became Japan's only option. Heavy losses at Guadalcanal so weakened the Japanese Navy that it could not stop the campaign to isolate the important base at Rabaul, which by April 1944 no longer posed a threat.

Between late 1943 and mid-1944, the advance in the South Pacific, combined with a drive in the Central Pacific, breached the Japanese defensive perimeter and opened the way for the liberation of the Philippines. While General Douglas MacArthur advanced through the South Pacific along New Guinea, the US Navy began the Central Pacific campaign, capturing bases in the Gilberts and the Marshall Islands. Carrier task groups shattered Japanese bases and intercepted their naval forces. The Gilberts were attacked and occupied in November 1943 and in February 1944 the main atolls of the Marshalls were overrun. As part of the assault on Eniwetok, the most westerly of the Marshall Chain, a huge two-day air strike on the Japanese navy base at Truk in the Carolines was carried out by the aircraft carriers in Admiral Raymond Spruance's 5th Fleet. Truk capitulated and the Japanese retreated, first to Palau and finally, in March 1944, to Singapore.

Chapter 13

The Battle of the Philippine Sea

> *Light has begun to break in the east through the scattered clouds. The clustered Hellcats are now mutually visible. We spread out a bit, floating effortlessly in space. The oxygen mask helps clear the mind, sharpen the eyes. This is the first combat air patrol of the day, on station ready for any early-morning attack on the fleet that might sneak out from some Japanese position. Our division leader's hand signals a 'trigger action', as if he is firing a pistol over his head. It's time to spread out and test fire guns to be sure everything is operational. Firing switches for the guns are flipped to 'on' position. A brief squeeze of the trigger on the stick and a bruummmmmp erupts from six .50-calibre machine-guns at the leading edge of the wings, jolting the Hellcat like a stiff wind. Phosphorus tracers stitch an arc through the clouds and the sky like a line sketched by an unseen hand. The beauty of the moment conceals the lethal nature of the reason for keeping guns alive. Billows of cloud create soft canyons through which we drift, disappear and reappear. The sun is bright now; sky is blue. War, home and memories are far away.*
>
> *Hellcat Dawn Patrol: Reminiscences of Carrier Duty in the Pacific*, **Evan Adams** of VF-23 on the *Langley*.

New, large *Essex*-class CV and light *Enterprise*-class CVL escort carriers, as well as amphibious landing craft, had helped make the American onslaught in the Pacific victorious. Newer, more powerful types of aircraft had also arrived late in 1943 onwards to replace the older fighter and torpedo bomber aircraft used in the early Pacific battles. The Grumman F6F Hellcat, which had first flown in prototype form shortly after the Battle of Midway on 26 June 1942, was now the standard fast carrier fighter in the US Navy. The Hellcat made

THE BATTLE OF THE PHILIPPINE SEA

its combat debut on 31 August 1943, being flown by VF-9 on *Essex* and VF-5 on *Yorktown* on strikes against Marcus Island. It was faster in level flight and the dive than the Mitsubishi A6M5 Zero. The Cyclone-engined FM-2 Wildcat, then in service aboard the small escort carriers, had benefited from experience gained by the Royal Navy. It had a better rate of climb than the earlier Wildcats and other improvements meant that it could hold its own against the A6M3 'Zero' and its descendants. The Grumman TBM/TBF Avenger, meanwhile, was the standard torpedo bomber aboard American carriers, while the Curtiss SB2C-1C Helldiver was on the verge of replacing the Dauntless SBD-5 dive bomber. The new dive bomber had its drawbacks though. It required more maintenance than the Dauntless and carried only the same bomb load with no improvement in range. Although it soldiered on until the war's end, plans were considered for re-equipping with SBDs again in July 1944.

Despite the harrowing defeats of late 1943 and mid-1944, Japanese naval forces in the Pacific were still far from finished. The A6M 'Zero' remained the standard carrier-borne fighter, for after attempts to bring the A7M Sam successor into service had failed, the A6M5 Model 52b, which was a cleaned-up version of the A6M3, was introduced at the end of 1943. The 'Zeke' 52 had a top speed of around 350 mph at 20,000 ft with more powerful 20-mm cannon and a 13 mm machine-gun complementing its other 7.7 mm machine-gun in the fuselage. Numerically, Japan possessed a much larger carrier force than the United States and their navy could call upon 1,700 land-based fighters if the American fleet could be lured to a suitable killing zone either in the Palaus or the Western Carolines where they were within air striking range from bases in the Netherlands East Indies, New Guinea, the Bismarcks, the Philippines and Singapore. Based on Tinian, Guam and Saipan in the Marianas were 484 aircraft, while a further 114 were based in the Western Caroline Islands. With such air and naval forces at their disposal, the Japanese admirals believed they could win a decisive sea battle and re-establish their naval supremacy in the Pacific.

The American admirals, however, had their own ideas. Plans had long been formulated for the invasion of the Mariana Islands and in June, they were put into effect. On 6 June 1944 Task Force 58, a huge carrier strike force composed of four self-contained task groups each with its own escorts and commanded by Vice Admiral Marc 'Pete' Mitscher, left Majuro for Saipan. TG58-1 was composed of *Hornet* commanded by Rear Admiral Joseph James

THE AIR WAR AT SEA IN THE SECOND WORLD WAR

'Jocko' Clark, *Yorktown*, *Bataan* and *Belleau Wood* with a total of 265 aircraft. TG58-2 consisted of *Bunker Hill* commanded by Rear Admiral Alfred Eugene Montgomery, *Cabot*, *Monterey* and *Wasp* with 242 aircraft. TG58-3 comprised the *Enterprise*, commanded by Rear Admiral John Walter 'Black Jack' Reeves Jr, the new *Lexington* (Mitscher's flagship), *Princeton* and *San Jacinto* with a total of 227 aircraft. TG58-4 was composed of the *Essex* under the command of Rear Admiral William Keene Harrill, *Langley* and *Cowpens* (affectionately known as the 'Mighty Moo') with 162 aircraft.

On 11 June, Task Force 58 began 'softening up' the Marianas with heavy gunfire while a fighter sweep by 211 Hellcats and eight Avengers was sent in to gain fighter superiority over the islands. 'Zeke' 52s tried to intercept the Hellcats over Guam, but 30 were shot down and Hellcats of VF-28 from *Monterey* destroyed six Mitsubishi G4M2 'Bettys' over Tinian. By 14 June, after four days of fighting, the US Navy pilots had destroyed almost 150 Japanese aircraft.

Meanwhile, on 8 June the US Northern Attack Force under the command of Vice Admiral Richmond Turner arrived at Eniwetok from Hawaii with 71,000 troops to capture Saipan, while the Southern Attack Forces, under Rear Admiral Richard Lansing Conolly arrived with 56,500 troops from Guadalcanal and Tulagi to assault Guam. The massive invasion fleet, which included 12 escort carriers, seven battleships and 91 destroyers set sail for Saipan, which was planned to be invaded by amphibious forces on 15 June. On 12 June Saipan and Tinian were shelled heavily. Two groups remained in the area to establish total air supremacy, while that evening, TG58-1 and TG58-4 sped 650 miles north to attack Chichi Jima and Iwo Jima. On 15 and 16 June Hellcats from TG58-1 and TG58-4 brought down about ten 'Zeros' in combat and destroyed 60 aircraft on the ground. The Japanese pipe dream of engaging the American fleet on their terms was vanishing into a fog of self-delusion. Vice Admiral Kakuji Kukuda, who commanded naval aircraft in the Central Pacific from his base on Tinian, omitted to tell Admiral Jisaburo Ozawa, who commanded the Japanese Main or First Mobile Fleet of the true losses.

On 13 June Admiral Soemu Toyoda, the commander-in-chief, ordered Ozawa's force to set course for the Philippine Sea where it was to rendezvous with the huge battleships *Yamato* and *Musashi* and six other vessels in a detachment commanded by Vice Admiral Matome Ugaki, who was told to abort an earlier mission to support Japanese forces fighting General Douglas MacArthur's troops on Bataan in the Halmaheras. On 16 June Vice-Admiral

THE BATTLE OF THE PHILIPPINE SEA

Jisaburō Ozawa rendezvoused with Ugaki's detachment. Next day was spent refuelling before the huge force resumed its easterly course towards the Marianas. The vast armada was composed of three forces. 'A' Force, made up of three large fleet carriers, *Shōkaku*, Ozawa's flagship *Taihō* and *Zuikaku*, had a total air strength of 430 aircraft. 'B' Force, commanded by Rear Admiral T. Joshima, comprising the fleet carriers *Hiyō* and *Jun'yō* and the light carrier *Ryūjō*, contained 135 aircraft. 'C Force was commanded by Vice Admiral Takeo Kurita, whose three light carriers contained only 88 aircraft but which was employed as a diversionary force for the other two groups. A defensive screen of destroyers, cruisers and battleships protected all the carriers in the three forces.

On 17 June Japanese aircraft based in the Carolines attacked American shipping. Nakajima B5N 'Kate' torpedo bombers from Truk attacked and sank an amphibious landing craft between Eniwetok and Saipan and in the evening, seventeen Yokosuka D4Y2 'Judys' and two Yokosuka P1Y1 'Frances' torpedo bombers escorted by 31 'Zeke' 52s made attacks on transports and escort carriers. Forty-two FM-2 Wildcats were flown off the small escort carriers and steamed into the attack. The Fighter Direction Officers were inexperienced and wrongly directed them to their targets. The Wildcats made fewer interceptions as a result, although they did shoot down eight of the bombers. Seven more were shot down by anti-aircraft fire. Bombs fell close to two other light carriers; the *Fanshaw Bay* was hit and was forced to retire from the operation.

That same evening, the US submarine *Cavalla* spotted part of the large Japanese force 780 miles to the west of Saipan, but the message did not reach Spruance until 0345 hours on 18 June. At this point, he could have ordered TG58-2 and TG58-3 to steer towards the enemy and launch an air strike, but Spruance did not want to split his forces. Spruance, with his 12 light carriers and the rest of the invasion fleet, decided to stay within 100 miles of Saipan in order to meet any enemy attack that should threaten the amphibious landing by the Marine Corps and US Army assault troops. The four American carrier groups rendezvoused at noon. Land-based reconnaissance aircraft and air searches from the US flat-tops failed to find the Japanese fleet, but enemy catapult-launched floatplanes succeeded in finding elements of Task Force 58 in the early afternoon. In 'C' Force, Rear Admiral S. Obayashi ordered 67 strike aircraft ready on deck, but the mission was cancelled on orders from Vice-Admiral Ozawa who wished to attack the next day.

Sixteen E13A 'Jake' seaplanes were launched from the decks of the Japanese carriers in 'C Force at 0445 hours on 19 June, followed by 14 more from

THE AIR WAR AT SEA IN THE SECOND WORLD WAR

Obayashi's aircraft carriers, half an hour later. At 0530 hours a D4Y1-C 'Judy' reconnaissance plane from Guam, which discovered the American carrier groups, was promptly shot down by fighters of VF-28 from *Monterey*. The first group was intercepted by the combat air patrol from TG58-4 who shot down eight of the seaplanes. The second reconnaissance group turned back for their carriers after failing to sight the American fleet, but at 0730 hours, on the way home, one of the seaplanes spotted ships of TG58-4 and flashed the sighting report to Vice-Admiral Ozawa. Ozawa acted immediately and the order was given to assemble an air striking force on the decks of his carriers. By 0830 hours 45e A6M2 'Zero' fighter-bombers, eight Nakajima B6N2 'Jill' torpedo bombers and 16 A6M5 Zero fighters from 'C Force were in the air. Close behind came 53 D4Y 'Judy' dive bombers, 27 'Jills' and 48 'Zeros' from A' Force, which began taking off around 0900 hours. At 0930 hours 'B' Force dispatched 25 A6M2s, 7 B6N2s and 15 A6M5 'Zeros'. While the aircraft of 'A' Force were taking off, the US submarine *Albacore*, lurking in the depths beneath the enemy, fired six torpedoes at Ozawa's flagship *Taihō*. A Japanese pilot who made a suicide dive on the tin fish before it could strike the carrier exploded one torpedo. Another torpedo struck the carrier and caused some damage to the forward elevator and some fuel lines, but the *Taihō* continued to launch her aircraft. At the same time the air strike force was fired on by nervous gunners in 'C' Force. Two aircraft were shot down and another eight were damaged before identification was correctly established.

Instructions for the attack were picked up by the R/T monitoring system on board the American flat-tops. It came as no surprise to the Hellcat pilots, therefore, when the eight B6Ns broke away from the main formation at 18,000 ft and descended to sea level to begin their torpedo attacks. The 'Jills' were intercepted in their dives by six Hellcats of VF-25 from *Cowpens* but they were too fast for the American fighters and only one of the torpedo bombers was brought down. Meanwhile, eight Hellcats of VF-15 from the *Essex* attacked the covering 'Zeros' at 25,000 ft and were soon joined by Hellcats of VF-2 from the *Hornet* and VF-27 from the *Princeton*. Japanese aircraft which managed to escape the Hellcats were met by VF-10 from the *Enterprise*, which shot down three aircraft before the anti-aircraft barrage opened up. By now the Japanese had abandoned any thoughts of attacking the carriers and the 20 survivors decided to hit the battleships of TG58-7, which were closer. One 550 lb bomb hit the *South Dakota*, killing 27 men in the explosion, but seventeen enemy aircraft were shot down by gunners on

THE BATTLE OF THE PHILIPPINE SEA

the ships. The fighters had had a field day, shooting down 42 of the enemy for the loss of only three Hellcats.

The second Japanese strike fared as badly as the first, although the dropping of 'chaff (thin metal strips designed to 'snow' enemy radar) proved successful and American interceptors were sent to the wrong location to attack the fake blips. Once again, the Japanese air leader took his planes into a circle and over the radio waves made his plans obvious to anyone listening. Eighty-one Hellcats already airborne intercepted the real raid about 55 miles from the carriers, while 33 more followed closely behind after being flown off the carriers. First to attack was Commander David D. McCampbell's six Hellcats of VF-15, which went after the dive bombers. Six minutes later, VF-14 from *Wasp* joined the fight, followed by 23 Hellcats of VF-16 from the *Lexington* and eight more from VF-27. Altogether, the Hellcats destroyed 70 aircraft for the loss of only four Hellcats. Lieutenant Alexander Vraciu of VF-16 shot down six 'Judy' dive bombers, making him the navy's leading ace with 18 'kills'. David McCampbell, who was to finish the war as the US Navy's top-scoring fighter pilot with 34 victories and the Medal of Honor, shot down four enemy aircraft in this engagement and three more in a second action on 19 June. Only about 20 enemy aircraft managed to break through the fighter defences and reach the American destroyer screen. The majority were brought down by intense anti-aircraft fire. A few of the bombers dropped their bombs and torpedoes, but those that did hit only caused minor damage to the aircraft carriers *Bunker Hill* and *Wasp*. By 1200 hours, it was all over and the 30 survivors began returning to their carriers.

Twenty minutes later, the submarine *Cavalla* struck again; this time, three of its torpedoes hit the *Shōkaku*, which caught fire and exploded three hours later, killing most of the 1,263-man crew. By coincidence the *Taihō*, which had been hit earlier, blew up at almost the same instant the *Shōkaku* was hit when vapour from its ruptured fuel tanks ignited, sending blasts throughout the carrier. Ozawa and his senior officers were taken off and transferred to a cruiser, but only 500 men from the 2,150 crew had been rescued when a further explosion signalled the end of the ship. The carrier capsized and sank beneath the waves.

At around 1300 hours, the Avengers and Helldivers that had been orbiting to the east of the carriers were unleashed on Orote Field on Guam. The bombers blasted the airstrip with 500 lb and 1,000 lb bombs until it was so badly cratered that it was of no use to enemy aircraft damaged in action against

THE AIR WAR AT SEA IN THE SECOND WORLD WAR

the Hellcats. Meanwhile, the Japanese air strikes continued. The 47 aircraft in 'B' Force had been sent too far northward. About 20 bombers turned to search for the carriers, but Hellcats of VF-1 from the *Yorktown* and VF-2 from the *Hornet* destroyed seven of the enemy and the survivors dropped their bombs hastily and at random without hitting anything, although the *Essex* was missed by only 30 yards. The third strike, involving 87 aircraft launched from *Zuikaku* and the three light carriers of 'B' Force, was also misdirected and the force flew too far to the south of the American fleet. The 18 'Zeros' from the *Zuikaku* turned for home. En route, three 'Zeros' were shot down when ten tangled with two Avengers and a Hellcat on a search patrol. Only a few bombers found the southern carrier group and the bombing was weak and ineffectual. Nine D4Ys and six A6M5s, unmolested, attacked the *Wasp* and *Bunker Hill* only to place their bombs well wide of the mark. Four of the dive bombers were shot down by anti-aircraft fire. Meanwhile, the remaining 49 aircraft in the enemy strike force was heading for Guam. They were intercepted by 41 Hellcats who shot down 38 aircraft in five minutes and damaged another 19 beyond repair.

By 1600 hours, the great air battles were over, although a skirmish between Hellcats of VF-15 and a dozen 'Zeros' shortly before sunset resulted in the loss of the CO, Commander Charles Walter Brewer and two of his wingmen. 'Charlie' Brewer was credited with 6.5 air-to-air victories. That night, Hellcats sought further combat over Guam and Rota but the only successes went to two F6F-3NS of VF(N)-77A from the *Essex* which shot down three enemy aircraft as they tried to take off. A dawn raid on 20 June by Hellcats from *Essex*, *Cowpens* and *Langley* destroyed or damaged a further 30 enemy aircraft.[85] Clearly, the great

---

85. On 11 May 1945, the *Langley* pulled out of the battle-line, where the carrier was with Task Force 58, the Fast Carrier Groups, and the ship was ordered to Hawaii and then to the USA, for repair and refitting. The *Langley* had been at sea continuously for 18 months without a port of call, other than advanced anchorage at Ulithi Atoll. Donald White, squadron skipper, had been shot down over Tokyo and assumed dead. He showed up in a prisoner-of-war camp near Yokohama, Japan, in September 1945. VF-23 returned to NAS Alameda at the end of May 1945. On return to San Francisco Bay, eight airmen - the fighter pilots - were assigned to reorganise VF-23 with a contingent of 20 new pilots, to train and reshape the squadron onto F4U Corsairs. This was intended to prepare for using Okinawa and other islands, as bases for the coming invasion of the Japanese homeland.

THE BATTLE OF THE PHILIPPINE SEA

battles on the 19th had revealed that the Japanese crews were not of the same calibre as those the US Navy pilots had confronted in the battles of the Coral Sea, Midway and the Solomons. Many who had completed their indoctrination were only half trained and some were still under training when they flew from Japan to the battle zone. The same appears to have been true among the gunners and fighter controllers on board the carriers. Ozawa had lost 243 aircraft and over 30 damaged out of 373 which had been dispatched against the American fleet, while other losses reduced the number of survivors to just 102. Fifty-eight land-based aircraft had also been shot down in the air and another 52 destroyed on the ground. Japan could not hope to replace the horrendous losses in pilots and crews, while American losses amounted to just 23 aircraft shot down (including 14 Hellcats and one Dauntless) and six more lost operationally. Hellcat pilots had accounted for 250 of the enemy aircraft shot down on 19 June.

Once again, in battle, the opposing American and Japanese fleets, sailing 400 miles apart, never faced each other or fired their massive guns at each other. Air power had once more decided the outcome of a major battle at sea and this time there would be no recovery for the Japanese. The US Navy had destroyed Japan's naval air power. All that remained was for Spruance to chase the Japanese carriers, narrow the 400-mile gap between them and then, when in range, send off his bombers to destroy them too. Unfortunately, American reconnaissance aircraft could not locate the enemy fleet and Spruance was also duty-bound to protect the bridgehead on Saipan. At dawn on 20 June, scouts were flown off the carriers to help aid the search, but they too drew a blank. Ozawa's force could have reached safety at this point by heading for Japan, but the Japanese commander, now aboard the *Zuikaku*, believed that the majority of his missing aircraft had landed on Guam and would be ready for another strike on what was left of the American carrier force. (Returning crews had reported hundreds of American aircraft shot down and at least four carriers sunk.) He decided to refuel and join the battle as soon as possible.

The time taken to refuel enabled Task Force 58 to close the distance sufficiently for an air strike on the enemy. At around 1600 hours, an Avenger reconnaissance aircraft from the *Enterprise* sighted the Japanese fleet and radioed its position to Mitscher. They were 300 miles from the American carriers. If Mitscher sent off his aircraft immediately, they could reach the seven remaining Japanese carriers, but it would mean they would have to land back on their carriers in the dark. He pondered for a brief moment, then turned to his staff on the bridge of the *Lexington* and said, 'Launch 'em'. At about 1630 hours, 50 Helldivers, 27 Dauntless dive bombers and 54 Avengers, escorted by 85 Hellcats, took off from the carriers and headed westwards in gathering darkness.

Half a dozen fuel tankers were spotted first and a section of Dauntlesses from *Wasp* broke away to attack and sink two of them. The rest of the force pressed on until 30 miles ahead it sighted the Japanese fleet protected only by about 40 Zero fighters. They fought well and succeeded in shooting down six Hellcats, four Avengers and ten Helldivers, but only about 15 'Zeros' survived the frenetic 20-minute air battle. Four TBM Avengers of Torpedo Squadron 24 from *Belleau Wood*, led by Lieutenant (jg) George B. Brown, made runs on the *Hiyō* and two hits were thought to have been made. Brown's aircraft was so badly shot up during the low-level strike that he ordered the crew to bail out. Brown stayed with his aircraft and a wing-mate tried in vain to lead him back to his carrier. Brown was last seen disappearing into cloud. The outnumbered but valiant 'Zero' pilots could not prevent the dive bombers causing several fires on board the *Zuikaku* either. The carrier *Chiyōda* was also ablaze and a cruiser and a battleship had also been damaged.

The American aircraft broke off their attacks and returned to their carriers, 300 miles distant. Few of the American pilots had ever made a night landing on a carrier before and hitting the rolling decks in the darkness would be well-nigh impossible. Mitscher threw caution to the wind and ordered all available lights on the carriers to be turned on to help guide the tired and over-anxious fighter and bomber pilots in. Low on fuel, they had but one chance to find the deck and land safely. Unfortunately, the assistance of searchlights, navigation lights and flight-deck floodlights and red masthead lights was not enough and 80 aircraft either crashed on the decks or splashed into the sea. The thirsty Helldivers suffered particularly badly and over 25 had to be ditched because of fuel starvation. Only five SBC2S landed back on board the carriers. The rescue services worked around the clock and managed to save the majority of pilots and crew. Overall, only 49 of the 209 aircrew were lost.

THE BATTLE OF THE PHILIPPINE SEA

The Battle of the Philippine Sea, as it was officially called, ended in victory for the US Pacific Fleet in what was the last carrier battle of the Pacific War. Once again, US Navy aviation had decided the outcome of the battle, which will forever be known as the 'Great Marianas Turkey Shoot'.[86]

---

86. At the Battle of Leyte Gulf in October 1944, aircraft of Air Group 20 (led by VF- 20) from the fast carriers (TF 38) were largely responsible for the sinking of the 64,000-ton battleship *Musashi*. The escort carrier *Gambier Bay* was sunk by guns fired by Japanese cruisers. *St Lo* was sunk by Kamikazes and suicide aircraft damaged six other escort carriers. Land-based Japanese attacks from airfields on Luzon sank the *Princeton* with bombs in Phase 1 of the battle on the morning of 24 October, and she became the first fast carrier lost since the original *Hornet* at the Battle of Santa Cruz. Finally, in Phase 4 of the battle, aircraft of VT-19 and VT-44 from the *Lexington* and the *Langley* together sank the *Chitose, Zuihō* and *Zuikaku*, the last of the six carriers that launched the attack on Pearl Harbor on 7 December 1941.

Chapter 14

The British Pacific Fleet

Before dawn on 19 April 1944 two Allied aircraft carriers, the USS Saratoga *and* HMS Illustrious *and 20 other warships of the British Eastern Fleet at anchor in Trincomalee Bay in Ceylon set sail for an air strike (Operation 'Cockpit') on the Japanese port and oil facilities and airfields on Sabang Island off the northern tip of Sumatra. It was the first major offensive raid by the Fleet Air Arm in the Far East since their retreat to the western side of the Indian Ocean in 1942. At 0650 hours, first light, thirteen Corsairs of 1830 and 1833 Squadrons and 17 Barracudas of 810 and 847 Squadrons from* Illustrious *and 53 SBD Dauntlesses, Hellcats and Avengers from* Saratoga, *were launched in a pre-emptive strike on the airfield from the carriers, catching the Japanese by surprise. The Corsairs and Hellcats destroyed 24 Japanese aircraft on the ground. Only one Allied aircraft - a Hellcat - failed to return, the pilot being picked up by a rescue submarine. During recovery aboard* Illustrious *four of 1833 Squadron's Corsair IIs, which were flying CAP, intercepted a Mitsubishi Ki-21 'Sally' reconnaissance bomber and shot it down in flames into the sea. On 17 May, Operation 'Transom', a joint air strike, was made on oil refineries and the port of Surabaya, Java, Dutch East Indies. As* Illustrious *and the rest of the task force returned to Ceylon for replenishment,* Saratoga *headed for Puget Sound Naval Shipyard for an overhaul. On 10 June aircraft from* Illustrious *again launched air attacks on Sabang, covered by ships of Eastern Fleet, as a diversion during US landings on the Marianas. On the return passage* Illustrious *launched air attacks on the harbour and airfield at Port Blair. On 22 July aircraft from* Indomitable, Illustrious *and* Victorious *returned to attack Sabang once more. When air strikes were launched on the 25th, Corsairs*

THE BRITISH PACIFIC FLEET

intercepted ten Japanese fighters and shot down 7 of them for loss of two Corsairs.

The Royal Navy was building its naval strength in the Indian Ocean, in preparation for joining the war in the Pacific and 'Transom' and 'Cockpit' would prove to be the first of several carrier raids on oil targets conducted by the British-led Eastern Fleet during 1944 and 1945 with the aim of disrupting fuel supplies to Japanese forces in the Pacific.

On 17 November 1944 the task force comprising *Illustrious* and *Indomitable*, three cruisers and five destroyers departed Trincomalee in Ceylon in Operation 'Outflank', the first combat operation by the British Pacific Fleet. Its commander was Rear Admiral Sir Philip L. Vian, who had recently arrived in the theatre to assume command of the 1st Aircraft Carrier Squadron at Trincomalee. Early on 20 November the carriers launched 27 Grumman Avenger bombers and 28 Vought Corsair and Grumman Hellcat fighters to attack Pangkalan Brandan, an important centre for oil production in the north-western part of Sumatra in the Dutch East Indies but the onset of bad weather forced the attackers to divert further south, to the secondary target, the oil installations of Belawan Deli. But the attacking aircraft were forced to fly through low cloud and squalls and the attack produced only minor damage to the port facilities. During the afternoon the carrier-borne aircraft attacked airfields near Sabang. There were no British losses, and the task force returned to Ceylon on 23 November.

On 20 December 1944 the primary target of Operation 'Robson' was once again the refinery at Pangkalan Brandan. The order of battle for the operation consisted of Force 67, the strike force, and Force 69, the oiler group. Rear Admiral Philip Vian had his flag aboard the *Indomitable* (21 Avenger IIs of 857 Squadron and 28 Hellcat IIs of 1839 and 1844 Naval Air Squadrons). Also in Force 67 were the *Illustrious* (21 Avengers of 854 Naval Air Squadron and 28 Corsairs of 1830 and 1833 Naval Air Squadrons), three cruisers, and five destroyers.

The strike force sailed from Trincomalee on 17 December, and met Force 69 the following day. Undetected, the fleet reached the flying-off position, north of Diamond Point, in the early morning of 20 December. For the strike force, *Indomitable* supplied twelve, and *Illustrious*, sixteen Grumman TBF Avengers, each with four 500-lb bombs. *Illustrious* supplied four Vought

THE AIR WAR AT SEA IN THE SECOND WORLD WAR

F4U Corsairs, each with two 500-lb bombs. Top cover was provided by eight Hellcats from *Indomitable*, middle cover by twelve Corsairs from *Illustrious*, and close cover by a further eight Hellcats from *Indomitable*.

At the flying-off position, low clouds and heavy squalls reduced visibility, prompting Vian to delay the launch for twenty minutes. The operation finally began at 0636 hours. One of *Indomitable*'s Avengers crashed into the sea after take-off, but its crew survived. The other Avengers and the escort force departed from the fleet at 0715, and the strike Corsairs took off shortly after. The strike force ran into thick cloud as they neared the Sumatran coast. Lieutenant Commander W. Stuart the Strike Leader, flew through a gap in the clouds to inspect the target but was unable to locate it and the attack was diverted to the secondary target, Belawan Deli, where the weather was not much improved. The Avengers bombed the wharves from 1500 feet, while the Corsairs strafed the fuel storage tanks and warehouses in the town. A train was also hit at nearby Kuala Simpang. Two of the Corsairs became lost and strafed a large storage tank at either Pangkalan Brandan or Pangkalan Susu. The defences of Belawan Deli were unprepared: the anti-aircraft artillery was ineffective and no fighters were put in the air, although one Mitsubishi Ki-21 was surprised and downed by a Hellcat. The raid ended in chaos, with complete loss of radio discipline.

It was not until 4 January 1945, during Operation 'Lentil' that Vian could properly carry out the first stage of attacks on oil refineries at Pangkalan Brandan. *Indomitable, Indefatigable* and *Victorious*, which were escorted by four cruisers and eight destroyers, had embarked a total of 88 fighters and bombers. At 0715 hours Rear Admiral Vian launched 27 Avenger torpedo and level bombers escorted by 28 Hellcat and Vought Corsair fighter-bombers. This was the first major naval action in which Fairey Firefly F.1 two-seat carrier-borne fighter-reconnaissance aircraft took part. Fireflies of 1770 Squadron flown off *Indefatigable* were tasked to carry out rocket attacks on Pangkalan Brandan between 1 and 7 January before the main Fleet action of 24 January, in which 48 Avengers, 16 Hellcats and 32 Corsairs played their part. Hellcats of 1839 and 1844 Squadrons flying from the carrier *Indomitable* provided close escort support during the early strike on Pangkalan Brandan (and again in the large operations against Palembang on 24 and 29 January when the 16 Hellcats were joined by 32 Corsairs of 1830 and 1833 Squadrons from *Illustrious*). However, finding their target at Pangkalan Brandan obscured by cloud, the strike aircraft attacked the port at Belawan Deli as an alternative, achieving only modest results as the target area was obscured by heavy squalls and low cloud. As the aircraft returned to their carriers, they attacked the airfields around Sabang, destroying several Japanese aircraft on the ground. On 2 January the first victory in air combat by a Firefly took place when Lieutenant Dennis Levitt of 1770 Squadron claimed a Nakajima Ki.43 Hayabusa (Oscar) fighter.

Considerable damage was caused to the Pangkalan Brandan refinery on 4 January. Only one aircraft, an Avenger whose crew was rescued, was lost. The fighter pilots claimed about a dozen Japanese aircraft as well as destroying another 20 on the ground. Despite the lack of discipline from some of the fighter pilots, who abandoned their main mission of protecting the bombers to engage in dogfights with the enemy, the attack on Pangkalan Brandan was pronounced a moderate success and follow-up attacks on Japanese oil production in the Pacific Theatre could now go ahead. Rear Admiral Sir Philip Vian intended to carry out a series of air operations on Sumatra in the Japanese-occupied Netherlands East Indies en route to Sydney, Australia to become the British Pacific Fleet commanded by Admiral Sir Bruce Fraser. In what would be the biggest ever opersation by the FAA in the Second World War, the targets, code named: 'Meridian I, II and III', were the Royal Dutch Oil Refinery at Pladjoe a few miles north of Palembang on the north bank of the Komerine where it joins the Musi, and the Standard Oil Refinery at Serongei Gerong at Palembang. Pladjoe was the larger of the two. Between them they were capable of meeting three-quarters of Japan's total requirement for aviation fuel. Crude oil was transported via pipelines to the large Pladjoe refinery. The confluence of the rivers, the town lying on the north side of the Musi River, some miles from its mouth and the huge refineries, all within an area of five square miles, was to make spotting the target straightforward. It proved the Royal Navy's heaviest assault on the Japanese to date.

On 13 January Task Force 63 left Trincomalee Bay at 1430 hours in the first stage of its planned deployment to Sydney. The Task Force comprised the battleship *King George V*, four cruisers and six destroyers and Vian's 1st Aircraft Carrier Squadron with the *Indomitable* (flag), *Illustrious*, *Indefatigable* and *Victorious* and 220 strike aircraft in total. On board *Indomitable* were 28 Hellcats and 21 Avengers, *Illustrious*: 28 Corsairs of 1830 and 1833 Squadrons and 21 Avengers, *Victorious*, 28 Corsairs of 1834 and 1836 Squadrons and 21 Avengers, *Indefatigable*: 40 Seafires, 12 Fireflies and 21 Avengers. Before the Force left Trincomalee, all four carrier-groups took part in a rehearsal attack on Colombo. An intensive mission briefing took place starting the day after TF 63 put to sea. The senior officers of the squadrons, after studying target models, then told their aircrews and worked out a plan of attack. They were told that there would be an attack on each refinery and if necessary, a third to mop up anything that was left undamaged. (The British Pacific Fleet was not capable of mounting simultaneous strikes against both targets.)

Task Force 63 was opposed by four fighter squadrons of the 9th Air Division of the Japanese 7th Area Army and by heavy AA batteries. Aircrews were warned that there would be stiff opposition from ack-ack and fighters. They would have however, 'plenty of fighter cover from the Hellcats and Corsairs.' Aerial reconnaissance showed that there were no barrage balloons but this was to prove false on the days of the attacks.

'Meridian I', the second half of Operation *Outflank*, and the first strike against Pladjoe, was originally scheduled to take place on 22 January. However, a prolonged tropical storm of high winds and driving rain on the night of 21/22 January and again on the night of 22/23rd each time caused a 24-hour delay. This did not do the aircrews' nerves, already strained with the thought of what might happen if they fell into the hands of this particular enemy, any good. The final approach was made on the night of Tuesday 23rd/Wednesday 24th. The low cloud lifted and the four carriers made another run into the flying position, about 70 miles east of Engano Island, for a take-off. The wind had dropped and the rain stopped but there was low cloud over the fleet. At 0630 launching of 43 Avenger bombers armed with 172 500 lb bombs began. Twelve rocket-armed Fireflies from *Indefatigable* were detailed to strafe the balloons during their rocket dives. Top cover and Fighter 'Ramrods' (strafing attacks on enemy fighter opposition on the ground by groups of fighters) on three airfields in the area were to be the tasks of 89 Corsairs and Hellcats. *Illustrious* and *Victorious* each contributed 12 Corsairs and *Indefatigable*, her Seafires, to create the 'Ramrods'. In order to prevent the enemy fighters from reacting in strength, four Avengers and six Hellcats of the fighter escort were to attack Mana airfield on the West Coast. Although a diversion, their main aim was to put out of action the runway and reconnaissance bombers which were known to be there.

Because of launching difficulties, the 12 Fireflies, which were detailed to provide low cover and then strafe the balloons ahead of the Avengers, left long after the main strike had disappeared towards the mountains of Sumatra and

THE BRITISH PACIFIC FLEET

joined only at the tail end of the action. This left just eight Corsairs of 1833 Squadron to provide the whole of the low cover for the Avengers. Lieutenant Commander Norman S. 'Hans' Hanson the Squadron CO was shot down and crashed into the sea half-a-mile astern of his carrier but, although being carried below the surface, unconscious and still strapped in his cockpit, he recovered before his Corsair finally sank, escaped from the aircraft and was picked up by a destroyer 35 minutes later.

The fighter-sweep destroyed 34 enemy aircraft on the airfields, but was unable to prevent about 20 Japanese fighters from getting airborne. The escort accounted for 14 enemy aircraft, for the loss of seven FAA aircraft from all causes. By 0940 the first planes started to land on the carriers and the fleet then withdrew to the southwest. Acting Lieutenant Colonel Ronnie Hay RM, the Air Co-ordinator thought that it had been one of the better strikes the Fleet Air Arm had ever accomplished. All told, Force 63 lost two Avengers, six Corsairs and a Hellcat in combat, while the pilots of a Corsair and a Seafire bailed out over the fleet. Production at the Royal Dutch Refinery at Pladjoe was halved for three months and all its storage burnt out. A few merchant ships were attacked in the course of the strikes; at Pladjoe one of Japan's largest surviving tankers was damaged beyond repair.

There was to be a second attack, on 29 January, on the second largest refinery at the Standard Oil Refinery at Serongei Gerong, also in the Palembang vicinity. 'Meridian II' benefited from the lessons of the earlier raid, but after 'Meridian I' the Fleet had to withdraw for refuelling and it was something of a shambles due to inexperience. To aircrews this was an awful waste of time and a five-day wait for the next attack was bad on the nerves. Meanwhile, the enemy, knowing that another attack was almost certainly imminent because the other refinery had been left untouched, strengthened their defences and brought down from the north some crack fighter squadrons to augment the local squadrons. This time the FAA fighter sweep would concentrate on the two major airfields. To cover Talangbetoetoe airfield *Victorious* despatched 12 Corsairs, while two Fireflies were sent up from *Indefatigable* to carry out an armed recce of Mana airfield.

Lieutenant Colonel Ronnie Hay, who was awarded the DSO for his part in 'Meridian' reported that on the strike against the oil refineries at Songei Gerong the return was without opposition of any kind. He concluded that 'Meridian' One and Two had been the most interesting and successful operations he had ever known and in both cases, they accomplished their objective. He singled out special praise for the determination of the Avenger pilots 'who bombed so accurately in the face of maximum discouragement. The fighter escort proved itself against the most serious air opposition it has so far met.'

'Meridian II' proved even more successful than the 24 January strike but enemy fighters were up in force and there were continuous air battles all the way to the target when the heavy and accurate AA took over. The strike was pressed home and the Standard Oil Refinery at Serongei Gerong was put out of action for two months and when it did start again it was at greatly reduced capacity. In addition to 38 enemy aircraft destroyed on the ground by the fighter sweep, over 30 were shot down by the escort. In the early afternoon, the CAP shot down a group of eight aircraft that intelligence officers learned were from the 'Special Army Attack Corps', or kamikazes and more attacks were expected. All told, on 29 January eleven Avengers and 19 pilots or aircrew were lost. Crews complained about lack of adequate protection. Altogether, 16 FAA aircraft were lost.

Force 63 was now due to carry out 'Meridian III' next morning (30 January) but how many planes would be ready by then was doubtful and the nerves of the pilots had worn thin. Many believed that the casualties would be appalling. Crews spent the morning of the 29th in a state of gloom but, at midday, the Tannoy blared out 'Meridian III has been cancelled'. The fuel situation would not allow more than one further attack. Crews felt 'as if a ton weight had been lifted from them'. The carriers and their consorts headed for Freemantle and Sydney having inflicted enormous damage on the refineries, the effects of which would last for months. The air groups had cut the aviation gasoline output from Sumatra to 35 per cent of its normal level, at a time when Japan was desperately short of oil in any form. Probably, the three strikes in January 1945 against Pangkalan Brandon, Pladjoe and Serongei Gerong were the British Pacific Fleet's greatest contribution to the ultimate victory. Sixty-eight Japanese aircraft were destroyed. British losses amounted to 16 aircraft lost in battle, eleven ditched, 14 destroyed in deck crashes - a total of 41 aircraft from 378 sorties. Personnel losses amounted to 30 aircrew.

The air strikes put both refineries out of action and neither recovered full capacity before the end of the war but the decision to attack the refineries on separate days had telegraphed the intention to return and the second strike suffered in consequence. Subsequent underway replenishment using the inefficient 'astern' method proved to be slow, with none of the carriers able to take on the amount of fuel oil they needed in the time available. Japanese aircraft located and attacked the BPF on 29 January, but combat air patrol (CAP) fighters shot down all of them. A total of 48 FAA aircraft were lost due to enemy action and crash landings and 30 aircrews were lost, some of them without a trace. Thirty Japanese aircraft were claimed 'destroyed' in the air and 38 on the ground. Three Fleet Air Arm crews (nine men) were captured by the Japanese during the Palembang raid. They were taken to Singapore where they were tortured and imprisoned. Finally, in August 1945, they were executed by the Japanese military authorities four days after the Japanese surrender.

The British Pacific Fleet's carriers would offer a capability that US planners could not ignore. Royal Navy aircraft losses were made good when the fleet arrived at Sydney on 10 February and on the 17th, *Illustrious*, *Indefatigable*, *Indomitable*, *Formidable* and *Victorious* joined Task Force 57, a part of the US 5th Fleet, which was destined for Operation 'Iceberg', the landings to capture Okinawa. Two afloat maintenance carriers - HMS *Unicorn* and HMS *Pioneer* with replacement aircraft and workshops able to prepare more planes for operations as they arrived in ferry carriers - would be based in the Admiralties and the Philippines, where air stations were ready just in time to provide shore-based facilities for the carrier squadrons.

During March to May 1945 aircraft of the 1st Aircraft Carrier Squadron of the British Pacific Fleet would mount an intensive bombing campaign on Japanese fighter bases on Formosa and islands south of Japan to assist the American landing at Okinawa. Ten fast carriers rotated in and out of TF 57, s. After stopping at Manus Island in the Admiralty Islands the BPF sailed with TF 57 for Ulithi Atoll in the Carolines. The BPF was to seal the six Japanese airfields on the Sakishima Gunto Island Group east of Formosa and south-west of Okinawa and the other Ryukyo Islands, whilst the Americans took Okinawa. The British Pacific Fleet would operate as a separate unit from the American task forces in Operation 'Iceberg'. Four US escort carriers would replace the British carriers when they were absent. Designated Task Force 57 (although it was only the size of an American task group) the BPF operated to the southwest of TF 58. Its task was to prevent the build-up of six potentially kamikaze staging airfields on the Sakishima Gunto Island group east of Formosa and southwest of Okinawa and the other Ryukyu Islands, using gunfire and air attack in cycles of two strike days followed by two days of replenishment. Supermarine Seafire fighters, naval versions of

THE AIR WAR AT SEA IN THE SECOND WORLD WAR

Spitfires that had been employed solely for CAP because of their limited endurance, had received improvised fittings so that they could carry large external fuel tanks, enabling them to carry out strike and escort missions and greatly increasing their usefulness.

TF 57 reached its flying-off position about 100 miles south of Sakishima Gunto on 26 March and the first strike went ahead using forty Avengers, twelve flak-suppression Fireflies and small formations of Corsairs and Hellcats. The air attacks were repeated on the 27th before the task force withdrew for replenishment. The airfields proved unrewarding targets, as the enemy repaired their runways, made of crushed coral, every night. The BPF's lack of night-flying capability was keenly felt, although some experienced Avenger pilots from the *Indomitable* flew predawn strikes to attack Japanese aircraft staging through the islands.

After a period of bad weather, on 1 April Japanese aircraft appeared over the invasion fleet in some strength. High-level bombers, followed by aircraft piloted by Kamikaze suicide pilots made their attacks and *Indefatigable* became the first British carrier to be hit by a kamikaze when a 'Zero' broke through the ship's CAP of eight Seafires and then carried out a front gun attack on *King George V* at about 0727 hours before making a feint diving attack on the *Indefatigable*'s starboard side, during which he was engaged by a Seafire. The 'Zeke' turned inside it and executed a 45° power dive from about 1,200 ft towards the carrier's port quarter. In the final dive the Seafire again engaged, but broke off when it seemed likely that he would follow the enemy into the ship. The 'Zeke' hit abreast the foremost barrier at the junction of the flight-deck and the island, burst on impact with the flight deck armour and rendered the other two barriers and the flight-deck, temporarily unserviceable. The siren pipes were cut, pneumatic tubes shattered, the Flight-Deck Sick Bay and Briefing Room were wrecked and a small fire was started in the roof of 'B' Hangar. Minor damage was caused by blast and splinters. Despite the damage and casualties of which eight - three of them officers - were immediately fatal, at 0742, fires in the island and hangar were reported under control and the after barrier was in action by 0800. At 0816, landing-on recommenced.

The British fleet carriers with their armoured flight decks were subject to heavy and repeated kamikaze attacks, but they proved highly resistant and returned to action relatively quickly. Unlike the wooden flight decks of the American carriers, the British ships had four-inch armoured flight decks

THE BRITISH PACIFIC FLEET

and any hole caused by an enemy attack was simply filled with quick drying cement.

At 0725 on 2 April a Japanese fighter - conflictingly reported as a 'Zeke' or 'Oscar' - made a strafing run over *Indomitable*, killing one rating and wounding two more. Another lone Kamikaze made a strike on *Indefatigable* and hit the base of the island, killing four officers and ten ratings and wounding sixteen. The carrier was put out of commission for a time but thanks to the armoured flight deck, no lasting damage was caused below. More Kamikaze attacks occurred on 6 April and a Zero got through to hit the island on *Illustrious* with its wingtip before crashing into the sea. During this suicide attack the Corsairs of 1830 Squadron and the Hellcats of 1844 Squadron shot down five Aichi D4Y Judys and a Nakajima P1Y 'Frances'.

Three minutes later, another lone kamikaze would slam into the base of *Indefatigable*'s island and put the carrier out of commission for a time but thanks to the armoured flight deck, which was only dented by about three inches, no lasting damage was caused below. Seafire pilot Sub Lieutenant R. H. Reynolds had engaged the kamikaze in its death-dive and reported hitting it repeatedly at long range, including on the wing root. He had to pull up sharply to avoid hitting the carrier himself. He was awarded a 'shared kill' credit on the kamikaze. Later, one 894 Squadron Seafires which had been diverted to *Victorious* while *Indefatigable*'s flight deck was unavailable, crashed on landing - killing its pilot. At 0755, a 'Zeke' - once again chased by Sub Lieutenant Reynolds in his Seafire - dropped a 500lb bomb close to the destroyer *Ulster*.

The USN liaison officer on *Indefatigable* commented: 'When a kamikaze hits a US carrier it means six months of repair at Pearl [Harbor]. When a kamikaze hits a Limey carrier it's just a case of 'Sweepers, man your brooms'.'

With *Indefatigable* back in action, a strike of 16 Avengers escorted by Corsairs was launched at 1215. The target was the airfields at Ishigaki. Later, TarCAP aircraft reported activity at Hirara and Isigaki. A 'Ramrod' was flown off and claimed three aircraft destroyed on the ground. A Corsair of 1834 Squadron was hit by flak and seen to make what appeared to be a perfect 'ditching'. However, he was not found by the ASR Walrus or an extensive sea and air search. At 1730 the fleet's radar again detected incoming hostile aircraft, this time at low level. The four suicide bombers from the Formosa-based 8th Air Division based at Schinchiku managed to slip past the CAP

Hellcats in cloud. They were not spotted again until they came within sight of the fleet. A single engine aircraft - it has not been established whether it was a 'Jill' or a 'Zeke' - made a dive on *Victorious*. Good handling of the ship by Captain Michael M. Denny saw the kamikaze strike a glancing blow when it touched a wing-tip to the flight deck before cart-wheeling into the ocean where it exploded harmlessly. The fleet then retired to the south-east to take up its night station. The day's FAA losses amounted to one aircraft in combat and three operationally.

When not flying CAP the Corsairs and Hellcats were tasked with strafing the airfields, but the runways were made of crushed coral and could be easily and quickly repaired after the strikes. On 12 April air strikes switched to the northern part of Formosa, where it was believed that a number of kamikaze attacks were waiting to be launched against the 5th Fleet. The first strike, by 48 Avengers and 40 Corsairs against the port of Kirun and airfields in the vicinity respectively, went ahead in bad weather. A few Corsairs found targets in the Shinchiku area and strafed aircraft on the ground. Later in the day a joint strike by Avengers and Corsairs succeeded in cratering airfield runways and destroying aircraft and buildings. Attacks on Formosa continued on the 12th when Corsairs of Nos. 1834 and 1836 Squadrons shot down three enemy fighters. Later in the day a CAP intercepted a kamikaze attack on the BPF carriers and four enemy aircraft were destroyed with six more damaged. Next day 8 Japanese aircraft were shot down during air strikes on the BPF.

By June 1945 the Royal Navy's Far Eastern Fleet came to its full strength and was divided into two parts - The East Indies Fleet (previously known as the Eastern Fleet) under the command of the Supreme Commander South East Asia Louis Mountbatten and the British Pacific Fleet (BPF) under the command of Admirals' Chester Nimitz and 'Bull' Halsey of the USN. The back-bone of the BPF was the 1st Aircraft Carrier Squadron, commanded by Rear Admiral Sir Philip Vian, which included all six of the *Illustrious*-class armoured carriers, although only four were in action at any one time.[87] There were 14 second line and fifty front line FAA squadrons, using both American and British manufactured aircraft. The Fleet Air Arm flew Fairey

---

87. In total there were 720 Royal Navy ships including 17 battleships 35 aircraft carriers, including six fleet carriers, five light fleet carriers and 24 escort carriers.

THE BRITISH PACIFIC FLEET

Firefly strike-fighters and Fairey Barracuda dive bombers, plus Corsairs, Hellcats and Avengers.[88] Supermarine Seafires were allocated the vital defensive duties of combat air patrol (CAP) over the fleet because of their good high-altitude performance, short range and lack of ordnance-carrying capabilities – compared to the Hellcats and Corsairs. The Seafires were vital in countering the kamikaze attacks during the Iwo Jima landings and beyond. The fighter's best day would be 15 August 1945, when pilots shot down eight attacking aircraft for one loss.

On 24 July Avengers of 848 Squadron on *Formidable* became the first FAA aircraft to attack the Japanese homeland, during a raid on Yokushima airfield when they were accompanied by Avengers of 828 Squadron on *Implacable*, which had taken part in the Battle of Truk in June. One of the last raids on Japan by Avengers was a strike in the Tokyo area carried out by 820 Squadron on 15 August. Between 17 July and 10 August, Corsairs of Nos. 1834 and 1836 Squadrons on *Victorious* and Nos. 1841 and 1842 Squadrons on *Formidable* carried out a series of strikes in the Tokyo area.

---

88. In the Pacific theatre, the Barracuda's performance was considerably reduced by the prevailing high temperatures; reportedly, its combat radius was reduced by as much as 30 per cent, which was a factor in the decision to re-equip the torpedo bomber squadrons aboard the BPF fleet carriers with Grumman Avengers. Another major problem hindering the Barracuda would be the need to fly over Indonesian mountain ranges to strike at targets on the eastern side of Java, which necessitated a high-altitude performance that the Barracuda's low-altitude-rated Merlin 32 engine with its single-stage supercharger could not effectively provide. Additionally, the carriage of maximum underwing bomb loads resulted in additional drag, which further reduced performance.

Chapter 15

Towards the Final Downfall

The sun and mist were breaking over the horizon as we continued to the target over an endless sea. I was nervous with anticipation over what was in store. It was hard to realize that I was actually on my way to attack the home islands of Japan as my eyes kept searching the sky for enemy aircraft and the ocean below for enemy ships or any sign of life. I calculated the force of the wind from the size of the waves and kept track of our course on my plotting board. If we were to encounter enemy planes and I was to get lost in the melee, it would be my only tool to help me find my way home to the fleet.

'*An hour of monotonous searching and checking had passed when suddenly through the mist appeared our target – Saeki Naval Base located on the shoreline of Kyushu. I forgot all the imaginary problems and concentrated on the target, arming my guns, bombs and setting my outboard rockets to fire. I checked all the instruments to make sure all were in working order.*

'*My adrenaline was really flowing as we pushed over in our attack. I went to the outside of the formation and a little behind Windy so that I could concentrate on the target. There were parked aircraft lined up on the runway and with the red 'Jap' meatball zeroed in on my gun-sight, I blasted away. I was almost mesmerized watching the first plane explode in a violent ball of flame and the second one fly apart as my bullets struck home.*

'*As we cleared the field, I saw a tanker cruising in the harbour. Resetting my eight rockets, I fired them in salvo while strafing the tanker. The rockets all smashed into its deck and hull. As I looked around, it was blowing and blazing and sailors were diving into the ocean: one less ship in the Jap navy. We made a few more strafing runs over the airfield and then CAG gave us the thumbs up and*

TOWARDS THE FINAL DOWNFALL

turned for home. I had not yet learned to conserve fuel while flying 'Tail End Charlie', which used much more gas than when flying lead. Pumping the throttle and flying wide in a turn would suck up your fuel all too quickly.

'Upon returning to the fleet, Intrepid was in the process of launching aircraft and was unable to land any planes. Many of us were running out of gas. The 'Big E' had just cleared their decks and had turned into the wind and they were prepared to take me aboard. As my fuel gauge showed my tanks to be nearly empty, I knew I would have to make the first approach a good one or go for a swim.

**Ensign Roy D. 'Eric' Erickson,
a Corsair pilot in VBF-10 on *Intrepid*.**

On 1 March 1945 carrier aircraft in Task Force 58 began strikes on Okinawa, a 60-mile-long island in the Ryukyu chain only 350 miles from Kyushu, before heading south to Ulithti lagoon in the Carolines. Then the US fast carrier force commanded by Admiral Marc Mitscher converged off Okinawa to begin softening up the Japanese defenders before the army and marine landing scheduled for Easter Sunday, 1 April. The Japanese troops defending Okinawa, under the command of Lieutenant General Ushijima Mitsuru, totalled some 75,000-100,000 men, augmented by thousands of civilians on the heavily populated island. American forces for the operation totalled 183,000 troops in seven divisions (four US Army and three Marine) under the Tenth Army. Finally, after an intense seven-day bombardment the main landings on Okinawa (Operation 'Iceberg') by the United States Tenth Army, comprising the US Army and Marine Corps divisions, took place at first light on 1 April, on the Hagushi beaches near the central part of the island's west coast. About 60,000 American troops landed on the first day and within a few hours, the 7th Infantry Division had taken their primary objective, Kadena airfield. Called Naka Hikojo by the Japanese, the airstrip was completed a short time prior to the amphibious landings. Kadena had a single runway constructed of crushed coral and measuring 1,500 metres in length. The nearby airfield at Yontan was also seized and the Marines pushed across the narrow waist of the island to cut it in two. There had been little opposition at the beaches as the Japanese had decided to meet the Americans farther inland out of range of naval gunfire.

THE AIR WAR AT SEA IN THE SECOND WORLD WAR

CVG-84 on *Bunker Hill* and aircraft on *Bennington* bombed and strafed beaches with napalm and gunfire as a prelude to more than 200,000 men being landed on Okinawa. Two days' later Kamikaze attacks off Okinawa threatened to disrupt the invasion and the American fighter shield was hard pressed to cope with the suicide planes. But 12 Corsairs of VMF-451 joined up with 16 Hellcats in an attack mission over Amami-Oshima and Kikai Jima and this was highly successful, the Corsairs destroying eleven of the Kamikazes while the Hellcats bagged the others. Then on the 6th and 7th the largest concentration of Kamikazes ever experienced so far appeared over the fleet. About 700 aircraft took off from Kyushu and of these 355 (230 navy and 125 army) were flown by suicide pilots bent on sinking a carrier or some other shipping. More than 200 of the Kamikazes were shot down by the fast carrier force and 50 more by the escort carriers; but 28 Kamikazes got past the combined air and sea defences and each hit a US ship, sinking three of them. On the first day Corsairs of VMF-221 'Fighting Falcons' and VMF-451 'Blue Devils' from *Bunker Hill* splashed 12 of the suicide planes and on the second day Corsairs from *Bunker Hill* and *Bennington* claimed seventeen of them.

It was impossible to intercept every Kamikaze, but the Marines' efforts saved countless lives and the aircraft they flew would earn the nickname the 'Sweetheart of Okinawa' for its contribution during Operation 'Iceberg'.

The primary mission of the Marine Corps fighters at Kadena was air superiority and air defence. Engineers attached to the 7th Infantry Division reconditioned the runway, adding extra coral to allow for the heavy fighters to operate from the newly captured airfield. Fighters at both Kadena and Yontan airfields were to conduct continuous combat air patrols to fend off the Imperial Japanese Navy and Army Air Force suicidal Kikusui attacks against the fleet. A total of ten Kikusui attacks were launched from 6 April to 22 June. The first major Japanese counterattack occurred on 6 and 7 April with attacks by kamikaze and 'Ten-Go' navy aircraft. A force, under the command of Admiral Seiichi Itō, consisting of the battleship *Yamato*, the light cruiser *Yahagi* and eight destroyers was assembled. This force was to be used as bait to draw away as many American carrier aircraft from Okinawa as possible, in order to leave Allied naval forces vulnerable to large scale Kamikaze attacks. The Japanese were short of fuel; consequently, the *Yamato* had only enough to reach Okinawa. Off Okinawa it was planned to beach the battleship and use her 18.1-inch guns to support the fighting on the island.

TOWARDS THE FINAL DOWNFALL

After being sighted by an American submarine and reconnaissance aircraft, naval attack aircraft were sent to attack the Japanese force. The 7th of April was one of the biggest days in the history of VBF-10. Early in the morning, two target CAPs from the *Intrepid* were launched over Okinawa. Commander John Hyland, commander of Carrier Air Group 10, who led one flight, shot down a 'Val' over the target and his flight then proceeded to Tokuno where they destroyed a twin-engine and a single-engine plane and damaged other grounded aircraft in revetments.

Meanwhile, aboard the *Intrepid*, considerable excitement was created by the report, made at 0830 by an *Essex* search plane, of a Japanese task group in the East China Sea steaming south towards Okinawa. It was composed of the super-battleship *Yamato*, an *Agano*-class cruiser, an *Oyodo*-class cruiser and seven destroyers. The *Yamato*, a 64,170-ton beast with nine 18.1-inch guns, had put to sea with only enough fuel for a one-way Kamikaze trip of her own. Among the 106 planes from TG58.4 that followed the main strike were 12 Corsairs of VBF-10, led by Lieutenant Commander Wilmer E. Rawie, a former Dauntless pilot who was also leader of the 75 planes of TG 58.4. One of the VBF-10 Corsairs was flown by Ensign 'Eric' Erickson, who clearly recalls this period.

'It was 1030. I was resting in my sack, having served as the duty officer for the early-morning 0600 flights, when suddenly over the squawk box I heard the message, 'Ensign Erickson report to the ready room!' I put on my pants and shirt and slipped into a pair of loafers. In case I had to go for a swim, I wanted to get out of my shoes fast. I hurried down the corridor, through several hatches, crossing the hangar deck and up the ladder to the ready room. The duty officer said, 'Get on deck.' One of my buddies, Ensign Ecker had injured his hand the day before and was unable to fly, so I took his place. They needed every available pilot. I didn't know who I was flying with and was completely unaware of the urgent situation. Jotting down 'point option' on my plotting board and putting on my flight gear, while noting the deck assignment for the aircraft, I left the ready room.

'Pilots were firing up their engines and many were already in the air. I crawled aboard my assigned plane and strapped myself in. The plane captain handed me a chocolate bar and a canteen of water. I said, 'What the hell is this for?' Never had I been treated with so much attention. He said, 'Haven't you heard? They have located the Jap fleet!' Suddenly, it dawned on me what the huge 1,000 lb bomb was doing under my plane.

THE AIR WAR AT SEA IN THE SECOND WORLD WAR

'I had never seen so much helter-skelter as the deck officer directed me forward. He rotated his flag violently and then pointed it down the deck. Pushing the throttle full forward, my plane rose from the deck. I joined up on a division that was missing a plane. I found myself flying wing on Lieutenant Wes Hays from Texas. Lieutenant (jg) Hollister and Ensign Carlisse filled the other two slots. On the way to the target, the sky became increasingly black due to rainsqualls and the heavy weather front the Japs were using as cover.

'At 0830, an *Essex* search plane sighted the *Yamato* force steaming south toward Okinawa. The Japanese were then shadowed by a pair of PBM Mariner flying boats, which held contact for five hours, despite being shot at by their prey. At 0915 Admiral Mitscher sent off 16 fighters to track the *Yamato* and at 0100, Task Groups 58.1 and 58.3 began launching a 280-plane strike. Included in this group were 98 torpedo-carrying Avengers. The *Hancock* was 15 minutes late in sending off their 53-plane contribution. We (TG 58.4) followed this main strike with 106 planes.

'Still groggy from this unexpected call to duty, I cranked off the cap to the canteen and took a swallow of water. I grabbed the candy bar that I had stuffed in a trouser leg of my flight suit and I thought about how thoughtful the plane captain had been. It provided me with a new surge of energy as I slid under the lead plane. Now the rainsqualls were getting worse and visibility was lessening. Looking down at the water, I could see white caps below and I estimated the wind to be around 25 knots, not a good day to make a water landing. No longer was the engine making imaginary noises as on my first combat flight, but was purring like a kitten. Checking all the instruments, the plane seemed to be functioning properly. We had travelled for over two hours searching the sea through this muck looking for the elusive Japanese Fleet. I hadn't been present at the briefing so I had no way of knowing exactly where we were headed, but by plotting the time and course, I knew we were somewhere south and west of Kyushu.

'At about 1330 my skipper, Lieutenant Commander Rawie ('Red One') was about ready to turn back. We were flying at 1,500 ft when, suddenly, through the scud, directly beneath me I saw a grey, massive structure. I was the first in our group to see the biggest damn battleship in the world – the mammoth 64,000-ton *Yamato*! It had been hiding under rainsqualls and low clouds. I transmitted the message to 'Red One' that the *Yamato* was directly below and Wes Hays signalled us to start our attack! We whipped into a fast 180° turn in an attempt to get on the *Yamato*! As we broke through the

1,500 ft ceiling, the *Yamato* appeared to be almost dead in the water, but still in a slow left turn. Smoking destroyers were all over the place and only two could be seen swiftly manoeuvring through the water. It was a navy pilot's dream with no enemy aircraft to repel our attacks.

'I had watched our task force shoot down Kamikazes like they were ducks in a shooting gallery and I thought, 'Oh my God! I'm now the sitting duck!' Now, I know how a Kamikaze pilot must have felt as he was preparing to make his final assault. How could all those ships down there miss when they were armed with all that sophisticated radar? It was a true test of courage! Even the *Yamato*'s 18.1 guns were shooting at the approaching aircraft (as they had in vain at the flying boats). In addition to her big guns, the *Yamato* was able to fire on us with her 24 5-inch guns and about 150 25-mm guns. The light cruisers and the destroyers joined in on the crescendo!

'We tried to get our sights on the battleship, but we had started our run so low it was impossible. I could see men scrambling all over the deck in what looked like mass hysteria! Where were they all going? Diving and pouring on the juice, we crossed over the *Yamato* and strafed the hell out of it. I could see bodies flying all over the place! In return, the sky was bursting with thousands of brass wires as the Japs' guns zeroed in on us! Looking down, I wondered why I wasn't getting hit; the tracers were so close you could smell the cordite! Black flak bursts were bouncing my plane violently from side to side and the sky was turning dark! I thought for sure this was the day for me to meet my maker!

'I could read the wake of the light cruiser *Yahagia*, an *Oyodo*-class cruiser, as it turned around toward the *Yamato* to help protect it. This was my first time to wing 'Wes', but I knew he was heading directly toward the cruiser! I moved in closer and closer on him and concentrated on his aircraft as we dropped our bombs in unison! After releasing our ordnance, we headed for cloud cover and then, as if on a roller-coaster, we dived back down and skimmed along the ocean floor strafing the destroyer *Isokaze* that lay dead ahead. Flashes of bright light were blinding us as the destroyer tried to elude our attack. Suddenly, the destroyer stopped firing as it went ablaze and dark black smoke poured from its deck. We passed over it and pulled up again into the low cloud cover. We thought we were out of range of enemy fire and as we looked back, no longer were the cruiser and destroyer in view. We circled at 5,000 ft and five miles from the *Yamato*. The clouds started to clear and we could see the battleship and the rest of our group making their attack.

THE AIR WAR AT SEA IN THE SECOND WORLD WAR

'While we were circling, I noticed great spouts of water rise from the ocean floor. My first thought was, some of us hadn't dropped our ordnance and were now doing so, but this was not the case. The damn *Yamato* was still shooting their big 18.1-inch guns at us - the largest guns in the world! Then, Air Group 10's dive bombers, torpedo planes and fighter-bomber pilots completed their run and a terrific explosion took place. Great billows of black smoke were sent skyward over 6,000 ft - the end of the biggest battleship in the world!'

Lieutenant Commander Wilmer E. Rawie's own division had scored two hits and one near miss on the *Angono* cruiser and his second division, led by 24-year-old Texan Lieutenant Robert 'Hal' Jackson, went one better. Known as the night watchman of the wardroom, Jackson, who was attending law school when Pearl Harbor was attacked, managed to sustain a completely bohemian existence amidst the otherwise regimented life aboard ship. Never on the flight-deck except to take off, the only way 'Hal' could tell whether it was night or day, was by the activity in the wardroom. He led his flight of four VBF-10 Corsairs as high roving cover and carried out a roller-coaster-type approach in order to avoid fire from the *Yamato*'s gunners. He wrote, 'The four of us came in at the *Yamato* at low level and delivered our bombs as we swept over the ship. The flak was very intense. Then we got the hell out of there as fast as we could, continuing our roller-coaster manoeuvring. One hit and several misses were observed on the ship. We circled the area below the overcast and shortly afterwards there was a tremendous explosion.' Hal's four Corsairs were the last aircraft to attack the *Yamato* and they were credited with a direct hit and two near misses on the battleship. They also strafed one of the destroyers, scoring many hits and starting a number of fires.[89]

Ensign 'Eric' Erickson concludes the report of this episode. 'The giant warship listed heavily to port and at 1423, disappeared underwater, followed by explosions of rupturing compartments and her magazines. It had taken ten torpedoes and five direct bomb hits to sink the *Yamato*. Her sister ship *Masashi* had required eleven torpedoes and 16 bombs to send her down in the Sibuyan Sea the previous October. Two light cruisers in the *Yamato* force were sent to the ocean floor. One destroyer was sunk outright; three others were so severely damaged that they were scuttled. The four other destroyers were damaged to varying degrees. Only 269 men survived the *Yamato*; 2,498

---

89. The attacks resulted in the sinking of the *Yahagi* and four of the destroyers.

TOWARDS THE FINAL DOWNFALL

including her captain and the force commander went down with her. Almost 1,200 more men were lost floundering in the sea. With the light cruiser and destroyers that were sunk, 3,700 lives were lost in the greatest Kamikaze sorties of all. In an incredulous comparison, TF 58's carriers lost three fighters, four dive bombers, three torpedo planes and a total of 12 fliers. One of the aircraft, a Corsair, was lost in a mid-air collision enroute to the attack. Our air group rendezvoused all its planes and headed for home. Not one of our aircraft was shot down and only a few tail feathers were lost in this auspicious attack.'

Okinawa would see the supreme effort made by the Kamikaze. Experienced Japanese pilots were now few and far between and barely enough were trained to be able to hit shipping by conventional means so a plan called 'Ten-Go' ('Heavenly Operation') was devised, whereby aerial attacks known as 'kikusui' or 'floating chrysanthemum' would be made on American shipping by the Kamikaze. Even though the Japanese air force was outnumbered and outclassed by Allied airpower, there would certainly be a surfeit of targets for the Kamikaze to aim for. Some 1,457 US ships would be involved in 'Iceberg', the operation to take the heavily fortified island.

More kamikaze attacks occurred on 6 April and on 8 April, a day after the USS *Hancock* was so badly damaged by a kamikaze hit that she had to return to the United States for extensive repairs, TF 58 commander Admiral Raymond Spruance requested that TF 57 strike at airfields on Formosa, believing that the armoured Royal Navy carriers would be less vulnerable than US carriers to kamikaze counterattack. Aircraft from TF 57's carriers conducted strikes against Formosan targets on 11 and 13 April. They damaged airfields, destroyed aircraft on the ground, hit road and rail targets and shot down at least 16 Japanese aircraft at the cost of three BPF aircraft lost. As TF 57 withdrew from Formosan waters, Spruance requested more BPF strikes against the Sakishima Islands, which the British command was again delighted to assist. In the fleet's absence, US escort carriers had not been able to maintain the same weight of attack as the Royal Navy carriers. TF 57 was no longer a 'flexible reserve'. Spruance's seasoned 5th Fleet now accepted the BPF as equals and an essential part of a coalition fleet under its commander's orders. On 14 April *Formidable* replaced the *Illustrious*, which had been steaming on only two of her three shafts, maintaining the number of TF 57's operational carriers at four. After strikes on 20 April, the task force sailed for Leyte Gulf to repair damage and replenish stores. It had been at sea for 32 days, the longest sortie by any British fleet since the days of sail.

It was on 8 April that Corsairs of VMF-224 destroyed three Kamikaze trying to dive on destroyers on picket duty moored off Okinawa to give radar warning of approaching aircraft. More Corsairs arrived from Guadalcanal, Espiritu Santo and Manus Island on CVEs during the first week of April to lend air support in the Battle of Okinawa. Fourteen US ships were damaged during the mass suicide attacks on 12-13 April by an estimated 185 aircraft. On 16 April, a massive air battle took place off Okinawa as the enemy put up masses of Kamikaze aircraft and Ohaka-piloted missiles. The carrier-borne Combat Air Patrol fighters destroyed 29 enemy aircraft without loss. Pride of place went to *Intrepid*'s VF-10 'Grim Reapers', which destroyed 20 Kamikazes over northern Okinawa. One VF-10 F4U-1D pilot, Ensign (later Lieutenant) (jg) Alfred Letch, shot down six Nakajima Ki-27 'Nates' and a 'Val' northwest of Okinawa. Two Kamikazes put his carrier out of action, with the loss of 20 fighters. Furthermore, ten men killed and almost 100 more injured and the *Intrepid* was forced to leave the area for repairs at Alameda. *Intrepid* took no further part in the Pacific War and VF-10 was decommissioned on 26 November 1945.

On 9 April the runway on Kadena was considered ready for fighter operations. Marine aviators were ordered to move from their carriers to 'Ruby Base', the allied code name for Kadena airfield.[90] The Marine Corsair squadrons based on Kadena were assigned to Marine Aircraft Group 33; a second group, MAG-31, was located on Yontan Field just north of Kadena. The first action came during the second Kikusui attack on 12 April. Pilots of a flight in VMF-312 led by Captain Dan H. Johnson intercepted 20 'Zeros' and four 'Jill' dive bombers and shot down eight Zeros and damaged six more. The enemy formation turned back before reaching their intended target. More than 185 Japanese aircraft took part in the raids between 12-13 April during which seventeen kamikaze aircraft hit allied ships. The mass kamikaze attacks were usually escorted by fighters and conventional sorties were flown

---

90. Pilots from Marine Fighter Squadron, or VMF, 312, the 'Checkerboarders' were the first to land their F4U-1D Corsairs on the field. The squadron was soon followed by VMF-323's 'The Death Rattlers', VMF-322's 'Fighting Gamecocks' and a single night fighter squadron, VMF(N)-543's 'Night Hawks', operating Grumman F6F(N) Hellcats.

TOWARDS THE FINAL DOWNFALL

against the allied invasion. Japanese ground forces shelled Kadena daily, while night-time bombing sorties were flown against the airstrip. Combat air patrols were launched from Kadena regardless of daily artillery fire.

Invariably, the US carrier pilots' targets were deep in enemy territory. Over several days, strikes by US Naval warplanes were mounted up and down the Nansei Islands. Large airfields aircraft and military installations were attacked by ground-level strafing and rocket attacks and factories bombed from low altitude by dive bombers. Japanese shipping was sunk whenever they could be found. While sweeps and strikes were hitting land targets, combat air patrols in the air fended off Kamikaze attacks, which dropped out of the skies on a one-way trip packed with explosives.

TF 57 sailed for further operations against the Sakishima Islands on 1 May. Three days later, as the Task Force came within striking distance of Japan the battleships *King George V* and *Howe* and five cruisers detached from the force's screen to close the islands and bombard their airfields. Despite the FAA Corsair pilots best efforts a kamikaze hit the *Formidable* at the base of her island, releasing what appeared to be a 500 lb bomb a second before impact. A sheet of flame rose to funnel height. The blast punched a two-foot-square hole in the armoured flight deck and eleven aircraft on deck were destroyed, Casualties were caused around the control tower and Sub Lieutenant Bell RNVR one of the pilots, was killed. Wally Stradwick, a 22-year-old pilot from Clapham, was flying his Corsair at 6,000 ft above *Formidable* when he saw a kamikaze pilot crash into its flight deck. In his diary he recalled: 'One of our carriers appeared to explode. I could only see the bows protruding from a colossal pall of black smoke in the centre of which was an ugly sheet of flame.' Remarkably, *Formidable* was fully operational again by the end of the day after a repair crew plugged the hole with a wood and cement patch, over which was tack-welded thin steel plates and flight operations resumed. *Formidable*'s captain grasped the arm of an American liaison officer standing alongside and, shaking his fist, asked, 'What do you think of our bloody British flight decks now?'

'Sir,' came the reply, 'they're a honey.'

Indomitable was the target of the second kamikaze attack that day. Billowing steam and smoke was already erupting from the impact on *Formidable*. Three minutes after this surprise attack another Zeke was seen flying low above the water, passing from forward to aft from over the starboard bow of *Indomitable*. Warned by the attack on *Formidable*, the fleet's gunners were now alert. The kamikaze was engaged at first by *Indomitable*'s 4.5-inch bow turrets and then by the light guns from the carrier and her escorts. The 'Zeke' evaded by climbing back into the cover of the clouds 3,000 ft above. It soon reappeared, this time in a 60° death-dive from the starboard beam. The fleet was already in an evasive turn to starboard under orders from Admiral Vian and the captain of the *Indomitable* now ordered his helm hard-over. The kamikaze was seen to be hit repeatedly by the Oerlikons and pompoms. While set afire, it was not knocked from its course. But *Indomitable*'s evasive action appeared to have been effective. The kamikaze pilot's aim was confused and he flattened out in what may have been an attempt to come around again, in the same fashion as had just occurred with *Formidable*.

'As a terror weapon, these kamikazes have a quality of their own,' one officer in *Formidable* later wrote. 'There is [still] something unearthly about an approaching aeroplane whose pilot is hell bent on diving himself right into the ship. Wherever you are, he seems to be aiming straight for you personally.' Another sailor, from Portsmouth, said: 'I remember thinking, I've been through the Blitz; we've had bombs, we've had incendiaries, we've had landmines thrown at us, but it's the first time I've had the bloody plane thrown at me as well. You feel that it's aimed at you, especially when he looks around and you think: can he see me?'

Five days later, on 9 May, following the return of a strike, a group of four kamikazes attacked TF 57 and *Formidable* was again hit by a kamikaze. It struck the carrier's flight deck, knocking out her single catapult and exploded among the full deck-park of aircraft destroying six Corsairs and one Avenger but the bomb did not penetrate the flight deck. The fires were soon under control but burning petrol seeped into the hangar deck and caused the loss of four more Avengers and 14 Corsairs. A second kamikaze also targeted the carrier, but Captain Michael Denny put his carrier's helm hard over as the Japanese pilot committed himself in the dive, resulting in the plane crashing through the aft deck park, bouncing off the armoured deck and landing about 200 yards off the port beam. Anti-aircraft fire destroyed the third kamikaze but the fourth slammed into the *Formidable*'s crowded aft deck park, destroying 18 aircraft though causing minimal damage to the ship. *Victorious* was also hit by two kamikazes, which killed three ratings and wounded 19, disabled the forward lift and destroyed four Corsairs on the deck.

During the attacks on the Sakishima Islands, the British Pacific Fleet spent 62 days at sea, with a break of eight days anchored in Leyte Gulf. In

TOWARDS THE FINAL DOWNFALL

that time aircraft from five of its fleet carriers flew 5,335 sorties and expended 1,000 tons of bombs and 500,000 rounds of ammunition and dropped 412 tons of bombs and fired 325 rockets, with the loss of 47 aircraft and 29 aircrew. The Corsairs and Hellcats destroyed 42 enemy aircraft in the air and more than 100 on the ground and prevented the Japanese from staging aircraft to Okinawa. In two months at sea TF 57 lost 44 officers and men killed on board ships and 41 aircrew and 73 aircraft in the kamikaze attacks and the fire aboard *Formidable*. A further 61 aircraft had been destroyed in accidents and 26 in combat with the Japanese. All its operational carriers needed dockyard repairs on their return to Sydney to make good defects and damage inflicted by the Japanese.

On 15-16 May, the Royal Navy carried out Operation 'Dukedom'; the 26th Destroyer Flotilla (composed of *Saumarez, Venus, Verulam, Vigilant* and *Virago*) sank the Japanese heavy cruiser *Haguro* in the Malacca Straits using torpedoes. 'It's a dirty war; all war is dirty, this one particularly so,' wrote 22-year-old Chris Cartledge, a Corsair pilot on 1842 Squadron in *Formidable* in a letter home on 16 May. 'Judging by the fanatical methods of defence used by the Japs they do not intend to give in however hard pressed...one cannot anticipate the reactions of a race so radically different from us. We can't apply our logic to them.'

On 18 May *Formidable* suffered more serious losses on her hangar deck when a Corsair's guns were accidentally fired into an Avenger, which exploded. The ensuing fire destroyed or seriously damaged 30 of her aircraft. The carrier left the battle area for repair in Sydney on 22 May and was followed by the remainder of TF 57 on 25 May. *Indomitable*, which needed a refit, was replaced later by *Implacable*, which had joined the BPF at Manus anchorage in the Admiralties in June and on the 12th, had joined in attacks on Truk in the Caroline Islands. The air attacks on Sakishima Gunto continued until the 25th, by which time Okinawa had been taken.

On 27 May Japanese suicide planes made 56 raids of two to four planes each throughout the day on the US fleet off Okinawa. Of the 1,900 Kamikaze sorties during the battle for Okinawa, only 14.7 per cent were effective, yet 25 US and RN ships were sunk, 157 were damaged by hits and 97 others were damaged by near misses. Total USN casualties on board ships in the Okinawa campaign were 9,731, of whom 4,907 were killed. Most of them were attributed to the Kamikazes.

THE AIR WAR AT SEA IN THE SECOND WORLD WAR

In the northern part of Okinawa American troops met light opposition and the area was seized within about two weeks. However, the main Japanese defences were in the southern part of the island. There was bitter fighting against well-entrenched Japanese troops, but US forces slowly made progress. The seizure of Shuri Castle on 29 May, the centre of Japanese resistance, represented both a strategic and psychological blow. Organized resistance was not over until 21 June. But many Japanese went into hiding and the campaign was not declared over until 2 July. The battle for Okinawa proved costly and lasted much longer than the Americans had originally expected. The Japanese had skilfully utilized terrain to inflict maximum casualties. Total American casualties were 49,451, including 12,520 dead or missing and 36,631 wounded. Japanese casualties were approximately 110,000 killed and 7,400 were taken prisoner. 94 per cent of the Japanese soldiers died along with many civilians. Kamikaze attacks also sank 36 ships of all types, damaged 368 more and led to the deaths of 4,900 US sailors, for the loss of 7,800 Japanese aircraft.

As Operation 'Iceberg' had progressed, Army Air Force B-24 Liberator heavy bombers and B-25 Mitchell medium bombers were stationed on Kadena and P-47 Thunderbolt fighters were based on Ie Shima. During the 82-day battle, Kadena airfield grew in size, staging for Operation 'Downfall', or the invasion of mainland Japan. Japan was still thought to have 10,700 operational aircraft left, half of them ready for suicide attacks. If the Japanese had carried on fighting and the Allies had been forced to invade Japan, the losses would have been incalculable.

In June *Implacable* and other BPF ships that had recently arrived in the Pacific carried out a series of strikes known as Operation 'Inmate' against Truk Atoll in the Caroline Islands. The *Implacable* subsequently joined the remainder of the British fleet off north-eastern New Guinea at the beginning of July. By then TF 57 had been redesignated TF 37, which formed an integral part of Admiral William F. Halsey's 3rd Fleet. Off the coast of Japan itself, the BPF's 1st Aircraft Carrier Squadron included the carriers *Formidable* as flagship, *Victorious*, *Indefatigable* and *Implacable*. The *Indomitable* remained in Sydney to become flagship of the newly arrived 11th Aircraft Carrier Squadron, which included the light fleet carriers *Colossus*, *Venerable*, *Vengeance* and *Glory*. The carrier squadron was to form the nucleus of a second BPF task force for the first phase of the invasion of Japan, scheduled for the autumn.

TOWARDS THE FINAL DOWNFALL

Task Force 37 joined USN TF 38 in attacks on Honshu, the largest of the Japanese Home Islands. It was the height of the typhoon season when attacks began on 17 July and the US Navy was forced to recall its first strikes. The FAA Corsairs and Fireflies however, carried on and they attacked airfield and railway marshalling yards in the northern part of the island. Next day, while the US Navy attacked the Yokosuka naval base, the largest in Japan, aircraft from the BPF were allocated targets to the northeast of Tokyo. Only their Corsairs were able to find their targets in the bad weather conditions prevailing and make their attacks. On 18 July, Lieutenant 'Wally' Stradwick took off from *Formidable* in his Corsair to strafe an airfield east of Tokyo. He was the first British aviator killed over Japan in the war. His last attack had been made four days' earlier, when Stradwick knew he was about to attack mainland Japan for the first time. 'We have been at sea for some time now, and for the last week have known where we are next striking – the full works, apart from getting out and saying "Hallo" to the yellow baskets,' he had written. 'I don't know if it is a particular fault of this Air Arm or not, but we have been on the ship so long, with long periods between ops, that I feel the full twitch over this coming "do". 'The whole thing hinges on strafing. God knows I'm just as scared as anybody flying on any op, but that disappears once the fun starts. 'However, I like the idea of fighting with brains and skill. Air to air fighting is the ideal. You have to use both whether the odds are for or against you.'

Indefatigable was delayed by mechanical problems and did not join the battle until 24 July, when airfields on Shikoku and coastal shipping in the Inland Sea were bombed and strafed. The airfield attacks were met by intense light flak and the shipping strikes were hampered by a low cloud base, but two Corsairs, six Avengers and two Fireflies carried out a successful attack on the Japanese escort carrier *Kaiyō*, leaving it crippled and burning. Further shipping strikes in the Inland Sea and against the naval base at Maizuru, on the northern coast of Honshu, were carried out during 28-30 July.

Operations early in August 1945 were cancelled because of bad weather. And then, on 6 August an atomic bomb was dropped on Hiroshima and three days later another was exploded over Nagasaki but Japan still refused to surrender. Attacks were resumed against Honshu on 9 August by aircraft from *Indefatigable*, *Victorious* (Corsairs of Nos. 1834 and 1836 Squadrons), *Formidable* (Corsairs of Nos. 1841 and 1842 Squadrons) and *Implacable*, when the second atomic bomb destroyed Nagasaki. Shortly before sunrise four Corsair fighter-bombers of 1841 Squadron led by 27-year-old Lieutenant Robert Hampton Gray RCNVR were flown off *Formidable* for an attack on enemy shipping in Onagawa Wan harbour.[91] When five Japanese destroyers and escorts were sighted Gray detailed two of the Corsairs to strafe anti-aircraft positions and a third to provide top cover while he dived on the escort sloop *Amakusa*, an *Etorofu*-class frigate. Gray's Corsair was hit repeatedly and it quickly burst into flames, but he continued his dive and his 500lb bomb sank the vessel. Gray was awarded a posthumous Victoria Cross for his action. It was only the second such award made to a FAA airman during the war and the last to be awarded for actions in the Second World War. The award was not announced until 21 August 1945 when the notice appeared in the London *Gazette* with the citation, 'For determination and address in air attacks on targets in Japan'.

After more air operations were flown on 10 August, when FAA strikes went ahead from dawn to dusk and further Japanese ships were sunk, the BPF had planned to withdraw to prepare for Operation Olympic (the intended invasion of Japan), but Admiral Halsey decided to prolong ongoing operations. Because the BPF's logistical group had insufficient fuel to keep TF 37 in action, the US Navy generously agreed to provide fuel for a smaller British force to remain on station so while the *Formidable*,

---

91. Born, 2 November 1917 in Trail, British Columbia 'Hammy' Gray had enlisted on 18 July 1940 at Calgary, Alberta. His brother John 'Jack' Gray died on 27 February 1942 while serving with the Royal Canadian Air Force. 'Hammy' Gray initially joined 757 Squadron at Winchester, England. He was then assigned to the African theatre, flying Hawker Hurricanes for shore-based squadrons, Nos. 795, 803 and 877, where he spent two years at Nairobi. He trained to fly the Corsair and in 1944 he was assigned to 1841 Squadron in HMS *Formidable*. On 18 July Gray led a strafing mission against airfields in the Tokyo area. On 24 July he led another flight to the inland sea which damaged one merchant ship and damaged two seaplane bases and one airbase. Gray earned a DSC for aiding in sinking a Japanese destroyer in the area of Tokyo on 28 July. From 24–29 August he took part in a series of unsuccessful raids against the *Tirpitz* in Norway. On 29 August he was Mentioned in Despatches for his participation in an attack on three German destroyers, during which his plane's rudder was shot off. On 16 January 1945 he received a further Mention, 'For undaunted courage, skill and determination in carrying out daring attacks on the German battleship *Tirpitz*.'

TOWARDS THE FINAL DOWNFALL

Victorious and *Implacable* left for Australia, the *Indefatigable*, the battleship *King George V,* some cruisers and a destroyer flotilla remained to form Task Group 38.5.

Finally, on 14 August the Japanese government surrendered unconditionally. On 15 August two carrier plane strikes were sent against Tokyo, but were recalled later when the surrender was announced. Meanwhile, dawn strikes that had been launched from the *Indefatigable* led to the last fighter combat of the war. After a dozen 'Zeros' intercepted a flight of the carrier's Avengers, ten Seafires in turn engaged the Japanese fighters, shooting down eight of the enemy planes for the loss of one of their own. The pilot, Sub-Lieutenant Fred Hockley, Royal Naval Volunteer Reserve, parachuted safely to the ground. But nine hours after Emperor Hirohito's radio broadcast at noon that day, announcing Japan's surrender and the cessation of hostilities, his Japanese army captors murdered him. Six soldiers were ordered into the mountains to dig a grave with pickaxes and shovels. At about 9 o'clock that night Hockley was taken to the grave blindfolded, his hands were tied and he was told to stand with his back to the hole. He was then shot twice and rolled into the hole, where he was stabbed him in the back with a sword to ensure that he was dead. His body was later exhumed and cremated. Two of the officers who instigated the killing were convicted of war crimes and hanged in Hong Kong on 16 September 1947 and a third was sentenced to 15 years imprisonment.

A Corsair pilot, Lieutenant Commander Thomas H. Reidy, acting CO of VBF-83, shot down a 'Myrt' to take his score of air-to-air victories into double figures before the recall. Probably it was the last enemy aircraft shot down in the Second World War. Reidy returned to the *Essex*, but as he made his approach, he discovered that he could not get his flaps down. He remained aloft while the rest of his squadron landed aboard and then came in for a safe landing. He eased the throttle to taxi away from the landing area, but there was no response from the engine and the prop just turned more and more slowly until finally it stopped. Reidy remarked, 'I guess the airplane knew the war was over.'

That same morning, Admiral Halsey was aboard the USS *Missouri* steaming in the North Pacific, south-east of Tokyo Bay, with the largest fleet ever assembled. There were seven carriers in the area of Japan and three more carriers were en route: *Intrepid* with CVG-10; *Boxer* with Air Group 93 and *Antietam* with Air Group 89. Admiral Halsey was having breakfast when his Air Operations Officer burst into the flag mess waving a message indicating that the Second World War was over and that President Truman had ordered all hostilities to cease. The war in the Far East was finally at an end without an air battle but with destruction on a massive scale.

One last shock awaited the British Fleet. When the carriers *Venerable* (with Corsairs of 1851 Squadron onboard) and *Indomitable*, two of the four carriers based in Sydney preparing for operations in the East Indies and the Philippines, were tasked to re-occupy Hong Kong on 31 August and 1 September, they were attacked by suicide boats. Corsairs, Avengers and Hellcats dive-bombed and strafed the attackers and finished off the rest that were hidden in the bays on the north of Hog King Island.

Next day, 2 September - VJ Day - the main British Pacific Fleet, now designated 38.5, was part of the allied fleet assembled in Tokyo Bay to witness the Japanese surrender aboard the *Missouri*.[92] Admiral Sir Bruce Fraser signed the Japanese surrender document on behalf of the United Kingdom. His flagship, the battleship *Duke of York*, was anchored close by and he hosted other Allied leaders at an emotional sunset ceremony on her quarterdeck that evening. They had every reason to celebrate and their soldiers, sailors and airmen too could rejoice for Operation 'Downfall' and its constituent parts, set to begin in November 1945, was no longer necessary. Operation 'Olympic' was intended to capture the southern third of Kyūshū with Okinawa to be used as a staging area. Later, in the spring of 1946, Operation 'Coronet' was the planned invasion of the Kantō Plain near Tokyo on the main Japanese island of Honshu. Airbases on Kyūshū captured in 'Olympic' would allow land-based air support for 'Coronet'.

If 'Downfall' had taken place, it would have been the largest amphibious operation in history. Depending on the degree to which Japanese civilians would have resisted the invasion, estimates ran up into the millions for Allied casualties.

---

92. In December 1945 the British Pacific Fleet was disbanded and its forces were absorbed into the East Indies fleet.

Index

Åandalsnes, 33
Abbott, Lieutenant Philip 'Bud', 122–4, 127–9
Abe, Rear Admiral Koki, 56
Acasta, HMS, 24, 27
Adams, Evan, 234
Admiral Hipper, 119
Admiral Scheer, 117, 119
Afrika Korps, 58
Air Group 89, 271
Air Group 93, 271
Akagi, 163, 206–207, 215–17, 219, 221
Akigumo, 229
Albacore, USS, 238
Aleutians, 204
Altenfjorden, 120, 122, 125
Antares, USS, 164
Antietam, USS, 271
Aorangi, SS, 20
Ardent, HMS, 24, 25
Ark Royal, HMS, 2, 17, 19, 21–2, 33, 41, 56, 72–3, 78, 85, 88, 91–3
Armistead, Major Kirk, 208
Armstrong, Leading Airman John Walker, 75
Auchinleck, General Claude, 21

Ault, Commander William Bowen, 199
Australia, HMAS, 156, 158, 161, 194, 197

Bailey, Sub Lieutenant Leslie RNVR, 104
Baker-Falkner, Lieutenant Commander Roy Sydney RN, 133
Bardufoss, 19, 22, 24
Barracuda, Fairey, 123, 125–6, 255
Bataan, USS, 236
Battle of the Denmark Strait, The, 77
Bayley, Lieutenant Gerald W., 49
Beamont, Sergeant Roland 'Bee', 98
Belawan Deli, 246
Bell, Sub Lieutenant RNVR, 265
Belleau Wood, USS, 236, 242
Bennet, Sub Lieutenant, 102–103
Bennington, USS, 258
'Berlin', Operation, 95
Best, Lieutenant Richard 'Dick' Halsey, 215–19, 221
Beynon, Sub Lieutenant William, 104, 110
Bickerton, HMS, 138–9
Biggin Hill Wing, 101

273

Biggin Hill, 103–104
Birkenhead, 71
Bismarck, 72–93, 95, 102, 104, 116–17
Black Watch, HMS, 144
Bligh, Sub Lieutenant Peter, 102–104, 110
Bonaventure, HMS, 59
Borgund, 30–1
Boxer, USS, 271
Boyd, Captain Dennis William DSC, 51, 58, 64–5, 67
Boyd, Edgar, 67
Boyd, Squadron Leader Finlay, 98
'Brawn', Operation, 130
Brest, 96
Brewer, Commander Charles 'Charlie' Walter, 240
Briggs, Pilot Officer Dennis Alfred, 83–4
Brinkman, Kapitän, 107
British Pacific Fleet, The, 244–6
Brooks, Flight Lieutenant Edward John, 3, 5
Brown, Lieutenant Commander W.L.M. 'Bruno', 8
Brown, Vice Admiral Wilson, 189, 192
Brunswick, 137
Bugeja, Lino, 57
Bunce, Naval Airman 1st Class Donald Arthur, 104, 109–10, 113
Bunker Hill, USS, 236, 239–40, 258
Buscall, Sub Lieutenant John Buscall RNVR, 44

C. A. Larsen, 129
Cabot, USS, 236
Calcutta, HMS, 38

Campania, HMS, 144
Campbeltown, HMS, 118
Cape Esperance, 226
Carline, Lieutenant G.A., 45
Cartledge, Chris, 137, 139–40, 142–3
Catapult Armed Merchantmen (CAMs), 145
Cavalla, USS, 237, 239
Chamberlain, Neville, 1
'Chariot', Operation, 118
Charlton, Lieutenant Commander Philip Noel RN, 121
Cheesman, Major Vernon Beauclerk George 'Cheese', 140, 143
Chichi Jima, 236
Chitose, 184–5, 243
Chiyoda, 242
Christ, Oberstleutnant Karl, 61
Churchill, Winston, 54, 116, 120
Ciano, Count, 54
Ciliax, Vice-Admiral Otto, 95–6, 107, 112–13, 118
Clark, Rear Admiral Joseph James 'Jocko', 235–6
Clifford, Lieutenant Edward W., 47–8, 51–2, 67–8
Clinton, Petty Officer William Johnson 'Clints', 102, 104, 106–107, 112
'*Cockpit*', Operation, 244–5
Collins, Captain James F., 208
Colossus, HMS, 268
Coltishall, RAF, 111
Conolly, Rear Admiral Richard Lansing, 236
Constable-Roberts, Wing Commander, 99, 102–103

INDEX

Coral Sea, Battle of, 189–204, 206, 222, 232
'Coronet', Operation, 272
Courageous, HMS, 9
Coventry, HMS, 38
Cowpens, USS, 236, 238, 240
Crace, Rear Admiral John Gregory RN, 194, 197, 199–200
Crombie, Flight Lieutenant Michael, 107
Cross, Squadron Leader Kenneth Brian Boyd 'Bing', 17–18, 22–3, 25, 30, 32
Cruickshank, Flying Officer John Alexander VC, 133–4
Crutchley, Rear Admiral Victor VC, 225
Cunningham, Vice Admiral Sir Andrew Browne 'ABC', 38, 41–2, 53–4, 56, 58, 135

Daniels, Ensign James G. 'Jim', 165, 170–5, 178, 229–30
Davao, 180–8
Day, Captain, 100
de Wiart, General Carton VC, 10
Deal, 104
Denny, Captain Michael, 254, 266
Dickinson, Lieutenant Clarence, Earle, 167–9, 214, 219–20
Dixon, Lieutenant Commander Robert, 199
Dolim, Abe, 176–7
Donaldson, Squadron Leader John W., 28
Donati, Lieutenant Marcus David, 6

Dönitz, Grossadmiral Karl, 91, 120, 130
'Donnerkeil-Zerberus', Unternehmen ('The Channel Dash' Operation), 94–115
Doolittle, Lieutenant Colonel James H. MoH, 179, 205
Dorsetshire, HMS, 91–2
Doungbrewer Farm, 137
Dover Castle, 98–100, 111
'Downfall', Operation, 268, 272
Doyle, Able Seaman 'Ron', 26, 30–2
Duke of York, HMS, 115, 119, 122, 131, 137, 141, 143, 272
'Dukedom', Operation, 267

Eagle, HMS, 37–8, 41, 56–7, 93
Earnest, Ensign Albert, 209
Ede, Flying Officer Herman Francis Grant DFC, 28
Eglinton, RNAS, 137
Emperor, HMS, 121, 126
Empire Lawrence, SS, 146–8
Eniwetok, 236–7
Ennever, Lieutenant Colin Croft, 104
Ennis, Pilot Officer J.M., 162
Enterprise, USS, 164–6, 169–72, 175, 178, 189–90, 192, 206, 208
Eriboll, Loch, 136
Erickson, Ensign Roy D. 'Eric', 257, 259, 262
Esmonde, Lieutenant Commander Eugene VC DSO, 78–80, 94–5, 101–104, 106–107, 112
Essex, USS, 70, 178, 190, 230, 232, 234–6, 238, 240, 259–60, 271

275

Eugéne, Prince, 74
'Excess', Operation, 57–71

Fairey Albacore, 118
Fencer, HMS, 126, 130
Fanshaw Bay, 237
Fenton, Lieutenant Commander J.E., 5
Ferrier, Harry, 209
Filton, 17
Fitch, Rear Admiral Aubrey B., 194, 200
Fieberling, Lieutenant Langdon K., 208
Fjaettenfjorden, 118
Fleming, Captain Richard Eugene MOH, 222
Fletcher, Rear Admiral Frank Jack, 189–90, 194–200, 203–204, 206, 208, 217, 225
Fliegerkorps X, 58
Formidable, HMS, 67, 71, 131, 135–9, 140–1, 143–4, 251, 255, 263, 265–70
Formosa, 263
Foster, Lieutenant Arnold, 100
Fraser, Admiral Sir Bruce, 122, 135, 247, 272
French, Sub Lieutenant [John Howard] RNVR, 142–3
Fuchida, Commander, 56
'Fuller', Operation, 98–9
Fuller-Wright, Sub Lieutenant Eric Herbert, 104, 110
Fulton, Sub Lieutenant R., 140
Furious, 2, 5, 8, 19–20, 35, 121, 129, 131, 137–41

Gallaher, Lieutenant Wilmer E., 215–16, 218–19
Galland, General der Jagdflieger Adolf, 97–8
Gallant, HMS, 59
Gallimore, Petty Officer, 124, 127
Gambier Bay, USS, 243
Gardiner, Lieutenant Commander Henry, 5
Gardiner, Pilot Officer Walter George, 11, 14–15
Garnett, Flight Sergeant Jack DFM, 134
Guadalcanal, 194–6, 224–7, 231–3, 236, 264
Gay, Ensign George H., 212–13
Gayler, Lieutenant Noel A.M., 220
Genda, Minoru, 56
General Botha, SATS, 148
Gibbs, Flight Lieutenant S. R., 157–9
Gick, Lieutenant Philip David 'Percy' DSC, 80–1, 102
Gleave, Wing Commander 'Tom', 103, 112
Gleneagles Hotel, 32
Glory, HMS, 268
Goddard, Lieutenant Noel Ernest, 75
Goering, Field-Marshal, 74
Going, Lieutenant G.R., 47, 51
Gneisenau, 3–4, 6, 24, 94–9, 102, 106, 108, 114–15
Glorious, HMS, 17, 19–21, 23–9, 31, 33, 37
Gonzenheim, 93
Good, Squadron Leader Duncan Charles Frederick, 6–8, 11–15

INDEX

Goodwin, Lieutenant D., 43, 47
'Goodwood I, II, III and IV',
  Operations, 135–6, 139, 141, 143
Grand Harbour, Valletta, 37, 57, 60, 66, 69–70
Gray, Lieutenant James S., 210, 212,
Gray, Lieutenant Robert Hampton
  VC DSC MiD RCNVR, 133, 269–70
Great Marianas Turkey Shoot',
  The, 243
Green, Sub Lieutenant R.A.F., 47
Gregory, Midshipman Mackenzie J., 156–7
Gribble, Leonard Reginald, 94, 115, 148, 156
Gruppe/Sturzkampfgeschwader, 61
Guadalcanal, Battle for, 224–6, 229, 231–3
Guam, assault on, 189, 236, 238–41

Hagger, Second Lieutenant, 96
Håkøybotn, 144
Hale, Lieutenant Commander John William 'Daddy', 43, 45, 47–8, 50, 52, 54
Hall, Lieutenant William E. MOH, 203
Halsey, Vice Admiral William F. 'Bull' Jr., 164–6, 171, 175, 178–9, 190, 192, 215, 254, 268, 270–1
Hamilton, Lieutenant Commander Weldon L., 198–9
Hancock, USS, 260
Harrill, Rear Admiral William Keene, 236

Hasty, HMS, 41–2, 65–6
Hatson, RNAS, 75
Hawkinge, RAF, 98
Hay, Acting Lieutenant Colonel Ronnie DSO RM, 249–50
Hay, Flying Officer Alastair James, 145–8
Hebel, 'Fritz', 172
Heidel, Kapitänleutnant Werner, 3
Henderson Field, 224–6, 231–2
Henderson, Major Lofton, 206, 211, 224
Henley, Lieutenant Robert S., 62
Hickam Field, 163
Hipper, *Admiral*, 5
Hiroshima, 269
Hiryu, 163, 206, 214, 217–18, 221
Hitler, Adolf, 74, 95
Hobart, HMAS, 194
Hockley, Sub-Lieutenant Fred, RNVR, 271
Hoffmann, Kapitän Kurt, 98, 107, 110
Holmberg, Lieutenant (jg) P.A., 214
Hong Kong, 272
Hood, HMS, 75, 77–8
Hornchurch Wing, 101
Hornchurch, 103
Hornet, USS, 179, 190, 205–206, 208, 210–12, 215, 218–19, 221, 226–31, 235, 238, 240, 243
Horsley, Terence, 59
Howe, HMS, 265
Huddlestone, Major Guy, 99–100
Hulbert, Jack, 96
Humphreys, Lieutenant 'Pat', 49–50

Huntington, Aviation Radioman Third Class Robert K., 212–13
Hyde, Squadron Leader Ernest Leslie 'Johnny', 3
Hyland, Commander, 259

'Iceberg', Operation, 257, 268
Ie Shima, 268
Illustrious, HMS, 38–43, 47–55, 57–66, 69–71, 244–8, 251, 253, 263
Implacable, HMS, 255, 267–70
Indefatigable, HMS, 131, 133, 135–41, 143, 246–9, 251–3, 268–71
Indomitable, HMS, 244, 245–7, 251–3, 265–8, 272
'Inmate', Operation, 268
Inouye, Admiral Shigeyoshi, 193–4, 199–200
Intrepid, USS, 257, 259, 264, 271
Ito, Admiral Seiichi, 258

Jackson, Lieutenant Robert 'Hal', 262–3
Jagdgeschwader 2 'Richthofen', 105
Jameson, Flight Lieutenant Patrick Geraint 'Jamie', 20, 23, 28, 32
JG 26, 105
Johnson, Captain Dan H., 264–5
Johnson, Leading Airman Ambrose Laurence 'Ginger' Johnson DSM, 104, 108
Johnson, Lieutenant Commander Robert R., 211
Jones, Sub Lieutenant P. D., 49

Joshima, Rear Admiral T., 237
'Judgement', Operation (Taranto), 36–56
Jun'yo, 230
Junack, Kapitänleutnant Gerhard, 72–3, 77, 89–91, 93

Kadena airfield, 257–8, 264–5
Kåfjorden, 122, 127, 130–3, 135–6, 138–9, 141–2
Kaga, 163, 206–207, 213–17, 219–21
Kaiyo, 269
Kajioka, Rear Admiral, 196
Kamikaze suicide attacks, 243, 250–5, 258–9, 261, 263–8
Kemp, Lieutenant Neil M., 45
Kenley, RAF, 98–9
Kent, HMS, 135
KG 26, 61
Kidd, Flight Lieutenant Gerald, 98
Kikusui suicidal attacks, 258, 263–4
Kimmins, Commander Anthony Martin, 124–6
King George V, HMS, 74, 247, 252, 265, 271
King, Admiral Ernest J., 189, 192
Kingcombe, Squadron Leader Brian, 104–105
Kingsmill, Sub Lieutenant Charles Major 'Pat', 104, 108–109, 113
Kirchberg, Oberbootsmann Kurt, 80
Kite, HMS, 141
Knight, Flying Officer Herbert H., 23
Kobayashi, Lieutenant Michio, 217
Kroeger, Lieutenant Edwin John, 215
Kukuda, Vice Admiral Kakuji, 236

INDEX

Kurita, Vice Admiral Takeo, 207, 237
Kurumba, HMAS, 194, 197

Langfjorden, 125, 127, 139
Langley, USS, 190, 234, 236, 240, 243
Lea, Lieutenant S.C., 49
Lee, Sub Lieutenant Edgar Frederick, 97, 104, 107–108, 112
Lee-on-Solent, 95, 99
Lehmann, Korvettenkapitän Walter, 73, 90
'Lentil', Operation, 246
Leslie, Lieutenant Commander Maxwell F. 'Max', 213–14
Letch, Ensign Alfred, 264
Levitt, Lieutenant Dennis Levitt, 247
Lexington, USS, 164, 189, 192–4, 196, 198–204, 206, 236, 239, 242–3
Leyte Gulf, Battle of, 243
Lindbergh, Charles A., 223–4
Lindemann, Kapitän zur See Ernst, 73–4, 78
Lindsey, Lieutenant Commander Eugene E., 169, 210, 213, 229
Lindsey, Robin, 229
Lossiemouth, 117
Luddington, Bill, 67
Lütjens, Admiral Günther, 74
Lützow, 119, 121
Lyster, Vice Admiral, Sir Arthur KCB CVO CBE DSO, 37, 41–2, 55–6, 58, 67

MacArthur, General Douglas, 233, 236

Macrihanish, 113, 121
MacLean, Lieutenant Neal Gordon, 80, 104
Makanaonalani, Dorinda, 163
Makigumo, 229
Malaya, HMS, 41, 55
Manning, Jay, 209
Maori, HMS, 91
Manston, 95–7, 101–105, 111–12
Marushige, Rear Admiral, 196
'Mascot', Operation, 131–3, 135
Massey, Lieutenant Commander Lance E. 'Lem', 213–14
Mattholie, Sub Lieutenant H.S. RN, 133
McCampbell, Commander David D., 239
McCarthy, Ensign John R. 'Mac', 167–8, 220
McClusky, Lieutenant Commander Clarence Wade, 170–1, 213, 215–16, 219
McGrigor, Rear Admiral Rhoderick, 131
'Meridian I', 248
'Meridian II', 250
'Meridian III', 250
'Meridian', Operation, 122
Meyer, Kapitän-zur-See Hans, 120, 129
Micklem, Lieutenant G.N., 133
Midway, Island, 164, 166, 204–22
Mikuma, 222
Millen, Sydney, 59–60, 63
Miller, William Cicero, 167–8
Milne, Leading Airman J.D., 75

Missouri, USS, 271–2
Mitchell, Lieutenant Commander Samuel G., 211
Mitscher, Admiral Marc 'Pete', 235–6, 241–2, 257, 260
Mitsuo, Fuchida, 163, 205
Mitsuru, Lieutenant General Ushijima, 257
Monarch of Bermuda, SS, 22
Monterey, USS, 236, 238
Montgomery, Rear Admiral Alfred Eugene, 236
Moore, Admiral Sir Henry, 131, 135, 137, 139
Moore, Group Captain M., 22
Morford, Lieutenant William Douglas, 47, 52
Mount Batten (10 Squadron RAAF), 3
Murmansk, 118, 147
Murray, James Francis, 218
Murray, Lieutenant J., 52
Musashi, 236, 243
Mussolini, Benito, 54, 56

Nabob, HMS, 135, 138–9
Nagasaki, 269
Nagumo, Vice Admiral Chuichi, 163, 179, 206–207, 210–12, 215, 231
Nairana, HMS, 144
Namsos, 33
Neale, Sub Lieutenant John W. 'Tweeny', 42, 46–7
Nelson, HMS, 33
Neugebauer, Pilot Officer Peter Hermann, 156–7, 159–62

New Georgia Sound (The 'Slot'), 225
Nichol, Lieutenant Commander Bromfield B., 166
Nicholetts, Wing Commander Gilbert, 9
Nimitz, Admiral Chester W., 189, 205–206, 254
Nordmark, 133
Norfolk, HMS, 76
Norfolk, Sub-Lieutenant Valentine Kay, 80
Norris, Major Benjamin W., 210, 221
North Weald Wing, 98
Norwich, 111

O'Hare, Lieutenant Commander Edward L. 'Butch' MOH, 192–3
Oban, 157
Obayashi, Rear Admiral S., 237–8
Oesau, Oberstleutnant Walter, 105
Ofot Fjord, 9
Oiled', Operation, 117–18
Okinawa, 122, 240, 251, 257–60, 263–4, 267–8, 272
'Olympic', Operation, 270, 272
Opie, John N. III, Lieutenant Commander, 47–8, 55
Orote Field, 239
Oxspring, Squadron Leader 'Bobby', 98
Ozawa, Vice-Admiral Jisaburō, 236–9, 241

Pacey, Leading Airman Maurice G. Pacey, 8
Paine, Sub Lieutenant S., 52

INDEX

Palembang, 122, 246–7, 249, 251
Pangkalan Brandan, 245–6
Parker, Pilot Officer Stanley Edgar, 104
Parkinson, Sub Lieutenant Robert Laurens, 104
Parks, Major Floyd B., 206, 208
Partridge, Captain Richard T. RM, 2
Patch, Captain 'Ollie' DSO, 43, 47
Pearl Harbor, 55–6, 163—79, 189, 192, 204, 206, 243
Peck, Sub-Lieutenant, 124, 127
Pembroke Dock, 3
Penelope, HMS, 6
Peterson, Chief Water Tender Oscar V. MoH, 203
Phelps, USS, 203, 220
Philippine Sea, Battle of, 234–43
Phillips, Flight Lieutenant, 33–4
Pioneer, HMS, 251
Pladjoe, 247
'Planet', Operation, 130
Pockley, Flight Lieutenant Harold Graham DFC, 149–52, 153–6
Pomeroy, Lieutenant-Commander Arthur Shubrook, 148
Port Moresby, 193–4, 196–200, 204
Pound, Admiral/First Sea Lord, Sir Dudley, 37, 101
Powers, Lieutenant John J. MoH, 203
Premier, HMS, 144
Prince of Wales, HMS, 75, 77
Prinz Eugen, 74–6, 78, 92–3, 95–7, 99, 102, 106–11, 114–15
Pumphrey, Lieutenant Commander Nigel, 96, 100–101, 110

Punjabi, HMS, 6
Pursuer, HMS, 121, 126
Pye, Vice Admiral William S., 189

Queen Elizabeth, HMS, 55
Queen, HMS, 144

Rabaul, 193-194, 196, 221, 224
Raeder, Admiral, 115
Raeder, Grossadmiral Erich, 117
Rajah, HMS, 137
Ramillies, HMS, 41, 55
Ramsey, Admiral Bertram, 100, 111–12
Ramsgate, 104
Ranger, USS, 190
Raw, Brigadier Cecil Whitfield, 99–100
Rawie, Lieutenant Commander Wilmer E., 191, 259–60, 262
Rayburn, Air Mechanic, 41, 52, 59–60, 63–7
Reeves Jr, Rear Admiral John Walter 'Black Jack', 236
Reidy, Lieutenant Commander Thomas H., 271
Renown, HMS, 38, 86, 91, 93
Reynolds, Sub Lieutenant R.H., 253
Rice, Petty Officer Frederick Charles, 8–9
Richardson, Admiral James O., 55
Richardson, Lieutenant Commander Archibald 'Arch' RNZAF, 140, 143
Ricketts, Lieutenant Milton E. MoH, 203

Ring, Commander Stanhope Cotton, 211
Robson, Operation, 245
Rodee, Lieutenant Commander 'Walt', 211
Rose, Sub Lieutenant Brian Westland, 97, 104, 107–108, 113
Rösselsprung', Unternehmen (Operation 'Knight's Move'), 119
Rotherham, Commander Geoffrey Alexander, 75
Ryujo, 183–4, 225, 237

Saalwächter, Generaladmiral Alfred, 115
Sainte-Nazaire, 118
Saipan, 235–7, 241
Sakishima Gunto Island group, 251
Samples, Sub Lieutenant Reginald McCartney 'Mac', 104, 109, 113
San Juan, USS, 231
Santa Cruz, Battle of, 226, 231–2, 243
Saratoga, 164, 189–90, 225, 244
Savo Island, The First Battle of, 225
Sayer, Petty Officer Leslie Daniel, 80–1, 102
Scapa Flow, 16–17, 19–21, 37, 74, 121–2, 130, 133, 137–8, 141
Scarlet-Streatfield, Lieutenant Norman John 'Blood', 43
Scharnhorst, 2–4, 6, 24–7, 33–4, 94–9, 101–102, 106–107, 110–12, 114–15, 120–1
Schmalenbach, Lieutenant Commander Paul, 106

Schöpfel, Gruppenkommandeur Gerhard, 105
Scott, LAC 'Bob', 152
Sealion, HMS, 96
Searcher, HMS, 121, 126, 144
Serongei Gerong, 249
Sewell, Sub Lieutenant Alfred 'Jackie', 62
Shaw, Captain T., 92
Sheffield, HMS, 38, 85–6, 121
Shima, Rear Admiral Kiyohide, 194
Shimazaki, Lieutenant Commander, 164
Shoho, 194, 196, 198–200, 203–204
Shokaku, 163, 169, 194, 199, 201–204, 206, 225–9, 237, 239
Short, Lieutenant Wallace C., 213
Sims, USS, 197–9
Slaughter, Henry J., 49
Smiley, Commander Curtis S., 191
Smith, Ensign Leonard B. 'Tuck', 83–4
Smith, USS, 231
Smith, Leading Airman William Grenville, 104, 110, 112
Solomons, Battle for the, 223–33
Soryu, 163, 206, 213–14, 216–17, 219
Source', Operation, 120
South Dakota, USS, 230–1, 238
Sparke, Sub Lieutenant Philip Donald Julian DSC, 43, 46
Sportpalast', Unternehmen (Operation 'Sports Palace'), 118
Spruance, Admiral Raymond, 191, 206, 208, 212, 217, 237, 241, 263

INDEX

St Lo, 243
Stark, Admiral Harold R., 55
Stradwick, Lieutenant 'Wally', 265, 269
Straight, Whitney MC, 18
Stretton, 137
Stuart, Lieutenant Commander W., 246
Suffolk, HMS, 10, 76
Sullom Voe, 2, 33
Supermarine Seafire aircraft, 251–2
Sutton, Alfred W.F. 'Alfie', 40, 48, 50–1
Svalbard Archipelago, 147
Svalbard II, 31
Swayne, Flight Lieutenant H.A.L., 44
Sweeney, Lieutenant Colonel Walter C., 207
Swingate radar station, 98
Swordfish aircraft, 36–7, 57–8, 115

Tain, 133
Tainan Kokutai, 224
Takagi, Rear Admiral Takeo, 194, 196, 198, 200
'Tallboy' bombs, 144
Tanaka, Admiral Raizo, 184
Tapping, Leading Airman Ernest, 104, 110
Taranto, 35–56
Task Force 8, 190–2
Task Force 11, 192, 196
Task Force 16, 226
Task Force 17/17.3, 190–1, 194, 197–8, 226
Task Force 37, 268, 270

Task Force 38, 243, 268
Task Force 44, 194, 196
Task Force 57, 251–2, 263, 265–8
Task Force 58, 251, 257, 263
Task Force 61, 225, 230
Task Force 63, 248
Taylor, Sergeant Bernard L.
Taylor, 23
Tedder, Air Chief Marshal, 59
Thach, Lieutenant Commander John S. 'Jimmy', 192–3, 213–14, 221
Thompson, Lieutenant John Chute, 104, 110
'Tiger Claw', Operation, 131
Tirpitz, 116–44, 270
Tokyo, 179, 205–206, 240, 255, 269–72
'Tokyo ('Cactus') Express', 225
Tomkinson, Lieutenant Commander Christopher Charles RNVR, 122
Tomonaga, Lieutenant Joichi, 207, 210
Tone, 207, 210–11, 227
Topp, Friedrich Karl, 120
Torrens-Spence, Lieutenant Michael Alexander 'Tiffy', 40, 48, 50
Tovey, Admiral Sir John, 74–5, 78, 86, 92
Toyoda, Admiral Soemu, 236
Transom, Operation, 244–5
Tribe, Leading Aircraftman Denis, 62
Trident, HMS, 115
Trincomalee, 245, 247

283

Tromsø, 16, 35
Trondheim Fjord, 3, 33, 35, 117
Troubridge, Captain Thomas Hope, 5, 17
Truk, 193–4, 202, 222, 228, 232–3, 237, 255, 267–8
Truman, President Harry S., 271
Trumpeter, HMS, 135–6, 138, 144
Tulagi, 193–6, 203, 224, 236
'Tungsten', Operation, 121, 130
Turner, Vice Admiral Richmond, 236

Ugaki, Vice Admiral Matome, 236–7
Ulithi Atoll, 251
Unicorn, HMS, 251

Vågsö, 144
Valiant, HMS, 38, 60, 65–6
Valletta, 57, 65
Vejtasa, 'Swede', 229–30
Venerable, HMS, 268, 272
Vengeance, HMS, 268
Vian, Rear Admiral Sir Philip L., 245–7, 254, 266
Victorious, HMS, 74–5, 77–9, 81–3, 86–7, 93, 118–19, 121–2, 124–7, 130–31, 144, 244, 246–9, 251, 253–5, 266, 268–70
Vincent-Jones, Lieutenant Desmond, 58–9, 66
Vindictive, HMS, 22
Volunteer, HMS, 148
von Loewenfeld, Frau, 74
Vraciu, Lieutenant Alexander, 239

Wake Island, 164, 166, 189, 191
Waldron, Lieutenant Commander John Charles, 211–12
Warburton, Pilot Officer Adrian 'Warby', 42
Warspite, HMS, 48, 65
Washington, USS, 119
Wasp, USS, 190, 236, 239–40, 242
Weber, Ensign Frederick Thomas, 169, 215
Wellham, Lieutenant John W.G., 49–50
Wheeler, Leading Airman Henry Thomas Albert, 104, 110
Wheway, Sub Lieutenant William Derek, 137
White, Donald, 240
Widhelm, Lieutenant Commander William J. 'Gus', 227
William B. Preston, USS, 182–4
Williams, Gaynor, 83
Williams, Lieutenant William Henry, 96, 104, 107, 112
Williamson, Lieutenant Commander Kenneth 'Hooch', 43–4, 46, 54
Wolf, Wilhelm, 112
Wood, Sub Lieutenant Cecil Ralph, 104, 110

X-Craft, 120–1

Yahagia, 261-262
Yamamoto, Fleet Admiral Isoroku, 56, 204–205, 207, 221
Yamato, 205, 207, 236, 258–62

INDEX

Yokushima airfield, 255
Yorktown, USS, 190–1, 193–6, 198–204, 206–208, 213–14, 217–19, 222, 235–36
Young, Howard L. 'Brigham', 166, 173–5, 191

ZG 26, 61
Zuiho, 206, 226–7, 243
Zuikaku, 163–4, 169, 194, 199, 201–204, 206, 225–28, 230–2, 237, 240–3